A Career with Meaning

Recreation, Parks, Sport Management, Hospitality, and Tourism

Cheryl A. Stevens
James F. Murphy
Lawrence R. Allen
Emilyn A. Sheffield

SAGAMORE
PUBLISHING

Publishers: Joseph J. Bannon/Peter Bannon
VP of Sales and Marketing: M. Douglas Sanders
Director of Development and Production: Susan M. Davis
Cover and Interior Design: Susan M. Davis

All photos by shutterstock or author collection unless otherwise indicated.

Library of Congress Catalog Card Number: 2010932156
ISBN: 978-157167- 526-2
Printed in the United States.

10 9 8 7 6 5 4 3

Sagamore Publishing, L.L.C.
www.sagamorepub.com

To Joe Bannon, Sr.,
for his lifetime of dedication
to improving the education
of recreation and park professionals

Contents

Acknowledgments

This complete revision of Kraus's *Career Perspectives* text would not have been possible without the collaborative efforts of many individuals. We started the project determined to produce a book that would introduce students to careers in recreation, parks, sports management, hospitality, and tourism by helping them link their passions to career possibilities. Like most major projects, this one required more time, creativity, and collaborative effort than initially anticipated.

Thanks go first to the editorial team: Emilyn Sheffield, who ignited my passion for the project by sharing her creative vision; Larry Allen, who proved adept at recruiting qualified authors and getting chapters completed; Jim Murphy, who provided necessary, ongoing mentoring, editorial, and visionary guidance.

Second, this book would not be what it is without retired park ranger and contributing author Tony Sisto's vision for the passions, pay and perks, preparation, and possibilities model, which he created in his first draft of the Outdoor Recreation chapter. It took a practitioner to show us (the academics) how to communicate clearly and concisely with our future recreation professionals.

We were committed to providing an edited book that was current, consistent in format, and aligned with our audience's needs. Toward this end, a meeting was held at NRPA in 2008, during which Larry Allen, Bob Barcelona, and Doug Kennedy provided valuable input that shaped the final format. Jim Murphy collaborated with me to produce the "Leisure Service Delivery System: Evolving Structure" model. This model is important because it allows us to place recreation-related careers on a continuum, which honors an emerging future where organizations have flexible boundaries. In chapter 15, Jim graciously shares his vision for forces shaping the future of recreation, parks, sport management, hospitality, and tourism.

Special thanks go to Dan Dustin, who came up with the "Career with Meaning" title concept; Craig Ross, who shared his expertise on career preparation; and Richard Williams, who allowed me to practice my editing skills with him. All of the contributors deserve special recognition for their time and patience with multiple revisions. Last, but not least, *A Career with Meaning* would not be what it is without all of the recreation, parks, sport management, hospitality, and tourism professionals who took the time to provide informational interviews, break-out box material, and quotes to make the book useful, informative, and interesting to read. I am grateful to my family and friends, especially Douglas Lamont, who supported me throughout this four-year project.

Our hope is that this text will help move the recreation-related professions toward a new status among undergraduate students: that of intended major rather than discovery major. Too many of our best alumni did not discover this major until they had been in college a while, changing from major to major, searching for the right fit. Eventually, someone pointed them in the right direction, and they "discovered" recreation, parks, sport management, hospitality, or tourism. Every day we hear, "Why didn't someone tell me sooner that I could have a career where I get paid to do this?"

Many thanks to all who contributed to *A Career with Meaning*, which we believe will help resolve this problem by helping students match their passions to the right possibilities earlier in their educational and career planning processes.

—**Cheryl Stevens**
Lead editor and contributing author

Preface

You are probably interested in this book because you enjoy things like sports, the outdoors, or travel, and you like the idea that you could have a career doing something you love. Who wouldn't want a job where they get up every day wanting to go to work? Plus, you probably have questions like: What kind of a job could I get? How much would it pay? What kind of education and experience will I need to meet my career goals? Perhaps the most important question you have is, "Would I really love it as much as I think?"

The purpose of this book is to connect you with top professionals in all aspects of recreation, parks, sport management, hospitality, and tourism careers so they can help you find the answers you need. Professionals in recreation-related careers tend to have passion for one or more of the following:

- Being outdoors and caring for the environment
- Helping people have a higher quality of life
- Playing games and sports
- Creating exciting events
- Entrepreneurism and being your own boss

There are few things we can say that apply to all careers in recreation, parks, tourism, and leisure because there are so many different kinds of opportunities. Since these careers cover many settings, skill sets, and populations, answers will vary from person to person. However, if you find you some (or all) of these qualities apply to you, keep reading:

- You think recreation is fun and exciting
- You want to make a difference
- You enjoy working with people
- You enjoy a challenge
- You're a problem solver and enjoy finding creative solutions
- You like being hands-on and involved in the action
- Sitting at a desk all day doesn't suit you
- You like doing many different things and being different places
- Being passionate about your career is important to you
- You are open-minded when it comes to people—their varied backgrounds, likes and dislikes, and needs and wants
- You can think on your feet without going off the deep end
- You can be both a leader and a team player, depending on what the situation calls for
- You don't mind flexible work hours and you're willing work when other people want to recreate, such as holidays and vacations
- You believe everyone in a community has the right to play and recreate
- You like the idea of helping to create and implement sustainable, eco-sensitive solutions for communities and our environment

- You would be thrilled to enter a career in which your knowledge and skills are transferable across many fields in recreation, parks, sport management, hospitality, and tourism, providing continual prospects for personal and professional growth

We, the editors and contributing authors, would like to promise you that a wide variety of good career opportunities exists—careers with pay and perks such as having a job you love, challenge and personal growth, high job satisfaction and benefits. What it takes is investing time and effort to do some investigation.

Prepare to actively engage in self-reflection and detective work so you can figure out which aspects of recreation, parks, sport management, hospitality, and tourism could be for right you. Once you figure out your specific interests, you'll be able to use the chapter on career preparation to make a plan to get the education and work experiences you need to build your ideal career.

As you read this book, you will discover possibilities you've never dreamed of, or perhaps, if you've thought of them you were unsure how someone could get a job doing "that." Each of these authors is passionate about what they do, and if one of their career areas is right for you, they would love to have you join their team!

Editors

Cheryl A. Stevens, Ph.D.
Associate Professor
Department of Recreation and Leisure Studies
East Carolina University

Dr. Stevens is a committed recreation educator who has been facilitating hands-on learning in recreation and outdoor leadership for over 25 years. She teaches undergraduate and graduate classes in leisure philosophy and recreation programming. As the recipient of five teaching awards, she continuously looks for ways to improve teaching materials and techniques. In addition to serving as lead editor for *A Career with Meaning* she has written a book titled *Service Learning for Health, Physical Education, and Recreation: A Step-by-Step Guide* and a number of other articles related to teaching and learning.

In addition to her teaching and research, Dr. Stevens has served as a member of the Council on Accreditation for Recreation, Park Resources and Leisure Services (COA), co-chair of the Symposium of Experiential Education Research (SEER), board member of the Society of Park and Recreation Education (SPRE), and editor of the Research Update column in Parks and Recreation Magazine

James F. Murphy, Ph.D.
Interim Associate Dean
College of Health and Human Services
San Francisco State University

Jim Murphy is Interim Associate Dean, College of Health and Human Services, San Francisco State University. Dr. Murphy received his B.A. in Recreation from San Francisco State University (1966), M.S. with Honors in Recreation and Park Administration from Indiana University (1967), and Ph.D. from Oregon State University (1972).

Jim has authored, co-authored, edited and co-edited seven textbooks including *Concepts of Leisure, Leisure Service Delivery System, Recreation and Leisure Service for the Disadvantaged*, and *Leisure Systems*. He has written many professional and juried articles and conducted numerous workshops and made many presentations at state, regional, national and international conferences. He served a total of six years on the SPRE Board of Directors, including one term as President. He was President of the Academy of Leisure Sciences (2008-09) as well as a Charter Fellow of the Academy of Leisure Sciences (1980). In 2008 Dr. Murphy received the Distinguished Colleague Award of the Society of Park and Recreation Educators, NRPA.

Lawrence R. Allen, Ph.D.

Dean
College of Health, Education, and Human Development
Clemson University

In May, 2003, Dr. Lawrence R. Allen became Dean of the College of Health, Education, and Human Development at Clemson University. From August, 2001 to May, 2003 he served as Interim Dean. He received his Ph.D. from the University of Maryland in recreation with a specialty area in counseling and his undergraduate degree in education from West Chester University of Pennsylvania.

Dr. Allen has been very active professionally for the past 34 years with memberships in several professional organizations. In 1987, he was elected to the Academy of Leisure Sciences, and in 1995, he served as the President of the Academy. In 1996, he was elected to the American Academy of Park and Recreation Administration. He has a very strong commitment to professional practice in leisure and tourism services and has served on various boards of directors, and state and national committees.

Dr. Allen has written extensively with his primary interest focusing on the impact of recreation and other out of school experiences on individual and community well-being. Along with colleagues at Clemson University, he has authored several articles and manuals revolving around the development and implementation of an outcome based model (Benefits Based Programming) of youth program delivery that enhances the youth's ability to overcome and cope with the stress and pressures they face in today's social environment. He has been instrumental in the development of a Master's degree in Youth Development Leadership at Clemson University and he is very interested in the integration of free-choice learning experiences with the more traditional educational systems employed within the United States and throughout the world.

Emilyn A. Sheffield, Ph.D.

Professor
Department of Recreation and Parks Management
California State University, Chico

Emilyn Sheffield loves every aspect of parks and recreation! She has worked in and taught about tourism, community recreation, fitness, special events, and conference planning in California, Texas, and Missouri. Working with industry sponsors, she develops service learning field schools around themes of national parks, community based stewardship, hospitality, and conference management.

Dr. Sheffield's interdisciplinary team of faculty, students, and field-based professionals complete destination projects for trails, heritage tourism, and scenic byways. The National Park Service, the USDA Forest Service, the Bureau of Land Management, the U.S. Army Corps of Engineers, the U.S. Fish and Wildlife Service are recent project sponsors and partners. She serves on the executive boards of the Association of Partners for Public Lands and the California Roundtable on Recreation, Parks, and Tourism.

Contributors

Dr. Robert Barcelona is an assistant professor in the Youth Development Leadership Program and the Department of Parks, Recreation, and Tourism Management at Clemson University. Dr. Barcelona received his doctorate from Indiana University after working professionally in the field of athletics and campus recreation. He has worked with numerous recreation and sport organizations in both programming and research efforts and is a member of the Society of Park and Recreation Educators' board of directors. Dr. Barcelona has won teaching excellence awards at both Indiana University and the University of New Hampshire, and he received a special citation award from the New Hampshire Recreation and Parks Association for his work with youth sports and coaching education. His research on sport and recreation management has been published in refereed journals, trade magazines, and textbooks. Dr. Barcelona is also the co-author of the textbook, *Leisure Services Management*.

Polly Crabtree has directed, or provided assistance with, hundreds of events for California State University, Chico in her role as associate director for the Office of Alumni and Parent Relations. These events have run the gamut from small, intimate affairs, to events for more than 1,000 attendees. Crabtree started her post-college career with 17 years of retail management, which provided a good training ground for the fast-paced and chaotic lifestyle of an event planner. Her current position provides her the capability and unique resources to train university students who are interested in becoming event planning professionals.

Dr. Yao-Yi Fu is an associate professor of the Department of Tourism, Conventions, and Event Management at Indiana University-Purdue University-Indianapolis. She received her Ph.D. from the Pennsylvania State University in Hotel, Restaurant, and Institutional Management. Prior to her current appointment with IUPUI, she taught courses in resort and lodging management and hospitality management at all levels at the Pennsylvania State University and at California State University, Chico. She has work experience in hotel and restaurant businesses, special events planning, and theme park planning. Her teaching and research interests include service failure and service recovery in the tourism and hospitality industry, measurement of customer satisfaction and service quality, tourists' travel decision-making, tourist behavior, and tourism destination development and marketing.

Dr. Morgan Geddie is a professor of Resort and Lodging Management in the Department of Parks and Recreation Management at California State University, Chico. Professor Geddie received his doctorate from Oklahoma State University in occupational and adult education with an emphasis in Human Resources Development. He also has an MBA with an emphasis in marketing from the University of Central Oklahoma and a B.S. in Hotel and Restaurant Management from Oklahoma State University. Before joining the faculty at Chico State, he taught at the University of Houston, Oklahoma State University, Eastern Illinois University, and Arkansas Tech University. He also has several years of hotel experience in the New York City, New York and Charlotte, North Carolina markets.

Professor Geddie specializes in the areas of lodging and cruise line management. He has published in many journals and trade magazines as well as being a featured speaker at several conferences.

Jim Greiner, founder and president of Wildwater Ltd. Rafting and Starfish Exuma Adventure in the Bahamas, is passionate and committed to outdoor adventures. In addition to his entrepreneurial ventures, Greiner has over 30 years of experience in three cities as a parks and recreation director, and he has been honored with numerous awards in the fields of municipal parks and recreation, tourism, and ecotourism. His wrote *The Middle Atlantic Region Campers Guidebook* and has been involved in leadership roles with a variety of outdoor recreation and adventure organizations such as the Virginia Recreation & Parks Association, Eastern Professional River Outfitters Association, America Outdoors Association (25 years), and Commercial Recreation and Leisure Businesses. Receiving his bachelor's degree in parks and recreation management from North Carolina State University, and a master's in leisure services management from Florida State University, Greiner's real-world experience and academic background provide a unique perspective.

Doug Kennedy is a professor and coordinator of the Department of Recreation and Leisure Studies at Virginia Wesleyan College. He also serves as the associate dean for Campus Recreation and oversees aquatics, fitness, recreational sports, and outdoor activities. Prior to his arrival at Virginia Wesleyan College, he gained experience in environmental resources, employee and campus recreation, fitness, and military recreation while employed in the public and private sectors. He has earned degrees from the University of Delaware, Southern Illinois University, and Temple University. He has also served as the president of the Virginia Recreation and Park Society and chair of the Council on Accreditation. As a three-time recipient of the Samuel Nelson Gray Distinguished Teaching Award, Virginia Recreation and Park Society's Fellows Award, and YMCA's Service to Youth Award, Dr. Kennedy has made over 100 presentations at professional events and led delegations to Uzbekistan to assist with recreation planning and democracy education.

Dr. Craig M. Ross is professor in the Department of Recreation, Park, and Tourism Studies at Indiana University and specializes in sport management. He has written 74 professional articles, five books, three book chapters, 28 technical reports and has delivered 44 teaching presentations, 47 guest lectures, and over 64 state, national, and international presentations. Dr. Ross has received the prestigious Indiana University FACET Award for exemplary teaching, the President's Award for Excellence in Teaching at the Indiana University, the Excellence in Teaching Award from the National Recreation and Park Association-Society of Park and Recreation Educators, the IU HPER Outstanding Teacher Award, the IU School of Continuing Studies Outstanding Teacher Award, the IU Board of Trustees Teaching Award in 2004 and 2005, and the Teaching Excellence Recognition Award from the IU Board of Trustees Award in 1997, 1998, and 2000.

Dr. Vinod Sasidharan serves as vice-president of the Great Western Travel and Tourism Research Association. He has also served on the Destination Marketing Association International Student and Educator Advisory Council. He was an invited member of the

International Advisory Committee for the World Leisure Consensus Project. Currently, he is an associate professor in the School of Hospitality and Tourism Management at San Diego State University. His research has included the evaluation and implementation of grass-roots tourism initiatives, involving local community participation in planning and decision making for sustainable tourism development in the Dominican Republic, Finland, Jamaica, Romania, Tanzania, and Turkey. His research specialty is in the area of sustainability assessment and corporate social responsibility evaluation in tourism. He holds a master's degree in Tourism Policy and Management from the University of Birmingham, UK, and a doctorate in Leisure Studies from the Pennsylvania State University.

Dr. Paige Schneider is an assistant professor in the Department of Recreation and Leisure Studies at East Carolina University. She is also an affiliate faculty with ECU's Center for Sustainable Tourism. Her primary interest is consumer behavior and tourism, specifically adventure and ecotourism. She has over 12 years of travel industry management experience, which offers her valuable insight and an understanding of the importance of translating research into practical application for the tourism industry. Schneider has worked with organizations such as the Adventure Travel Trade Association (ATTA), Sustainable Travel International (STI), and Conservation International conducting research of both the supply side (providers of tourism goods and services) and demand side (consumers/travelers) of the tourism industry. As a long-time participant and advocate of adventure and ecotourism, she believes these types of travel experiences promote cultural understanding, fulfill personal dreams, and encourage environmental sustainability.

Dr. Kindal A. Shores is an associate professor at East Carolina University in the Department of Recreation and Leisure Studies where she also serves as the director of the Recreation and Park Administration and Recreational Therapy Administration Master of Science degree programs. Dr. Shores draws on her research experience in both exercise science and leisure studies to investigate the contribution of community parks and recreation for healthy, active living. She has worked on funded research projects linking parks and health for the Robert Wood Johnson Foundation, the Association for Prevention and Teaching Research, Be Active North Carolina, the Be Active Appalachian Partnership, the Centers for Disease Control and Prevention, and numerous county commissioners. Dr. Shores is an associate editor for the academic journal, *Journal of Leisure Research,* and has been recognized with multiple university awards for teaching and scholarship.

Tony Sisto is a retired park ranger with over 32 years of experience in the National Park Service. He stays involved with park issues in his volunteer work with the U.S. Association of National Park Rangers (www.anpr.org) and with the International Ranger Federation (www.int-ranger.net). When not traveling to world-protected areas, he lives in California.

Dr. Asuncion Suren is an assistant professor in the Department of Recreation, Parks, and Tourism at San Francisco State University. She also directs the campus-wide Youth and Human Services Nonprofit Certificate program. In these capacities, she teaches multiple courses on recreation and leisure, and nonprofit administration. In addition to her years in higher education, Asuncion is considered a multifaceted professional with 15 years of recreation and consulting experience combined. She has facilitated numerous community service needs in the areas of assessment planning, program development, and evaluation. She attributes gaining these transferable skills while working in Armed Forces Recreation. Asuncion has served as a director and program director for community recreation centers both stateside and abroad. She directed the Youth Services Center for Edwards Air Force Base in the Mojave Desert and the 2-2-0 Recreation Center in Korea.

Dr. Clifton E. Watts, Jr. is an assistant professor in the Department of Recreation and Leisure Studies at East Carolina University. Dr. Watts's research and scholarly interests are directed to: (1) evaluating how and to what extent communities enact collaborative, interdisciplinary approaches to address the needs of youth; (2) understanding what contexts and transactions are linked to positive youth development; and (3) examining how parks and open spaces promote healthy behavior and environmental awareness in youth. He has an extensive background as an evaluator; assisting with the design and execution of studies for a range of prevention and intervention programs aimed at high-risk youth. He has worked with community-based programs emanating from municipal recreation and park departments, schools, hospitals, criminal justice, and other grassroots agencies. He is a member of the National Recreation and Park Association, and also serves as an associate editor for the academic journal, *Leisure Sciences*.

Dr. Richard Williams is an associate professor in the Department of Recreation and Leisure Studies at East Carolina University in Greenville, NC. He teaches primarily in the Recreational Therapy curriculum but also teaches leisure theory and philosophy and research methods courses. His research interests are varied but are currently focused on the investigation of effectiveness of recreational therapy services for people with spinal cord injuries, stroke, and other disabilities.

Dr. Jo An M. Zimmermann, CPRP, has a BS in Recreation and Park Administration from Western Illinois University, an MBA from Olivet Nazarene University, and a Ph.D. in Parks, Recreation and Tourism Management from Clemson University. She is currently an assistant professor in the Department of Health and Human Performance at Texas State University–San Marcos. Her professional experience includes recreation program development/management and training and developing training materials while working for and consulting with recreation agencies in both the Non-Profit and Community sectors. Dr. Zimmermann is a Certified Park and Recreation Professional, was named the Al Hattendorf Professional of the Year by the Illinois Park and Recreation Association in 1999 and received a Special Recognition Award from the American Camp Association in 2002. Dr. Zimmermann has traveled extensively, allowing her to investigate many different approaches to the delivery of recreation services and programs.

"

Recreation improves awareness, deepens understanding, stimulates appreciation, develops one's powers, and enlarges the sources of enjoyment. It promotes individual fulfillment. It encourages self-discovery. It helps give meaning to life.

—DAVID E. GRAY, 1972

"

1

Recreation and Leisure in North American Life

CHERYL A. STEVENS
East Carolina University

FOCUS QUESTIONS

Q: *I understand why this book covers careers in recreation, parks, sport management, hospitality, and tourism, but why is leisure important?*

A: If you think of leisure as being lazy or idle time, it won't seem important, but when you consider that leisure experiences are where people can feel free, present, and integrated, you start to understand how it is integral to quality of life.

Q: *I heard someone say that recreation is associated with humanism. What does that mean?*

A: Humanism, as a school of thought, attaches great importance to human dignity, concerns, and abilities. Social and environmental justice issues and services for important, and sometimes underserved, populations such as youth, elderly, and people who are economically disadvantaged continue to be of the utmost importance. Also, since many North Americans are stressed because they feel rushed and harried, recreation and leisure have the potential to greatly enhance quality of life for all.

Q: *What motivates a person to enter a recreation-related profession?*

A: Recreation-related professions provide a great opportunity to align your life's work with something you truly enjoy. Individuals who are attracted to careers in recreation, parks, sport management, hospitality, and tourism all love some aspect of recreation activities themselves, and they also have a strong commitment to helping others, the outdoors, play, and/or entrepreneurism.

Q: *Why do people invest significant amounts of time and money in recreation and leisure experiences?*

A: Scientific studies have documented numerous tangible, important benefits to leisure experiences, including things like: stress management, improved physical and mental health, personal growth, spirituality, reduced crime and social alienation, economic growth, and environmental stewardship. Perhaps even more importantly, recreation and leisure experiences add to quality of life and life satisfaction.

KEY TERMS

Leisure	Tourism
Time free from work	Play
Freedom from	Humanism
Freedom to	Recreation-Related Profession
State of mind	Direct service
Recreational activity	Inclusive service
Public recreation	So-importants
Recreation	Benefits
Public park	Purple Recreation
Hospitality	

INSPIRATIONAL EXPERIENCES

Stories are a great way to begin to connect with reasons why people are so passionate about recreation, parks, sports management, hospitality, and tourism experiences:

A Senior Leisure Experience: I currently live in a nursing home because I had a severe stroke about a year ago. I can honestly say the only reason I have not gone into a severe depression is our leisure encounter group. The recreational therapists are great and they keep me busy. It's helped me make new friends, tested my endurance, and it's something I can look forward to every day.
—*Female, African American, Age 72*

What's Great About Being a Camp Counselor: Camp was a lot more than I expected because I learned so much about myself. I learned to take leadership for a group of teens and not be afraid of them and what they think of me. I got the chance to make connections with people from different countries and from all walks of life. I got to see the campers overcome their greatest fears and that put a smile on my face. Some were afraid of horses, others didn't know how to swim, and some didn't want to try a new activity. I learned to gently push them to their limits without making them push back in the wrong way. Some mornings I didn't want to get up, but I did. That says a lot about camp life and the positive state of mind you develop while in the company of your camp family.
—*Female, Caucasian, 4-H Camp Counselor, Age 22*

Enjoy Work and It Becomes Leisure: I love computers. I have a degree in computer engineering, and I really love spending hours in front of the computer screen. I asked my sister if I could put a computer inside her computer. She had no clue what I was talking about, but she let me do it. It took me hours—uploading, downloading different files and applications—but I had a blast. When I finished, I presented it to her with a smile on my face, and then I showed her how to work her two computers in one.

—Male, African American, Age 27

Competitive Sports: I played women's competitive softball for four years. I have so many great memories from the games. Nothing compares to sharing time with friends and others with a common interest; we laughed all the time. I'm very competitive, so that aspect of the game gave me both a release and a chance to show my skills. The tougher the game, the better I liked it. It was such an adrenaline rush. One thing I really miss now is the fitness—I could run, hit, throw, and exercise in a way that felt more like fun than work.

—Female, Caucasian, Age 50

FRAMING THE DISCUSSION

These personal stories illustrate benefits that recreation and leisure experiences have for individuals and the professionals that provide them. An important first step in understanding the career options covered in this book is carefully considering the meaning behind some of the terms used in the profession, including leisure, play, and humanism. It's also important to understand what we mean by each of the words in the book's subtitle, "Recreation, Parks, Sport Management, Hospitality, and Tourism." Leisure is the broadest term, so we'll start there.

What Do You Mean by Leisure?

Don't be too hasty in dismissing leisure as unimportant. The word leisure can get a bad rap when it is equated with being lazy or idle time that is left over when everything important gets finished. However, the meaning of the word leisure is rich and complex, and you should become familiar with these deeper meanings in order to understand what's meant by "leisure services."

Alison Link, Leisure Education Consultant tells us that: "**Leisure** has many different definitions—some involving time, some relating to an activity being done, some relating to state of mind. Personally, I am most at leisure when I feel free, present, and integrated. I like this definition for myself, because it allows me to experience leisure at any moment, even in just a few minutes" (cited in Alboher, 2008).

Leisure and Freedom

Leisure has been associated with **time free from work** since Ancient Greece, when the best life was seen as one where male citizens who didn't have to labor had time to pursue truth and self-understanding (Dare, Welton, & Coe, 1998). The Greeks called this time *schole*—note its close association with "school"—because learning for the Greeks was considered to be a part of the best life and a privilege. Since Greeks that had *schole* did not have to work (in the sense of physical labor), they were able to enjoy learning and thinking freely about interesting questions such as "How should we best live?"

Today, however, we tend to associate school with work, or at least earning our way to a better paying job. In part, this shift in viewpoints happened when the meaning of leisure shifted during Roman times to one that viewed work and leisure as opposites. While Ancient Rome did spread many of the classical ideals in knowledge, arts, music and literature across the European continent, the majority of Roman authors viewed leisure as

WHY DO WE STAY SO BUSY?

Americans' training for a perpetual sense of obligation and productivity starts early, and it doesn't just affect older adults with mortgages. Consider this narrative written by a soon-to-be college graduate who reflected on leisure, productivity and guilt:

"Work and school consumed so much of my life for many years, so even walking my dog has been done more for exercise than as a leisure activity. When I moved to Florida recently, I bought an annual pass to Disney World, and I have been three times. One Saturday, my boyfriend and I spent the day at Blizzard Beach studying, and then we walked around Magic Kingdom afterwards. I have to admit that I get a sense of guilt when I engage in an activity merely for pleasure, so being productive on my trip to Disney World by doing some homework seemed like the perfect way to spend my time."

— (H. Chapman, personal communication, June 8. 2009)

otium, which translates as rest and recreation (Neulinger, 1974). This implied that leisure was a time of non-activity that was useful for recovering/restoring for work. Leisure was also viewed as a well-earned rest and reward for a lifetime of hard work (*negotium*).

This work-leisure dichotomy is how modern leisure is viewed today; that is, that work and leisure are opposite concepts. The Romans believed a person needed to earn his right to rest and relaxation by first working hard. Today, people think about leisure only casually, and continue to view leisure and work as opposites, because the most commonly understood definition of leisure is time free from work. However, it's important to consider more complex understandings of leisure in order to understand the value of leisure services.

Bregha (1982) expands our understanding of the connection between leisure and freedom when he urges us to consider that leisure can be both "freedom from" and "freedom "to." **"Freedom from"** is associated with time seen as free from constraint, oppression, or manipulation. For example, if a person views his or her job as controlling of time and choice, he or she will not have a leisure experience while working. However, if a person has a high-autonomy job and feels he or she is in control of, and enjoying, work (which can be creative and meaningful), then he or she may experience leisure and meaning during at least some of the work.

Joe Pavelka (2000), author of *It's Not About Time: Rediscovering Leisure in a Changing World*, notes that some people get more meaning and satisfaction from their work than from their non-work time. Ann Hochschild, author of *The Time Bind*, explains: "today's managers have successfully engineered the workplace to serve as surrogate family, and while workers will state they value family more than work, they often find work more personally gratifying than home" (cited in Billitteri, 2005). Bear in mind that many people face constraints imposed by many outer and inner forces other than work. For example, a person may make choices that result in a prison term; a child is required to be in school; a person may feel guilty if he is not doing something society thinks of as productive; a person who is unemployed may feel he or she has no right to enjoy time not working because he or she has not earned that right. In sum, a person's perception of "freedom from" constraints, which is necessary for leisure, is much more complicated than just being off of work.

From a different perspective, thinking about leisure as **"freedom to"** brings us closer to the deeper meaning of leisure that was implied in Ancient Greece; that is, freedom to engage in something meaningful, significant and authentic to self. Dare et al. (1998) state that,

> To live life to its fullest is to live creatively and to understand the freedom which underlies human existence. To understand and accept this freedom is to be authentic. To live meaningful lives we must understand who we are—that is, we must have reflected on our lives and our projects (p. 243).

Finding meaning in one's life is central to satisfaction. Victor Frankl (2006), concentration camp survivor and author of the book *Man's Search for Meaning*, concluded that "Life is not primarily a quest for pleasure ... but a quest for meaning. The greatest task for any person is to find meaning is his or her life" (p. x). And leisure can be the context in which people connect with whatever is meaningful to them. As Pavelka (2000) notes, "leisure is not so much about time as it is the personal meaning of time" (p. 30).

Bregha cautions us to realize that embracing leisure as "freedom to" can be our greatest opportunity as well as our greatest challenge, because it requires the self-knowledge and wisdom to know what we truly want. In order to embrace freedom, we must be willing to consciously choose goals that will bring long-term happiness and affirm our unique character. This is not always easy in a world where most of us feel our discretionary time is scarce and subject to restrictions. Most people feel they are under a lot of time stress.

In sum, you might be tempted to think that leisure isn't really very important in our society, but this is only true if you continue to equate leisure with laziness or idle time. As you continue to learn more about leisure, I urge you remember how leisure as "freedom to" is associated with quality of life. Meaningful leisure has the potential to improve anyone's quality of life because we are human *beings*, not human *doings*. Alison Link hints at the importance of leisure in one's quality of life when she tells her clients, "Leisure can be experienced every day, even if we only have five minutes. Even small amounts can turn 'surviving' into 'living.'" John de Graaf (n.d.) drives this point home when he states that the well-being of people in North America is linked to far more than Gross Domestic Product, and we would do well to ask, "What's the economy for, anyway?" This line of questioning can urge policymakers to consider the importance and value of health, equality, savings, and sustainability. Thus, one's attitude toward leisure can make a tremendous difference in quality of life, and this is good news, because personal attitude is something each person can control.

Leisure as a State of Mind

The leisure as a **state of mind** perspective provides a useful way to move past our tendency to view leisure and work as opposites, for if a person is enjoying meaningful work, it is leisure for them. Alison Link describes how leisure can be viewed subjectively as a state of mind, when she says, "Leisure can happen when we are in various [mental] states: artistic or creative, physical, intellectual, social, spiritual, learning new things, volunteering, active, passive, or as a spectator or participant. One can be emotionally connected and engaged or not. And we can even have leisure at work and be more productive, healthy, and creative" (cited by Alboher, 2008). The essence of the "leisure as a state of mind" view is that leisure is a special attitude; in fact, time and activity are irrelevant, because it is personal feelings that matter (Russell, 2009). Therefore, if a person perceives her experience as leisure, then it is leisure for her. Viewing leisure as a state of mind is appealing because it gives value to the individual's subjective feelings about an experience. If your state of mind tells you that "This experience is meaningful and I choose to do it because it has value to me," no one can disagree, because leisure depends on your perspective.

Leisure as Recreational Activity

A third view is that leisure is a **recreational activity** that people choose because they expect to enjoy it. Leisure activities may provide personal benefit, reduce stress, and restore peace of mind. Recreational leisure activities can be virtually anything—going for a drive, playing cards or computer games, cooking, or bird watching. People choose different activities for various reasons, and "expecting to have fun" is just one. Other reasons may involve socializing or obligation. For example, we may go to a movie because our friends or family ask us to (i.e., social reasons), or sometimes we go to a "fun" event because it's expected of us, such as your boss inviting you to a Christmas party (i.e., role obligations). In reality, many people have multiple reasons for choosing a particular activity. For example, a trip to the gym may be motivated by many reasons, such as the desire to lose weight and reduce stress, meeting up with a friend, and the intrinsic joy of moving and feeling powerful.

The main advantage to viewing leisure as activity is that researchers can count it by asking people to record activities time diaries. This way, they can find out how much leisure time people have and what activities they prefer. Time diaries are useful, but they are less than perfect. The primary downside to viewing leisure as recreational activity is that people have different perspectives on the same activity. For example, some people find running enjoyable and meaningful, and for others, it's work. The leisure as recreational activity view also excludes non-active leisure experiences we may choose for relaxation such as taking nap or daydreaming.

LEISURE'S MULTIPLE DIMENSIONS

Recreation

The National Recreation and Park Association defines **public recreation** as activities that take place at a public park or facility, such as sports, physical activities, experiences in nature or exposure to arts and culture, among other things. Recreational activities can be passive or active and can be engaged by visitors on their own time or they may be organized/conducted by employees of a recreation agency or business. DeGraff, Jordan, and DeGraff (1999) inform us that **recreation** can be viewed as any activity a person freely chooses that has the potential for achieving some desirable outcome. DeGraff et al. define recreation as "an activity that takes place during one's free time, is enjoyable, freely chosen,

> " SOMETHING WILL HAVE GONE OUT OF US as a people if we ever let the remaining wilderness be destroyed; if we permit the last virgin forests to be turned into comic books and plastic cigarette cases; if we drive the few remaining members of the wild species into zoos or to extinction; if we pollute the last clean air and dirty the last clean streams and push our paved roads through the last of the silence, so that never again will Americans be free from noise, the exhausts, the stinks of human and automotive waste. And so that never again can we have the chance to see ourselves single, separate, vertical and individual in the world, part of the environment of trees and rocks and soil, brother to the other animals, part of the natural world and competent to belong in it.
>
> We simply need that wild country available to us, even if we never do more than drive to its edge and look in. For it can be a means of reassuring ourselves of our sanity as creatures, a part of the geography of hope.
>
> —Wallace Stegner "

and benefits the individual emotionally, socially, physically, cognitively, and spiritually" (p. 3). Thus, while recreation and leisure are often used interchangeably, recreation is more easily linked to measurable benefits because it involves people engaging in activities with specific goals, or outcomes, in mind. We will discuss the benefits of recreational activities later on in this chapter.

Parks

The National Recreation and Park Association tells us that a **public park** is any area, or portions of areas, that are dedicated by any federal, state, or local agency primarily for public recreational use. Therefore, parks include: boardwalks, green spaces, and playgrounds close to people's homes where they visit on a daily basis; metropolitan and state parks near to urban areas where people can go for weekend visits; and they include large tracts of land such as the National Parks that have been reserved for all. Parks are very important to quality of life even when we are not visiting them on a daily basis because we like knowing the park is there for our enjoyment, as well as the potential enjoyment of future generations. There is something about being outdoors that brings peace of mind and connects us with our sense of place in the universe. As author Rachel Carson noted, "Those who contemplate the beauty of the earth find reserves of strength that will endure as long as life lasts."

Sport Management

According to Dr. Robert Barcelona, Clemson University, **sport management** is a term that is incredibly wide in scope, and it refers to any one of a number of professional careers that involve planning, organizing, leading, and controlling sport events, programs, personnel, and facilities (see chapter 9, "Sport Management and Sports Teams"). McLean, Hurd and Rogers (2008) tell us that sport management is not restricted to any one sector, so it's important for any individual interested in a sport management-related career to think outside the box. There are some career possibilities that may come to mind immediately such as collegiate, semi-professional, professional, and amateur sports, but be aware that jobs in these settings often require specialized skill sets and are highly competitive. If you love sports, you should also think broadly about career possibilities to include areas of sport management such as: sport marketing, guest services and sports clubs (see chapter 9, "Sport Management"); sports arenas, coliseums and stadiums (see also chapter 10, "Events"); intramural sports (see chapter 8, "Campus Recreation"); community recreation youth athletics programs (see also chapter 3, "Community Recreation"); youth sports programs in non-profit agencies and religious organizations (see also chapter 4, "Non-Profit Recreation); sports programs in military morale, recreation and welfare (see chapter 5, "MWR"), and commercial businesses involving sports facilities and sporting goods (see chapter 13, "Commercial Recreation").

Hospitality

Simply put, the term **hospitality** is providing food, beverage, lodging accommodations, and entertainment (including recreational activities) to guests. The hospitality industry is comprised of many businesses including hotels, resorts, cruise ships, theme parks, clubs, and restaurants. Typically, hospitality is considered to be a component of the tourism industry since all travelers will need hospitality upon their arrival. Hospitality, however, has its own niche, since dealing with guests face to face where they sleep and eat comes with its own special set of opportunities and challenges. Consider that lodging must be available to meet the demands of all types of travelers, whether its families, people with pets, people with special needs and interests, people who want luxury, or those traveling on a budget. In addition to the food, beverage, lodging, and entertainment, recreation specialists also provide activities programs for children and families at destination resorts, timeshares, and campgrounds. If you are interested in providing quality customer service and working in a fast-paced industry that advances people more quickly than many, consider hospitality (see chapter 11, "The Hospitality Industry" as well as chapter 10 "Events," chapter 11 "Commercial Recreation Businesses," and chapter 12, "Tourism").

Tourism

Tourism can be defined as travel that takes place for recreational, leisure, or business purposes. The World Tourism Organization (1995) defines tourists as people who "travel to and stay in places outside their usual environment for more than twenty-four (24) hours and not more than one consecutive year for leisure, business, and other purposes not related to the exercise of any activity remunerated from within the place visited" (p. 14).

Today, tourism is big business and is recognized as an expanding field within recreation and leisure services, and many argue that it should be seen as a profession in its own right. However, most agree that it is a growth industry, and it is motivationally tied to our recreation behaviors and leisure interests (Sessoms & Henderson, 1994). The World Tourism Organization (UNWTO) (n.d.) informs us that in 2008, international tourism grew by 2% to reach 922 million. This is up 18 million over 2007, and international tourism generated 944 billion U.S. dollars and accounted for 30% of the world's service exports. Further, UNWTO forecasts that there will be 1.6 billion tourist arrivals worldwide by the year 2020. Because tourism is a very significant business today, and due to its obvious tie to recreation activities and leisure experiences, tourism is addressed along with more traditional recreation and leisure services in this book on careers (see chapter 12, "Travel and Tourism" as well as chapter 10, "Events," and chapter 11, "Hospitality."

Play

Play is so integrally connected with having fun that our discussion about the meaning of recreation and leisure would be incomplete without it. All people know what play is from personal experience, and play occurs wherever people find it—play can happened anytime, anywhere. As the Non-Sequitur cartoon by Wiley Miller illustrates, children's play today involves both virtual and in-nature experiences, but both types of activity are play.

Johan Huizinga, author of one of the original studies of play and culture tells us that play has seven defining elements:

1. All play is voluntary activity, and hence, play is linked to freedom,
2. Play is not ordinary, or real life—it is only pretending for fun,
3. Play is limited within time and space in that it has a beginning and an ending,
4. Play creates order by bringing a temporary and limited perfection,
5. There is an element of tension and uncertainty in play,
6. All play has rules that determine what "goes" in the temporary world of play, and
7. Play surrounds itself with an air of secrecy; that is, "we are different and do things differently when we play (p. 12)."

Play can involve participating in a game of pretend, playing soccer, or playing World of Warcraft, and it can occur anywhere—at home, at work, on vacation, and even in a prison, because it occurs in a temporary world constructed by the players.

Questions about play have fascinated people for centuries. Why do people play? What benefit is there in play? Ellis (1977), a recognized play expert, explains that people play for two reasons: (1) to have optimal experiences, and (2) to gain a sense of competence and control. Consider, for example, a girl "playing" teacher with her dolls—she creates the rules of the pretend classroom and has fun handing out rewards and punishments to her "students" She has placed herself in control (a role she cannot take in real life), and her play world affords her the opportunity feel competent and effective, just as she perceives her teacher to be.

As to how people benefit from play, many people think of play as the activity of childhood. Bregha (1982) confirms that's how it starts: "It is a generally accepted belief that, as children, we first discover freedom, its delights and dangers, in playing" (p. 1). However, researchers and managers are increasingly discovering that play is very important to adults too. Adult partners who seek novelty and play together, stay together. Play also fosters creativity during work by facilitating the cognitive and affective dimensions, as well as the motivational and skill conditions, of the creative process (Mainemelis & Ronson, 2006). For example, Google erases some of the artificial dichotomizations between work, leisure, and play by expecting employees to spend 20% of their time on non-core projects, which they are expected to explore without allowing considerations of profitability or marketability to hinder their efforts. Why sanction play at work? Because companies are finding that building play into work culture adds to the bottom line by creating more innovative products and employee satisfaction.

Clearly, play adds to one's life at any age. As playwright George Bernard Shaw once stated, "We don't stop playing because we grow old; we grow old because we stop playing." So, play is important to quality of life at any age, because all humans gain joy from having peak (optimal) experiences and feeling competent and effective, even if only in the moment.

Leisure, recreation and play are clearly linked to optimal human experience. The next section will explain, from a philosophical perspective, what humanism means to recreation.

Leisure, Recreation, and Humanism

Humanism can be described as a philosophical perspective that attaches great importance to human dignity, concerns, and abilities. Humanists believe that, on a deep level, every person has good inside of them in the form of human spirit, or conscience. Whether or not a person is in touch with, or uses, his or her conscience is another matter (which we will not debate here), but suffice it to say that recreation and leisure service providers have a long history of striving to help people develop their most human qualities.

A humanistic approach to recreation and leisure services is of paramount importance in today's increasingly stressful and troubled world. As de Graff (n.d.) points out, economic success can no longer be measured in just economic terms like Gross Domestic Product. We must start taking into account other values that constitute the greatest good—health, happiness, knowledge, kindness—for the greatest number—equality, access to opportunity—over the long run—in a healthy democracy and sustainable environment (p. 1). Parks and recreation visionary David Gray noted back in 1972 that "America is turning inward. We are reexamining our thoughts, our ideas, our motives. Our method is introspection and our goal is self-discovery ... the motive is a deeper participation in life" (p. 18). Before you dismiss Dr. Gray's commentary as potentially outdated, consider its keen relevance to today's issues:

- Most North Americans believe they face too many demands on their time on any given day and they feel rushed and overwhelmed (Pavelka, 2000)
- For most of the final quarter of the 20th century, Europeans gained relative to Americans in almost every quality of life measure (de Graaf, n.d., p. 2)
- Many people face days filled with tension, boredom, feelings of powerlessness, monotony, and frustration and have increasing problems related to physical health (i.e., heart disease, obesity, diabetes) and emotional health (i.e., anxiety, depression, addiction, and alienation).
- While technology and connectivity have increased work efficiencies, they are merely tools and they will not solve problems with the human condition.

A humanistic ethic is of central importance to the delivery of recreation, parks, sport management, hospitality, and tourism in today's world. What this means, in a practical sense, is re-conceptualizing recreation from a humanistic perspective. This means making it our business to promote health and well-being. It means keeping people well versus curing them after they are sick. It means helping people who get sick back to a path where quality of life is of the highest priority. It means viewing recreation as a psycho-emotional-physical response that is independent of the activity. The activity becomes the medium, but from a humanistic perspective recreation is the individual's internal, pleasurable response to the activity. As Dr. Gray aptly put it:

> Recreation is an emotional condition within an individual human being that flows from a feeling of well-being and self-satisfaction. It is characterized by feelings of mastery, achievement, exhilaration, acceptance, success, personal worth, and pleasure. It reinforces a positive self-image. Recreation is a response to esthetic experience, achievement of personal goals, or positive feedback from others. It is independent of activity, leisure, or social acceptance (p. 19).

A growing number of people in North America are seeking new ways to experience the fullest of what life has to offer. Grass-roots movements and the self-help industries are burgeoning with advice to help people improve the quality of their lives by slowing down, focusing on health and well-being, establishing greater intimacy with others, and creating sustainable lifestyles. These approaches to the good life embrace the fulfillment of individuals' inner experiences rather than the acquisition of things. This is ultimately the work of recreation, parks, sport management, hospitality, and tourism professionals. Humanistic values are not new to recreation; in fact, they have been with the profession since the beginning.

Next, we are going to take a brief historical tour so you can understand, in a general way, where the profession came from and where it's going. This overview illustrates how recreation and leisure services in America had its beginnings in social services and how the profession has expanded, over time, to meet the needs of many, varied client groups. The good news is this expansion has opened the door for many diverse career options within the recreation, parks, sport management, hospitality, and tourism professions and meeting humanistic needs is more important now than ever! Note that we will explore the detailed history of each career area in chapters 3 through 13, because we believe history is more interesting and relevant when studied in context.

A Brief History of Recreation, Parks, Sport Management, Hospitality, and Tourism

The notion of providing recreational activities and parks in America has its roots in social services and human needs. The profession was established around the late 1800s as the urban population doubled and the Industrial Revolution and immigration resulted growing social welfare concerns. Early social reformers, who were mainly private philanthropists, saw play and recreation as anecdotes to all nature of ills—physical health could be improved by fresh air and physical activity, and moral character and social skills could be learned through organized recreation and play. As you can see from the break-out box, "Our Radical Roots," the need was great. Consider that in 1890, there were 350,000 children living in New York City, and there were no organized places for them to play (McLean, et al., 2008).

> ❝   In many ways, [our founders] were the radical counterparts of Eldridge Cleaver, Jane Fonda, Caesar Chavez, Gloria Steinem, and Ralph Nader. They continually fought city hall, organized labor strikes, marched in the streets, gave public speeches, and wrote award-winning articles deploring the living conditions of the poor. The issues and problems they faced were well defined: slavery, the aftermath of the Civil War, thousands of new immigrants, slums, child labor, disease, the suffrage movement, World War I, and a rapidly industrializing nation. America was striving to develop its abundant natural resources and was also enjoying a booming economy. The work ethic and the free-enterprise system flourished, thus creating a paradox of strong economic growth at the expense of human suffering and exploitation.
>
> Our founders faced these issues. They were not meek and mild, easily intimidated or swayed by local politicians. They worked in, around, and with the political system. The political battles they fought gave them the skills needed in order to establish the park, playground, and recreation services we enjoy today (p. 331).
>
> — MARY DUNCAN
> excerpted from *Our Radical Roots* (1991) ❞

Jane Addams and Joseph Lee are two examples of the profession's prominent founders. Jane Addams, the daughter of a wealthy man, helped organize support for immigrant settlers and poor laborers. A settlement house, called the Hull House, opened in 1889 in Chicago slums as a neighborhood center to provide multiple social, educational, and recreational services. According to Duncan (1991), Ms. Addams channeled her life's energies into programs like the Hull House in order to create a more humanistic society. She touched the lives of many, including Joseph Lee, the father of the American playground movement. Like Addams, Lee came from a wealthy family. He was "appalled by the jailing of children for playing in the streets, [and] he established, at his own expense, an experimental playground in Boston" (Duncan, 1991, p. 335). Philosophically, Lee believed recreation should be an integral part of everyone's life (both adults and children). He wrote an influential book called *Play and Education*, which described the relationships between play, recreation, and the social problems facing our cities (Duncan). Lee and Addams both served as officers in the Playground Association of America, founded in 1906, which is the forerunner to today's National Recreation and Park and Association (NRPA).

Other events that dramatically shaped the nature of the emerging recreation and parks movement happened concurrently. Central Park was established in 1857 as the first major city park, Yellowstone was set aside as the first national park in 1872, and more than 80 cities initiated their own parks and playgrounds between 1880 and 1900. Thus, the stage was set in America for a peculiar and uniquely democratic vision that sanctioned the use of public funding to provide for recreational activities, facilities (like playgrounds), and parks on a local and national scale. On a national scale, it was deemed that these activities, facilities, and parks should be as available and accessible to the average citizen, not just the wealthy, because they were good. That is, they were good for individuals, good for society, and good for the country as a whole. Accordingly, recreation agencies, facilities, and parks took on an accepted social role across the country as people came to gradually accept recreation, parks, and leisure services as a valid social good in a democratic society.

As the recreation and parks professions matured and diversified, it became accepted that leisure was an end in itself to be enjoyed by all. Public recreation drifted away from a social welfare model (with specific goals to help those in need) toward a model where services were provided for everyone who wanted them (DeGraaf, Jordan, & DeGraaf, 1999). Hence, new kinds of recreation and leisure service providers, which targeted the health and wellness benefits, emerged. These more specialized areas included: armed forces recreation, therapeutic recreation, campus recreation, and employee recreation. In addition, commercial recreation and leisure businesses such as retail sales of recreational vehicles, boats, and equipment and destinations like Disneyland became increasingly popular in post-WWII prosperity and beyond. Of course, non-profit agencies and public recreation and parks continued to operate as well.

As America and other developed countries moved from manufacturing toward a service economy in the latter half of the 20th century, a more specialized class of recreation, parks, and leisure services began to emerge in response to continuing social service needs and people's growing ability and desire to pay for recreation and leisure. The hospitality industry added value with organized recreation and leisure programs to attract and hold repeat visitor interest. Sports management evolved out of a growing interest in recreation and management opportunities in youth and professional sports. Meeting planning, conference services, and the entertainment industry provided a convergence for business and pleasure. Travel and tourism continued to grow on a national and international scale. Many of these specialized areas are considered professions in their own right, but they are also considered part of the **recreation-related professions.**

In the 21st century, our recreation and leisure-related professions face tremendous challenges and opportunities. The need for social services and programs that support social justice and the demand for leisure experiences at all points in the cost spectrum has never been greater. People from all walks of life are beginning to reexamine their priorities and consciously seek higher quality leisure experiences. All recreation, parks, sport management, hospitality, and tourism organizations are being challenged to operate ethically, sustainably, and to respond to the needs of diverse populations.

Individuals who are attracted to careers in recreation, parks, sport management, hospitality, and tourism all love some aspect of recreation activities themselves, and they also have a strong commitment and attraction to one or more of the following: helping others, love of the outdoors, play, and entrepreneurism and excitement. Let's take a closer look at these four motivations so we can better understand what drives recreation, parks, tourism, and leisure services professionals.

What Motivates Recreation, Parks, Sport Management, Hospitality, and Tourism Professionals?

Those who work in recreation-related professions are especially passionate about one or more things that give them great satisfaction in their chosen career. Many students searching for a major discover the recreation field and feel like they've landed in a gold mine because it's obvious to them that "This degree will prepare me for a job where I can look forward to going to work every day!" Recreation-related professions provide a great opportunity to align one's life's work with something that corresponds with one's authentic self. Thus, the recreation professionals whose profiles you'll be reading throughout this book didn't arrive there because they were trying to get rich—that might be a secondary outcome—but their first love was something else.

First and foremost, recreation professionals have an intrinsic attraction to some activity or leisure experience that "turned them on" in their youth. What do you love? Maybe it's soccer, baseball, backpacking, scouts, sailing, summer camp, travel, or kayaking. Mike Gamache, the Director of the Oyster River Youth Association (ORYA), tells us how his passion connects him with his profession: "I played sports and was involved with sports all my life. I've always been interested in sports and fitness. I majored in recreation management with a focus in sport studies. I had a chance to interview with the former Executive Director following my internship, and he hired me. I wanted to be at ORYA because I believed that I would be able to make a difference in people's lives, and learn a lot in the process." Maybe you love many kinds of recreation and leisure, and the possibilities are truly unlimited.

We're going to lead you through some exercises in chapter 2 to assess your passions, but we'd like to get you started thinking about what drives your recreational career interests right away so you can see how what motivates you can help you choose the recreation-related career options that may be right for you.

Helping Others

Recreation professionals are all about making a difference in people's quality of life. That difference can be helping others by working directly with clients or helping many on a broader scale (inclusive service). Tom Carr, Certified Therapeutic Recreation Specialist and Program Coordinator for the Northeast Passage Athlete Development Center, talks about what it's like to provide **direct service** to others: "Helping to make a difference was a big thing for me. I like to be involved with beginners, and seeing the instant gratification when they are introduced to a sport and get a positive experience. But I do a lot of my work with high level, competitive athletes. What is even more rewarding is seeing their long-term growth. Seeing them begin a sport, and then 10 years later, they are competing in the Paralympics on the national and international stage."

Sandy Dhuyvetter, the founder, executive producer, and host of TravelTalk MEDIA, provides the type of **inclusive service** that has a broader effect. She states, "The greatest part about my job is to hear from guests about how we have added value to others' lives. Travel positively affects people personally and socially, and our world benefits economically as well. Meeting people and connecting people from all over the world is pure joy" (www.traveltalkradio.com). As you can see from Sandy's comment, some recreation professionals help others on a broad scale.

Matt Postein, from the New England Outdoor Center in Maine, serves both directly and inclusively: "First, there is the satisfaction of seeing our guests have a really great time and feeling the enrichment they are receiving from the experience. The second is being a part of helping our community economically, socially, and environmentally by bringing in visitors who are eco-sensitive, and sharing the beauty and wonder of this wilderness area with them. We do all this while creating jobs and revenue that supports the community."

Many recreation professionals are driven by the desire to make a positive difference. Our society has many **"So Importants,"** such as programs, services, and organizations that address social and environmental justice issues. For example, youth need healthy developmental opportunities; the aging and elderly populations deserve active, high-quality lives; persons with mental, physical, and emotional disabilities can be reached through recreation and leisure experiences in ways that they cannot be reached by clinical treatment; people and communities that are coping with crime, poverty, and racial tensions can use recreation and leisure to build common bonds; communities can be strengthened through sustainable tourism; and, the environment can be preserved and enjoyed simultaneously when we follow sustainable practices. There are no limits to the needs and opportunities for those interested in using recreation and leisure experiences as a means to improve quality of life.

Love of the Outdoors

Are you drawn to the great outdoors? When you are in nature, do you feel at peace? Those who love working in the outdoors have a strong bond with nature. Some people would love nothing more than to work outdoors. They may be particularly interested in preservation and protection, providing positive outdoor experiences, or both. Maybe you can relate to this anonymous blogger who wrote, "I love taking long walks, collecting my thoughts as I enjoy the sights and sounds of nature. I like camping, looking up at the stars, breathing in fresh air. The beauty of nature is unmatched, and we should take the time to appreciate it."

Ginny Alfriend, Park Specialist for the City of Eugene Parks and Open Space in Oregon, states, "We are outside most every day of the year and time all of our activities to the weather and season. It is a real treat to have my 'office' share space with a Pileated Woodpecker!" So, if you love the outdoors in an extraordinary way, the recreation professions provide a number of ways you can work in and for the out of doors.

Play for Life

Earlier in the chapter we talked about how play is a universal human experience. If you are one of those people who have kept your childlike passion for play as an adult, you may be motivated to share it with others. Jack Wise, the CEO of Wildwater Rafting, talks about the value of having fun: "I would have to say that the most rewarding [thing about my job] is to have new and exciting experiences in a special environment. It's also a bonus to be able to be involved in all these fun experiences myself." Given that the desire to play-hard/work-hard is a wide-spread phenomenon in American culture, it's not surprising that many would love to have a job where they can do just that!

Entrepreneurism and Excitement

An entrepreneur is a special type of person who is drawn to the excitement of combining innovation and risk taking to create and sustain a business venture. He or she provides the leadership for the venture and assumes a significant amount of accountability for the risks and outcomes inherent in that enterprise (O'Sullivan & Sheffrin, 2003). Phrases that describe entrepreneurs include: innovator, creator, risk taker, problem solver, and catalyst for change. Starting and maintaining innovative business ventures is not for everybody, but entrepreneurial skills are increasingly needed in all sectors of the economy. That is, public, non-profit and for-profit enterprises increasingly rely on entrepreneurial skills because financial sustainability is no longer a given for any type of organization. Indeed, as we move to a more social economy (more on this concept in chapters 2 and 15), an increasing number of professionals will be called on to blend their entrepreneurial abilities with their passion for making a difference.

John Hope-Johnstone, the CEO of Corvallis Tourism, is one such entrepreneur in a recreation-related profession. John tells us, "I started my tourism career as a travel agent, then as a tour wholesaler, then as a hotelier, then owned my own bed and breakfast in Hawaii, and now I am finishing my tourism career in destination marketing." John goes on to explain how innovation permeates what he does: "Travel and tourism always stays on the cutting edge. When the Internet search engines started to blossom as a marketing tool in the '90s, many of the first online e-commerce businesses were travel-based."

If you have entrepreneurial abilities, crave the excitement of solving problems and being on the cutting edge of innovation, you will find a number of recreation-related careers that appeal to you, including: sport management, the hospitality industry, travel and tourism, event management, and commercial recreation businesses. Depending on your unique abilities and interests, you may also find ways to combine your entrepreneurial aptitudes with other passions, such as becoming the head of a non-profit organization dedicated to preserving and protecting open space.

Now that you've become familiar with motives for working in a recreation-related profession, let's take a look at what motivates clients to engage in recreation and leisure experiences. Understanding the benefits of recreation and leisure experiences will help you better understand how these experiences help people acquire knowledge, skills, and abilities that help them live more satisfying lives.

MOTIVATION FOR RECREATION AND LEISURE PARTICIPATION

Generally speaking, people are motivated to engage in recreation and leisure experiences because of a mix of intrinsic and extrinsic motives. For example, I may attend my department's softball game because it's expected of me as part of my work-role (extrinsic motive—I feel I have to be there because my boss asked me to come), but I may also think it will be fun (intrinsic motive—I go because I want to enjoy myself). In most cases, people choose recreation experiences because they anticipate receiving one or more benefits

According to Bev Driver (2008), the recognized expert on outcomes and benefits of recreation and leisure experiences, there are three types of **benefits** we should be aware of. First, there are those benefits that are associated with an improved change or condition (p. 4). This implies that a new state is viewed as more desirable than a previous state. These changes could occur within individuals, groups, or biophysical and cultural resources. Examples include improved health, learning, social bonding, improved economic viability, and improvements in natural or man-made environments. A second type of benefit is the maintenance of a desired condition, prevention of an undesired condition, or reduction of an undesired condition (p. 4). An example is protecting natural resources in order to provide opportunities for visitors to maintain their physical and mental health. A third type of benefit is, quite simply, the realization of a satisfying recreation experience (p. 4). It is very important to place a high value on people having satisfying experiences regardless of whether or not any improved conditions can be easily discerned or measured. As pointed out by Estes and Henderson (2002), "Professionals shouldn't forget … that the outcomes related to enjoyment are still at the core of what makes our profession unique and valuable among other human service areas—we facilitate fun and intrinsically motivating experiences. Although the values of our profession go beyond 'fun and games,' enjoyment is, at all times, central to our work" (p. 22). Driver classifies benefits into four types: Personal, Social/Cultural, Economic, and Environmental. See Table 1 to better understand these potential positive benefits.

Documentation of benefits has only come about fairly recently since recreation and leisure experiences tend to be very personal, and often subjective, in nature. However, as you gain more education and experience in recreation, parks, sport management, hospitality, and tourism, you will gain a better understanding of benefits and how they can be used to manage the best possible recreation and leisure experiences for your clients. While most people are motivated to engage in recreation and leisure experiences for positive benefits like those shown in Table 1.1 (e.g., fun, relief from stress, physical health, being with friends and so on), it is also important to be aware of the darker side of recreation motivation.

TABLE 1.1

Selected Benefits that Have Been Attributed to Leisure by One or More Scientific Studies
(adapted from Driver, 2008, p. 10-11)

I. **Personal Benefits**
1. Mental Health and Maintenance of such:
    - Holistic sense of wellness
    - Stress management
    - Prevention of and reduced depression, anxiety, and/or anger
    - Positive changes in mood and emotion
2. Personal Growth and Development
    - Self-esteem
    - Self-confidence
    - Value clarification
    - Leadership ability
    - Teamwork/cooperation
    - Balanced living
    - Acceptance of one's responsibility
    - Academic and other mental performance
3. Personal Appreciation and Satisfaction from:
    - Sense of freedom
    - Self-actualization
    - Sense of adventure
    - Perceived quality of life/life satisfaction
    - Nature appreciation
    - Spirituality
4. Pyschophysiological
    - Cardiovascular benefits, including prevention of hypertension and strokes
    - Better muscle functioning and strength
    - Decreased obesity
    - Increased life expectancy
    - Improved perceived quality of life
    - Reduced need for medications

II. **Social Cultural Benefits and Improvements**
    - Community identity, satisfaction, and morale
    - Reduced social alienation
    - Reduced crime
    - Ethnic social integration
    - Family bonding/better life
    - Conflict resolution/harmony
    - Prevention of social problems by at-risk youth
    - Developmental benefits in children
    - Increased independence of older people
    - Increased longevity and quality of life

TABLE 1.1 CONT.

III.   **Economic Benefits**
- Reduced health costs
- Increased productivity
- Less absenteeism
- Local and regional economic growth
- Local amenities help attract industry
- Employment opportunities
- Promotion of places to retire and associated economic growth
- Increased property values

IV.   **Environmental Benefits**
- Stewardship and preservation
- Improved air quality through urban forestry
- Understanding human dependency on the natural work
- Public involvement in environmental issues
- Environmental protection
- Ecosystem sustainability
- Preservation of particular natural sites/areas
- Promotion of ecotourism

Living Near Green Spaces Positively Influences Health

There is new evidence that living near a green space has health benefits. New research published in the ***Journal of Epidemiology and Community Health*** indicates that living near green spaces has tangible benefits to human health. The best health benefits come from living less than one kilometer (3/5 of a mile) from a green space. The research shows that the impact is particularly noticeable in reducing rates of depression.

Other health indicators that benefit from proximity to green spaces include: coronary heart disease; neck, shoulder, back, wrist, and hand complaints; depression and anxiety ; diabetes; respiratory infections and asthma; migraine and vertigo; and stomach bugs and urinary tract infections.

While people often report that time in nature reduces their stress and helps them feel better both physically and mentally, this is the first study to demonstrate that proximity to nature translates into fewer health problems.

Researchers looked at the health records of 195 family doctors and 350,000 individuals across the Netherlands, and tracked how often patients were diagnosed with 24 different disease types. Researchers mapped the amount of green space near each patient's household by using postal codes and land use data.

The study: Maas J, Verheij RA, de Vries S, et al. (2009) Morbidity is related to a green living environment. Journal of Epidemiology and Community Health. 2009.

Taken from: "Community Health Priorities: Join the Conversation". Retrieved December 13, 2009 from www. communityhealthpriorities.org/conversation/comments/living_near_greenspaces_proven_to_positively_influence_health/

The Darker Side of Motivation

Let's face it—not everyone engaging in recreation and leisure experiences has moral, health-enhancing benefits in mind. Humans are driven to seek pleasure, and they are often hedonistic—that is, self-indulgent and reckless—in their choice of activities. In fact, our cultural belief system tells us that when we have worked really hard for a long time that we have earned the right to play hard. In other words, we are prone to thinking, "Thank goodness that's over, now it's time to go blow off some steam." Left to one's own devices (which means the individual is free to do what he or she wants), many will choose experiences that are potentially harmful to self, others, or society.

Curtis (1988) believed that any recreation professional preparation program should include consideration of **purple recreation**. He coined the term "purple recreation" to refer to "those activities and interests indulged in by youth and adults during non-work, non-study free time that do not fall within the parameters of what society generally views as wholesome or good" (p. 73). Curtis points out that many purple recreation activities are not starkly bad or evil, as they may be victimless crimes, such as a college students drinking too much after final exams (assuming they make it home safely). They've harmed no one but themselves, and the harm may be minimal in the form of a hangover. However, some purple recreation can be quite harmful even when the person did not intend harm. Consider drinking and driving, binge drinking, heavy drug use, dog fighting, compulsive gambling, pornography, prostitution, and so on.

Our intention here is not to engage in a lengthy discussion about hedonistic behavior, but rather to acknowledge its existence and explain why this knowledge is important for future recreation professionals. Dustin, McAvoy, and Shultz (1991) point out that the only virtuous act is one that is freely chosen. Therefore, our role (as recreation professionals) is not to go around forcing people to do only moral, beneficial activities. However, it is our job to ensure that recreation and leisure experiences provided by our agencies are as safe and beneficial as possible. In many instances, recreation, parks, sport management, hospitality, and tourism organizations will be providing healthy activities that promote positive benefits and moral character development. In other cases, agencies may provide mild purple recreation activities—especially when the paying customer desires them. However, in these cases, it's important that we, as recreation professionals, always remain aware of the potential for harm and practice good judgment about what activities we willingly provide and practice good risk management to minimize harm.

CONCLUSION

In conclusion, recreation, parks, sport management, hospitality, and tourism professions are rich with meaning, history, and benefits. There are many young professionals who will find a career under this umbrella who will love their jobs and look forward to going to work every day. To a certain extent, all recreation professionals are leisure educators, too. This is a growing and diverse field, rich with challenges and opportunities. The desire to make a positive difference while doing something one loves is indeed a unique opportunity for leaders in this profession to embrace opportunities to improve quality of life for all.

FOR FURTHER INVESTIGATION

For More Research

A growing number of people in North America are seeking new ways to experience the fullest of what life has to offer. Grass-roots movements and the self-help industry are burgeoning with advice to help people improve the quality of their lives by slowing down, focusing on health and well-being, establishing greater intimacy with others, and creating sustainable lifestyles. Do some research via the Internet to locate at least five facts about Americans' views of time, work, and leisure. Which public policy agenda items are the most intriguing to you? What do you think about these grass-roots movements? Six websites you should explore are listed here:

Take Back Your Time
(http://www.timeday.org/)

Right2Vacation.org
(http://www.timeday.org/right2vacation/default2.asp)

Families and Work Institute
(http://familiesandwork.org/site/about/main.html)

MomsRising.org
(http://www.momsrising.org/)

Common Good: Restoring Common Sense to America
(http://commongood.org/)

The USA Affiliate of the International Play Association: Promoting the Child's Right to Play (http://www.ipausa.org/index.html)

Active Investigation

1. Collect your own stories about people enjoying recreation and leisure experiences. Ask one or more individuals to tell you about what recreation or leisure they enjoy the most and what they got out of it (benefits). Write a paragraph for each story. Identify the person by sex, age, and ethnicity (e.g. Female, age 25, Caucasian) to share with others in your class. Classify the story into one of the following types of experiences:

- Someone enjoying an eudaimonic-type leisure experience (i.e., something that involves good action and no goal other than enjoyment; the experience is an end in itself)

- Someone who is benefiting from a youth recreation program (i.e., after school, summer camp), a person with disabilities, or elderly person

- Someone benefiting from a recreational experience (i.e., play, sports, etc.)

- Someone (or the environment) benefiting from outdoor recreation experience, preferably a park

- Someone enjoying a commercial recreation/leisure experience (i.e., concert at an arena, Disneyland, etc.).

- Someone enjoying a vacation at a resort or adventure travel experience

- Someone enjoying a virtual leisure experience (i.e., electronic game, social networking)

- Someone enjoying a hedonic leisure experience (i.e., drinking alcohol, gambling)

REFERENCES

Alboher, M. (2008, May 5). Why leisure matters in a busy world. *The New York Times* Retrieved November 24, 2009 from www.nytimes.com/2008/05/05/business/smallbusiness/05shift.html?_r=1&adxnnl=1&oref=slogin&adxnnlx=1210522088-/lw8fJjht4DGgSk5dLH7Sg

Billitteri, T. J. (2005). Time crunched: How busy schedules are sapping our spirit. *U.S Catholic, 70*(5), pp. 12-17.

Bregha, F. J. (1982). Leisure and freedom re-examined. In T. L. Goodale, & P. A. Witt (Eds.), *Recreation and leisure: Issues in an era of change.* State College, PA: Venture.

Curtis, J., E. (1988). Purple recreation. *SPRE Annual on Education, 3*, 73-77.

Dare, B., Welton, G., & Coe, W. (1998). *Concepts of leisure in western thought* (2nd ed.). Dubuque, IA: Kendall/Hunt Publishing.

DeGraaf, D. G., Jordan, D. J., & DeGraaf, K. H. (1999). *Programming for parks, recreation and leisure services: A servant leadership approach.* State College, PA: Venture.

de Graaf, J. (n.d.). What's the economy for, anyway? New American Dream Retrieved November 27, 2009 from New American Dream at www.newdream.org/newsletter/economy_for.php

Driver, B. L. (2008). Why outcomes-focused management is needed. In B. L. Driver, (Ed.), *Managing to optimize the beneficial outcomes of recreation* (pp. 1-17). State College, PA: Venture.

Duncan, M. (1991). Back to our radical roots. In T. L Goodale, & P. A. Witt (Eds.), *Recreation and leisure: Issues in an era of change* (3rd ed.). State College, PA: Venture.

Dustin, D. L. McAvoy, L. H., & Schultz, J. H. (1991). Recreation rightly understood. In T. L. Goodale, & P. A. Witt (Eds.), *Recreation and leisure: Issues in an era of change*(3rd ed.), (pp. 97-110). State College, PA: Venture.

Gray, D. E. (1972). Exploring inner space. *Parks & Recreation Magazine, 12*(12), pp. 18-19, 46.

Ellis, M. J. (1973). *Why people play.* Englewood Cliffs, NJ: Prentice-Hall, Inc.

Estes, C. A., & Henderson, K. (2003, February). Research Update: Enjoyment and the Good Life. *Parks and Recreation Magazine, 38*(2), 22-31.

Frankl, V. E. (2006) *Man's search for meaning: An introduction to logotherapy.* Boston, MA: Beacon Press.

Huizinga, J. (1950). *Homo ludens: A study of the play element in culture.* Boston: The Beacon Press.

Mainemelis, C., & Ronson, S. (2006). Ideas are born in fields of play: Towards a theory of play and creativity in organizational settings. *Organizational Behavior: An Annual Series of Analytical Essays and Critical Reviews, 27*, pp. 81-131.

McLean, D. D., Hurd, A. R., & Rodgers, N. B. (2008). *Kraus' recreation and leisure in modern society* (8th ed.). Sudbury, MA: Jones and Bartlett Publishers.

Neulinger, J. (1974). *The psychology of leisure: Research approaches to the study of leisure.* Springfield, IL: Thomas.

O'Sullivan, A., & Sheffrin, S. M. *Economics: Principles in action.* Upper Saddle River, NJ: Pearson-Prentice Hall.

Pavelka, J. (2000). *It's not about time: Rediscovering leisure in a changing world.* Ontario, Canada: Creative Bound, Inc.

Russell, R. V. (2009). *Pastimes: The context of contemporary leisure* (4th ed.). Champaign, IL: Sagamore.

Sessoms, H. D., & Henderson, K. A. (1994). *Introduction to leisure services* (7th ed.). State College, PA: Venture.

World Tourism Organization. (1995). *Technical manual: Collection of Tourism expenditure statistics, No. 2.* Retrieved November 27, 2009 from pub.unwto.org/WebRoot/Store/Shops/Infoshop/Products/1034/1034-1.pdf

World Tourism Organization. (n.d.). *Fact and figures.* Retrieved November 27, 2009 from www.unwto.org/index.php

"

At the end of the day, it's really a job about a place and a mission to believe in. Yellowstone, and the other national parks, provide people outstanding places to visit and experience, but we must do this in a way that leaves the parks 'unimpaired' for future generations, not just this one, to enjoy. What could be more inspiring than working for the future?

—COLLETTE, PARK RANGER
Yellowstone National Park

"

2

Understanding Careers in Recreation, Parks, Sport Management, Hospitality, and Tourism

CHERYL A. STEVENS
East Carolina University

FOCUS QUESTIONS

Q: *What do you mean by careers in recreation, parks, tourism, and leisure services?*

A: There are solid opportunities or professional careers with good salaries, benefits, and opportunities for advancement. The good news is recreation, parks, tourism, and leisure services is a broad umbrella that includes a wide variety of career opportunities.

Q: *I love recreation, but how can I know if I would like a career in recreation, parks, or tourism?*

A: A passion for recreation is a great place to start. Another essential quality is being passionate about helping people to have the best experience possible. This chapter will guide you through some self-assessment exercises to help you answer this question.

Q: *What kind of person enjoys working in a recreation and leisure profession?*

A: Recreation is a hands-on profession. By "hands on" we mean working with people, planning, facilities, parks, etc. You might be out front, working directly with people, or behind the scenes, making it all happen. If you see yourself as a doer, and if you are a person who likes to be in the middle of what's going on, you'll probably like recreation.

Q: *This sounds really great, why haven't I heard about this before?*

A: As we mentioned earlier, the good news is the recreation, parks, sport management, hospitality, and tourism professions cover a very broad range of opportunities. That's also the bad news. Recreation-related professions cover so many career possibilities that many people are not aware of how easy it is to build a career doing something they love.

Q: *What kind of education would I need, and once I finish my education, will I be able to get a good job?*

A: Most recreation professionals have a degree, whether it's an associate, bachelor's, master's, or even a Ph.D. Whatever level of education you plan to pursue, most recreation, parks, and tourism degree programs build in practical experiences and internships that help you get the experience you need to land a full time position once you've completed school.

KEY TERMS

Leisure service delivery system
Traditional, ownership-based
Public, government-sponsored
Public good
Non-profit, community-based
Social services
Specialized recreation and leisure services
Needs-driven
Commercial, for-profit
Private enterprise
Emerging

Permeable boundaries
Globalization
Virtual leisure
Fourth sector
Hybrid organizational models
Generalists
Preferences
Passions
Continuum approach
Four Ps (Passions, Pay and Perks,
    Preparation, Possibilities)

INTRODUCTION

The good news about recreation and its related professions is that it covers a broad array of career possibilities. The downside of this is that it can be hard to figure out where the careers are because there is so much variety. The authors of this book believe the key to unlocking your career path is matching your passions and personality to potential careers, and this book is dedicated to helping you do it!

Maybe you are a student like Shayna, who is considering becoming a recreation major, so she goes to see her academic adviser for career advice. For starters, she tells her adviser she loves basketball. Basketball is her authentic passion, and she wants to prepare for a job doing what she loves most. Is recreation the right major for her?

Shayna's passion for basketball is a great place to start, but her career adviser needs to know more in order to give her a clear sense of direction. The adviser may ask, "Where do you want to work?" We are aware that some people want to be an integral part of a smaller community, others see themselves in the middle of big-city life, and still others have a passion for exotic locations and travel. The adviser might follow up with "What kind of clients do you see yourself working with?" because we know some people have a passion for helping young people develop their athletic skills, others see themselves working with professional athletes, some really want to help youth at risk or senior citizens, and still others really like travel and vacation spots where sports are popular. It turns out Shayna really likes youth sports, and she'd like to stay and help young people in her hometown of Wichita Falls. She might find a great match for her passions and abilities within community recreation, non-profit recreation, or sports management.

Shayna and her adviser have more to talk about, but I think you get the picture. Whether or not you have an academic adviser to serve as your guide, you can now use this book to help you select and pursue a career path in recreation, parks, sport management, hospitality, or tourism that's perfect for you. Any interested student's passions and interests can be matched with potential career opportunities in a recreation-related career once he or she knows the right questions to ask. The purpose of this chapter is to guide you to find your own answers so you can begin to connect with the right combination of education and experiences in order to have a career doing something you love.

As you begin your personal exploration of recreation-related careers, you first need to understand the unique and varied ways recreation and leisure services (RLS) have been, and are still being, delivered in North America. Consider the phrase: tradition matters and it's a changing world. Those who don't know the basics run the risk of choosing a focus prematurely only to find that they've later got to correct their course because they've spent unnecessary time and resources moving in a direction that's not their best fit. Think of understanding the leisure service delivery system as the key that unlocks the first door. Once you get through this door you'll be able to find which road you want to travel as you hone in on more specific areas that are right for you. Interested yet? Read on!

LEISURE SERVICE DELIVERY SYSTEM: TRADITION MATTERS AND IT'S A CHANGING WORLD

What we mean by **leisure service delivery system** is the vast network of government-sponsored, non-profit, for-profit, and specialized organizations that provide recreation, park, sport management, hospitality, and tourism experiences for people. The system is highly diverse, ranging from the federally owned National Park Service, to non-profits like the YMCA, to for-profits like sports teams, hotels, and resorts, to specialized service providers like college intramurals and hospitals.

Traditional Leisure Service Delivery System

In recreation, parks, sport management, hospitality, and tourism, tradition still matters, but it's a rapidly changing world. Historically, recreation, parks, sport management, hospitality, and tourism services were organized around a **traditional, ownership-based** model, where more formal, defined organizational boundaries were based on ownership (ownership refers to the primary owner).

Before going into detail about who these owners are, let's look at some important background on the traditional RLS delivery system. Before World War II (WWII), most recreation providers in North America could be classified as either public, government sponsored, or non-profit, community-based organizations serving youth and other people in need of sponsored services. During this time, the owners of recreation and parks organizations were the taxpayers (i.e., National Park Service) and not-for-profit social service agencies (i.e., YMCA). It was fairly easy to understand the purpose and mission of each organization. However, while the National Park Service and the YMCA still have the same primary missions, these organizations look very different today, and the forces affecting them are similar to those affecting all areas of the economy, and hence recreation.

Following WWII, and through the 1990s, recreation, parks, sport management, hospitality, and tourism organizations diversified into four service delivery categories but still remained within fairly clear organizational structures based on ownership, mission, and purpose (see Figure 2.1). They include:

1) **Public, government-sponsored** parks and recreation services are those agencies primarily owned by the federal, state, or local government for the good of all citizens. This is known as providing parks and recreation for the **public good**.

Why were public, government sponsored parks and recreation established?

As the American frontier moved west, it became evident if the government did not preserve land for the public good, Americans would lose access to wilderness, national treasures, and green space to play near their homes. Yellowstone, the first national park, was founded in 1872 "as a public park or pleasuring ground for the benefit and enjoyment of the people" and it was placed "under exclusive control of the Secretary of the Interior" (Mission, n.d.). The founding of Yellowstone set off a worldwide national park movement. The recognized need for preservation of timber and water resources and space for play impacted state and local governments and space was set aside for parks, forest preserves, and city parks, with Central Park in New York City being formally established in 1856 for the "refreshment of the mind and the nerves for city dwellers" in the midst of heavily populated areas. Preserving national treasures, wilderness, green space close to people's homes, and recreation opportunities remains a priority for the recreation and parks profession today.

2) **Non-profit, community-based** organizations that provide recreation services, mainly for children and youth, were founded as private, non-profit organizations beginning around the mid-1800s to meet social service needs. **Social services** are activities and programs designed to promote people's social well-being, and they are provided by philanthropic organizations.

Why were non-profit, community-based organizations recreation providers established?

Around the mid-1800s, private citizens noted there were great social needs among the poor, many of whom were immigrants. Some organizations, like the YMCA, rose from the founders' desires to promote Christian principles through direct service to those in need. Other agencies, such as settlement houses, were started to help poor people, especially immigrants, find their way in America. The work of these organizations and social service pioneers was considered radical and controversial as they fought against child labor, crowding, disease, and other ill effects of industrialization in a rapidly growing nation. Jane Addams, the social work pioneer who founded the Hull (settlement) House in Chicago was once called "the most dangerous woman in America" (Duncan, 1980) for her work, which included providing supervised play facilities. Not surprisingly, many of these organizations still provide recreation and leisure services today by continuing to respond to social service needs such as addressing urban ills and the difficulties facing youth who are considered at risk.

3) **Specialized recreation and leisure services** are recreation service providers that meet clients' specific needs such as therapy and campus recreation that cannot be classified as public, non-profit, or for-profit. **Needs-driven** refers to an organization that is charged with designing and delivering recreation and leisure services based on clients' needs.

Why were specialized recreation providers established?

While there are numerous public and non-profit agencies providing all types of recreation, park, sport management, hospitality, and tourism services, additional service providers arose driven by social and individual needs that did not fit with the missions of public and not-for-profit agencies. Since a healthy leisure lifestyle is an essential component of a high-quality life, and people are willing to pay for recreation and leisure services, a number of specialized professional areas have emerged. There is often a cost involved to participate, but insurance companies, employers, or educational fees may cover (or highly subsidize) the cost. Examples of specialized recreation providers include recreational therapy (treating individuals with disabilities, injuries and illness), employee recreation (serving employees where companies see recreation for employees as central to their mission), and campus intramurals and sports (serving students at schools, colleges and universities who are interested in health, wellness and recreational sport).

4) **Commercial, for-profit** recreation providers are private enterprises owned by individuals or share holders who make a profit providing recreation and leisure experiences that people are willing to pay fair market price for. **Private enterprise** refers to privately owned business operated for profit in a competitive system.

What are some examples of for-profit recreation providers?

People have long demonstrated that they are willing to pay for spa and resort experiences, and companies providing for all aspects of recreation and leisure experience have flourished in recent years. They range from small, family-owned businesses to franchises and major corporations. For-profit recreation providers include hotels, resorts, travel agencies, theme parks, health and fitness clubs, spas and resorts, manufacturers of games, recreation, and equipment, sports franchises, and entertainment venues like coliseums and arenas. Ecotourism and adventure tourism are examples of growing leisure services oriented business enterprises.

While reading this section, you probably noted that the public, government-sponsored and non-profit community-based recreation and leisure services have been around a little longer than the specialized service provides and commercial enterprises. We're not suggesting that people didn't receive recreation that was therapeutic or pay for recreational experiences at resorts prior to World War II. As we discussed in chapter 1, recreation started being thought of as a profession around the time of the playground movement in the 1800s, and like all other professions, over time it's become more specialized and diversified (and popular!). By the 1990s, recreation was a major force in our national and local economies and responsible for millions of jobs in such varied fields and national, state, and local government, sports participation and viewing, youth programs and organized camps, military welfare and recreation, travel and tourism, and many kinds of businesses that support recreational hobbies. And by the year 2000, recreation was big business. For example, Golf 20/20, a project focusing on the golf industry and its growth and run by the World Golf Foundation, estimates that as of the year 2000, the golf industry was worth $62 billion. This staggering sum includes golf facility operations, investments in courses, supplies, media, tournaments, and charities as well as hospitality, tourism, and real estate associated with golf (Buelow, 2007), and a lot of people working in these organizations are recreation professionals.

We call these four categories of recreation and leisure services traditional because they have traditionally met the needs of particular groups. The plus side of a traditional organization is that its mission and services are clear and specific, which makes it easier to hold the organization accountable. However, a limitation of traditionally organized service providers is that they may not be as quick to innovate because they tend to be limited by bureaucracy. However, as we will see next, changes in society are resulting in a blurring of boundaries as organizations experience the need to be more flexible and form partnerships across boundaries in order to stay viable and meet their clients' needs.

Emerging Leisure Service Delivery System

It's a new era, and a new leisure service delivery system has evolved, **emerging** from the traditional structure. Factors such as the need for financial and environmental sustainability, increased accountability, continuing needs of hard-to-reach population and the need for services that fit post-modern lifestyles have created a new face to recreation, parks, sport management, hospitality, and tourism. In the mid-1990s, a number of important forces started blurring the boundaries of the traditional leisure service delivery system. Social justice and programs for the underserved were still greatly needed and there are growing trends to focus more on community, family, the environment, sustainability, and well-being. Local governments and non-profits still fill an important niche in recreation, but they can only respond to some needs with their limited funding. In the current global economy, the demand for innovation, efficiency, and effectiveness affects all sectors—not just for-profit enterprises as in the past.

Consider how change is accelerating and you'll start to get some idea of how it's affecting the recreation profession. The world continues to face increasingly rapid change, and the degree to which people can predict what their future holds is even less now in the 21st century than ever before. The transition from hunting and gathering societies to agrarian societies can be measured in thousands of years, and the transition from agrarian society to industrialized society can be measured in hundreds of years (Dare et al., 1998). The transition to an information-based society took place in decades, and the transition to a global economy in less than a decade. While this rapid change can be unsettling, it is also a time of great opportunity.

As a result of the forces affecting society, the lines that once existed between traditional recreation and leisure service providers have become **permeable boundaries** as leisure expression occurs across traditional lines and partnerships between different types of agencies are formed. Recreation and leisure occurs wherever people want it and find it. Traditionally, leisure service delivery was organized according to ownership and purpose and could be easily classified as public, non-profit, specialized, or commercial. While these classifications are still relevant today, these traditional agency structures are becoming spring boards for innovative, blended organizational structures. Let's consider a few examples:

- The name of Mesa Arizona's Parks, Recreation and Commercial Facilities reflects a blending of public services with for-profit ventures. Their stated mission is "to fill our facilities and programs with satisfied guests" (www.mesaaz.gov/parksrec/). You may be interested to know that the term "guests" was popularized by commercial recreation industry to refer to the way paying customers should be viewed and treated.

- The City of Anaheim, the tenth largest city in California and home to Disneyland, formed partnerships between previously separate departments to form a new department called Community Services. This innovative restructuring was driven by the need to better coordinate service-delivery to hard to reach populations. Anaheim's Community Services of today encompasses golf, libraries, recreation and human services, parks, urban forestry and neighborhood services (http://www.anaheim.net/section.asp?id=29).

- More than 650 for-profit concessionaires operate businesses and trips in national parks, and in 2005, concessionaires, working in conjunction with national parks and forests across the country, grossed more than $34 billion in sales and put $72 million back into the federal government in the form of usage fees alone (www.jobmonkey.com/parks/html/concessionaires.html). Coca Cola is an official sponsor of the non-profit National Parks Foundation.

- Gap Adventures, which grew from a one-man show to an award-winning company of over 700 employees, created the non-profit Planeterra to demonstrate its 20-year commitment to triple-bottom-line sustainability and giving back through travel (www.gapadventures.com/about-us/gapadventures/). Planeterra (www.planeterra.org) is dedicated to support sustainable community development through travel and voluntourism, and Planeterra partnered with The International Ecotourism Society (TIES) to host a convention in 2010.

As illustrated in Figure 2.1, the "Leisure Service Delivery System: Evolving Structure," the forces affecting this emerging structure can be described as follows:

- The need for financial and environmental sustainability—When public funding and non-profit donations are tight, agencies look to innovative ways to fund their programs, such as forming partnerships with for-profits. Another way agencies increase their financial sustainability is partnering with other public and non-profits to avoid duplication of services. Community grass-roots efforts, such as starting a new Boys & Girls Club with funding from private donations, help communities find the support for the programs they need and want. Further, everyone is going green, and as people direct their time and money toward causes they support, all types of agencies benefit from improving the environment. An example would be a non-profit kayak and canoe club sponsoring a river clean-up day. River clean-up recruits may come from schools, the community, and local businesses.

- Increased accountability and connectivity—People want to know that their money is going to accomplish something they believe in. Measuring and reporting the positive outcomes from recreation and leisure services is more important than ever before. It used to be enough to report how many people attended a program, but now stakeholders want to know things like whether or not a youth program is connected to dropping crime rates and increased graduation from high school. Regarding connectivity, all types of agencies are making use of forums such as YouTube, Twitter, and other automated messages sent through cell phones or the Internet. If the local baseball game is called on account of weather, a quick message on Twitter can reach parents and coaches before they leave home.

- The need to create outreach programs for hard-to-reach populations—The problems facing youth including gang involvement, drug use and addiction, dropping out of high-school, violence, suicide, and mental illness are increasing rather than decreasing. Recreation programs enhance their traditional youth development role through emerging programs like roving leader outreach. In a roving leader program, the leaders move around so they can interact with youth where they are in their communities instead of waiting for them to show up at a program site (do a quick Google search of "Roving Leader" to learn more).

- Service-delivery is increasingly driven by clients' needs and lifestyles—People have high expectations and busy lifestyles so they expect top-quality programs that occur when they want them. This may mean opening the gym at 5:00 a.m. or even being open 24 hours a day. Increasingly, businesses are providing multiple, cutting-edge service options in one place, like the giant Vaughan Mall near Toronto, Canada, that has turned mall shopping into a real event by adding a bowling alley, NASCAR Speedpark with an arcade, Laser Tag, and family-friendly racing, including seasonal outdoor tracks (http://toronto.about.com/od/mallsshoppingcentres/p/vaughanmills.htm).

Evolving Leadership Roles

Leadership roles for recreation, parks, tourism and leisure services professionals under emerging structure include program facilitator, information referral, developmental leader, outreach specialist, and facilitator. In general, leadership roles are requiring professionals to: go where the clients are (rather then expecting them to come to a program site), provide programs that respond to each clients' specific needs; and create liaisons between different service providers in order to meet clients' holistic needs. Packaged programs will become a thing of the past as each professional is expected to adapt to ever evolving situations and clients' needs.

Parks Make Life Better!

The California Recreation and Park Society (CPRS) has recognized the need to have a brand that is easily recognizable, like the Starbucks logo, and stands for something essential to communities. The CPRS has developed a brand as part of its 21st Century VIP project (Vision ... Insight ... Planning) to help member agencies position themselves as essential community services.

"In 2009, CPRS conducted an extensive public opinion research study. This research was used to create our profession's brand promise:

Parks and recreation make lives and communities better now and in the future by providing access to the serenity and inspiration of nature; outdoor space to play and exercise, facilities for self-directed and organized recreation; positive alternatives for youth that help lower crime and mischief; and activities that facilitate social connections, human development, therapy, the arts, and lifelong learning.

The brand promise became further condensed into our memorable slogan/tag line:

Parks Make Life Better!"

The grand launch of the brand occurred at the 2010 conference in Palm Springs, CA. This event illustrates how recreation and parks professional organizations are expanding their interpretation of mission, goals and service delivery mechanisms to embrace change in the 21st Century. See www.cprs.org for more details.

Future Leisure Service Delivery System

Factors such as globalization, virtual leisure, and the rise of a fourth sector, are shaping organizations delivering recreation, parks, tourism, and leisure services. Thomas Friedman, author of *The World is Flat* (2005), tells us that in the 21ˢᵗ century we are experiencing a world with a level playing field in terms of commerce. This phenomenon, called **globalization**, has resulted from the convergence of personal computer usage, global fiber-optic micro cable, and work flow software. These have resulted in the widespread use of open sourcing, outsourcing, offshoring, insourcing, and informing. Friedman points out that while the global playing field is being leveled, Americans are not ready and are falling behind.

The profileration of personal electronic devices is responsible for another trend that we predict will continue to grow. **Virtual leisure** experiences such as gaming, music, video, interactive fitness, Internet sports, interactive sites, simulation technologies, blogging, social networking, and virtual tourism continue to grow as access to technology and connectivity increase.

As we discussed earlier in the chapter, it's difficult to predict the future, but we believe that future organizational models will be collaborative and relatively boundary-free as boundaries between traditional sectors continue to blur and may eventually disappear (refer to Figure 2.1). According to FourthSector.net the boundaries between public, private and non-profit sectors have been blurring and a **fourth sector** is emerging as many pioneering organizations in the three traditional sectors have been blending social and environmental aims with business approaches (Fourth Sector, n.d.).

According to FourthSector, there are two sets of events in action driving the convergence of the three traditional sectors into this fourth sector: (1) A Shifting Purpose in the Private Sector, and (2) Shifting Method in the Public and Social Sectors. The first event, shifting purpose, is characterized by businesses dedicating more resources to delivering social and environmental benefits. Some phrases that FourthSector.net identifies as buzzwords that reflect this trend include:

- Corporate Social Responsibility
- Cause-Related Marketing
- Cause-Related Purchasing
- Carbon Offsets
- Corporate Philanthropy
- Socially Responsible Investing
- Triple Bottom Line
- Employee Ownership
- Sustainability Reporting
- Transparency

The second event, shifting method in the public and social sector, is characterized by buzzwords such as:

- Effectiveness
- Efficiency
- Market-discipline
- Accountability and Measurable Impact
- Venture Philanthropy
- Social Investing
- Program Related Investments

- Mission Related Investing
- Earned Income Ventures
- Economic Sustainability
- Privatization
- Reinventing Government
- Social Return on Investment.

While it is beyond the scope of this book to address the fourth sector in great detail, be aware that other terms used to describe the fourth sector include For-Benefit Sector, Quaternary and Quinary Sector, and Social Economy. FourthSector.net identifies a number of **hybrid organizational models** that arise as organizations consciously blend attributes and strategies, thus forming organizations that resist classification into one of the traditional three sectors. Each of these hybrid organizations share two common characteristics: (1) the pursuit of social and environmental goals, and (2) the use of business methodology. A few terms you may see as you explore organizations delivering recreation, parks, tourism, and leisure services include: civic and municipal enterprise, cross-sectoral partnership, faith-based enterprise, non-profit enterprise, sustainable enterprise, community wealth organization, social enterprise, blended value organization, and social economy enterprise

As fourth sector organizations evolve, they have little choice but to operate within the constraints of the three traditional sectors (Fourth Sector, n.d.). Thus, traditional structures may limit potential for those organizations on the cutting edge of innovation. At present, powerful institutional and structural barriers continue to resist change (Supportive Ecosystem, n.d.). However, it is predicted that as organizations continue to challenge conventional thinking about capital, markets, legal and regulatory rules, ownership and leadership a more supportive ecosystem will evolve and innovative organizations unbounded by traditional models will be better supported, perhaps to the extent that the traditional sectors no longer exist (Supportive Ecosystem, n.d.).

While we will comment more on the future of recreation, parks, sport management, hospitality, and tourism services in chapter 15, we expect the following trends to continue to and bring about change in current organizational structures:

- Organizational models will become increasingly diverse and continue to be driven by individual and community needs.

- There will be a continuing need for the dual goals of financial and environmental sustainability will bring out more public-private partnerships.

- Both virtual and real-life recreation and leisure experiences will be valued.

- Consumers will further expand their influence on organizations because they will use virtual connectivity to explore all their choices so they can allocate their time and money exactly where they choose.

- Leadership roles will continue to evolve and professionals in recreation, parks, tourism and leisure services will become change agents/advocates, servant leaders, guides, collaborators and experts in sustainability.

FIGURE 2.1

LEISURE SERVICES DELIVERY SYSTEM: EVOLVING STRUCTURE

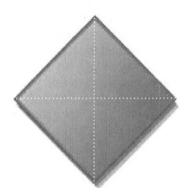

TRADITIONAL	EMERGING	FUTURE
(Clear Boundaries)	*(Permeable Boundaries)*	*(Flexible Boundaries)*

ORGANIZATIONAL CHARACTERISTICS

• Public good • Social service roots • Capitalism	• Engaging hard-to-reach populations • New partnership models for a more social economy • Need for financial and environmental sustainability	• Collaborative, boundary-free organizational structures • 4th Sector Organizations • Public-Private, eco-friendly, sustainable programs programs

LEADERSHIP ROLES

• Packaged programming • Direct service • Facility manager • Resort attendant • Activity specialist	• Program facilitator • Information referral • Developmental leader • Outreach specialist • Facilitator	• Change agent/advocate • Servant leader • Eco-tourism guide • Collaborator • Sustainable living

In the Traditional diamond, the four quadrants are labeled: Public, Government-sponsored; Non-profit, community-based; Commercial, for-profit; Specialized rec.+ leisure services.

MAKING THE CONNECTION TO THE RECREATION-RELATED CAREER THAT'S RIGHT FOR YOU

Career possibilities in recreation, parks, sport management, hospitality, and tourism are dynamic, meaning they are always in motion. Whether you choose a major in Recreation Management, Therapeutic Recreation, Leisure Studies, Sport Management, Outdoor Recreation, Resource Management, or Hospitality and Tourism, you will find a variety of potential careers under the broad umbrella of possibilities. Rest assured that you don't have to know exactly what you want to be when you grow up just yet. If you put some time and effort into self-assessment, you will be better able to hone in on your recreation-related career choice by the time you choose an internship.

The broad array of possibilities may seem a bit overwhelming, but the self-assessment exercises that follow will help to prepare you to find one or more good career matches in the chapters that follow. If you have a passion for recreation, want to make an impact, enjoy a challenge, and love working with people or behind the scenes to make events happen, you can be reassured that you're starting in the right place.

Identifying Your Preferences and Passions

The first step toward making the right choice for you is assessing your preferences and passions so you can best connect your profile to the right career area as you read the chapters that follow. While it's beyond the scope of this book to conduct an in-depth personality and values assessment, you'll find guidance on how to conduct more in-depth assessments in the "For More Research" and "Active Investigation" sections of this chapter.

What Kind of Person Will Enjoy a Recreation-Related Career?

There are a few characteristics that we can say all professionals in recreation, parks, sport management, hospitality, and tourism have in common. Look at the following information so you can get familiar with what recreation, parks and tourism professionals love most about their jobs.

- Recreation, parks, sport management, hospitality, and tourism professionals are people-oriented. If you don't like working with people, this is probably not the right profession for you. Professionals should have friendly, outgoing personalities. This does not mean some of us are not a little introverted, and there are some jobs where we work behind the scenes with parks, facilities, animals, and the like, but we still like to get out there and connect with people, too!

- Recreation, parks, sport management, hospitality, and tourism professionals value meaning in their work, and these venues provide a medium whereby professionals can improve people's quality of life. Whether you are part of a helping profession like youth development, recreational therapy, or parks, or involved in providing premium experiences at a resort, gym, golf course, or sporting event, you can be a part of giving people joy for a moment or teaching them skills that may improve their lives for a lifetime. The smiles on their faces and expressions of joy give recreation professionals frequent, positive feelings about the work they do.

- Recreation, parks, sport management, hospitality, and tourism professionals are willing to put in a good deal of effort and hard work for things they believe in. Day-to-day operations tend to be complex and involve a lot of hard work. Clients don't see the behind-the-scenes work that is necessary to put of a top-class program or orchestrate the perfect leisure experience. One of the most exciting things we do is conduct an event from start to finish and we get to see the participants' satisfaction, accomplishments, and enjoyment.

- Recreation, parks, sport management, hospitality, and tourism professionals can handle autonomy and they need to be flexible. Using their skills and resources to solve problems and working irregular hours doesn't bother them. With a few exceptions, these professionals often work long hours during peak times. This can include weekends, holidays, nights, and when everyone else had vacation like 4th of July and Labor Day. We often love the excitement of putting in extra hours before and during the event.

- Recreation, parks, sport management, hospitality, and tourism professionals enjoy being hands-on people who apply their knowledge in practical ways to meet people's needs, solve problems, and make things happen. A recreation professional's toolbox contains knowledge about a whole lot of diverse things: motivational theory, teaching/coaching, teamwork, facilities and equipment, risk management, budgets, transportation, marketing, program design, assessment, outcomes research, the latest trends … and they need to be able to apply that knowledge to solve myriad problems at a moment's notice. If you need certainty, predictability, and want to stick to using just one skill set, then recreation may not be for you.

- Recreation, parks, sport management, hospitality, and tourism professionals find it energizing that a typical day often means performing a number of different assignments. They might be analyzing customer surveys before lunch, teaching a parent youth-sports education program at noon, inventorying and buying equipment, and then coaching or refereeing at night. This youth recreational sports scenario is only one of many possibilities—but most recreation professionals do a variety of different things during a day. You probably saw some things in the paragraphs above that appeal to you. The next step is to get to know yourself better by exploring your preferences.

Preferences: Get to Know Yourself Better

It can be said that careers in recreation appeal to people who are **generalists**—this means that there are common qualities shared by most recreation, parks and tourism professionals, but there are a multitude of settings where they can be expressed (e.g., park ranger, guest services for the Yankees, youth recreational services director, tour guide). More than 80% of people in the overall population can be considered generalists. If you are a generalist, you may feel like it's been hard to directly answer the question, "What do you want to do when you graduate?" If the concept of generalist describes you, you will be relieved to know that most people feel the same way. The best way for a generalist to approach a career choice is to learn more about his or her **preferences**, and then use that knowledge to look for career areas are a potential match. In simple terms, a preference is something you favor or prioritize over something else. What this means to you is that there will likely be more than one career option that will match your profile. Chances are you'd be happy in any of them, and you can make a more informed choice once you understand which career options fit well for you and why.

Read the following list of general qualities of recreation professionals and rate them according to how well they describe you. After you finish the list, go back and review it and select the top five things you prefer most. Make sure sure you list them in the order of how important they are to you.

	Not like me	Somewhat like me	A lot like me
You think recreation is fun and exciting	☐	☐	☐
You want to make a difference	☐	☐	☐
You enjoy working with people	☐	☐	☐
You enjoy working behind the scenes	☐	☐	☐
You enjoy a challenge	☐	☐	☐
You're a problem solver and enjoy finding creative solutions	☐	☐	☐

	Not like me	Somewhat like me	A lot like me
• You like being hands-on and involved in the action	☐	☐	☐
• Sitting at a desk all day doesn't suit you	☐	☐	☐
• You like doing many different things and being different places	☐	☐	☐
• Being passionate about your career is important to you	☐	☐	☐
• You are open-minded when it comes to people—their varied backgrounds, likes and dislikes, and needs and wants	☐	☐	☐
• You can think on your feet without going off the deep end	☐	☐	☐
• You can be both a leader and a team player depending on what the situation calls for	☐	☐	☐
• You don't mind flexible work hours and you're willing work when other people want to recreate, such as holidays and vacations	☐	☐	☐
• You believe everyone in the community has a right to play and recreate	☐	☐	☐
• You like the idea of helping to create and implement sustainable, eco-sensitive solutions for communities and our environment	☐	☐	☐
• You would be thrilled to enter a career in which your knowledge and skills are transferable across many fields in recreation, parks, sport management, hospitality, and tourism, providing continual prospects for personal and professional growth	☐	☐	☐

Preferences Worksheet
List, in order, your top five preferences:
1.
2.
3.
4.
5.

Chances are a lot of these general preferences that describe recreation, parks, sport management, hospitality, and tourism professionals are a fit for you, so we'll have you get more specific in the next section.

Passions: What Matters Most to You
   Passions are things people feel intense emotion about. Passions can also be thought of as objects of enthusiasm. As you read through the next checklist, rate how passionate you are about each item. After you finish the list, go back and review it to select the top five things that matter most to you. Make sure you list them in the order of how important they are to you.

	Not like me	Somewhat like me	A lot like me
• Being part of a mission-driven organization and helping people excites you	☐	☐	☐
• You see yourself working to make a difference with a particular group (choose one):			
–Children	☐	☐	☐
–Teens	☐	☐	☐
–Young adults	☐	☐	☐
–Older adults	☐	☐	☐
–Other (i.e., race, ethnicity, religion etc.)	☐	☐	☐
• Social justice and positive community development are very important to you	☐	☐	☐
• You'd like to help improve quality of life for people with disabilities	☐	☐	☐
• You'd be happy working within the boundaries of a mission-driven non-profit or government agency	☐	☐	☐
• You'd like to have the structure provided by a regular schedule	☐	☐	☐
• You absolutely need autonomy and flexibility to do your best work	☐	☐	☐
• You're happiest when you have lots of variety and you actually like multi-tasking	☐	☐	☐
• You're happiest when you get to use the skill set you've developed without having to respond to ever-changing situations	☐	☐	☐
• Resolving problems, crises, and conflicts energizes you	☐	☐	☐
• You really enjoy teaching people about … _____ (sports skills, the environment, art, fitness etc.)	☐	☐	☐
• Working long hours is great so long as you get to play hard later	☐	☐	☐
• You'd really like to own your own business some day	☐	☐	☐
• The thought of being in charge of a large event excites you	☐	☐	☐
• You would love to work outdoors most of the time	☐	☐	☐
• You'd rather be hands-on with facilities, planning, or parks than programs	☐	☐	☐
• You'd really enjoy being a part of creating sustainable, eco-sensitive solutions	☐	☐	☐
• You are highly skilled at and/or especially passionate about a particular aspect of recreation or leisure:			
Playing or coaching one sport (or several sports)	☐	☐	☐
Fitness, health, and wellness	☐	☐	☐
Outdoor Adventure and Adventure Sports	☐	☐	☐
Art	☐	☐	☐
Theater	☐	☐	☐
Watersports	☐	☐	☐

	Not like me	Somewhat like me	A lot like me
Other:			
• You'd like to live and work in a smaller community	☐	☐	☐
• You'd live and work in a large city	☐	☐	☐
• Traveling as part of your job is exciting to you	☐	☐	☐

Passions Worksheet

List, in order, the top five things that matter to you most:

1.
2.
3.
4.
5.

HOW TO USE THIS BOOK

The Continuum Approach to Understanding Recreation-Related Careers

Due to blurring boundaries, it's no longer possible to neatly classify career areas according to traditional sectors (public, non-profit, specialized and for-profit), so we've organized them using a **continuum approach**. Career types start with the government funded, non-profit areas, move through specialized areas, and end with commercial enterprises. Traditional sectors, such as community-based recreation and recreation in non-profit organizations, have been around a long time, and other specialized areas, such as therapeutic recreation and event management, are newer on the scene. As previously discussed, partnerships between agencies and sectors result in more possibilities and you'll notice a lot of blending between sectors as you progress through the continuum.

CAREER CONTINUUM IN RECREATION, PARKS, SPORT MANAGEMENT, HOSPITALITY, AND TOURISM

Government-funded/ non-profit	Chapter 3	Community Recreation and Leisure Services
	Chapter 4	Recreation in Non-Profit Organizations
	Chapter 5	Morale, Welfare, and Recreation
↕	Chapter 6	Outdoor Recreation in Federal, State, and Local Parks
	Chapter 7	Recreational Therapy and Therapeutic Recreation
Specialized	Chapter 8	Campus Recreation, Leisure, and Intramurals
↕	Chapter 9	Sport Management and Sports Teams
	Chapter 10	Special Event Management: Meeting Planning, Conference/ Exposition Services, and Entertainment Events
	Chapter 11	The Hospitality Industry
Commercial	Chapter 12	Travel and Tourism
enterprises	Chapter 13	Commercial Recreation and Leisure Businesses

If a career in a recreation-oriented profession appeals to you, you'll want to make sure to explore the entire continuum, because you'll likely find potential matches in unexpected places. For example, if you love sports, it will obviously be covered in chapter 9, Sports Management, but you will also find exciting opportunities for a sports-oriented professional in Armed Forces Recreation—and if you want to see the world, this might be a perfect niche for you. However, don't stop reading there, because you'll also want to consider the many other sports-related opportunities in that appear in chapters 3, 4, 7, 8, 10, 12, and 13 to make sure you don't leave any stone unturned while looking for your best match.

The Four Ps: Passions, Pay and Perks, Preparation, and Possibilities

Each career chapter presents career-specific information using a model we're calling the **four Ps: Passions, Pay and Perks, Preparation,** and **Possibilities**. Each author addresses careers in their topic area by describing the four Ps as they relate, in general, to all careers in the chapter. The passions section tells you what people who work in the career area feel strongly about. The pay and perks section tells you, in a general way, about pay and typical perks that come with these jobs. You may notice that we don't list specific salaries. This was intentional, because it's best for you to research what salaries are like for certain positions in your region, because salaries differ a lot by location. The preparation section tells you information about the kind of education and experience professionals in the career area typically pursue in order to be successful. You'll also find a wealth of information on professional organizations, certifications, and other resources towards the end of each chapter to help you prepare to market yourself successfully. The last P is possibilities. This section is designed to inform you about where to look for internships and jobs. Each possibilities section expands to provide details about a several more specific career tracks. Each career track describe continues using the four Ps model by including a brief discussion about the passions, pay and perks, preparation, and possibilities specific to that track. What better way to select a career focus that will likely be a great fit for you!

CONCLUSION

This book is designed to help the interested student link their passions, preferences, and interests to career possibilities. Each career chapter begins with fascinating interviews with professionals currently working in the field so you can get in touch immediately with what they love about their jobs—just by reading this book you'll get great advice from 22 active recreation professionals, not to mention the expert advice from the contributing authors. The four Ps model provides you a consistent frame for determining how well your own passions, preferences, and interests fit with a particular career area. Each chapter also contains ideas for ways you can conduct more research, get involved in active investigation, plus ideas about where to get experience so you can starting building a strong resume immediately.

FURTHER INVESTIGATION

For More Research

There are several on-line career assessments you can take for free. Self-assessment will help you learn more about yourself by helping you further define your core interests, values, personality, and skills. No one assessment can resolve all your career-related questions, but you should use them as tools during your career selection process.

1. **Take the Keirsey Temperament Sorter II**

   http://www.keirsey.com/

   Click on Take the KTS-II free sorter access and free temperament report. This assessment is designed for college students and adults to provide a brief summary of the user's temperament and career options matching the personality. Free registration is required to take the test.

2. **Complete an iSeek Skills Assessment**

   http://www.iseek.org/

   iSeek is Minnesota's career, education, and job resource site. Click on "Assess Yourself" under the "Careers" heading to take the iSeek Skills Assessment complete with matching jobs listing. Users are asked to rate skills positively or negatively according to preference.

3. **Get to know more about your work values and motivations**

   http://www.lifeworktransitions.com/

   Life Work Transitions.com is the companion website for the book by the same name, and the website has worksheets that are useful and free, whether or not you buy the book. Go to the website, click on "Career Assessment Exercises" and scroll down to chapter 3, "Redefining Your Self: Passions, Preferences, Purpose" to access online worksheets corresponding to the book. The worksheets on work values and motivating factors are particularly useful.

Active Investigation

1. Visit your school's career center and find out what assessments they have that you can use to explore, evaluate, and measure your various attributes. Self-assessment will help you learn more about yourself by assisting you with defining your core interests, values, personality, and skills. No one assessment can resolve all your career-related questions, but they are definitely useful tools during your career-selection process. The Myers-Briggs Type Indicator is especially helpful for gaining understanding of how your personality matches with occupations. If your school doesn't offer Myers-Briggs, or something like it, you can take a similar test for a fee from www.personalitypathways.com.

2. Informational interviewing is a great way to learn first-hand about career possibilities that interest you. It involves setting up an interview with a professional who currently has a job in a career you might be interested in. These interviews can be done in person, by phone, or by E-mail. When setting up these interviews, it's important that you are clear that you are not seeking a job and are asking for information and advice only. A side benefit of informational interviews is that you will be familiar to potential employers and they might remember you if an internship or job becomes available. You will be pleasantly surprised how many people will enjoy talking with you about what they do and how willing they are to offer advice to an interested student (instructions adapted from The Career Center, n.d.).

What the interview is: a way of gaining valuable information and advice from a professional in a field that interests you. You conduct the interview for the purpose of seeking information and advice only. A side benefit of informational interviewing is networking with potential future employers.

What the interview is not: it is not an interview for a job. It's important to be crystal clear from the beginning that asking for a job during an informational interview is inappropriate.

How to Conduct an Informational Interview:

1. Be clear about your objective before you contact the professional. Write a brief script that explains why you are calling, what you want to know, and rehearse what you will say. Select between eight and 12 questions from the list of potential questions to use during your interview. You may want to write out some back-up questions in case time allows.
2. When you call (or E-mail) explain why you are calling, be polite, positive, and businesslike.
3. Be flexible. Be prepared to conduct the interview right when you call, understanding that the person may be busy and want to set up an appointment at a future time. Be considerate of their time and keep the interview to 30 minutes as a courtesy. Chances are you may not get to ask all of your questions so know which ones are the most important to you.
4. Whenever possible, schedule a face-to-face meeting so you can gain exposure to the work environment and culture as well as make a positive impression.
5. Ask your contact to recommend others you might speak to in the field or industry
6. Always send a thank you note by mail (not E-mail) after your call or visit. If appropriate, include your phone number or E-mail address. Ask the contact to let you know if more information becomes available or if they become aware of opportunities.
7. After you get your internship or first job, notify all your networking contacts. Tell them briefly about your new position, thank them again for their help, and give them your updated contact information.

Questions About the Career Field:

*   How did you get into this career?
*   What do you do at work on a typical day? What are your responsibilities?
*   What do you like most about your job?
*   What are the biggest challenges you face in your job?
*   How do you make a difference in people's lives?
*   What advice do you have for someone preparing for a career in this field?
*   What kind of formal education do you recommend?
*   What experience is necessary to get an entry-level job in this field?

Questions about the Organization/Industry:

*   How did you get into this organization? What other organizations have you worked for?

- What would you say is unique about your organization?
- What is your work environment like?
- When there are job openings or internships, where are they advertised and how are they filled? Is this typical of other similar organizations?

Questions about Future Opportunities and Salary:

- What are the employment prospects for entry-level employees?
- Are internships common in this industry? What do interns typically do?
- What is the growth and promotional potential in this field?
- What areas are growing/changing in this field?
- Are there some regions/countries that have a higher demand than others?

Follow-up Questions:

- Can you recommend other professionals in this field with whom I should speak? May I use your name when I contact them?
- Is it okay if I contact you again if I have further questions?
- Which professional organizations/publications and other resources do you consider relevant?

REFERENCES

Buelow, C. (July 28, 2007. *How much is the golf industry worth?* Retrieved from www.ask. com on February 26, 2009.

Dare, B., Welton, G., & Coe, W. (1998). *Concepts of leisure in western thought* (2nd ed.). Dubuque, IA: Kendall/Hunt Publishing.

Duncan, M. (1980). Back to our radical roots. In T. Gooddale, & P. Witt (Eds.), *Recreation and leisure: Issues in an era of change*. State College, PA:Venture.

FourthSector (n.d.). *The Emerging Fourth Sector*. Retrieved from http://www.fourthsector. net/learn/fourth-sector on August 31, 2009.

Mission. (n.d.) *The National Park System: Caring for the American Legacy*. Retrieved from http://www.nps.gov/legacy/mission.html on March 2, 2009.

Supportive Ecosystem. (n.d.). *The Emerging Fourth Sector.* Retrived from http://www. fourthsector.net/learn/supportive-ecosystem/ on September 2, 2009.

The Career Center. (n.d.). *Career Success Guide 2008-2009: East Carolina University.* Retrieved from http://www.ecu.edu/e3careers/img/CareerSuccessGuide.pdf on September 4, 2009.

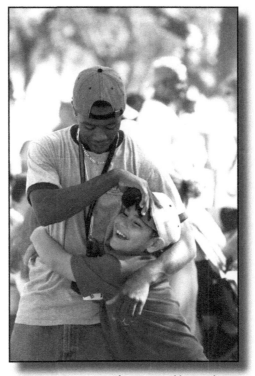

Photo courtesy of the City of Austin,
Parks and Recreation.

" **"**

The kids are a huge reason for me loving my job. I love talking with teenagers. I work with kids from all types of backgrounds.

—CHRIS GOLDBECKER

Teen Services Program Supervisor, Fairfax County, VA Department of Community and Recreation Services

"

3

Community Recreation and Leisure Services

CLIFTON WATTS
East Carolina University

KINDAL SHORES
East Carolina University

FOCUS QUESTIONS

Q: *Do you have a passion for helping others?*

A: Having passion to help others through recreation services is what motivates many who work in this field. This commitment to serving others is rooted in the belief that strong communities need supportive structures to hold these communities together. Providers of community recreation services are an important link in the overall service structure that supports communities.

Q: *Do you have to like working with people and have strong communication skills?*

A: Community-based recreation and leisure services jobs require constant interaction with residents, other staff members, and recreation workers in complementary agencies (e.g., other local and non-profit recreation providers). Being calm, comfortable, and responsive during communications is an important skill to cultivate for a career in community recreation.

Q: *Are you a patient person who's willing to go with the flow and put the needs of people first?*

A: If you are considering a career working with youth, you will need many of the skills of a good parent and friend—patience, understanding, enthusiasm, and more patience! Even good kids can sometimes get out of hand—and you can expect this to happen when they come to your recreation programs. They come to cut loose!

Q: *Are you willing to work a flexible and varied schedule?*

A: Especially at the beginning of your career, you may be called upon to work during evenings or weekends. After all, since you will be providing leisure for others, you sometimes have to work when they want to play!

Q: *What's more important to you—a secure job with benefits and opportunities for advancement or a high salary?*

A: You can make a comfortable living in local, county, school, and inclusive recreation careers, although the entry-level salary for these careers is often lower than your starting pay in other careers. The good news is that you can often rise quickly within an agency. Your increased experience and responsibility will pave the way for increases in your income.

Key Terms

Discover the Benefits
Senior Games
Inclusive recreation
Risk behaviors
Resilience
Positive youth development (PYD)

Site-based programming
Roving leaders
Pro-social values
21st Century Community Learning
   Centers

Profile 1: Could This Be You?

Deirta "Dee" Crandol (dcrandol@greenvillenc.gov) is a recent graduate with a Bachelor of Science in Recreation and Leisure and has begun work in her native North Carolina for Greenville Recreation and Parks Department. She coordinates inclusive recreation services, which puts her in charge of recreation offerings for city residents who have mental and physical disabilities. I recently met with Dee at work and asked her a few questions.

Q: *What are your favorite tasks at work?*

A: I really have a passion for physical activity and sports. Some kids, particularly some of our kids with disabilities, have never played sports before. It is really cool to see the look on their faces when they realize they can be active, sweat, and play—they get to see what they can do instead of focusing on what they can't. I love getting kids started in athletics and also with kids training for Paralympic events. Their passion gives me passion.

Q: *What advice do you have for students considering a career in community recreation and leisure services?*
A: You need patience, energy, and basic computer skills! But really, if you like people and parks, this is a great career. People come to you to have fun. Their attitude is infectious.

Q: *What do you like most about your job?*

A: All of the people I've met seem to enjoy coming to work. It is a relaxed atmosphere—there's a good mix of energy and excitement without a lot of pretension. I've only been out of college two years and the people I have met—residents and co-workers—make me look forward to going to work.

PROFILE 2: COULD THIS BE YOU?

CHRIS GOLDBECKER is Program Coordinator Teen Services for the Fairfax County, VA Department of Community and Recreation Services. Chris started as a seasonal employee out of high school and through his college years. During college, Chris worked in seasonal programs like summer camps and community recreation. Following college, Chris worked with the Fairfax County Park Authority as a marketing and sales manager, and then returned to direct service working as an outdoor education specialist at George Mason's Hemlock Overlook Outdoor Education Center. He also worked as a ski instructor in the winter at Lake Tahoe. For the past four years, he has worked full time as a Teen Service Program Coordinator.

Q: *What do you do at work on a typical day? What are your responsibilities?*

A: That's kind of a lot. The first things I do are administrative in nature, such as checking my e-mail, procuring goods, entering part-time staff work hours, turning in receipts to the finance office, responding to different community partners, responding to staff needs and requests, and checking county announcements. For example, when checking county announcements, you are looking to see if there are any closings or special government mandates such as flags flying at half mast, etc. Then I review the itinerary for the day and check on equipment and supplies needs for programs and services. When I finish that, I meet with my staff to review plans for the day. Then from there, the day gets kind of easier, as I am monitoring programs to ensure that the programs are going okay. Monitoring means I am observing programs, talking to teens, and filling in where needed throughout the program day. At the end of the day, it's what you would expect; you clean up, put things away and lock up.

Q: *What do you like most about your job?*

A: There are three things I love about this job: the freedom to program, the teens, and my coworkers. First, Fairfax County gives me a tremendous amount of freedom to design my programs. For example, I designed an outdoor adventure camp in the Shenandoah Mountains, which I worked four years on to secure funding.

The kids are also a huge reason for me loving my job. I love talking with teenagers. I work with all kids from all kinds of backgrounds—those with special needs related to developmental and physical disabilities, youth who are adjudicated, youth who are identified or being treated for substance use, and youth from subsidized housing units. I think it helps that I can connect honestly with teens, and this helps a great deal when trying to help them with planning and designing programs that they want or need. Finally, my coworkers and the people who work in this industry (in general) are some of the best people you could meet. These are very nice people who share with me a commitment to this work and a belief in what they are doing. It is clear to me that these individuals believe in helping the community through their work.

Q: *What are the biggest challenges you face in your job?*

A: The challenges are mostly related to juggling hours during the week. My day-to-day work hours are typically 10 a.m. to 6 p.m. or 1 p.m. to 10 p.m., depending on what the focus of the day is. Another big challenge is related to working with teens. I love to work with this age group, but it is also an age where trends come and go, and where their preferences can be kind of fickle. They can get bored very fast, and keeping the program fresh with limited resources and standard facilities is always a challenge for our centers.

Q: *How do you make a difference in people's lives?*

A: I think the value of my role is that I am someone with whom teens can talk about the things in life that they are experiencing for the first time. Our role is to be an external asset who is seen as a resource by the teens we serve.

Q: *What need does your program and services fill in the community?*

A: Often, many of our teens are from homes where parents are not involved. The bottom line is that we get a lot of teens off the streets. We have a theme that relates to our programming, "P3R." P3R refers to what we want our programs to instill—personal development, practical skills, professional development, and resiliency. We give teens a place to go; we aren't teachers and we are not parents, but what we do is support teens through our work. If someone needs services beyond what we provide, we make an appropriate referral to a community provider. We often work to organize other service providers through fairs and community events, and this represents a form of outreach, as we seek to connect communities to what is offered in human services.

Q: *What are the employment prospects for entry-level employees?*

A: I worked for many years as a seasonal employee before landing a full-time position with Fairfax County. Many of these seasonal jobs represented what one would expect as an entry-level recreation leader in the field. There are full-time, entry-level jobs, but I found it easier to string together seasonal work before entering the supervisor level in this field.

Q: *What advice do you have for someone preparing for a career in this field?*

A: Early in your career, you may need to be flexible as I was with seasonal employment. These experiences can pay off and lead to a great job down the road. Once you get that great job, be prepared give 100% to your job. Show up, be prepared. and have fun.

Q: *What kind of formal education do you recommend? What experience is needed?*

A: I am pretty firm about the idea that you need to have a Recreation Management degree. Having a minor in Psychology, Sociology, or Criminal Justice is very helpful for those who want to work with youth. You need to be a jack of all trades in this field. You have to know how to run games and develop programs. You have to know how to market and reach out to people for whom you are designing services. A recreation degree does all of that.

COMMUNITY RECREATION AND LEISURE SERVICES

Like Deirtra and Chris, many people who work in county, local, youth, and school recreation choose to do so because they had positive experiences with parks and recreation in their daily lives. Maybe you want to give others an opportunity to receive the benefits of community-based parks and recreation that you enjoyed in your hometown. The idea that recreation offers benefits to users and that a community should provide parks and recreation for its residents is not a new idea. In fact, researchers have traced the origins of United States' local parks, recreation programs and youth activities back to the Industrial Revolution!

History of Community Recreation and Leisure Services

Since the early 1800s in the United States, community-based parks and recreation has grown and developed in response to worldwide changes in work, politics, and finance. Community-based parks were first established in the United States during the Industrial Revolution. This period in time was marked by rapid immigration from Europe into U.S. cities. Cities also became a domestic hub for jobs as citizens moved from the countryside into cities for jobs in factories. Both young children and adults worked and jobs typically required long hours, regimented tasks, and took place in dirty and unsafe working conditions. This concerned residents and community leaders in New England and New York factory towns. To give children a safe place to play and families a place to gather and refresh themselves for work, towns set aside and landscaped green spaces—the first U.S. parks. The playground movement in these areas expanded nationally and by the start of the 20th century, more than 80 "sand gardens" or modern day playgrounds were established.

Community-based recreation expanded over time. In addition to an attractive environment, people realized that children could be taught skills and responsibility through games and recreation programs. These early recreation programs were designed to assimilate recent immigrants to U.S. culture. Later, in the 20th century, recreation programs were expanded to teach adults useful skills. For example, community recreation providers taught women to cultivate "victory gardens" to support troops during World War II and taught hobbies and skills to men who were unemployed during the Great Depression.

A Timeline of Community Recreation and Leisure Services

1885	The Boston Sand Garden, the first U.S. playground designed for children opens
1889	Jane Addams and Ellen Gates Starr open the Hull House Settlement, a model for providing basic human services (including recreation) to recent immigrants
1889 – 1891	The New York Society for Public Parks and Playgrounds open two small model playgrounds
1898	New York Public Schools opened as evening recreation centers
1906	The Playground Association of America is established
1965	The National Recreation and Park Association (NRPA) is established
1995	NRPA kicks off the "Benefits Are Endless" campaign, a movement
1998	The 21st Century Community Learning Centers Initiative is funded; which brought significant attention to the value of recreation and parks to communities making it the only federally funded initiative to support after-school programs.

Today, community-based programs are more diverse and far reaching than ever. These services are designed to meet the needs of specific groups within the citizenry (e.g., youth, seniors, families, recent immigrants), as well as the general public. Delivery of these services has also changed as partnerships with other community-based services (e.g., public health, schools, social work) provide the opportunity to reach those who most need these services. We will explore how these services function to support communities.

Community Recreation—Discover the Benefits

As part of a movement to emphasize the value of recreation, and particularly, community recreation, the National Recreation and Park Association (NRPA) developed a campaign focusing on the benefits associated with recreation and leisure services. The Benefits Are Endless campaign was formally launched in 1995 and focused on the benefits of recreation and parks to individuals, communities, the economy, and the environment. The campaign continued into the 2000s with a slight name change: **Discover the Benefits.** The focus on a benefits-based framework was an important movement that sparked a major resurgence in regard for community-based recreation services. Recreation services were repositioned from being viewed as ancillary to being regarded as valuable resources for meeting the needs of communities throughout the U.S. Examples to emphasize each are provided below.

Healthy Livable Communities

One benefit of community recreation services is that they provide opportunities for residents to improve and maintain their health. This contribution has been increasingly important with the escalating incidence of obesity and lifestyle diseases in the United

States. In 2005, the National Recreation and Park Association initiated the Step up to Health Program in collaboration with the National Football League Youth Football Fund and the Centers for Disease Control and Prevention. The basic premise of the initiative is to help community recreation and leisure services contribute to healthy lifestyles and livable communities. Achieving healthy livable communities is possible by making incremental improvements to ongoing practices, advancing collaboration with other community agencies such as the public health departments and city planners, and engaging citizens on individual, family, neighborhood, and community levels. In its first five years, NRPA conducted 32 Step Up to Health Summits, trained 2,250 individuals, and enrolled over 850 communities in the Step Up to Health Movement.

This recent initiative is not the first time our nation has addressed livability and public health concerns with a commitment to parks and recreation. The heritage of the park and recreation movement includes the development of parks to beautify urban communities, improve air quality, reduce the risk of various diseases, and to provide a place for play, physical activity, and social engagement. Today, community recreation and leisure service agencies are again being asked to enhance existing programs to encourage physical activity and outdoor play for active recreation. Also, community-wide events hosted by recreation providers are being infused with physical activity. Local parks can be designed to increase physical activity among passive users. Finally, population-specific programs are being developed to encourage physical activity. Thus, more than 100 years later, community recreation and leisure services are offered by an estimated 6,000 municipal and county recreation and park systems nationwide that manage approximately 500,000 parks and recreation facilities available to support emerging public health and community livability goals.

Seniors

One population-specific program that supports healthy active living is the **Senior Games**. In 1985 in St. Louis, Missouri, a group of seven men and women formed the original leadership for what was initially known as the National Senior Olympics Organization. The organization was dedicated to motivating senior men and women to lead a healthy lifestyle through the senior games movement. In the fall of 1985, they hosted a meeting of individuals who were currently conducting sports and games for seniors in their 33 states. That group planned the first National Senior Olympic Games, held in 1987 in St. Louis, Missouri. The games were a great success, with 2,500 competitors. Today, the organization does business as the National Senior Games Association and holds its signature event, the Summer Games, which has grown to one of the largest multisport events in the world with over 12,000 competitors.

Local recreation and leisure departments who offer senior sports teams, practices, and arrange local and statewide competition most often manage this nationwide event.

Senior adults can participate in their state in events year-round that will keep them motivated to achieve greater value and quality in their lives by staying healthy, active, and fit. The Senior Games recognizes that residents of all ages need opportunities to be healthy and active—community recreation providers can provide access these opportunities.

Inclusive Recreation

The mission of **inclusive recreation** is to create recreation opportunities where all people, regardless of their abilities or disabilities, may achieve their potential and develop their artistic, civic, social, and leadership abilities. Inclusive recreation supports valuing and including all citizens. It goes beyond tolerance and accommodation to allow for full participation and integration into programs. Programs are not separate, and include all people. This may require services to make adaptations to equipment, facilities, or within programs. At times, it will also require recreation leaders to advocate for individual rights, teach skills and develop strategies to empower individuals in leisure, and assure that other participants respect and include others.

In some cases, community-based recreation and leisure service providers will employ Certified Therapeutic Recreation Specialists (CTRS). CTRSs are trained to implement therapy and techniques to promote skill development, improve function in physical abilities, and meet the needs of clients with disabilities, mental illness, and other challenges. You can read more about the work of CTRSs in chapter 7, Recreational Therapy and Therapeutic Recreation.

Inclusive recreation may also connect community members to unique opportunities through adapted sports. Almost every sport you can imagine can be adapted to allow participation. Skiing, basketball, and road racing are among the most popular competitive adapted sports. Adaptive sports have grown in popularity with the improvement of technology and advent of universally designed facilities.

Community Youth Services and Positive Youth Development

In 1992, the Carnegie Council on Adolescent Development published a report titled: *A Matter of Time—Risk and Opportunity in the Non-School Hours.* This report had a significant bearing on community recreation services for youth, as research demonstrated that youth were more likely to engage in **risk behaviors** (e.g., juvenile crime, substance use, etc.) between the hours of 2 - 7 p.m. Other research showed that youth were protected from risk when they had access to positive non-parental adults and structured extracurricular activities (e.g., after-school and recreation programs). Access to adults and structured activities was linked to the promotion of **resilience**, or a state of being where youth feel hopeful about the future, perform well in school, and avoid risk behavior. The promotion of resilience continues to be a common goal for many recreation-based programs for youth.

Since 2000, the focus of many programs has evolved from the promotion of resilience into a broader, positive youth development framework. **Positive youth development (PYD)** promotes principles to develop youth as assets, and this approach is in opposition to past approaches that focused only on preventing problems or addressing deficits. Similar to the notion of resilience, this perspective examines how youth succeed and develop to be healthy adults who are involved within their communities. Karen Pittman (2000), a noted advocate of PYD, sums up the PYD approach by stating that "problem free is not fully prepared" and "fully prepared is not fully engaged." This orientation suggests that youth service workers are charged with preparing youth for adulthood by providing opportunities to lead, make choices and learn from these choices within a supportive environment— leading to substantial benefits to youth, their families, and their communities.

Site-Based Programming

Over the last twenty years, community-based recreation has experienced growth in the area of **site-based programming**. Site-based programming is an intentional effort to bring programs to communities where need is most prevalent and where services and facilities are limited. Site-based programs often occur outside public park and recreation facilities. This strategy emerged because of the need to engage and retain underserved youth who reported dropping out of programs due to difficulties with transportation or safety concerns with travel to sites managed by public recreation programs. We will focus on two site-based programming methods: roving leaders and 21st Community Learning Centers.

Roving Leaders. In general, **roving leaders** are employees of municipal park and recreation programs. These individuals work in underserved communities and meet with youth in the nonschool hours. Often, service provision is developed organically. This means that programs and services are developed along with youth, who identify what services are needed or wanted within communities. To this end, roving leaders provide meaningful experiences in safe environments, and they also reinforce messages about staying school, making positive choices, and working to develop **pro-social values** such as trust, respect for others, and cultural awareness.

The history of roving leaders can be traced back to the birth of the recreation movement when church and charity leaders worked with youth who spent the day living and being exposed to the dangers of the streets of emerging American cities. This model continued into the twentieth century with programs offered in Chicago (e.g., 1930s), which were followed in the 1950s by programs in New York and other cities. The practice re-emerged in the 1980s, and is still offered in areas where juvenile crime (particularly violent crime) is a concern. This model is also being applied into areas where the presence of new immigrants is high. Often times, new immigrants function outside the dominant culture, because of limited opportunities, resources, and understanding from the dominant culture. In these cases, it is important to engage youth and families with services, as it may lead to broader access to the dominant culture and other needed services.

The work of roving leaders is often challenging. It can often be difficult to program based on individual needs and preferences. Roving leaders need to have a keen sense of how to respect youth voice and choice, while being able to adapt to new ideas, wants, and needs over time. While challenging, the work of roving leaders can be extremely rewarding.

The 21st Century Community Learning Centers Initiative. The **21st Century Community Learning Centers** (CCLCs) initiative was developed in 1998 to target children attending high-poverty, low-performing schools. These centers share an interesting history with the Lighted School Houses of Milwaukee. Founded in 1911 by Dorothy Enderis, the Lighted School Houses were developed to enrich the lives of immigrant families through the provision of physical games, dance,the arts, and opportunities for socialization. Today's 21st Century programs offer similar opportunities for families living in underserved communities.

Since 2002, funding for CCLCs is managed at the state level and falls under the No Child Left Behind Act. As the name implies, these centers promote learning within communities through after-school programs that support academic enrichment. In addition to academic support, CCLCs offer a broad array of services such as activities to support math and science education, the arts, recreational services, and programs to support promote parent involvement and family literacy. To meet these service needs, CCLCs often partner with community-based and non-profit recreation and leisure service providers. This program is an excellent example of how community-based recreation service provision has evolved into site-based service provision, as recreation leaders utilize facilities that fall under the purview of another community agency (i.e., public schools) and not those managed by a public park and recreation department.

The 21st CCLC initiative is just one example of how social policy has created opportunities for partnerships between recreation programs and other community-based service providers. Many programs have emerged in the past ten years. These include the Safe Schools/Healthy Students Initiative, the School to Community Action Grants, and other initiatives introduced outside of government by philanthropies and private, non-profit agencies. Funding tied to these initiatives is often designed to promote collaboration between various community-based services, and recreation often plays a substantial role in the services and programs that emerge from these efforts.

As public funding becomes increasingly competitive and limited, it is important for leaders in community-based recreation and leisure services to understand the extent to which their services fulfill needs in the broader community. This requires a thorough appraisal of existing human services, and the ability to explain to what extent recreation providers can complement, partner, or fulfill gaps that exist within the broader service structure. This also requires entry-level employees to understand that their work does not exist in isolation. Those within the recreation profession need to develop a multidisciplinary perspective or a view that incorporates an understanding that reflects the broader spectrum of community services. Recreation leaders who realize these objectives can be very effective in developing long-term, beneficial services to communities.

CAREERS IN COMMUNITY RECREATION AND LEISURE SERVICES

The majority of the more than estimated 140,000 full-time local recreation and park employees work for a city department of recreation. Today, approximately one-third of the leisure service careers are in community recreation and leisure services. These include programs offered in local communities, counties, and that programs that are inclusive, youth-focused, and offered through schools. The key goal of community recreation providers today remains the same as it was during the inception of parks and recreation: To provide benefits of parks and recreation in people's daily lives that will help individuals achieve their potential. Whether a school provider is trying to get kids active or a recreation supervisor is providing older adults opportunities to socialize, the common goal is to help people achieve their potential and enjoy the process along the way!

Passions

Similar to many of the careers in leisure services you have read about so far, employees in community recreation and leisure services are focused on balancing people's enjoyable experience and sustaining the environment in which this experience takes place. However, two things separate careers in community-based leisure services from many other public recreation careers.

First, in community-based recreation, you interact on a very frequent (sometimes daily) basis with park and recreation users. For example, as a school recreation provider, you might work with a group of 20 youth every day after school for a year. This frequent personal contact is in stark contrast to the experience of a wildlife manager in a National Park who interacts most often with tourists visiting the park for short stays.

Second, as you may have guessed, community-based leisure service providers live in the communities that they serve. This means that you will be providing facilities and services for residents, who will include your friends, family, neighbors, and co-workers.

The desire to give back to the community is a driving force for many professionals in local, county, inclusive, and youth leisure services. In fact, public leisure service providers work hard to provide opportunities for all residents, regardless of their abilities, wealth, background, age, or religion. Public leisure services are for everyone!

Pay and Perks

Pay for many entry-level positions in community recreation and leisure services vary based on the job type. Many departments offer seasonal employment to mature high school and college students, and these positions are desirable because they often pay well above minimum wage and offer field experience. Full-time, entry-level positions usually require a minimum of an associate's degree with some prior experience as a part-time or seasonal employee. The pay for these positions varies by region. Pay increases with education, experience, and nature of responsibilities (program supervisor vs. a city manager). Perks for entry-level employees include flexible schedules and flexible duties over the course of the year. Many community-based programs offer fixed site programs during the fall, spring, and winter months with special events, day camps, and other off-site opportunities occurring in the summer months. Other perks for those working in community recreation and leisure services include the potential of working in one community over a long period of time and the ability to advance within that community. There are also possibilities for those looking to move to other communities through networks in professional organizations.

Preparation

As you think about what makes careers in community-based recreation different from other leisure services, these unique characteristics will help you make a list of personal attributes that are important for employers. Thus, good communication skills, patience, responsiveness, and openness to diversity are key attributes for a career in community-based recreation and leisure services. In addition to these personal attributes, a career in community-based recreation also requires specific knowledge, skills, and abilities related to the management of people, recreation activities, and facilities.

While in school, you can make big strides that will put you in position for a local, county, inclusive, school, or youth position upon graduation. The first step is to earn your bachelor's degree. A bachelor's degree in recreation and leisure studies or park and recreation administration is preferred, although training in business administration, community development, family studies, or employee services will provide you the minimum qualifications to apply for entry-level positions. Also, an associate's degree will meet the qualifications for numerous entry-level positions.

In addition to your major coursework and sampling work in the field, specialized training or experience in a particular field such as youth development, business administration, physical fitness, or gerontology, will be an asset for many jobs. Consider earning a minor in these areas or acquiring available certifications. Some jobs will require certification. For example, a lifesaving certificate is a prerequisite for teaching or coaching water-related activities. A facility manager may be required to be a certified pool operator. Most (if not all) employers will require First Aid and CPR Certification. Certification in the recreation field itself may be helpful for advancement. Following graduation from an accredited four-year program and after two years of work experience, you may sit for the Certified Park and Recreation Professional exam (CPRP). The National Recreation and Park Association offers this paper and pencil test to professionals seeking recognition and certification by the national governing body of parks and recreation.

Finally, because there are fewer upper-management positions than entry-level positions with local government leisure service providers, you may consider pursuing a Master of Science degree in recreation or a related field to improve your opportunity of advancing into the ranks of higher salaried administration jobs. Those with graduate degrees should have the best opportunities for supervisory or administrative positions.

Possibilities

Now that we have covered the basics of entering the community-based park and recreation profession, we will take a closer look at specific hiring trends within the ranks of local, county, school, youth, and inclusive recreation.

According to the Bureau of Labor Statistics, a U.S. federal agency that tracks career paths and progressions, employment of local and county recreation workers is expected to keep pace with other occupations through 2014. However, special sectors of the local, state, and school recreation field can expect growth at faster than average rates.

The Importance of Finance, Planning, and Partnerships in Community Recreation and Parks

by Jamie S. Sabbach, M.S., CPRP
President of 110%, LLC in Boulder, CO ...
committed to advancing parks, recreation, and related services through education
(www.110percent.net)

GP RED: Research, Education and Development for Health, Recreation and Land Agencies (A Non-profit Organization)

"Given economic and social realities, cities across the country are grappling with budget problems brought on by a nationwide financial crisis and recession, and ever-changing social circumstances that lead many to believe that the systems of yesterday are antiquated and ill-equipped to adapt to today's conditions. As a result, many municipal parks and recreation agencies and others are experiencing unprecedented budget reductions in the midst of heightened expectations. Regardless of governments' financial challenges, citizen interest has not diminished relative to quality of life services. The belief is that municipal parks and recreation, libraries and others that contribute to or enhance the human condition should be sustained or expanded to meet the needs and desires of increasingly diverse populations. Many organizations have had to make difficult decisions due to budget reductions including eliminating recreation programs, "mothballing" parks, or permanently divesting of long-held assets.

Due to these economic realities, new professionals must be better prepared when it comes to a myriad of competencies. Among these are financial management, communication and ethics. These competencies are being vigorously tested in all sectors primarily due to budget reductions and resulting constituent and customer anxieties about how these reductions may affect them and their personal interests.

These competencies can be developed and enhanced through the ability to develop, manage and monitor budgets; the ability to identify and solicit alternative funding sources such as grants, donations, sponsorships and other non-traditional methods of generating revenues other than charging and/or raising fees for services; an ability to apply logical pricing methods rooted in fair and equitable strategies; the ability to communicate candidly and diplomatically in diverse settings including political charged venues; and an ability to adhere to ethical principles when presented with ethically conflicting situations."

On one hand, the leisure services field is expected to grow as retiring Baby Boomers bring their disposable incomes, free time, and passion for continued education and health to our facilities. Across the United States, city and county recreation services that provide general adult offerings are now adding senior-specific offerings and creating new positions to meet the expected demand from active seniors reaching retirement age.

On the other hand, the aging of our customer base means that employment opportunities will rise as these same Baby Boomer s are expected to retire from local and county recreation jobs in large numbers between 2004 and 2016.

A second national trend, America's youth obesity epidemic, is also shifting demand in community leisure service providers. Previously content to provide neighborhood parks, crafts, camps, and sports leagues, local and county governments are increasingly turning to park and recreation providers to help get kids healthy and active within their communities. Graduates from recreation curricula with supporting coursework and experience in exercise science, pedagogy (teaching), public health and nutrition are attractive to employers who are meeting this new need.

What is most exciting about working in community-based recreation and leisure services is the variety of populations served. Community-based service providers work with the population of a community. This means that one may work across different groups (e.g., seniors, youth, families), or specialize in a specific area of programming (e.g., promoting youth development, active living). There are five common career areas for community recreation providers to consider.

General Recreation Programming

Imagine your day begins with overseeing a group of seniors who participate in low-impact aerobics and social games. Your early afternoon is spent in meetings with different community groups—schools, public health, and neighborhood associations. The focus of these meetings is related to how your center can integrate efforts to provide a cohesive system of services within the community you serve. The afternoon features after-school programs and teen groups until 6 p.m. The remainder of your day is helping the night staff members prepare for family evening programming. Seems like a busy day, right?

General recreation programming is a catch-all term used to describe the many duties of community recreation and leisure service specialists. In many small communities, program budgets do not allow for specialized services, such as those for youth, families, seniors, and people with disabilities. In these cases, recreation programmers are often the "jacks of all trades" who serve the broader population in specialized and inclusive settings. Many of these individuals have worked for as seasonal or part-time employees with several different populations over time.

Passions—A strong affinity for people; A belief in the benefits of recreation services for communities.

Pay and Perks—Salaries vary widely. Employees can be seasonal staff assistants in high school to city or county park and recreation managers. Oftentimes, community-based recreation specialists live in the communities where they work and become strongly connected to members within that community. These positions also allow for movement if one wishes to climb the management ladder.

Preparation—Seasonal employment can begin as early as the late high school years. Full-time, entry-level positions with benefits often require a college degree and work experience. Supervisors often have five years experience beyond college. City managers have at least ten years experience beyond college and a Master's degree.

Possibilities—Positions are most abundant in suburban and urban communities. Communities are also where the potential for growth is highest.

Youth Sports/Athletics

Youth sports and athletics is a specialized area that often falls under recreation programs that are city- or county-based. These programs introduce sports to youth in a safe, fun, supportive environment. Youth sports are also an opportunity to promote physical activity and the character values of teamwork, respect for others, and persisting through challenges. If this career area interests you, make sure to read chapter 9 on Sports Management for more details on a sports-related career.

Passions—A love and value of sports, instruction, and management of sports facilities.

Pay and Perks—Pay for entry-level employee positions is comparable to other community-based service personnel. Some communities employ a Director of Athletics who has several years of experience. In many cities and suburbs, good youth athletic facilities and programs off an opportunity to host county, state-wide and regional tournaments. As sports are generally valued, these programs enjoy good support within communities. Tournaments and other special events related to athletics, also have the potential to offer tremendous economic benefit to communities.

Preparation—Similar to other community-based services, positions in youth athletics and sports can range from seasonal to more formal, benefited positions. Positions with benefits require a bachelor's degree with classes or concentration in youth sport, recreational sport management or youth leadership.

Possibilities—Sports remain very popular in the U.S., and these programs are well supported in suburban and urban communities.

After-school and Teen Centers

After-school (sometimes called Out-of-School) programs serve a variety of community needs. The majority of after-school programs offer academic enrichment, which provides homework support and tutoring. In addition to academic enrichment, after-school programs offer opportunities to participate in athletics, arts, crafts, theatre, and programs where recreation activities embed learning. For example, we once observed a program that focused on boat making. Students learned the craft of making wooden boats, but they also learned a lot of math, too!

Teen Centers are a type of after-school program that caters specifically to this age group. Teen Centers offer many of the same activities as other after-school programs, but they are designed to appeal to teen interests and community involvement. These programs may offer the opportunity for teens to develop and implement a community-based project such as a food drive. Teen Centers also offer sessions where teens can talk to each other about problems or work directly with mentors. Teen Centers represent many of the ideals of positive youth development, where youth have the voice to speak their minds, and the choice to make decisions in a supported environment.

Passions—Contributing positively to the development of children and teens. Having beliefs about the value of "giving back" to a community. Having an orientation that supports mentoring and positive development for youth.

Pay and Perks—Part-time positions are available for college students looking for work experience. Recent college graduates often fill formal youth leader positions. Some communities have recreation departments have parallel tracks for general community-based programs and youth programs.

Preparation—Educational preparation mirrors that described earlier in community-based recreation services. Specialized coursework in youth development, psychology, and grant writing is a plus for those looking to work in this area.

Possibilities—Public funding for youth programs is currently at historical highs. These emphasize growing public support for developing youth as assets and future community leaders.

Facility Manager

Many larger towns and counties employ facility managers to oversee the day-to-day operations of arenas, amphitheatres, ballfields, and other built environmental structures. In addition to maintenance and upkeep, facility managers are often responsible for scheduling facility use, developing risk-management plans, and managing facility staff. In many cases, facilities become symbols for the communities in which they are housed. If being a facility manager interests you, make sure you read the chapter on Outdoor Recreation to learn more about working in parks.

Passions—Budgeting, personnel management, risk management, maintenance, scheduling, complex organizations, planning, marketing.

Pay and Perks—Salaries for facility managers depends upon the size and number of facilities and experience of managers.

Preparation—Bachelor's degree in recreation or a management-related field. Specific training and aptitude in personnel management and facility maintenance is essential.

Possibilities—Recent growth in the south and southwestern U.S. means that more opportunities for new construction and new facilities will be in these areas. Cities and towns that have increasing populations of young families and seniors in retirement will be those that have the most potential for new facilities and services.

Seniors

A recreation professional who works with older adults must be confident in a wide range of programming (from crafts to travel to fitness) and have strong social skills. Beyond organizing and promoting senior activities to a wide age of seniors, this professional needs to be a good listener and friend to the seniors who attend their programs. Because of this, individuals who enjoy learning about people, hearing their stories and sharing their own experiences are likely to enjoy working with older adults. A professional in senior recreation may be employed by the local recreation and park departments, in assisted living communities and may liaise with resident care facilities.

Passions—An appreciation for older adults, their experiences and history.

Pay and Perks—Entry-level positions in both community and senior resident settings allow new employees autonomy as they often have responsibility for both the design and delivery of programs that they choose.

Preparation—Bachelor's degree in recreation with coursework in gerontology and health promotion is preferred. An aptitude for program planning and organization is essential.

Possibilities—The largest generation of older adults, the baby boomers are beginning to enter retirement. These older adults are healthier and wealthier than in any previous generation. Employment prospects working with seniors are at an all-time high and should continue to grow for the next 20 years.

Inclusive Recreation

Inclusive recreation specialists are called upon to adapt existing programs and facilities to meet the needs of people with disabilities. In addition, you will have the opportunity to design services for all ages of residents with special needs to ensure that all people can enjoy their leisure time in ways that enhance their health, well-being, and independence.

Passions—Creative, flexible approach to work (each day and resident will be different); Universal design, adapted sports, community outings

Pay and Perks—Pay varies by state and if employees are Certified Therapeutic Recreation Specialists (CTRSs). This work is often personally rewarding, as it is often focused on empowering individuals through skill development and education.

Preparation—A bachelor's degree in recreation management or therapeutic recreation is preferred (see the chapter 7 on Recreational Therapy). Entry-level and seasonal positions are available to individuals with an associate's degree, although advancement will require a four-year degree in recreation or a related field (child development, social work, adapted physical education). To successfully compete for a supervisory or administrative position, it will be beneficial to complete a master of science degree. Volunteer and seasonal work experience in community recreation, education, or clinical settings is a must. Many staff members begin their path to inclusive community recreation by serving as a volunteer or coach for the Special Olympics.

Possibilities—Inclusive recreation programming is slowly but steadily becoming a more prominent feature of our local communities. Also, new opportunities to work with veterans through Wounded Warrior programs have increased the number and diversity of inclusive recreation programs nationwide.

FUTURE OPPORTUNITIES, ISSUES, AND CHALLENGES

The future of community recreation and leisure services (CRLS) appears to be ripe with potential. The needs of communities continually change, but we know the need for recreation and leisure is important to developing healthy communities, supporting families, and contributing to the overall welfare of a community. We have identified four areas that present special opportunities and challenges for community recreation and leisure services.

SUMMARY OF COMMUNITY RECREATION AND LEISURE SERVICES CAREER POSSIBILITIES

Career	Passions	Pay and Perks	Preparation	Possibilities
General recreation programming	Community service, giving back	Varies. Seasonal employment, entry level to upper management	Varies from high school (seasonal) to master's degree (management)	Superintendent, director, supervisor, coordinator, seasonal
Youth sports/athletics	Values of sport to skill development	Varies. Seasonal employment, entry level to upper management	Varies from high school (seasonal) to master's degree (management)	Director, supervisor, coordinator, seasonal
After-school/teen centers	Mentoring young people	Paraprofessional leaders and assistants, professional entry and management	High school and community college for paraprofessional; minimum four-year degree for professional	Director, supervisor, coordinator, youth leader, staff assistant
Facility management	Planning and risk management	Salaries depend upon the size and number of facilities and experience.	Bachelor's degree in recreation or management-related field, and work experience in facilities	Director, supervisor, crew member
Seniors	Working with older adults, personal history	Paraprofessional and professional tracks. Demonstrate your creativity.	High school and community college for paraprofessional; minimum four-year degree for professional	Director, supervisor, program staff, staff assistant
Inclusive Recreation	Helping others, new challenges	Paraprofessional and professional tracks	High school and community college for paraprofessional; minimum four-year degree for professional	Director, supervisor, program staff, staff assistant

Promoting Healthy and Active Lifestyles

Regardless of age, the need to engage communities in becoming more active is greater than ever. During the past four decades, the obesity rates have at least tripled for youth. Over two-thirds of adults are now considered overweight or obese. Diabetes, heart disease, and many cancers are tied to inactivity and obesity—making it the most pressing challenge for community recreation services providers today.

Meeting the Needs of an Increasingly Diverse Population

Communities continue to change and grow with populations becoming more ethnically diverse. Community-based recreation has a long history of serving recent immigrants and their families, and this historical practice will continue into the future. Inclusive recreation practices will ensure service to those with diverse backgrounds. These practices may also lead to a broader "spillover" into mainstream culture as the historic and cultural traditions from those in minority status groups become integrated into the broader population.

Interdisciplinary Collaboration

The need to streamline service and limit duplication requires recreation professionals to continually identify opportunities for collaboration with other community partners. Community-based recreation services have a role in schools and after-school programs, public health, social work, and other human service areas. Recreation professionals need to work closely and collaboratively with their community partners if they are to be valued and called upon as partners.

Senior Programs

As described above, the senior population will experience a "spike" with the aging of the Baby Boomer generation. In addition to being prepared for the retirement of this group, recreation programmers need to be aware of this group's unique needs. "Boomers" are better educated and in better health than their previous cohorts, and this means that their preferences and needs may be different.

RESOURCES AND GETTING INVOLVED

Professional Organizations

National Recreation and Park Association
http://www.nrpa.org is the single largest professional organization for recreation professionals in the United States.

American Alliance of Health, Physical Education, Recreation and Dance (AAHPERD)
http://www.aahperd.org. and the subordinate association, the American Association for Physical Activity and Recreation (AAPAR): http://www.aahperd.org/aapar.

Both AAPHERD and NRPA have state chapters that do an excellent job of being responsive to regional and local communities. State chapters are also great places for professional networking.

Certifications, Licenses

Certified Park and Recreational Professional (CPRP)
http://www.nrpa.org/Contentaspx?id=412
CPRP is a professional certification offered through the National Recreation and Park Association. Many park and recreation agencies recommend or require CPRP certification when hiring for certain positions.

Certified Therapeutic Recreation Specialist (CTRS)
(refer to chapter 7 on Recreational Therapy for detailed information).
CTRS is a professional credential designed to ensure professional and ethical standards of practice for Therapeutic Recreation Specialists.

Where to Get Experience

A large number of temporary, seasonal jobs in are available in youth sports, event planning and execution, officiating, facility maintenance, youth camps, craft and fitness courses, and in community centers. As a general rule, for every full-time position in local government leisure services, there are two or more part-time positions available. Volunteering with local agencies during college and back home during vacation periods can help you select an area of community recreation and leisure in which you would like to specialize. These experiences will also give you an advantage when looking for your preferred internship and job at the end of your studies. The contacts you will make "in the field" will provide you with a professional network for job seeking and advice as your establish your leisure service career.

Additional Online Resources

American Association of Adapted Sports Programs
http://www.adaptedsports.org/
This organization works in partnership education agencies to establish programs, policies, procedures, and regulations in interscholastic adaptive sports

National Alliance for Youth Sports
http://www.nays.org/
NAYS is America's leading advocate for positive and safe sports and activities for children.

National Senior Games Association
http://www.nsga.com/DesktopDefault.aspx
This is a national organization that promotes healthy lifestyles for seniors through sport and physical activity. It is the national body that oversees the Senior Games programs throughout the U.S.

National Intramural-Recreational Sports Association
NIRSA, http://www.nirsa.org//AMTemplate.cfm?Section=Welcome
NIRSA is the leading resource for professional and student development, education, and research in collegiate recreational sports.

Active Living by Design
ALbD, http:activelivingbydesign.org
ALbD creates community-led change by working with local and national partners to build a culture of active living and healthy eating.

Conclusion

Working in community recreation and leisure services is for those who enjoy working with people from all walks of life. One of the important perks of this job is related to the connections one develops within the community. If you value work that positively impacts the lives of the people you serve, your neighbors, and the broader community, then a career in community recreation and leisure services might be the career choice for you. Along with the traditional mission of serving the unique recreation needs of communities, those working in community recreation will play important roles in promoting health through active living, contributing positively to the development of youth, and ensuring equal access to leisure for all citizens.

For Further Investigation

For More Research

1. Check the website of your local recreation and parks department, and make note of what types of services are provided. See if you can find information on the types of staff members that are employed. Are there specialists in youth development, senior programming, and inclusive recreation? If not, who handles these duties? Go to a smaller or larger city's website and try to do the same. What differences in services offered or staffing?
2. Go to the Internet and look for state schools that feature degrees in recreation and parks. What are the concentrations within the degree program? Do these have coursework to support working with seniors, youth, sports and/or inclusive recreation?

Active Investigation

1. Visit a local recreation center in your area. What services does it provide? List the services and then segment by population served. Note any particular focus (more family oriented, more seniors oriented).
2. Interview five youth served at the local after-school or teen program and find out: Why they attend this program? How often they attend the program? What do they like best about it?
3. Volunteer with a special event or program. What tasks were performed by center staff? How did the tasks of the permanent staff differ from the tasks volunteers were asked to undertake?
4. Interview Activity: Identify and ask a recreation professional at the center for an information interview. The questions provided below will assist you with the interview. Refer to the Informational Interview instructions under "Active Investigation" in chapter 2 for more information before conducting your interview.

1. What is the title of your position?
2. What are your responsibilities?
3. What responsibilities do you like most and least?
4. What are your work hours? Does this change during the year?
5. Does your job have a set routine or does it change frequently?
6. In 10 years, what types of services or programs do you feel will need to be offered to the community? Please explain your answer.
7. What advice would you have for someone interested in a career in community recreation and leisure services?

Recommended Reading

Crompton, J. (2007). *Community benefits and repositioning: The keys to park and recreation's future viability.* Ashburn, VA: National Recreation and Park Association.
This book demonstrates how to market park and recreation services based on repositioning. Repositioning is the practice of changing the identity of a product. This text focuses on ways that recreation programs can shed the identity of an ancillary service by identifying benefits associated with them, and marketing services based on benefits to the community.

DeGraaf, D., & Jordan, D. (2003). Social capital. *Parks & Recreation, 38*(11), 20-27.
This article identifies ways in which recreation programs and services can be used to create social capital within communities.

Schleien, S.J., & Miller, K.D. (2008). *Search for Best Practices in Inclusive Recreation: Phase One Report.* Greensboro, NC: Department of Recreation, Tourism, and Hospitality Management, University of North Carolina at Greensboro. Accessed 1/15/10 at: http://www.uncg/rth/phaseonereport.pdf
This monograph identifies practices that administrators and direct leaders can implement to develop more inclusive recreation programs and services.

Wellman, D., Dustin, D., Henderson, K.A., & Moore, R. (2008). *Service living: Building community through public parks and recreation.* State College, PA: Venture.
A must read for anyone considering community recreation as a career, this book underscores the vital role these services play within communities.

REFERENCES

Afterschool Alliance. (2010). *21st Century Community Learning Centers Federal Afterschool Initiative.* Accessed 1/22/10 at: http://www.afterschoolalliance.org/policy21stcclc.cfm

Dattilo, J. (2002). *Inclusive leisure services: Responding to the rights of people with disabilities* (2nd ed.). State College, PA: Venture.

McClean, D., Hurd, A.R., & Rogers, N.B. (2008). *Recreation and leisure in modern society* (8th ed.). Sudbury, MA: Jones & Bartlett.

Murphy, J.F. (1975). *Recreation and leisure service: A humanistic perspective.* Dubuque IA: William C. Brown.

Pittman, K.J., Martin, S., & Yohalem, N. (2006). Youth development as a "big picture" public health strategy. *Journal of Public Health Management Practice*, November (Supplement), s23-s25.

Witt, P. A., & Caldwell, L. (2005). *Recreation and youth development.* State College, PA: Venture.

Witt, P.A., & Crompton, J.L. (1996). The at-risk youth recreation project. *Journal of Park and Recreation Administration, 14*(3), 1-9.

" *For most people in the nonprofit sector, their work is not just a 'job.' It is part of a life of meaning that depends, in no small part, on building a career that makes an impact for good.*

—SHELLY CRYER
The Nonprofit Career Guide:
How to Land a Job that Makes a Difference
"

4

Recreation in Non-Profit Organizations

JO AN M. ZIMMERMANN

Texas State University–San Marcos

FOCUS QUESTIONS

Q: *What makes a non-profit recreation agency different from a public or for-profit agency?*

A: The biggest difference between the three types of agencies has to do with the purpose of the agency. While all of them provide recreation programs and/or services, non-profit agencies are more **mission-focused**, meaning they are established to provide a very specific type of service based on the organization's purpose. Many non-profit recreation agencies provide programs and services for people and groups of people who have limited resources and/or specific needs that are not being met by public or for-profit agencies.

Q: *What sort of place do you want to live and work, and what kind of people do you want to be around?*

A: The cool thing about working with non-profit agencies is that you can find them anywhere in the world. You can work for a very small agency or a huge multinational organization such as the YMCA. You can also choose to work with particular population groups such as people with disabilities, children, senior adults, low-income or at-risk youth, etc.

Q: *Would you enjoy working in a mission-focused environment?*

A: The best thing about working in a mission-focused environment is that everyone is trying to achieve the same outcomes. People affiliated with the agency are passionate about either the population group or the particular type of programs offered or both. It is exciting to work with people who are passionate about what they are doing rather than just doing a job.

KEY TERMS

Mission focused
Non-profit leisure organization
Volunteers
Vision statement
Social justice
Service provider
Advocate
Facilitator
Unstructured recreation

Structured recreation
Recreational sports
Instructional sport
Out-of-school-time programs
Youth development
Seasonal
Vulnerable populations
Backcountry

PROFILE 1: COULD THIS BE YOU?

MARGARET KAY-ARORA has worked with YMCA (Young Men's Christian Association) Canada for the past 20 years. After graduating from the University of Toronto, Canada, with a bachelor's degree in Physical and Health Education she worked for the YMCA of Greater Toronto as the Assistant Director and then Director of Health, Fitness, and Recreation in four different facilities over a 10-year period. She then received an opportunity to implement YMCA Canada programs at the YMCA of Metropolitan Singapore. This two-year project provided her with the chance to adapt health, fitness and recreation programs to a new culture and to learn about health issues in the Singaporean environment. When she returned to Canada, she moved to the east coast and managed the Dartmouth YMCA in Halifax for three years before going international again with the YMCA of Hong Kong, where she managed their Physical and Health Education and Camping programs. In this position, she was able to oversee two large facilities as well as develop partnerships with schools, clubs, and government organizations. Now that she's back in Canada, we got together with Margaret to catch up on her career.

Q: *You've been with the Y a long time and traveled all over the world. What are you doing now?*

A: My newest position is with YMCA Canada in the Management Resource Centre where I get to provide training, programs, and direct strategic projects for the 14 YMCAs in the Eastern region of Canada. It's an exciting time, because our objective is to increase capacity in all the facilities and to leverage our resources to enhance efficiencies, improve productivity, and support association growth throughout the region.

Q: *You've been with the Y ever since you graduated from college. How has that worked?*

A: I have been very fortunate to grow and develop within the YMCA environment. I started out being the person who implemented programs on the front line with our clients, and now I'm developing strategic initiatives within Canada as well as in other countries. When I took my first job with the YMCA, I never envisioned that I would have so many amazing opportunities to try new things, visit new countries, and meet new people.

Q: *I had no idea the YMCA was so big. What can you tell me about its mission?*

A: The YMCA is a worldwide movement that strives to develop the body, mind, and spirit of individuals. This can take many forms depending on the community and its issues and focus. For example, in Hong Kong, the YMCA offers a wide variety of programs and services to the community including extensive health, fitness, and recreation programs, employment skills training for immigrants coming from mainland China, secondary school, youth programs, etc. The YMCAs in Canada are all independent Associations that meet community needs in a number of ways: Youth Environmental Internship programs, exchange programs for students in the Quebec province (French speaking) to exchange with English speaking students in other areas of Canada, employment and skills training for unemployed and underemployed, residential and day camps, health, fitness and recreation, and international partnerships with YMCAs in other parts of the world.

Q: *You clearly have a passion for what you do. How would you say the Y makes a difference in people's lives?*

A: Our slogan is "We develop strong kids, strong families, and strong communities." Through all of our programs we strive to make a difference in everyone that we touch, so that overall our communities become stronger. Whether it's teaching a child to swim or helping an adult lose weight, the aim is to do so in a positive and long-term lifestyle modifying way. We also integrate values into all programs so that through the activities, caring, honesty, respect and responsibility are taught and demonstrated. As a result, not only do participants learn physical activity skills and benefit from improved health, but they also learn how to effectively interact with others in society.

PROFILE 2: COULD THIS BE YOU?

ELTON FITE JR. is the Unit Services Coordinator for the Boys & Girls Clubs of South Central Texas located in San Marcos, Texas. He has been in that position for three years. Prior to working at the Boys & Girls Clubs, he coached little league baseball starting at age 16 and then worked at an extended daycare program while pursuing his bachelor's degree from Texas State University in San Marcos, Texas. The Boys & Girls Clubs of America focus on enabling all young people to become productive, caring, and responsible citizens through proven character and leadership programming.

Q: *What exactly is a Boys & Girls Club?*

A: A Boys & Girls Club provides a safe place to learn and grow by facilitating ongoing relationships with caring, adult professionals, life-enhancing programs, and character development experiences as well as hope and opportunity (http:// www.bgca.org/whoweare/mission.asp). The Clubs meet in a dedicated space located within communities or neighbourhoods. For example, a neighborhood may be lacking a recreational locale such as a park or recreation center close by. This would be an ideal location for a Boys & Girls Club, and they would seek to establish a meeting place initially, perhaps using a school, church, or even a conference room in a community building.

Q: *How do you make a difference through your work?*

A: Being connected to the Boys & Girls Club, I have the opportunity to influence young lives. In many cases, I have become the only positive adult that our members, children ages 5 to 18 years, have. Through being positive and encouraging, I (along with other staff and volunteers) am able to teach values and promote active and healthy lifestyles to disadvantaged youth.

Q: *What do you love about your career?*

A: My career as a youth development professional is very rewarding. I am helping prepare young people to live life productively through the same values once taught to me. Daily, we demonstrate social standards and concepts like manners and respect, which are becoming less and less commonplace in our members' homes. These are only a few things among many that we do to help our youth improve. It's a great feeling to see our youth on a day-to-day basis and have them know that someone is here for them.

Q: *How did you get into this profession?*

A: I have been working and volunteering for kids programs since I was 16 years old. Three years ago, I was asked to apply for this position because I was teaching writing at a charter school that is on the same property as the Boys & Girls Club. I knew many of the kids in the program, and it seemed like a natural choice for me.

Q: *If you could give a young professional interested in this career area one piece of advice, what would it be?*

A: This career path is all about being able to share your experiences to make a great impact in a young person's life. You have the opportunity to become the role model that you once had or have heard people speak about.

NON-PROFIT RECREATION AND LEISURE SERVICES: YOU CAN MAKE A DIFFERENCE

A **non-profit leisure organization** is a legal entity that "in some way promotes a public service orientation or mission" (Edginton, Jordan, DeGraf, & Edginton, 1998, p. 251). There are four primary characteristics that distinguish a non-profit organization from a public or commercial agency. First, most non-profits use very altruistic language when discussing why they exist and what they are trying to achieve. Some of the core values found in non-profit agencies include: respect for a diversity of people, fairness, stewardship, volunteerism, building community, and service to others. Second, they have a public service mission. They are seeking to improve the lives of the population they have chosen to serve. Third, non-profit organizations have tax-exempt status, and therefore do not have to pay taxes. Finally, the governance of non-profit agencies is set up to eliminate self-interest and private financial gain.

The provision of recreation and leisure services by non-profit agencies parallels quite closely the development of the recreation industry in the United States. The next section will look more closely at the development of non-profit recreation and leisure services in North America.

History of Non-Profit Recreation and Leisure Services in North America

Recreation and leisure programs emerged in the mid-to-late 1800s as a means of addressing social and general welfare issues. Several key organizations were established to serve specific populations. A number of well-known and recognized organizations had their beginnings during this time. For example, the Young Men's Christian Association (YMCA) was first introduced in Boston in 1851 with the formation of the National YMCA following in 1866, the Boys & Girls Clubs of America started as a single Boys Club in Hartford in 1860, and the Young Women's Christian Association (YWCA) began in Boston in 1866. Another early provider of recreation programs was The Hull House, which was started by Jane Addams

> " The **Young Men's Christian Association** was founded in London, England, on June 6, 1844, in response to unhealthy social conditions arising in the big cities at the end of the Industrial Revolution (roughly 1750 to 1850). Growth of the railroads and centralization of commerce and industry brought many rural young men who needed jobs into cities like London. John Mott, a leader of the YMCA movement in America, received the Nobel Peace Prize in 1946. Mott's award was in recognition for the YMCA's role in increasing global understanding and for its humanitarian efforts
>
> —HTTP://WWW.YMCA.NET "

in 1889. She designed Hull House to be a center of community life. In many cases, these agencies' services were provided by "idealistic young middle class men and women who committed to live for an extended period of time in urban slums" (Jordan, DeGraf, & DeGraf, 2005, p.16). Although not all of the non-profit recreation and leisure agencies discussed later in this chapter have been around as

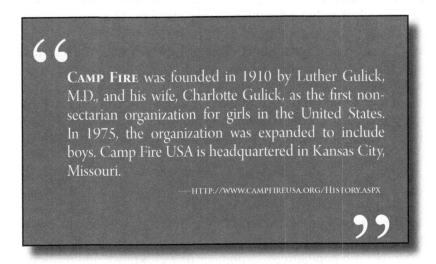

> " **Camp Fire** was founded in 1910 by Luther Gulick, M.D., and his wife, Charlotte Gulick, as the first non-sectarian organization for girls in the United States. In 1975, the organization was expanded to include boys. Camp Fire USA is headquartered in Kansas City, Missouri.
>
> —HTTP://WWW.CAMPFIREUSA.ORG/HISTORY.ASPX "

long as the ones mentioned here, most have a long and interesting history of service to their local communities and beyond.

It should be noted that the formation of public recreation departments began in 1850, when the state of Massachusetts passed legislation that granted taxing authority to local governments for the provision of recreation programs and services. Non-profit organizations were initially developed in order to provide services that communities saw as being important but were not included by the guidelines for those agencies that received taxpayer support. Generally speaking, the same is still true today. By law, all money that a non-profit agency makes must go into the operation of the programs and services that the organization provides. Non-profit agencies do not have taxing authority and they still focus on serving specific segments of the population.

What You Should Know about Non-Profit Agencies

There are a great number and wide variety of non-profit leisure service agencies, but they share a number of things in common. "These organizations focus on social welfare and benefits to members in terms of enriched living, community building, character building, and citizenship"(Edgington, Hudson, & Lankford, 2001, p.14).

In many cases, one person or a small group of people who see a need that they feel they can meet through a non-profit agency found a non-profit organization. Since most non-profits start out small and are designed to serve one specific population or provide one specific program or service, they are often able to experiment with new ways of providing services. Although it is possible to exist for a while as just a group of people trying to accomplish a specific goal, if they want to grow or expand, they will likely find it necessary to develop a constitution and register as a corporate entity. At this point in time, the organization needs to name a board of directors who will then be responsible for ensuring that the agency meets all of its legal obligations. According to BoardSource (2004), the basic responsibilities of non-profit boards are to: 1) determine the organization's mission and purpose, 2) select the chief executive, 3) provide proper financial oversight, 4) ensure adequate resources, 5) maintain accountability, 6) ensure effective organizational planning, 7) recruit and orient new board members, 8) enhance the organization's public standing, 9)

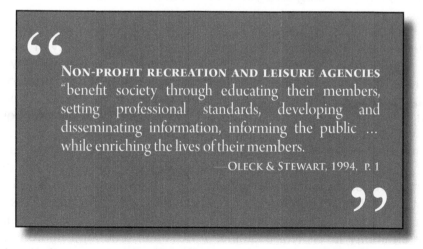

> **NON-PROFIT RECREATION AND LEISURE AGENCIES**
> "benefit society through educating their members, setting professional standards, developing and disseminating information, informing the public ... while enriching the lives of their members.
> —OLECK & STEWART, 1994, P. 1

determine, monitor and strengthen programs and service, and 10) support the chief executive and assess his or her performance. The success of a nonprofit agency is measured in two ways. First, the board of directors will compare the achievements of the organization to its established goals. Second, they will assess how well it has managed to generate "enough revenue and other resources (e.g., volunteers) to stay in operation and continue benefiting their specialized markets" (Brayley & McLean, 2008, p. 7). Obtaining funding so that organizational goals can be met is a continuous challenge for many small non-profits. Sources of funding include grants, membership fees, donations, fundraising, and earned income. The use of **volunteers**, people who offer their time and skills to an organization without the expectation of being paid, are the mainstays of many non-profits' operating staff.

Non-profit recreation and leisure agencies "benefit society through educating their members, setting professional standards, developing and disseminating information, informing the public ... while enriching the lives of their members" Oleck & Stewart, 1994, p. 1).

Other Characteristics of Non-profit Agencies

One characteristic that sets non-profit recreation and leisure organizations apart from both public and commercial agencies is the importance of the agency mission statement. A mission statement gives an agency direction as it describes what the agency is about, the essence of what it is striving to accomplish. Later in this chapter, you will find information about a lot of non-profit recreation and leisure organizations. Included in the information about each of the agencies is either a mission or **vision statement**. A vision statement is a bit more global than a mission statement, because it describes what the agency wants to be in the future. Having an understanding of what an agency stands for and believes in is always important, but is even more so when you are working in the non-profit sector. Most non-profits will want to know that you can and will support what they are trying to accomplish and not just on paper, but in your actions as well (both on and off the job). As one YMCA professional stated: "You can work here for a little while without completely buying into what the Y believes in, but if you don't carry the values through to your daily life, you won't be able to make a career here."

Who Non-Profit Agencies Serve

Non-profit recreation and leisure agencies serve a wide variety of age groups, specific populations, and income levels. For example, it is possible to work with very young children (and parents or caregivers), preschool age, primary school age, teens and adolescents, young adults, adults, and even the elderly. If you are not committed to working with one particular age group, many positions will require you to work with several different age groups. Beyond considering various age groups, you should also consider specific populations with which you may be interested in working. Many non-profit organizations offer programs and services to individuals with some level of disability (and perhaps family members as well). In addition to organizations focusing on those with a disability, some may target most of their programs to the general population but also make them available on an integrated basis for all ability levels (for example, YMCA and scouting). Sporting and arts organizations will most likely work with all ability levels as well. Finally, there are non-profit organizations set up to assist people who need recreation programs and services but who may not be able to afford them. Non-profits are driven by the desire to facilitate **social justice,** which is striving to distribute the benefits and hardships in society so disadvantaged groups can receive the same benefits as other groups have in a community (www.answers.com). So, if you have a desire to help individuals who may otherwise be excluded, you definitely need to look at a career in non-profit work.

Where Non-Profits are Located

Non-profit agencies are located wherever there are both people who need services and programs and where there are people who want to help meet those needs. You might consider working in a non-profit right in your own community. Local agencies may be very small and depend on a large number of volunteers or have a number of part-time paid staff. Most serve the interests and needs of a clearly defined local group of people. In addition, they might "stand alone" and therefore not be connected or affiliated with a national or regional organization. An example would be a community organization that is established primarily to provide after-school care to a specific area. If staying local is not something that sounds interesting to you, consider working or volunteering for a non-profit agency that has state, regional, national, or even international affiliations. Examples include Camp Fire Inc., Boy and Girl Scouts, YMCA, YWCA, and Boys & Girls Clubs. Sporting groups tend to have regional or state affiliations in order to provide statewide or regional competition.

Non-Profits Fill Varied Roles within their Communities

It might be easy to assume that all non-profit recreation and leisure agencies play a similar role within society. However, nothing could be further from the truth. There are four primary roles an organization might play. The most common role is the one of **service provider**. This type of agency has as its primary role to develop and deliver programs and/or services directly to a constituent group, for example – summer camps, dance classes, sports teams, swim lessons, etc. There are other non-profits who serve the role of **advocate**. Their primary purpose is to advocate for the rights of those who cannot do it themselves. For example, there are non-profits set up specifically to champion the needs and rights of people with disabilities to participate fully in recreation programs and services. The third type of role is one of **facilitator**. Agencies in this role assist people to access programs and services but will not necessarily be providing any through their own organization. This approach is frequently used with specific populations such as individuals who are disabled, youth at risk, and the elderly. For example, in Melbourne, Australia, there is an organization called Rec Link, whose primary function it is to connect people with disabilities with appropriate recreation programs. Finally, the agency may exist in order to provide facilities. There are some non-profits that only provide facilities or maintain outdoor areas for recreation activities. In this case, they would not necessarily be offering any specific programs or services.

Variety of Programs

Non-profit agencies offer a wide variety of programs that fall under the umbrella of recreation and leisure services, including sport programs, educational institutions, and youth development. Recreation and leisure services encompass many different types of activities and programs that can range from unstructured to highly structured experiences. A person walking on a trail through a park is experiencing what most professionals would call **unstructured recreation**; participants only need the space or appropriate area and they do their own thing. **Structured recreation** is provided for people who prefer to have activities planned and organized for them. Activities can be loosely structured with participants making many decisions all the way to a highly structured activity where most components are prescribed.

Sport programs are offered on a variety of levels depending on the skill level and preference of the individual involved. **Recreational sports** are offered for those merely wanting to have fun in an active way. There is minimal focus on coaching or technical skill development. **Instructional sport** is designed for those who want to develop their skills in a specific area, and competition is frequently offered for individuals who demonstrate a minimum level of skill. Within the instructional sports area, organizations may focus on various levels of skill as well as competition.

In addition to traditional recreation and leisure non-profit agencies, many schools offer **out-of-school-time programs**, which include a variety of recreation and/or sport experiences. Programs may be offered as before- and after-school programs, intramural sports or weekend/vacation activities and may be academically oriented. In most cases, each school offers programs that will benefit their students and perhaps members of the local community.

Youth development generally refers to those programs and services directed at adolescents or young adults. The primary objective is to assist young people in becoming healthy, successful adults who make positive contributions to their community and society as a whole. The range of programs that may be offered is extremely diverse and may encompass sports, the arts, outdoor programs, high adventure, and many others. Many of these types of services are offered by public, government-supported agencies and for-profit agencies, so be sure to refer to the chapters on Community-Based Recreation and Sports Management for additional information.

CAREERS IN NON-PROFIT RECREATION AND LEISURE SERVICES

The non-profit sector in America employs a steadily increasing segment of the North American working population, and the numbers of those employed in the non-profit sector has doubled in the last 25 years. Non-profit employment

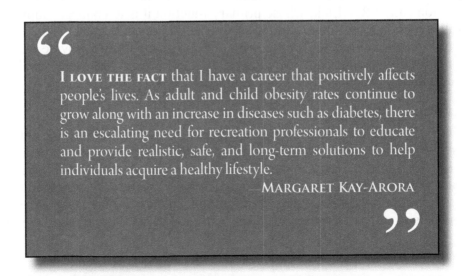

"

I LOVE THE FACT that I have a career that positively affects people's lives. As adult and child obesity rates continue to grow along with an increase in diseases such as diabetes, there is an escalating need for recreation professionals to educate and provide realistic, safe, and long-term solutions to help individuals acquire a healthy lifestyle.

—MARGARET KAY-ARORA

"

represents 7.15% of total employment in the United States, with total employees numbering 10.9 million (Independent Sector, 2001). Students interested in a career in the non-profit sector have many choices including arts, culture and recreation, nursing homes, religious congregations, and social services organizations.

Passions

If you enjoy working with people in a place where the overriding mission is to improve the quality of life of individuals and communities, then a career in a non-profit agency may be for you. According to some studies, people working in the non-profit sector tend to have a higher level of job satisfaction than either the public or commercial sectors. David Mason has had a long career managing local, regional, and international non-profit agencies. In speaking with non-profit professionals over the years, he found that their organizations had provided "direct personal gratification, satisfying activities, and opportunities for cultivating friendships, having one's ego stroked, and socializing" (Mason, 1996, p. 3). When reflecting on his own career he realized that for the past four decades he "awoke every morning eager to grasp opportunities, wrestle with problems, create new solutions, and mobilize people" (Mason, 1996, p. 286). Now that is someone who is passionate about what he does!

Pay and Perks

There are numerous opportunities all over the world to have a career in non-profit recreation and leisure services. People who work part-time or **seasonal** jobs while going to school may have a foot in the door for future jobs. If you are working in a seasonal or part-time position, you can expect to be paid slightly above minimum wage but will probably not receive any benefits in the traditional sense of the word. Some agencies have the capacity to offer some pretty amazing perks such as housing and food (perhaps coupled with lower than minimum wage), flexible time schedules, the ability to bring children (and sometimes dogs) to work with you, free professional development and/or certification opportunities, and perhaps some paid travel to attend conferences. Many people have had long and fulfilling, full-time careers in non-profit organizations. For example, maybe you have heard of career scouts? They are people who have been active in either Boy or Girl Scouts for most of their lives, starting as participants, moving on to volunteer work, then into paid positions. Many organizations, such as the YMCA, have a promote-from-within philosophy that enables workers to move up in the agency as they develop skills, as illustrated in the chapter opener by Margaret Kay-Arora. Most non-profit agencies have come to appreciate that you get what you pay for and have thus been improving their rate of pay over the past 10 years or so. If you are in an entry-level position, you should expect to make about what local teachers are making. The higher the position, and the more experience and/or certifications you obtain will influence how high your salary may go. Although you are unlikely to get rich, it is quite possible to make a comfortable living doing something you love by working the non-profit sector of recreation and leisure services.

> **66**
>
> **ACCORDING TO NANUS AND DOBBS** (1999) successful leaders of non-profit organizations possess the following four characteristics: 'being **honest, forward looking, inspiring**, and **competent**' (p. 22). **99**

Preparation

Like many areas within the recreation field, professionalism in non-profit organizations has become very important. There is a new perspective on how important education is compared to work experience. In the past, enthusiasm and experience may have gotten you quite far, but today most organizations are looking for both experience and education. Today's world requires all agencies to be accountable to those they serve and this includes employees being able to demonstrate professional competence in such areas as financial management, comprehensive assessment and evaluation of programs and services, and a complete understanding of risk management in all areas of operation.

Most full-time jobs in non-profit leisure services require some level of higher education. Depending on the agency and the position, this may be only a 15 credit hour certificate in a specific area, or it may require an associate's or bachelor's degree in a specified area. In many cases, you will also be required to have first aid, CPR, and other safety qualifications. Working with people who have disabilities or working in a therapeutic environment may require special training such as the Certified Therapeutic Recreation Specialist certification (refer to the chapter on Therapeutic Recreation for more information).

Working in the outdoors or in a specialized facility of any kind (aquatic, gymnastics, tennis, rock climbing, etc.), may require other certifications. If you are interested in a particular area, you should visit its website and talk with a manager about specific job requirements (refer to chapters 6 through 9 for more information about outdoor and specialized recreation opportunities).

Educational requirements are generally paired with a requirement of experience, either with a population group or program type. The best thing that you can do while you are in school is to volunteer for at least one nonprofit organization. Agencies use volunteers in a variety of ways, from helping out with the phones and office work to one-time special events. Figure out what can fit into your schedule and get out there!

Possibilities

According to Salamon (1999), there are two million people employed with non-profit organizations in the recreation and arts field, with the majority (93%) of those in sports, recreation, and entertainment. "Nonprofit organizations hire for all types of positions, from chief executive officer to receptionist" (Vaugan, 2005, p. 1). Examples of jobs with non-profits within recreation, leisure, and sport include: counselors, teachers, program officers, development directors, public relations managers, administrative staff, and many others.

Further, non-profit agencies vary tremendously in terms of size, service area, and focus:

- Agencies range in size from having only one person working part-time to multimillion dollar operations.
- Agencies may serve a local community, or they may have a state, regional, national, or even international focus.
- Agencies may be direct program or service providers, serve an advocacy role for others, facilitate the participation of people in certain programs, or simply be a facility provider.

The potential for employment varies greatly based on the specific type of program and/or population in which you are interested. Large organizations like YMCAs are frequently looking for seasonal staff to lead various programs or work at the customer service desk. The Scouts, on the other hand, have fewer paid positions at the local level. If you are waiting for a position to open in the non-profit agency next to your house, you could be waiting a long time. If you are willing to move across town or to another geographic area, your chances of finding full-time employment improve dramatically. Obviously, the larger the agency, the more frequently full-time positions are available. Many organizations will hire full-time program directors that will be responsible for specific areas of programming such as aquatics, early childhood, sports, arts, and so on. Additionally, once you have gained experience, there may be opportunities for administrative roles higher up within the organization.

Most non-profit organizations have numerous part-time and/or seasonal positions. If you are interested in a career in non-profits, as stated earlier, one of the best things to do while attending school is to work or volunteer at different types of agencies to see if they will be a fit for your future career. Additionally, by having part-time or seasonal positions with one or more organizations, you are gaining the experience that many employers will be looking for when filling full-time positions. Let's look at four types of umbrella areas where you could consider looking for a job in a non-profit recreation and leisure service agency.

Youth-Serving Non-Profit Agencies

Although non-profits can serve any population group, one of the primary target markets is children and youth. Generally, this means working with people from birth through about 18 years of age. The mission of youth serving non-profits tend to center around the youth in their service area gaining outcomes related to self-esteem, specific skills, and social competencies. For example, the mission of the Boys & Girls Clubs of America is "To enable all young people, especially those who need us most, to reach their full potential as productive, caring, responsible citizens." (http://www.bgca.org). Job opportunities range from short-term volunteer work to full-time career path positions.

As a charity that's over 150 years old, the **YMCA** continues to serve people of all ages, backgrounds, and abilities and through all stages of life. No one is turned away from participating in YMCA activities. To me this is very important because health and recreation should be attainable to all. In order to make this a reality, the YMCA fundraises to ensure that economic challenges are not a barrier to participation. I enjoy being part of an environment that provides opportunities for personal growth and the ability to help others and the community in general.

—MARGARET KAY-ARORA

Passions—People working in this area are passionate about advancing the interests and capability of youth. They may have been a youth who received help from a program in the past or know someone who has. Others are appreciative of what they have and want more youth to have some of the opportunities.

Pay and perks—Historically, positions in youth-serving agencies (particularly non-profit) have paid less than other areas of recreation or leisure. However, this has been changing over the last 10 years or so. Society is increasingly recognizing the value of providing quality programs to children and youth. As the requirements for education have increased, so has the pay. Perks have not changed much over the years. People work in this area because they love children and want the best for them. If you can do something you love and make a living at it, what more can you ask for? One of the biggest perks to this career area is that you will have many opportunities to play and stay current with what kids are into. Joyce Taylor, a long-time early childhood teacher once said, "How can I get old or feel bad when I have these smiling faces to look forward to every day?"

Preparation—This area especially requires experience at the leadership level before moving into administration. Children and youth are **vulnerable populations,** therefore particular care is taken when hiring staff for this area. A vulnerable population is any group of people not necessarily capable of making decisions regarding what is in their best interest. In order to work with children it is likely that you will need to pass a background check, either by the police or the FBI.

Possibilities—Listed below are examples of key non-profit agencies to give an idea of the range of opportunity.

YMCA (Young Men's Christian Association) is recognized for its strength in helping bring people together; programs and facilities are for people from all faiths, races, ages, abilities, and incomes. Building strong kids, strong families, and strong communities is what the Y stands for—worldwide. Y s are at work in more than 120 countries around the world, serving more than 45 million people.

Every Y is unique because it is designed to meet the needs of the community it serves. Because every Y is different, there are different job opportunities in every community. Examples include: swim lesson instructors and lifeguards, camp counselors (both day and residential), sports instructors and coaches, child care workers, customer service staff, health and fitness trainers, and working in community outreach to teens, disadvantaged youth, and the homeless. There are many full-time career paths in the Y, some tied to the program areas listed above, but there are many other managerial opportunities such as in human resources, facility management, marketing, fundraising, information systems, and finance. Additional information can be found on the Y website http://www.ymca.net under "Employment."

Boys & Girls Clubs of America. The mission of the Boys/Girls Clubs of America is "To enable all young people, especially those who need us most, to reach their full potential as productive, caring, responsible citizens"(http://www.bgca.org/). Club programs and services promote and enhance the development of boys and girls by providing a safe place to learn and grow, all while having fun. There are four key characteristics that the organization believes are critical in exerting a positive impact on the life of a child: 1) having a dedicated youth facility, 2) being open daily; 3) hiring professional staff; and 4) making sure program are available/affordable to all youth.

Boys & Girls Clubs offer many opportunities for volunteering and employment. At the local club level, you may be able to work as a sports instructor or coach, swim instructor, life guard, health and fitness instructor, camp counselor, homework tutor, art instructor, computer instructor, community outreach and much more. There are frequently full-time positions available that offer a career path in the professional areas of youth development, management, and executive leadership. An example of an entry-level full-time position with the Boys & Girls Clubs is a program director who would be responsible for a particular area of programming such as teens, aquatics, or health/life skills. Additional information can be found on the website http://www.bgca.org/ under "Career Opportunities."

Community Youth Services. In almost any good-sized community across the United States, you will find Community Youth Services. Generally, they receive some level of funding from the United Way. Listed below is information from one such agency to give you an idea what a Community Youth Service agency is about.

Community Youth Services (CYS) in Olympia, Washington, was founded in 1970. "It has grown steadily, responding to the diverse and ever-changing needs of our community" (http://www.communityyouthservices.org/). Currently, CYS offers a variety of programs that serve nearly 4,000 children, teens, and families each year. The Mission of CYS is to support youth and families in meeting their needs for health, safety, security, and community. Community Youth Services currently operates a number of programs: AmeriCorps, Career TREK, Choice for Change, Diversion, Family Reconciliation and Preservation, Foster Care, Haven House and Safe Shelter, Independent Living Skills and Readiness to Learn.

Girls Incorporated is dedicated to inspiring all girls to be strong, smart, and bold. Since 1864, "Girls Inc. has provided vital educational programs to millions of American girls, particularly those in high-risk, underserved areas"(http://www. girlsinc.org/). Today, the organization concentrates on innovative programs to help girls confront and deal with societal messages about their value and potential, and prepare them to lead successful, independent, and fulfilling lives. Individual clubs encourage girls to try new things and to master physical, intellectual, and emotional challenges. Currently, their major programs address math and science education, pregnancy and drug abuse prevention, media literacy, economic literacy, adolescent health, violence prevention, and sports participation.

Although there are centers operated by Girls Inc., programs can be offered anywhere including schools, churches, community centers and housing projects. Many of Girls Inc. centers are located in low-income areas. Girls Inc. needs volunteers and staff to conduct the many programs they offer such as: instructors in science, math and technology skills; leaders and mentors in the prevention of teenage pregnancy; instruction in media and economic literacy; instructors in personal safety skills; sports coaching; and mentoring as well as general leaders. There are full-time positions within this organization on a fairly regular basis. You may look on the website http://www.girlsinc.org/ or contact individual clubs for information.

4-H Clubs. The National 4-H Council Mission is "to advance the 4-H youth development movement to build a world in which youth and adults learn, grow, and work together as catalysts for positive change"(http://www.fourhcouncil.edu). 4-H is funded in multiple ways, including federal and state and some groups are forming non-profits. Within its mission, 4-H is focusing on three priority areas: science, engineering, and technology; healthy living; and citizenship. 4–H offers a number of programs including environmental stewardship, rural youth development, family strengthening, health, wellness and safety, and many others. 4-H Afterschool is an example of one of the programs offered by the organization. The program is designed to increase young people's opportunities to have fun while developing lifelong skills through experiential learning in safe, healthy, and enriching environments. If you are looking for jobs with the national office, they are shown on the website. Go to the "about us" page and look under "about Council" Careers.

Camp Fire USA. Camp Fire USA's mission is to build caring, confident youth and future leaders. The organization serves nearly 750,000 boys and girls from birth to age 21 on an annual basis. Youth participate in comfortable, informal settings that allow them to learn and play. They have a commitment to providing inclusive, fun programs to all children and families. Programs include youth leadership, self-reliance, after school groups, camping and environmental education, and childcare. Camp Fire USA's programs are designed and implemented to reduce sex-role, racial, and cultural stereotypes and to foster positive intercultural relationships.

There are many volunteer and part-time opportunities at the local club level to help plan and lead activities, educational programs, and events. Seasonal positions are available at more than 100 day and residential camps nationwide and will include counselors, kitchen help, specialty instructors, and aquatics staff. Full-time positions are available and may be located on the website http://www.campfireusa.org/.

Big Brothers Big Sisters. The mission of Big Brothers Big Sisters is "to help children reach their potential through professionally supported, one-to-one relationships with mentors that have a measurable impact on youth"(http://www.bbbs.org). The main focus of the organization is the one-to-one matching between children and youth ages 6-18 and adult volunteers in a professionally supported mentoring program. The program can be either community based or site based, but both involve regular weekly interaction between a "big" (volunteer) and a "little" (child or youth). Although most of the opportunities in Big Brothers Big Sisters are volunteer, they do have full-time professional-level positions both at the local and national levels. Local-level positions would be program directors, program specialists, matching specialists, and development officers. National-level positions are in areas including Executive Leadership, Fund Development, Program Management, Marketing and Communications, and Information Technology. See the website http://www.bbbs. org and look at "Careers" in the "About Us" section for more information.

Religious-Affiliated Agencies

Many religious organizations are not only interested in reaching their current members, but are looking for ways to reach out to the community around them. Sport and recreation programs provide an excellent venue to provide practical support and life-changing experiences within neighborhoods and communities.

Passions—Recreation and sport is seen as one of many tools that might be used in reaching the world with a particular religious belief or perspective. The common theme in this area of service provision is the opportunity to advance your faith while pursuing a career you may be passionate about.

Pay and perks—Many would assume that the pay in religious organizations would be a bit low compared to a similar position in local government, and while they may be correct, the working conditions can make up for it if they appeal to you. The hours of work tend to be concentrated on weekends and afternoons or evenings. Like many other jobs in recreation, you need to work so that others can play during their time off from school and work. One of the biggest perks offered in this type of position is the alignment with your own spiritual beliefs. People who work in this area really appreciate working with others who have a like mind-set.

Preparation—Although a religious degree is not necessary for working in church recreation, you will need to believe in and accept the philosophy of the organization for which you work. Churches will want a person skilled in the area of recreation and sport but who is also able to discuss issues of faith with participants.

Possibilities—Job opportunities in this area can be found in a number of settings from local churches to organizations with large networks of service. Listed below are examples of key agencies.

Church Recreation. Many local churches offer some level of recreation or sport for their members, whether it is focused only on children and youth or incorporates the entire family. Examples of activities within a church are: outdoor activities such as picnics and camps; social gatherings; vacation schools; workshops stressing arts, crafts and music; fellowship groups and clubs; sports leagues; study and discussion groups; and innovative worship programs (Carlson et al., 1979). In small churches, volunteers would probably conduct recreation programs, although in some communities, churches band together and all contribute in order to employ a qualified person. Larger congregations may have multiple positions in recreation services. If you are interested in this area, you should look for information under specific denominations or check with your local clergy.

Salvation Army. "The Salvation Army objectives are 'the advancement of the Christian religion... of education, the relief of poverty, and other charitable objects beneficial to society or the community of mankind as a whole'"(http://www.salvationarmyusa.org). The basic social services are a visible expression of the Army's strong religious principles. In addition, new programs that address contemporary needs have been established. Recreation or community centers owned and operated by the Salvation Army can be found in many communities. Examples of programs and services that may be offered are: disaster relief services; day care centers; summer camps; holiday assistance; services for the aging; AIDS education and residential services; medical facilities; shelters for battered women and children; family and career counseling; vocational training; correction services; and substance abuse rehabilitation. Depending on the local corp (the name for a local Salvation Army group), you will be able to find jobs working with sports leagues, child care, after-school programs, various summer and holiday camps, senior citizens programs. Full-time positions may be found at each local corp, while positions at the national headquarters are listed on http://www.salvationarmyusa.org under "contact us".

Jewish Community Centers (JCC). "JCC Association is the continental umbrella organization for the Jewish Community Center Movement, which includes more than 350 JCCs, YM-YWHAs, and campsites in the U.S. and Canada" (http://www.jcca.org). JCC Association supports the largest network of Jewish early childhood centers and Jewish summer camps in North America, and also is a U.S. government-accredited agency for serving the religious and social needs of Jewish military personnel through JWB Jewish Chaplains Council. Due to the size of this national organization, there are frequently full-time jobs available. You may check with the local center in your area or browse the website http://www.jcca.org under JCC Employment, where they not only offer a listing of available jobs but also tips on interviewing and preparing applications.

Outdoors and Camping Organizations

Although many non-profit organizations are tied to specific populations such as children and youth or people with disabilities, there are perhaps equally as many that are identified with the outdoors.

Passions—People who work in outdoor, camping, and resource-related organizations are generally passionate about spending time in the out-of-doors. Not only do they want to do all they can to preserve the natural wonders of the world, but they are convinced that nature can assist people with personal growth in ways that that other facilities cannot.

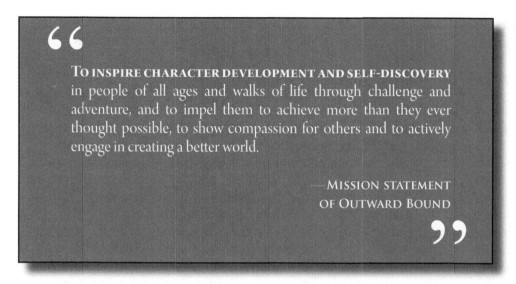

Pay and Perks—Pay may be structured differently for agencies in this group. For instance, if you are working at a camp, you may have housing and/or food covered, which may be considered part of your pay. A side benefit to working at a camp is that it's easy to save money because you don't have much to spend your paycheck on. It is also possible that you may be hired on a contract basis to complete a specific task such as leading Outward Bound expeditions. You will get paid, but it wouldn't be calculated on an hourly basis. In some cases, an organization will provide you with specialty gear, but others will expect you to purchase it on your own. Many organizations offer a pro rate (professional rate) that allows employees to obtain a significant discount on brand-name gear. If you truly love spending a lot of time in the outdoors, you may not want to pass up the opportunity to work in the natural environment, hopefully with a population group you enjoy. Breathing clean air on a regular basis and getting plenty of exercise is a great health benefit!

Preparation—There are many safety aspects to working in the outdoors. If this is your chosen career area, you will want to investigate the specific requirements for what you want to do. Depending on where you work, you will need specific knowledge of various population groups as well as be able to teach skills or lead activities. Expect that most organizations will require you to have personal experience in the environment you want to work in, in addition to your formal education. If you are going to work in a **backcountry** setting, you may need special certifications such as wilderness first responder and training or certification in specialized sports such as rock climbing, whitewater rafting, or ropes courses.

Possibilities—This section will discuss specific organizations in scouting; international opportunities; camping and retreat centers; parks and reserves; and advocacy groups.

Scouting. Scouting has a long tradition that can be traced back to the early 1900s in both America and England. Since that time, scouting has become one of the primary means of introducing young people from all backgrounds to the outdoors. Listed below is information on Boy Scouts and Girls Scouts. Information on international scouting programs is listed under international opportunities.

Boy Scouts of America (BSA). Boy Scouting is a year-round program for boys age 11 to 17. It is a program of fun outdoor activities, peer group leadership opportunities, and a personal exploration of career, hobby and special interests, all designed to achieve the BSA's objectives of strengthening character, personal fitness, and good citizenship. Local councils operate and maintain Scout camps. The National Council operates high-adventure areas at in New Mexico, Minnesota, Canada, and the Florida Keys. About 70 councils also operate high-adventure programs. These outdoor centers provide many seasonal positions for everything from counselors to cooks to specialty instructors and aquatics staff. If you are interested in a career in scouting, you should check with your local council, because most employ full-time executive directors as well as other positions such as a director of special needs. If you are new to scouting or have trouble locating a local council, check out the website http://www.scouting.org/ under employment opportunities as they have a council locator feature.

Girl Scouts of America—"Girl Scouts of the USA is dedicated solely to girls where, in an accepting and nurturing environment, girls build character and skills for success in the real world"(http://www.girlscouts.org/). Girl Scouts offer programs that have the potential to change the way girls see the world and their place in it. The overall objective of the programs is for girls to learn the importance of personal responsibility, the value of goal-setting, the spirit of teamwork, and the thrill of accomplishment. The Girl Scout program is based on four fundamental goals that encourage girls to: develop to their full potential; relate to others with increasing understanding, skill, and respect; develop a meaningful set of values to guide their actions and to provide for sound decision-making; and contribute to the improvement of society. In addition to seasonal jobs at the local level, Girl Scouts offers many career opportunities at both the local and national level. They employ 400 people in the national office and over 9,500 in local councils in areas such as marketing, program development, technology, research, advocacy, publishing, fund development, sales, and many others. To see what opportunities await you, go to the website http://www.girlscouts.org/ and look under "careers."

International Opportunities—As mentioned at the start of this chapter, many nonprofit organizations have international connections. YMCAs, Boy Scouts, Girl Scouts, and many others feature international branches to their operations. Listed below are examples of two other organizations; both operate worldwide and offer many opportunities for careers in nonprofit work. If you are really interested in pursuing an international job or career, check out the Global Directory of Nonprofit websites (The Idealist) at http://www.idealist.org/. The site provides links to more than 10,000 nonprofit websites in 120 countries.

World Scouting is an international, non-profit organization composed of recognized national scouting organizations around the world. According to the organization's website (http://www.scout.org), scouting is about much more than the outdoors. Scouts are involved in a vast number of issues facing the local communities in which they operate. A large component of scouting involves working with other community groups to achieve mutual objectives. Although volunteers carry out most of the work of scouting, there is a small staff of full-time professionals in 12 offices around the world. Current openings at the world level are shown on their website http://www.scout.org under "employment."

Outward Bound International is an umbrella organization for Outward Bound Schools worldwide. Outward Bound has schools on six continents and offers courses for individuals, families, corporate groups, and other organizations. Programs can vary widely depending on the country and the environment. Outward Bound is recognized as a world leader in outdoor experiential education. Although there are not really any full-time job opportunities with the international office, they can help connect you with job openings in one of the schools operated in 32 countries in addition to the United States. If you want to know what the possibilities are, go to the website, http://www.outwardbound.net, and look under "Staff Resources." where there is a job link.

Camps/Retreat Centers. Organizations and programs that fall under this heading typically will have some meaningful and intentional relationship to the natural environment. There are too many job and career possibilities to list in one small section in a chapter of a book. There are literally thousands of seasonal positions available across the United States where you can do anything from cooking the food, to being a camp counselor, a specialty instructor or a program or unit coordinator. There are many full-time positions with camps and retreat centers as well. A starting point would be the American Camp Association, as they provide accreditation programs for both day and residential camps as well as conference and retreat centers. Check out their website, http://www.acacamps.org/, and register for their job notification service.

Parks/Preserves. National, state, and local parks and forests and related non-profit organizations such as The Nature Conservancy and Sierra Club as discussed in the chapter on Outdoor Recreation in Federal, State and Local Parks.

Other Career/Leisure Service Areas

In addition to the major career areas already discussed, there are many other opportunities available to you in the nonprofit sector. The section will discuss three such options.

Out-of-School-Time Programs (may also be called after-school programs). This area has developed rapidly in the past two decades as work patterns in the United States have changed and more families are either headed by single parents or in the case of having two parents, both are working full-time. Programs for school-age children can be found in most communities and may be offered by schools, local recreation departments, or non-profit organizations set up for that specific purpose.

Although some agencies might rely on volunteers, most now employ people on either a part or full-time basis as they have realized the value of consistency in staff. The best way to find jobs in out of school time programs is to check the local paper. In addition, there are several organizations listed in the professional organizations section of this chapter that you will find helpful. The topic of youth development is discussed in more detail in the chapter on Community-Based Recreation and Leisure Services.

Drama, Theatre and the Arts. This is an area where the non-profit sector has traditionally taken the lead. Most towns and cities will have at least one (if not many more) non-profit organizations dedicated to various forms of art, including performance arts (dance, drama, music); visual arts (painting, photography, ceramics, and many more); and folk arts. A search on the Internet reveals literally hundreds of thousands of organizations around the world. While many organizations survive due to volunteers, do not make the mistake of thinking there are no jobs available in this area; you would be wrong! Just think about the number of theatres, museums, and art centers in any metropolitan area, and you will realize that they all need people to conduct programs, organize events, manage staff, develop marketing programs, and much more. Jobs in the arts area tend to be listed at a more local level than what this section is going into. At the end of this chapter in the section for further research, several arts organizations are listed. Follow the links to local or regional groups and that is where you will find the jobs.

Sports Organizations. As mentioned in the focus questions, sports programs are offered on a variety of levels depending on the skill level and preference of the individual involved. Non-profit agencies organize many youth sports for competition and instruction, for example baseball, softball, soccer, football, swimming, and golf. websites for a few sports organizations are listed in the further resources section of this chapter. More information on sports is available in the chapter on Sports Management and Sports Teams.

SUMMARY OF NON-PROFIT ORGANIZATIONS CAREER POSSIBILITIES

Career	Passions	Pay and Perks	Preparation	Possibilities
Youth-serving non-profit agencies	Advancing the interests and capability of youth	May start out a bit low, but the more education or experience required, the higher the pay.	Experience at the leadership level before moving into administration. Must pass background checks.	Seasonal positions are widely available. Permanent full-time jobs are competitive.
Religious-affiliated agencies	Advancing your faith	Similar to teaching, flexible work hours	Positive educational requirements, belief in the organizational philosophy, experience important.	A variety of settings, various opportunities at the lower levels, perm-anent full-time positions are compe-titive.
Outdoors and camping organizations	Preservation of natural wonders	Varies from minimum wage to contracts including housing and gear.	Positive educational requirements, experience important, some specialty certifications	Seasonal positions almost limitless, permanent positions can be difficult to get.

FUTURE OPPORTUNITIES, ISSUES, AND CHALLENGES

This chapter has covered information about the various types of non-profit agencies in recreation and leisure services. While it is an interesting and exciting sector that offers a lot of diversity in terms of jobs and careers, there are some challenges that need to be addressed. The non-profit sector of recreation has long faced many challenges. We will explore three major challenges facing non-profits today including funding, efficient operations, and locating volunteers and staff.

One of the biggest challenges faced by most non-profits is a lack of funding and financial sustainability. Because many non-profits start out as small organizations serving a specialized need of a population group, the sources of funds have traditionally been limited. Today this is being overcome in a number of ways. First, small groups have begun to band together in order to gain efficiencies of operation as well as a voice in the public sector. By forming partnerships with agencies providing similar services or working with similar population groups, they also benefit from knowledge gained by others. Another funding source that has benefited many non-profit organizations is the availability of government grants or contracts for providing specific social services. However, these funding sources often specify how and where services must be provided. Local, state, and federal government agencies are all being challenged to operate in a more efficient manner, and in many cases they are no longer providing all services themselves but are contracting with specialized agencies. Contracts are a great way to increase funding for non-profits as long as the funded efforts are consistent with their mission and core business. Students wanting to work in non-profit organizations will need to gain an understanding of how contracts are managed, be comfortable working in partnerships as well as know how to conduct traditional fundraising activities.

Most non-profits are started by a group of people with good intentions, but "they do not necessarily have the necessary skills to manage their resources effectively"(*Directions*, 2001, p. xv). One of the key ingredients to long-term success for a non-profit is a clear vision of what it hopes to achieve and a sound strategy for achieving it. Once the vision and strategy are in place, there is a great need for sharp business skills so that finances and other resources, such as volunteers and staff, are managed properly. Large organizations with a long history will probably have more developed management systems, but this is not always the case. One of the best things students can do if they are planning to work in a non-profit organization is to obtain some business skills. Most current position descriptions will ask for some sort of business knowledge and experience.

The third big challenge facing non-profits is locating, training, and retaining quality staff and volunteers. Volunteers are the lifeblood of an organization. Without them, the agency would have no hope of achieving its vision. There are two types of volunteers—those who believe in the mission of the organization and will help with anything and those who are only interested in helping with specific projects. Both are needed for sustained success, so it is important to understand what motivates a person to volunteer. As you are investigating the possibilities of working in the non-profit sector, you can be a volunteer for one or more organizations. If you let someone at the agency know you are interested in a career in non-profits, it is likely they will be willing to share their knowledge and expertise about the sector.

Resources and Getting Involved

Professional Organizations

One good way to find out more about the non-profit sector is to join a professional organization. These membership agencies have been established to support people working in specific industries or sectors and can offer many educational and networking benefits to a student. Listed below are some you may want to consider. Keep in mind that there are many more that can be located by searching the Internet.

The American Camp Association
http://www.acacamps.org.
If you are interested in organized camping, this is an excellent organization to join. They offer leadership institutes, certification programs, and assistance with finding jobs.

American Humanics
http://www.humanics.org.
This is a good organization to consider if you are interested in non-profit work as they offer training and certification for students as well as professionals.

Art in the Public Interest (API)
http://www.apionline.org/.
The organization is part of the Community Arts Network and offers a monthly newsletter as well as publishes a quarterly magazine focused on the arts.

Association for Experiential Education
http://www.aee.org/.
The Association for Experiential Education (AEE) is a nonprofit, professional membership association dedicated to experiential education and the students, educators, and practitioners who utilize its philosophy. They offer publications, conferences, accreditation for programs, and postings about jobs.

The Charity Channel
http://www.charitychannel.com/
This is an online subscription resource that allows you to connect to nonprofit professionals around the world. You can take online classes, subscribe to various newsletters and alerts as well register for a career search feature. Even though there is a small fee, they have stated that they will not turn anyone away for their inability to pay.

Christian Camping International
http://cciworldwide.org/default.aspx.
CCI is an alliance of Christian camping associations throughout the world, helping each association to be more effective in serving its membership of Christ-centered camps, conference and retreat ministries, to the glory of God and for the building up of His Church.

Idealist.org also known as Action without Borders
http://www.idealist.org.
Idealist is one of the most popular communities of nonprofit and volunteering resources on the Web and offers information for non-profit professionals, students, parents, and teachers. One of the prime benefits of the site is the access to searchable nonprofit job, internship, and volunteer opportunities (U.S. and international). They also offer tips and resources for nonprofit job seekers.

International Association of Conference Center Administrators (IACCA)
http://www.IACCA.org.
This professional organization offers a student membership, provides conferences, has a certification program, and offers listing of current job postings as well as allowing members looking for positions to post their details on the website.

The National AfterSchool Association (NAA)
http://www.naaweb.org.
This organization offers accreditation programs for programs and sites, conferences and training programs, as well as numerous resources to assist the practitioner. The website also features a section for affiliated organizations to post job openings.

National Council of Nonprofit Associations (NCNA)
http://www.ncna.org.
This organization does not serve individual members but rather advocates that professionals and organizations join their state associations as the primary means of professional development and networking. Many NCNA state associations have job boards on their websites where non-profits advertise job openings. Accessing the website will assist you in locating the association representing non-profits in your state._

National Institute on Out-of-School Time (NIOST)
http://www.niost.org/
NIOST provides resources and training for practitioners working in the field as well as provides technical assistance to programs having difficulty with particular issues. One of the best features of their website is the links page, which offers a variety of resources including information on national and international organizations, funding sources, education, public policy and advocacy, as well as professional development.

Outward Bound
http://www.outwardbound.org/.
Outward Bound is a non-profit educational organization that serves people of all ages and backgrounds through active learning expeditions that inspire character development, self-discovery and service both in and out of the classroom.

Wilderness Education Association
http://www.weainfo.org/.
The mission of the WEA is to promote the professionalism of outdoor leadership through establishment of national standards, curriculum design, implementation, advocacy, and research driven initiatives.

Certifications/Licenses

American Humanics National Certification in Nonprofit Management and Leadership
http://www.humanics.org
The American Humanics Certificate is granted upon the verification of an AH-affiliated college or university that a student has demonstrated attainment of essential nonprofit competencies, practical experience in nonprofit organizations, and leadership in student organizations. For information: CPR, first aid and automated external defibrillator (AED) training are all available from the Red Cross: http://www.redcross.org/

Wilderness First Responder and Wilderness First Aid
http://www.nols.edu/wmi/courses/wildfirstresponder.shtml
This is a nationally recognized program that trains participants to respond to emergencies in remote settings. The 80-hour curriculum includes standards for urban and extended care situations.

Leave-No-Trace/Leave No Trace Training
http://www.lnt.org
Master Educator courses train people to become comprehensive Leave No Trace educators, or Master Educators. Master Educators, in turn, teach people who become Leave No Trace Trainers. Trainers (or Master Educators) are then able to conduct Awareness Workshops, which are designed for the general public and promote Leave No Trace.

Aquatics Certifications include Certified Pool Operator, Water Safety Instructor, and Lifeguard. Information on these and other specialized certifications can be obtained by doing an Internet search.

Where to Get Experience

As mentioned earlier in the chapter, it is very important that you gain experience while you are going to school. Doing so will help you make good decisions about future employment opportunities, including field placements and internships. Even if you have a very busy schedule, try to find some time to volunteer at local events, whether it is a plant sale at the local community garden or a fundraiser for the local chapter of the Boys & Girls Clubs. If you have a little more time and can volunteer on a more regular basis, why not coach a soccer team for the YMCA or help out with a local Boy Scout troop? You are also encouraged to consider seasonal positions with non-profit agencies. There are many opportunities to work at both day and residential camps during the summer. Non-profits are always looking for enthusiastic staff with a passion for service. Everything you do helps build your understanding of the non-profit sector and builds your resume for a future career.

Conferences

Conferences are a great way to meet people in a particular industry or sector of work. As was mentioned in the section on professional associations of this chapter, there are many conferences available to people working in the non-profit sector. The real advantage that you have as a student is that many offer reduced fees and membership rates for students who want to attend. Some organizations even offer full scholarships if you are willing to volunteer some time at the conference. To search for conferences, start with professional associations, talk to people in the field and look on the Internet.

Volunteer Opportunities

Volunteering involves you giving up some of your free time and skills to assist your community or an organization. The commitment could be a one-time thing, or it could be an ongoing involvement. As discussed earlier in this chapter, most non-profits lack resources, both financial and human. You can make a difference in helping an organization to achieve its mission or vision! It is not just a one-way street though; the organization will benefit, but so will you. Helping others feels good, and you will gain a broader perspective on life at the same time you are gaining valuable experience to add to your resume. There are literally millions of opportunities for you to volunteer with non-profit organizations. Start with your local area, and you will see much that you can do in your own backyard. Need more info? Put the word "volunteering" into any search engine on the Internet and see what happens; you will be overwhelmed! Another great way to locate opportunities is check with your school's volunteer center. Volunteer centers are dedicated to connecting people with their community's volunteer needs. http://www.idealist. org/kt/volunteer.html#SEC26 has links to volunteer centers around the world.

CONCLUSION

This chapter has provided a glimpse into the exciting work that is being done in recreation and leisure services by non-profit organizations throughout the world. There are a wide variety of opportunities in this area, everything from small neighborhood programs to large international organizations and everything in between. If you are still not sure about working in this sector (or even if you are) be sure to check out the final section of the chapter, which offers information for further investigation including numerous websites and additional resources that you should find interesting.

FOR FURTHER INVESTIGATION

For More Research

If you are interested in looking for employment in the non-profit sector, try these websites in addition to the recreation-specific websites listed in the chapter (note that these websites are not recreation specific):

Energize, Inc.
http://www.energizeinc.com/placements.html
Jobs and internships involving volunteer management.

Jobfindersonline.com
http://www.planningcommunications.com/jf/index.htm
Find jobs and publications on careers.

Community Career Center
http://www.nonprofitjobs.org/
Search jobs, post jobs through this website.

The Chronicle of Philanthropy
http://philanthropy.com/jobs/
Browse jobs by position, receive career advice.

Nonprofit Career Network
http://www.nonprofitcareer.com
Offers a complete one-stop shop for job seekers in the non-profit sector

The Nonprofit Times
http://www.nptimes.com
Whether you're looking for a new job, or ready to take the next step in your career, this is the website for you.

Philanthropy News Network Online
http://www.philanthropyjournal.org
Allows you to search job openings by region or category.

For more information on non-profit organizations in the arts and sport industries, try these websites:

Art Search
http://www.artsearch.us/
This unique website offers listings of art galleries, artists, art museums, art services, art supplies, education, jobs, and much more. This is a perfect jumping-off point to learn more about the art world.

ART for the World
http://www.art-for-the-world.com/
The mission of this organization is "to create, through the universal language of art a meaningful and enduring dialogue among diverse peoples, cultures, and world views in order to encourage tolerance and solidarity and to foster education as a human right."

National Alliance for Youth Sports (NAYS)
http://www.nays.org/
NAYS partners nationwide with more than 3,000 community organizations in order to promote the value and importance of physical activity and sport. The website offers an excellent list of resources for parents, coaches, officials, and anyone interested in youth sport.

Sports Outreach USA
http://www.sportsoutreachusa.com
This organization seeks to use sport as a means of reaching communities through the local church, with an overall goal of reaching kids, connecting families, and equipping leaders through providing vision, training, and resources.

Active Investigation

Throughout the chapter, you have seen mission and/or vision statements for a lot of different non-profit recreation and leisure agencies. Most non-profits will want to know that you can and will support what they are trying to accomplish and not just on paper, but in your actions as well (both on and off the job). The message is: knowing what you believe in makes it easier to decide if you can work in an agency that has strong beliefs about how and why they function. You should be thinking about and developing a personal philosophy about recreation service provision and be able to clearly state it to potential employers.

Try writing a personal philosophy statement:

A. Start by writing down three to five things that are very important to you.
B. Explore non-profit agencies further by doing the following:

1. Look back through the agencies listed in the chapter and find two or three that seemed particularly interesting to you.
2. Go to each of their websites and really look at what the agency stands for and what types of programs and services they offer to what type of people.
3. Write down key phrases or statements from each that stand out or strike you as being personally meaningful.
4. Once you have finished with several websites, look and see what you have written down; that should give you a starting point for refining and expanding what you first wrote down into a personal philosophy statement.

RECOMMENDED READING

Borrup, T. C. (2006). *Creative community builder's handbook: How to transform communities using local assets, arts, and culture.* St. Paul, MN: Fieldstone Alliance Publishing.
This book offers tools that may be used in communities to bring together individuals and groups from diverse backgrounds, perspectives and skills to build upon the strengths within a community to make it a better place for all to live, work and play.
Cryer, S. (2008). *The nonprofit career guide: How to land a job that makes a difference.* Saint Paul, MN: Fieldstone Alliance.
This book explores rewarding career opportunities in the nonprofit sector beyond those in recreation, parks, sport management, hospitality & tourism.

Duncan, M. (1980). Back to our radical roots. In T. Goodale, & P. Witt (Eds.), *Recreation and leisure: Issues in an era of change.* State College, PA: Venture Publishing.
Duncan tells the little known history of five early pioneers in the recreation field and the challenges they faced in making recreation spaces and programs available to all members of society rather than just the upper classes of society.

Putnam, R. C., & Feldstein, L. M. (2003). *Better together: Restoring the American community.* New York: Simon & Schuster.
This book takes the reader on a journey around America to learn about organizations and communities that are being strengthened through making connections with people, establishing bonds of trust and understanding and building community.

REFERENCES

BoardSource. (2004). Ten basic responsibilities of non-profit boards, www.ncnb.org.
Brayley, R. E., & McLean, D. D. (2008). *Financial resource management: Sport, tourism and leisure services.* Champaign, IL: Sagamore.
Carlson, R. E., MacLean, J. R., Deppe, T. R., & Peterson, J. A. (1979). *Recreation and leisure: The changing scene* (3rd ed.). Belmont, CA: Wadsworth Publishing Company, Inc.
DeGraf, D. G., Jordan, D. J., & DeGraf, K. H. (1999). *Programming for parks, recreation, and leisure services: A servant-leader approach.* State College, PA: Venture.
DIRECTIONS Nonprofit Resource Assessment Model. (2000). Edginton, C. R., Hudson, S. D., & Lankford, S. V. (2001). *Managing recreation, parks, and leisure services: An introduction.* Champaign, IL: Sagamore.
Edgington, C. R., Jordan, D. J., DeGraf, D. G., & Edginton, S. R. (1998). *Leisure and life satisfaction: Foundational perspectives* (2nd ed.). Boston, MW: WCB/McGraw-Hill.

Jordan, D. J., DeGraaf, D. G., & DeGraaf, K. H. (2005) *Programming for parks, recreation, and leisure services: A servant leadership approach* (2nd ed.). State College, PA: Venture.

Mason, D. E. (1996). *Leading and managing the expressive dimension: Harnessing the hidden power source of the nonprofit sector.* San Francisco: Jossey-Bass Publishers.

Nanus, B., & Dobbs, S. M. (1999). *Leaders who make a difference: Essential strategies for meeting the nonprofit challenge.* San Francisco: Jossey-Bass Publishers.

Oleck, H. L., & Stewart, M. E. (1994) *Nonprofit corporations, organizations and associations* (6th ed.). Englewood Cliffs, NJ: Prentice Hall.

Salamon, L. M. (1999). *America's nonprofit sector: The primer.* (2nd ed.). New York: The Foundation Center.

Vaugan, A. (2005). Career options in the nonprofit sector. http://www.learningtogive. org, (3 October 2006).

Veal, A. J., & Lynch, R. (2001). *Australian leisure* (2nd ed.).Frenchs Forest, NSW, Australia: Pearson Education Australia Pty Limited.

"

After spending two years on the U.S.S. Nimitz aircraft carrier in the middle of the Gulf—where I provided recreation and leisure for 5,500 military personnel—I knew the services that I provided served a valuable purpose of building camaraderie as the soldiers maintained a stance of combat readiness.

—KERRIE SMITH
Athletic Director

"

5

Morale, Welfare, and Recreation

ASUNCION T. SUREN
San Francisco State University

FOCUS QUESTIONS

Q: *What is Morale, Welfare, and Recreation (MWR)?*

A: MWR is a comprehensive network of support and leisure services designed to enhance the lives of military personnel, their families, civilian employees, retirees, and other eligible participants.

Q: *Are MWR programs similar to recreation programs in civilian communities?*

A: MWR departments operate in a similar manner as civilian recreation agencies. Many of the programs such as entertainment, outdoor adventure, club sports, and fitness trends mimic those offered at civilian recreation agencies.

Q: *Why choose a career in MWR?*

A: A career with MWR allows the recreation professional to contribute to the strength and readiness of military commands by offering comprehensive services designed to enhance the quality of life as that of the citizens they are pledged to defend.

Q: *How can I get started with a career in MWR?*

A: The key to selecting a rewarding career with MWR is to do your homework. Start by conducting a thorough overview of which branch of service best meets your interest; for instance, are you interested in working for the Navy because of its mission to defend our nation's waterways and to support the Army, or are you interested in the Air Force because of its mission to protect the United States from the air and cyberspace? You will then want to identify at least three program service areas (e.g., fitness and aquatics, travel and tourism, youth and child development) that will not only meet your career goals, but will also satisfy your personal recreation and leisure needs. With this preliminary information in hand, do an Internet search by linking to your selected branch of service's Civilian Personnel Office.

Q: *Do I need to complete an internship with MWR in order to secure a position?*

A: Don't be concerned if you want to intern with an agency or company outside of the Armed Forces; you will be just as marketable. The key is to seek work opportunities to gain the traits and characteristics necessary to be successful in the MWR system. Use your internship to gain a well-rounded experience that will prepare you to be competitive in multiple program service areas (e.g., budgeting, supervision, programming, marketing, computers, etc.). You should select meaningful projects at your internship site that will expose you to public speaking opportunities, apply customer service techniques, and lead different target groups through programs and activities.

KEY TERMS

Department of Defense (DoD)
Morale, Welfare, and Recreation (MWR)
Armed Forces recreation
Esprit de corps
National Security Personnel System (NSPS)

Branch of service
Joint service facilities
Nonappropriated fund (NAF)

PROFILE 1: COULD THIS BE YOU?

TANYA MCCORMICK works for the Department of Defense Morale, Welfare, and Recreation (MWR). She is the fitness center director at the 60th Services Squadron Fitness Center at Travis Air Force Base (AFB) in California. Tanya oversees a variety of fitness and sports programs for the base personnel, which includes active duty, dependents, retirees, reservists, **Department of Defense** (DoD) civilians. She manages a $12 million-dollar full-service fitness center with all the services and equipment one would find at a private club. She is responsible for maintenance and program delivery for three softball fields, a soccer field, four tennis courts, and one track. Tanya is responsible for a wide variety of recreation-related programs, including:

- Intramural and extramural sports programs
- Group exercise classes
- Special events
- Self-directed fitness programs
- Trendy and specialized activities

Q: *What do you like most about your role in MWR?*

A: Well, I believe it would be the amount of responsibility. I enjoy being able to make decisions about all aspects of the facility and programs. My favorite part is working on facility remodeling projects. For example, we added 30,000 square feet to the fitness building, and I worked up the floor plans with the contractor during the design phase. I got to decide every aspect of paint, carpet, flooring, etc. I also enjoy developing program ideas and implementing them. Offering good quality programs that most customers can enjoy and that are current with trends found in the private sector.

Q: *It sounds like you have a variety of important things to do as a director. What are some of the things you may not like as much?*

A: Government bureaucracy can make things complicated at times. You have to follow chain of command to get a response to a question; because of this you may not get your answer as quickly as you need.

Q: *You must really believe in supporting military personnel and their families. In what ways do you get to improve their lives?*

A: Everyone needs some sort of recreational outlet. Intramural sports is great for *esprit de corp*. I love to play sports and compete and others get that same joy. I know units enjoy camaraderie and being competitive with co-workers. Now, we are also focusing more on families being fit, so we are expanding our offerings to include more children into our facility and programs, and not limiting it to an adult-only facility as much as it was before. Our programs are important to the quality of life for military personnel (McCormick, personal communication, March 24, 2008).

PROFILE 2: COULD THIS BE YOU?

PAMELA LAW has worked for MWR in different service areas since 1995, when she launched her career following two internships. She has worked in Diego Garcia, a British Indian Territory as an athletic director; Atsugi, Japan, as a community activities director; Vicenza, Italy as a pre-teen director; and Hickam Air Force Base, Hawaii, as an outdoor recreation programmer. She has been successful at building supervisory skill sets and applying them to enhance the Navy, Army, and Air Force MWR programs. As the fitness and aquatics manager for Commander Fleet Activities in Sasebo, Japan, Pamela's duties include:

- Operation of two pools
- Operation of two facilities
- Maintenance of fitness equipment
- Coordination of lifeguard and water safety classes
- Coordination and leading fitness classes
- Special events planning and implementation

Q: *Your career with the Navy has allowed you to travel quite a bit. What is it like supervising MWR staff overseas?*

A: I enjoy working with the staff, and seeing them learn why I want things done in a certain way. I have bilingual staff, so that is a huge challenge for me. I have lived in Japan for more than seven years total, and I still don't know enough of the language—something to work on! I also enjoy creating new events. I like hearing ideas from customers and making their ideas come alive. When you listen to your customers and then they see the results, it makes everyone happy.

Q: *You are learning from your staff and customers. What do you like least about working for MWR?*

A: Budgets! The Navy doesn't require us to be responsible for the budget. I really enjoy knowing how my programs are doing financially whether it's good or bad. In MWR, there is always a need for qualified staff who knows about recreation and leisure.

Q: *As a Navy MWR career professional, do you think you're making a difference in the lives of the people you serve?*

A: I know I make a difference every day! Being able to let people know that they are cared for and appreciated can set the tone in the community. I will have commands ask for me to help with swim lessons or physical training sessions. I have run a contest similar to the television show *Biggest Loser*. The participants came back several months later to show me their waistlines and tell me that what I taught them really does work. Their smiles, in return, make me want to do a better job (Law, personal communication, February 18, 2008).

DID YOU KNOW?

Morale, Welfare, and Recreation (MWR), also known as military recreation, or **Armed Forces Recreation**, is a multifaceted operation where each branch of service (Army, Navy, Air Force, and Marine Corps) offers a variety of program and service career options throughout the United States and overseas. MWR personnel contribute to the readiness, productivity, **esprit de corps**, and overall quality of life for soldiers and their families. MWR exists because the Armed Forces are committed to the well-being of the military community who stand ready to protect the nation. Thousands of MWR employees worldwide are dedicated to implementing the highest quality programs and services at each of the Armed Forces installations. Career opportunities are available for any recreation professional interested in family and youth programs, single solider services and events, sports and fitness, or information, travel, and tourism (http:// www.armymwr.com/portal/about/).

Do You Know How MWR Got Its Start?

Legend has it that the MWR tradition was born one rainy, cold World War I day, on the front lines in France, when a Salvation Army soldier cooked up the first batch of doughnuts to go with a homesick Arkansas soldier's hot coffee (Gibbs, 2007). "It wasn't until July 1940 that the Morale Division—later named Special Services—was established within the Adjutant General's Office. Between 1946 and 1955, the core recreation programs were established and staffed by a combination of active duty military and civilians". (http://www.armymwr.com/portal/about/) By the mid-1980s, soldiers and officers held military positions in Special Services; as those occupational specialties were changed, civilians operated MWR programs with oversight from military officers. By 1984, the U.S. Army Community and Family Support Center, for example, was established as the headquarters for MWR operations. This newly formed structure was instrumental in providing oversight and policy support, as well as the management of the Armed Forces Recreation Centers. As the system evolved, the Family and Morale, Welfare and Recreation Command were established by the Department of the Army in 2006 resulting in numerous recreation and leisure career options (http://www.armymwr.com/portal/about/).

What is MWR Like Today?

Today's Armed Forces MWR continues to thrive in its mission to support the combat readiness of military personnel through myriad programs and services designed to meet specific needs of single soldiers, or the single parents, for instance. To accomplish its mission, a strong emphasis is placed on the professional development and growth of MWR professionals through trainings and continued

> ### Wounded Warriors Take Healing Process Outdoors
>
> For Soldiers of the Warrior Transition Unit on Caserma Ederle, a day trip to the waters of Laghi Verdi (Green Lakes) delivered a chance to unwind, while enjoying a fishing tournament with friends under sunny skies. Organizer Richard Boudreau, who was supported by numerous people and organizations on post, said he searched for an event that would benefit injured members by "getting them out of the barracks for some fun."
>
> His solution: a fishing excursion to the nearby community of Valproto di Quinto Vicentino. "I figured (it) would be the easiest way to get the most soldiers involved," he said. One of Boudreau's first stops was to visit Outdoor Rec's Chris Wolff, explaining what was needed was for MWR to cover the cost of licenses and fees. "(Our participation) was a no-brainer for us," said Wolff. "This was a great way to help out our wounded soldiers and to invest our resources in a way that all of them could readily enjoy (Kieffer, Jan. 29, 2008 USAG Vicenza Public Affairs).

educational opportunities; thus to stay abreast of program trends found in civilian communities, and rapidly changing technologies and forms of social media prevalent in society. In the 21st century, the DoD hiring format shifted from a Grade Scale (GS) structure to the **National Security Personnel System (NSPS)**. NSPS is a civilian workforce structure that is centered on professional competency skill sets and employee performance. It drives the hiring and promotion process by putting skilled people in highly demanding, business-oriented positions. In 2009, you will find recreation professionals operating multimillion dollar state-of-the art fitness facilities and managing exotic resorts worldwide. For instance, Armed Forces recreation center (AFRC) resorts career opportunities are highly desired by recreation and special events graduates across the nation. AFRC resorts are operated by the Family and Morale, Welfare and Recreation Command and are located at popular vacation destinations, making this operation one of the most sought after career tracks within the MWR system.

CAREERS IN MORALE, WELFARE, AND RECREATION

Based on the **branch of service**, careers in recreation and leisure can be found on small tropical islands, in large urban cities, on ships, and under water on submarines—in other words, worldwide. Recreation professionals can find career opportunities under such categories as: Family and Morale, Welfare, and Recreation with the Army; or Fleet and Family Readiness with Navy Morale, Welfare, and Recreation; or Combat Support and Community Service with the Air Forces; or

Marine Corps Community Services. Each branch of service has myriad program service areas for students to pursue either as an intern, or to establish professional career tracks that will allow them to move from one branch of the service to another branch and from one program service area to another. Overall, MWR professionals work hard so that military personnel and their families can have fun and enjoy life at any time of day or week (Temple & Ogilvie, 2006).

Passions

If you have a sense of duty to mankind and believe in a holistic approach to enhancing the well-being of men and women whose mission in life is to protect and serve, then you have the passion needed to be successful in MWR. For instance, do you embrace the Army's philosophy, which is that soldiers are entitled to the same quality of life as the citizens they are pledged to defend? If you answered yes to the above question you only need to continue reading to explore more fully what a career professional like Mr. John Kelly Powell believes to be the core ingredient necessary for a long-term career in military recreation.

"Working in military recreation is the most challenging and the most rewarding experience a person can choose to perform within the recreation and leisure career field, but it is definitely not for everyone. Entering into military recreation can be a very difficult task and discouraging for some people. However, once in the system, the ability to climb any of the career ladders is only inhibited by the individual's desire to excel. A performance management system is set up to foster a high-performance culture that rewards employee performance for going above and beyond the usual job responsibilities. The rewards, both intrinsic and extrinsic, abound for the right person. Additionally, both personal and professional development opportunities flourish for anyone wanting to accept the challenge that could include living and working in various countries across the world. If you are the type of person that wants to make a difference and impact people's lives with your work, then working in MWR might be your ticket" (personal communication, February 20, 2008).

Preparation

Securing a degree in recreation and leisure with an emphasis in either sport management, fitness and wellness, commercial, outdoor, tourism, nonprofit, or even therapeutic recreation will give you a solid foundation for a career in military recreation. Most colleges and universities require field experience prior to pursuing an internship. When selecting an agency for field experience, make sure you gain the necessary skills as described above; however, success is predicated upon your willingness to experience and practice the following:

- Program planning and creativity
- Budgeting and financial management
- Team building and partnerships

- Leading activities and people
- Risk management planning
- Conducting inventories
- Exhibiting sound customer service
- Developing and maintaining databases and registrations
- Writing and documenting
- Encouraging accountability and integrity
- Listening and effective verbal communication

Mr. Powell stresses what traits or characteristics a student should gain in preparation for a career in military recreation:

"An individual wanting to work in this setting must be extremely motivated, flexible, multitalented, hardworking, and have the uncommon ability to perform with little or no supervision. The individual must also be a total team player with the highest standards of self-confidence, integrity, dependability, and knowledge of program delivery. Additionally, the person must demonstrate a greater customer service concern and the willingness to go the extra mile for the people and the organization he or she serves that is rarely seen today."

Further, get any and all recreational programming experience possible. Volunteer with a local recreation center, for example, to gain experience assisting customers in all facets of the operation. Learn all you can in the area of personnel, interpersonal relations, and finance (understand budgeting). Become as computer savvy as possible and become comfortable with public speaking. Most importantly develop sound principles and philosophy that you can carry with you throughout life (personal communication, February 20, 2008).

Advancing Your Career with MWR

To be competitive for career opportunities with MWR, you may want to consider the **Nonappropriated Fund** (NAF) Management Training Program. This program is designed to train college students in select program service areas (e.g., hospitality, marketing, and recreation) and then hires them for full-time employment. Trainees are placed at various military installations within the United States to complete up to 18 months of on-the-job training (OJT). After successfully completing the OJT, trainees are encouraged to compete for permanent placement worldwide. To be competitive for the MWR training program the following qualifications are required:

- College graduate with a degree in the specialty sought (require college transcript)

- Overall grade point average (GPA) of 2.9 or Major GPA 3.5 (on the 4.0 scale)

- Must be able to relocate to a regional training site, successfully complete the 18 months of OJT

- Upon successful completion of training, be willing to relocate to a permanent placement location nationwide

  (http://www.campuscareercenter.com/students/honorroll_detail.asp?company_id=1036).

Pay and Perks

A career with MWR has a very competitive salary at different professional levels ranging from student intern to supervisory classification, and benefits package that includes medical, dental, and life insurance, 401(K) savings plan, and a comprehensive retirement plan. Recreation professionals will earn a salary under the National Security Personnel System or NSPS (with salary pay bands or step increases). This system values performance and contribution, supports broader skill development, and promotes excellence in the workplace (http://www.cpms.osd.mil/nsps/documents.html). Through this system, career MWR personnel ranked at the professional level (one of the highest performance levels) can earn an average pay of $75,000 annually. Other benefits derived through this performance-based system include:

- Annual pay raises and/or bonuses on performance and contributions.
- High-performing employees can get higher base pay raises and/or bonuses

(Civilian Personnel Management Service, Wage and Salary Division, January 2008).

Questions about positions and employee benefits can be directed to:
The Department of Defense
Civilian Personnel Management Service
1400 Key Boulevard
Arlington, VA 22209-5514

Possibilities

Recreation and leisure career opportunities are available in such areas as special events, marketing, youth services, fitness and wellness, and much more can be explored in the Armed Forces. If you have a love of the arts, or building classic automobiles, or boxing you can build a career around your personal interest, skills, and talents. If you are a person who seeks adventure through travel and tourism, then working for the MWR Information, Travel, and Tourism program might be right up your alley. While there are traditional recreation and leisure program service areas across the Armed Forces, there are some unique service areas available just for your individual career interest and talents.

EXAMPLE MWR PROGRAM SERVICE AREAS

Physical Fitness	Recreation Centers
Outdoor Recreation	Youth Recreation
Single Soldier Recreation	Special Events and Entertainment
Child Development	Information, Travel, and Tourism
Library Services	Resort Management - Hospitality
Auto Hobby Shop	Golf Course
Aquatics	Music and Arts/Crafts
Arts and Crafts	Sports and Intramural Clubs
Food and Beverage	Marketing and Public Relations

Army MWR - Armed Forces Resort Center (AFRC)

"Whether strolling barefoot on the sands of Waikiki Beach, sightseeing historic European castles, shopping Seoul's exciting shopping district or visiting the enchanting Walt Disney Resort; there is a vacation getaway that will leave you with fresh memories and new perspectives" (http://www.armymwr.com/portal/travel/recreationcenters/default.asp).

How would you like to be the hospitality professional to write a similar advertisement to invite military personnel for a relaxing yet exhilarating vacation experience? Hospitality professionals are hired to organize and plan relaxing yet exhilarating vacation experiences for military personnel and their families at one of five AFRC resorts worldwide. These resorts are operated by the Army Family and Morale, Welfare and Recreation Command. Much like other civilian resort destinations, AFRCs offer a full range of hotel opportunities and amenities. Please refer to chapter 11, The Hospitality Industry, for additional information that complements this career option.

Passions—Friendly and team-oriented, enjoys working with all types of people, freely engages in public speaking and skilled at creative writing, program planning, special events coordination and customer services; enjoys facilitating relaxing and memorable vacation experiences.

Pay and Perks—Depending on a number of factors such as previous work experience in the hospitality industry, education, and time in the military system will determine the annual salary range. Professionals working for AFRCs may earn an average salary, at the low end, from $30,000 but can go up to $60,000. Wages are comparable with industry standards. Depending on the AFRC resort location, professionals may be eligible for meals programs, dormitory-style housing accommodations, and access to the amenities during down time.

Preparation—Bachelor's degree in recreation, special events planning, or hospitality management.

Possibilities—AFRCs are (**Joint Service Facilities**) resort hotels located in five vacation destinations: Florida (Shades of Green–Walt Disney World), Hawaii (Hale Koa Hotel–Diamond Head), Korea (Dragon Hill Lodge–Asia Style), Germany (Edelweiss Lodge and Resort), and Virginia (Cape Henry Inn–Atlantic Coast). As a professional with the AFRC, you will provide high-quality yet affordable resort experiences with a focus on endorsing the Army's mission to provide rest, relaxation, and recreation to foster combat readiness and retention (http://www. armymwr.com/portal/travel/recreationcenters/default.asp).

Marine Corps Community Service–Single Marine Program (SMP)

The well-being and recreation needs of single soldiers have become a vital service component of MWR programs for more than a decade. The Single Marine Program (SMP) or Better Opportunities for Single Soldiers (BOSS), for the other branches of service, is a highly energetic

program designed to identify and address issues and concerns affecting the living environment of the soldier. Additionally, it gives a voice to single soldiers in the development of recreational events that best meets their needs (http://www.mccslejeune. com/smp.html).

Passions—Program planning, needs assessment, and evaluation; provide opportunities for single individuals to participate and contribute to local community efforts and recreational activities; facilitate efforts to improve conditions to enhance the well-being of others; and enjoys advocacy work and organizing fundraising events.

Pay and Perks—Professionals working in the SMP/BOSS program are usually considered recreation specialists (single soldier coordinator) under the community activity center. Pay range for recreation specialist usually ranges from $40,000 - $50,000 annually. Positions with SMP/BOSS program are available worldwide. One of the perks of working in the SMP/BOSS program is that it allows recreational professionals to assume a leadership role on base and to work closely with military leaders on base. Standard perks include a generous retirement program, flexible work environment, alternative work schedules, paid employment-related training, education, and possible student loan repayment. Other incentives include assistance with paying tuitions for academic degrees, pay band bonuses, and performance awards.

Preparation—Bachelor's degree in recreation and leisure with competencies in the areas of leadership and team building, budgeting, and financial management. The recreation specialist working for the SMP/BOSS program must also exhibit the highest standard of self-confidence, integrity, dependability, and knowledge of program delivery. A significant amount of time spent through either an internship or volunteer experience gaining skills in the area of needs assessment and evaluation is essential.

Possibilities—The Single Soldier Coordinator will work closely with the soldier, senior military personnel, and other essential community service staff to ensure the best possible quality of life for single and unaccompanied men and women in the Armed Forces. Career advancement is available worldwide.

Navy MWR – Fleet Recreation

Because being at sea for lengths of time can be difficult and demanding for sailors, quality leisure time activities that fit into the limited space available aboard ship are essential. Therefore, recreation professionals are expected to provide holistic leisure experiences for sailors whether in port or overseas. For instance, these career professionals provide a variety of individual and group activities to include tours, picnics, athletic competitions, fitness, and wellness. The recreation professional working for Navy MWR is generally responsible for the development of programs and services, as well as provides resources such as equipment for 5,000 or more Navy personnel. Please refer to chapter 3, Community-Based Recreation and Leisure Services, for details on similar jobs.

Passions—Very passionate about sailing and living in coastal communities; an independent thinker while also embracing team camaraderie; interested in special events planning, fitness and wellness, sports, and budget management; and enjoys marketing and public relations.

Pay and Perks—Depending on a number of factors such as job responsibilities specific to programming activities or managing budgets, the average salary for a recreation specialists will range from $30,500 to $40,000 annually. A primary perk of working for the Navy MWR Fleet recreation is extensive travel.

Preparation—Bachelor's degree in the field of recreation management from an accredited university or college. Recreation specialists working for the Navy should be knowledgeable of activities suitable for individuals or groups of various ages, interests, and capacities based on participant interests and needs. Further, the ability to effectively communicate both verbal and in writing is of the upmost importance. Consider gaining experience from an internship or volunteering at local agencies on managing people and material resources.

Possibilities—Career options are available at fleet sites around the world if you are interested in shipping out to sea and providing quality recreation and leisure programs for hard-working sailors (http://usmilitary.about.com/library/milinfo/allhands/blnavymwr.htm).

Air Force Combat Support and Community Service–Outdoor Recreation

Outdoor recreation programs provide military personnel (airmen) and their families with opportunities to participate in the outdoors by planning and offering activities and adventures. Emphasis is placed on outdoor recreation skill development and opportunities for airmen to acquire lifetime leisure skills that assist them in remaining combat ready. In many cases putdoor recreation specialists are charged to assist base commanders in maintaining readiness by providing varied outdoor adventure training opportunities (http://www.apgmwr.com/recreation/odr/index.html). Chapter 6 on Outdoor Recreation has additional information that will be helpful if this is a career area that interests you.

Passions—If you have a passion or interested in the great outdoors, natural resources, adventure, and skill building, then MWR outdoor recreation will be the best path to pursue a career in the military system. Other areas of interests might be rock climbing, skiing, sailing, kayaking, and camping

Pay and Perks—The average salary for MWR outdoor recreation specialists is approximately $31,000 annually. Similar to other recreation specialist positions within the MWR system, perks includes generous retirement program, flexible work environment, alternative work schedules, and paid employed related training and education. The variety of programs and services ranging from planning an outdoor adventure excursion to managing family camp groups can be a fantastic perk for the outdoor enthusiast.

Preparation—Bachelor's degree in outdoor adventure, park management, or recreation management. Exposure to experiential learning opportunities in the out of doors will serve you well in this area of military recreation.

Possibilities—All branches of the service have thriving outdoor recreation and adventure programs; however, based on geographic location, availability of natural resources, and patron demand you may find yourself managing a riding stable, marina, picnic areas, outdoor equipment checkout centers, and family campgrounds.

As you learn more about careers in military recreation, you will quickly see there are numerous position titles for you to explore and learn about the specific duties and responsibilities. In general, however, you will see that jobs fall at one of three different levels:

Entry Level—These are either part-time or full-time positions with minimal management responsibilities. With this type of position, the employee would be asked to assist the director or specialist with activity planning, and will maintain basic day-to-day customer service operations such as equipment check-outs and activity registrations.

Mid Level—These are full-time positions with responsibility to manage people, programs, services, and facilities. This level generally requires a college degree and some experience in the program service area for the position. With a pay band increase, the MWR professional may be in charge of approximately 10 employees.

Upper Level—These are full-time director positions where the MWR professional would oversee duties of mid-level personnel. At this level, the director is expected to oversee budgets, understand and apply all military operating standards, and ensure the NSPS employees are adequately trained to apply their skills in an efficient and effective manner.

"Career advancement generally follows a path from entry level, through the intermediate level, to managerial or executive positions. Individual progression depends on a variety of factors including demonstrated performance, assignments completed, formal education, functional and geographical mobility, and completion of training programs"

(http://www.campuscareercenter.com/students/honorroll_detail.asp?company_id=1036).

The above information covers general career areas available within military welfare and recreation. For information about specific Armed Forces Recreation program service areas visit the following websites:

Navy MWR
http://www.mwr.navy.mil/

Marine Corps Community Services
http://www.usmc-mccs.org/

Army and MWR Family Command
http://www.armymwr.com/

Air Force Combat Support and Community Service
http://usafservices.com/_

Armed Forces Recreation Center Resorts
http://www.armymwr.com/recleisure/default.aspx

SUMMARY OF MORALE, WELFARE, AND RECREATION CAREER POSSIBILITIES

Career	Passions	Pay and Perks	Preparation	Possibilities
Army MWR-Armed Forces Resort Center (AFRC)	Friendly and team-oriented, customer service	Ranges from entry-level pay similar to educators to administrative levels.	Bachelor's degree in recreation or special events planning	Various opportunities in fine vacation destinations.
Marine Corps Community Service-Single Marine Program (SMP)	Program planning, needs assessment, and evaluation	Ranges from entry-level pay similar to educators to administrative levels.	Bachelor's degree in recreation and leisure services	Career advancement is available worldwide.
Navy (MWR) Fleet Recreation	Passionate about sailing and be an independent thinker	Pay level similar to educators, depending on education and experience.	Bachelor's degree in the field of recreation management	Career options are available at fleet sites around the world.
Air Force Combat Support and Community Service	Great outdoors natural resources, adventure, and skill building	Pay level similar to educators, depending on education and experience.	Bachelor's degree in outdoor adventure, park management, or recreation management	All branches of the service have thriving outdoor recreation and adventure programs.

ARMED FORCES RECREATION SOCIETY (AFRS) works on behalf of military recreation professionals around the world to improve the quality of life for sailors, soldiers, Marines, Air Force personnel, Coast Guard men and women, and their families. AFRS is committed to attracting and developing MWR professionals; implementing innovative training and professional development opportunities; and networking, designing, and implementing programs that enhance cross-cultural relations. By doing this, NRPA members in these settings contribute to mission readiness and retention of the men and women in uniform who protect our country.

FUTURE OPPORTUNITIES, ISSUES, AND CHALLENGES

According to John Kelly, working in military recreation is the most challenging and rewarding experience a person can choose to perform within the recreation field, but it is not for everyone (personal communication). MWR career professionals like Tanya McCormick and Pamela Law told you that this career track can be satisfying yet challenging. The military has an obligation to provide for the well-being of its personnel and their families during peacetime and times of war, so if you choose to join, it is important to have a genuine commitment to uphold the mission of the military. While military recreation offers career opportunities at exotic resort destinations, it also provides career opportunities for the passionate person during times of war. Historically, mission-essential DOD civilians were needed to maintain combat readiness during times of crisis. Since high morale is critical to the success of military personnel, there are special career opportunities available to the recreation professional if he or she elects to be deployed to a foreign country to work in safe areas within war zones.

To promote their commitment to skilled professionals, the MWR system offers:

- Transitions from one branch of service to another (e.g., from Navy to Army)
- Trainings to keep MWR professionals abreast of trends and issues in the field of recreation
- Deployment bonuses and housing
- Promotions and pay raises through the National Security Personnel System

It is evident that recreation is needed at all times to develop, maintain, or enhance the morale of military personnel. In the 21st century, recreation professionals can also find positions with Veteran Hospitals and Centers designing programs and services to meet the needs of veterans returning home to the United States. Because of the significant number of injured military personnel returning from Afghanistan and Iraq, the need for inclusive recreation is paramount. The "Inclusive Recreation for Wounded Warriors" program is an innovative training program designed to help the recreation professional address the many needs of returning military personnel.

The Benefits of an MWR Internship

According to John Prue, recreation division head and internship coordinator, "Interns can target one or more specific areas of the MWR Department or experience a number of recreational areas. We allow the students to decide what type of experience they wish to receive from their internship. Our main goal is to provide them with a positive learning experience." He said that over the past few years, the Navy has been recruiting qualified recreation students for internships at bases all over the world, and a number of these successful interns are then hired as MWR recreation professionals. Prue added, "This MWR internship will look really good on my resume because it's a worldwide organization. It really legitimizes my previous collegiate experience." Other internship advantages include a stipend of $75 per week and room and board, which works out to approximately $1,300 per semester (Mohr, 1997, *Parks and Recreation*).

"The [inclusive recreation] program will provide the knowledge, tools, and resources recreation managers need to integrate active-duty wounded warriors into their existing recreation programs. During previous wars, these men and women might have been discharged or retired. This is no longer true. Current military policies permit wounded warriors to remain on active duty" (McIlvanie, 2008).

MWR faces challenges as well. Despite economic hardship and war, a myriad program service areas exist (worldwide) for students to consider. Much like civilian recreation centers, MWR bases are facing issues of high turnover in staff and dwindling budgets. However, MWR remains committed to seeking future professionals who possess competitive skill sets and a passion for helping the military protect our nation.

RESOURCES AND GETTING INVOLVED

To remain competitive and move up the ladder from a recreation assistant position, for example, to a recreation center director or specialist position, you will have ample opportunities to gain new skill sets from trainings via workshops, specialized courses, or by attending national conferences. Individual professional development is a high priority for the military, so much so that they have a training center known as the MWR Academy. "It provides employees with quality management and customer service training, in support of continuous professional growth and meeting the MWR mission" (http://www.mwraonline.com). MWR professionals can select from more than 50 courses and training programs through this system of professional development. Many of these courses will not only help you with continuing education units, but also help you earn college credits.

Professional Organizations

You may want to also consider joining a professional organization such as the National Recreation and Parks Association (NRPA) or the Armed Forces Recreation Society, a branch of NRPA (visit: http://www.nrpa.org/). As you become more familiar with a specific program area and develop a passion for what you're doing to meet the military mission, it will be essential to connect with a professional association. There are many professional associations at the state and national levels where you network with others in your area of expertise to stay abreast of current trends and practices. Being an active member will help with pay band increase and subsequent pay increases.

Certifications and Licenses

There are no licenses or certifications that are specific to MWR, but you should investigate those that relate to your specific area of interest. These will be covered in other chapters such as Community Recreation, Outdoor Recreation, Therapeutic Recreation, and Sports Management.

Where to Get Experience

MWR internships are educational experiences designed to give college students studying recreation and leisure or related curriculums an opportunity to gain real-life experience while earning credits toward their degree. Universities are committed partners with MWR departments from any of the four branches of service. Through this partnership, students gain practical, hands-on experience before graduation, while MWR program departments bridge the gap between theory and practice students learned while in school. The benefit of this partnership is the enhanced service to military personnel and their families (http://www.mwr.navy.mil/mwrprgms/trngann/internmanual.pdf).

CONCLUSION

MWR departments provide a viable service to military personnel, their families, civilian personnel, military retirees, and other eligible participants. MWR exists because the Armed Forces are committed to the well-being of the military community of people who serve and stand ready to defend the nation. MWR offers comprehensive recreation and leisure services areas ranging from sports and fitness to travel and tourism, to single soldier special events, and much more. Thousands of MWR employees worldwide are committed to delivering the highest quality programs and services at each of the Armed Forces installations. A career with MWR allows the recreation professional to contribute to the strength and readiness of soldiers by offering services that reduce stress and build skills and self-confidence.

There are numerous positions for students who are interested in earning a degree in recreation and leisure or a related discipline with Morale, Welfare, and Recreation throughout the Continental United States and overseas. To be competitive for career opportunities with MWR, consider the Nonappropriated Fund (NAF) Management Training Program and join a professional organization such as the Armed Forces Recreation Society.

To fully comprehend the vast structure of MWR, its hiring structure, job opportunities, and employee benefits, you must think critically about what program service area you are interested in and do your homework by asking specific career planning questions. Further, you should do your homework with the notion in mind that MWR services are equivalent to recreation and leisure services found at civilian agencies. If you have a passion for helping others and working to uphold the ultimate mission of keeping U.S. soldiers combat ready, then military recreation should be a strong consideration for your future career.

ACTIVE INVESTIGATION

In preparation for an internship with military recreation, or to determine if you are interested in making a three-year commitment to the nonappropriated fund management training program, conduct an informational interview with any career professional within the MWR system. See chapter 2 for more details on conducting this type of interview, and consider the following questions to help guide your personal quest to secure an MWR position:

1. What can I do right now to prepare myself for a career with MWR?

2. Are there specific skill sets I should gain that will make me competitive for position as a recreation specialist?

3. What should I consider before pursuing a position overseas?

4. Are there financial perks available to me if I qualify for and accept an overseas position with MWR?

5. What is the best professional association for me to join to help improve my chances of upward mobility within the NSPS?

6. Once I secure a position with MWR, how can this experience help me if I want to pursue a position with a civilian agency or a corporate business?

FOR FURTHER INVESTIGATION

To help you address these questions and others, you will want to surf the following websites and their links:

Air Force Services Career Program
http://www-p.afsv.af.mil/CR/

Army Civilian Personnel On-Line
http://www.cpol.army.mil/library/naf/

Civilian Personnel On-line
http://www.cpol.army.mil/

Department of Defense's Civilian Employment Center
http://www.godefense.com

Fundamentals of NSPS: An Overview of Proposed Regulations
http://www.cpms.osd.mil/nsps/

MWR Training Academy
http://www.mwraonline.com

Naval MWR Internship Program
http://mwr.navy.mil/mwrprgms/intern.html

Navy Morale, Welfare and Recreation Overseas Positions
http://federaljobs.net/overseas.htm

Nonappropriated Funds Employment Opportunities
http://acpol.army.mil/employment/naf.htm

USAJOB.com
http://www.usajobs.gov/

USAF Services

http://usafscrviccs.com/_AFSVA/About.htm

Recommended Reading

Lankford, S., & DeGraaf, D. (1992). Strengths, weaknesses, opportunities, and
    threats in morale, welfare, and recreation organizations: Challenges of the
    1990s. *Journal of Parks and Recreation Administration, 10* [1], pp. 31-45.
This recommended reading by Lankford and DeGraaf, while written in the 1990s,
lends much to the reader on the topic of trends and issues in MWR. The authors
provide strategies to aid Armed Forces Recreation directors on how to best
assess future leisure service delivery systems. This reading provides an excellent
framework for MWR trends and issues young professionals might face in the 21st
century, as well as effective methods for making operational decisions.

McLean, D. D., Hurd, A. R., & Rogers, N. B. (2005). *Kraus' recreation and leisure
    in modern society.* Sudbury, MA: Jones and Bartlett.
This textbook provides a brief yet thorough overview of six specialized leisure
service areas to include Armed Forces Recreation. Chapter 9 will offer the reader
insight into how the military is an untapped industry, and why recreation students
should consider it as a career option.

Human Kinetics. (Ed.) (2006). *Introduction to recreation and leisure.* Champaign: Human Kinetics.

Temple and Ogilvie, authors of the "Recreation in the Armed Forces" section, discuss the similarities between military and civilian recreation in this introduction to recreation and leisure textbook. See chapter 11 for more in-depth reading on the history of morale, welfare, and recreation. The interested reader will also get a peak at the educational credentials and career path taken by Mr. John Kelly Powell. There is a brief discussion on Canadian Armed Forces and recreation principles as well.

Stars and Stripes (2009). "MWR plays vital role" Available http://www.stripes.com/article.asp?section=125&article=65994

Stars and Stripes is the military and MWR civilian personnel's best kept secret. It is steeped in long tradition of keeping the military community abreast of current trends and issues. The reader can consider their online newspaper for what happening in the Armed Forces stateside and abroad. The reading on "MWR plays vital role" is one example of pressing news that showcases the importance of recreation in maintain the physical, mental, and psychological well-being of soldiers fighting during a time of war. Since World War II, Stars and Stripes has provided cutting edge news, but now the reading will find blogs, multimedia events, and even select television episodes

REFERENCES

Aberdeen Proving Ground Family Morale, Welfare, and Recreation. Available: http://www.apgmwr.com/recreation/odr/index.html   June 25, 2008.

Armed Forces Resort Centers. Section Destination Paradise. Available: http://www.armymwr.com/portal/travel/recreationcenters/ May 23, 2008.

Armed Forces Resort Centers. Section Mission Relaxation. Available: http://www.armymwr.com/portal/travel/recreationcenters/mission.html May 23, 2008.

Campus Career Center: Morale, Welfare, and Recreation. Section NAF Management Training Program. Available: http://www.campuscareercenter.com/students/honorroll_detail.asp?company_id=1036 June 25, 2008.

Civilian Personnel Management Service, Wage and Salary Division. (January 2008). Available: http://www.cpms.osd.mil/WAGE/WAGE_index.aspx. June 30, 2008.

Gibbs, H. K. (2007). MWR 2007: This is not your father's morale, welfare, and recreation program. Available: http://www.ameriforce.net/PDF/AF2007_Summer/18-20_AFmag.pdf June 2008.

Kieffer, G. (2008, Jan 29). Wounded Warriors Take Healing Process Outdoors. USAG Vicenza Public Affairs. Available: http://www.army.mil/-news/2008/01/29/7169-wounded-warriors-take-healing-process-outdoors/ February 10, 2008.

Marine Corps Community Services Camp Lejeune. Section Single Marine Program. Available: http://www.mccslejeune.com/smp.html June 15, 2008.

McIlvanie (2008, November 11). Penn State University, Army MWR, DOD Promote Inclusive Recreation Training for Recreation Professionals. Available http://old.armymwr.com/portal/news/display.asp?NEWS_ID=891 July 8, 2010

Mueller, Ingrid. Navy MWR Programs and Services Help Meet Fleet Support Challenge. BNET Business Network. Available http://findarticles.com/p/articles/mi_pnav/is_200303/ai_2927822261 February 10, 2008.

Mohr, C. (1997). The benefits are endless for IPCC veterans and college interns –Intensive Psychiatric Community Care veterans and college interns brought together by the Morale, Welfare, and Recreation Department at the Naval Training Center, Great Lakes. Parks and Recreation. Available: http://findarticles.com/p/articles/mi_m1145/is_n12_v32/ai_20127498 June 25, 2008.

National Recreation and Parks Association. Section AFRS. Available: http://www.nrpa.org/content/default.aspx?documentId=526 June 30, 2008

Navy Fleet and Family Readiness Internship Program Manual. Section Internship. Available: http://www.mwr.navy.mil/mwrprgms/trngann/internmanual.pdf June 29, 2008.

Navy MWR. Section Fleet Recreation. Available: http://usmilitary.about.com/library/milinfo/allhands/blnavymwr.htm February 12, 2008.

Temple, J., & Ogilvie, L. (2006). *Recreation in the armed forces: Introduction to recreation and leisure.* Champaign, IL: Human Kinetics.

U.S. Army MWR. (2008, April 3). Section Army MWR. Available: http://www.armymwr.com/portal/about/ April 9, 2008.

“
We simply need that wild country available to us, even if we never
do more than drive to its edge and look in. For it can be a means
of reassuring ourselves of our sanity as creatures, a part of the
geography of hope.

—WALLACE STEGNER
Author and advocate for Utah's landscapes, people, and culture

”

6

Outdoor Recreation in Federal, State, and Local Parks

TONY SISTO
National Park Service (retired)

CHERYL A. STEVENS
East Carolina University

FOCUS QUESTIONS

Q: *Do you really love parks and are you comfortable spending time with just yourself in the outdoors? Do you also enjoy being with other people?*

A: Those who love working in the outdoors have a strong bond with nature. If you don't know whether that's you, spend extended time alone in the outdoors and find out. Some parks jobs can be isolated and require employees to work alone in the outdoors for sustained periods of time. If you would like a job with a lot of variety that balances the peace and quite of the natural world with the noisier world of park visitors, this may be the job for you.

Q: *Do you like working with people in the role of teacher or educator?*

A: Many park jobs require working with visitors who may have little understanding about how to behave in the natural world so that its beauty and serenity can be sustained for future users. Park employees emphasize visitor education about appropriate park uses through media or personal contact before any use of law enforcement. This often requires patience and a positive attitude because new visitors with the same questions come every day.

Q: *Are you willing to work on creative solutions to create a sustainable future for outdoor recreation areas?*

A: Funding will continue to challenge outdoor recreation professionals who must continually find new and innovative ways to secure funding and resources in a shifting landscape of support from the public sector, non-profits and private enterprises.

Q: *Do you have a particular interest or passion related to the outdoors that drives you?*

A: If you find yourself attending rallies or meetings in which people are trying to change governmental policy to promote environmental sustainability, you will discover many non-profit organizations and entrepreneurs with similar interests who partner with government outdoor recreation agencies.

Q: *How important are financial rewards to you?*

A: Although most career positions in outdoor recreation will pay comparable salaries to similar non-recreation jobs, you almost certainly will not get rich in this profession. It's important to know this at the beginning of your career. Many people find the perks of living close to nature and doing what they love are more important to them than large financial rewards.

KEY TERMS

Village greens
Boston Common
Central Park
Frederick Law Olmsted
Landscape architecture
Yellowstone National Park
Secretary of the Interior
John Muir
Forest Reserve Act
President Teddy Roosevelt
Gifford Pinchot
Forest Service

Department of Agriculture
Multiple Use Sustained Yield Act
    (MUSY)
Non-profits
Stephen T. Mather
For-Profit Concessions
Carrying capacity
Interpretation
Government Land Management
    Agencies
Non-Government Organizations
    (NGOs)

PROFILE 1: COULD THIS BE YOU?

COLETTE DAIGLE-BERG is a park ranger in Yellowstone National Park (she is the one in back!). Colette works with the United States National Park Service. As a park ranger in the world's first national park, she is responsible for a wide variety of outdoor duties, including:

- Bear research, trapping, and relocation
- Backcountry patrol, by foot, horseback, and aircraft
- Fire fighting
- Search and rescue
- Law enforcement and poaching investigations
- Medical technician

Q: *What do you like most about your career?*

A: The variety is great. I can start the day working in the campground and talking to campers, then work a bear jam or deal with a bear rambling through the housing area, respond to a medical call at the lodge, throw in an ambulance run or orchestrate a helicopter med-evac, spend some time with park visitors who are watching wolves as it gets dark, then wrap it up by shooing a bison or two away so I can get into my house.

Q: *That sounds pretty great. What are some of the things you may not like as much?*

A: There is a bunch of paperwork and E-mail and budgeting and scheduling to contend with, and it gets hectic; but when you look back, it's the great people, the wildlife, and amazing country that you remember. The job changes with the seasons and I love that. Backcountry patrols in the fall are spectacular.

Q: *So, you must think that this career can make a real difference in people's lives?*

A: Absolutely! At the end of the day, it's really a job about a place and a mission to believe in. Yellowstone, and the other national parks, provide people outstanding places to visit and experience, but we must do this in a way that leaves the parks unimpaired for future generations, not just this one, to enjoy. What could be more inspiring than that, working for the future?" (For further information about the National Park Service, and Yellowstone National Park, see http://www.nps.gov/yell/).

PROFILE 2: COULD THIS BE YOU?

VIRGINIA "GINNY" ALFRIEND is a Park Specialist IV for the City of Eugene Parks and Open Space in Oregon. She coordinates the everyday functioning of Hendricks Park, which she describes as a beautiful piece of land, rising above the east side of town, with mature native oaks and firs setting the tone. The park is 79 acres and includes 60 acres of woodlands, six acres of rhododendron gardens, a native plant garden picnic areas, lawns, trails and parking lots. Her crew of three, plus contract staff and a host of volunteers, manages the entire park. We contacted Ginny recently about her career in municipal parks.

Q: *What is a typical day like for you and your crew?*

A: Everyday starts out with "chores"—cleaning the place up and making it ready for another day of visitors. This time gives us a chance to look over the whole park to see if anything is wrong or needs to be attended to immediately. Then our focus shifts to the many tasks needed for on-going management of the park, including: gardening, grounds, amenities, irrigation maintenance, forest restoration, public outreach and education and volunteer coordination. As you can see, we keep really busy.

Q: *What do you like most about your job?*

A: I enjoy the variety—everyday is different! It is a bit like working on a farm—lots of daily problem solving and plenty of opportunities to figure out how to get things done on a limited budget. I also really love the seasonal aspect of the work. We are outside most every day of the year and time all of our activities to the weather and season. It is a real treat to have my "office" share space with a Pileated Woodpecker!

Q: *What are the biggest challenges you face in your job?*

A: There are increased pressures on natural and built areas due to increased public use, global warming, invasive species, and shrinking budgets. Finding creative, cost effective ways to preserve and enhance this beautiful place can be quite challenging at times.

Q: *What areas are growing/changing in this field?*

A: Funding issues continue to be a challenge, and following the money usually shows where the employment opportunities lie. For example, federal money to support storm water management has created several new jobs within parks to manage riparian and wetland areas. There has also been a shift in the public sector from relying solely on tax funding to pursuing grant monies and public/private partnerships. And, in other cities, routine maintenance duties (such as restroom maintenance and garbage/litter pick up) are now contracted out to the lowest bidder. While this may save money for the municipality, it creates a lower class of employees (and taxpayer!) and forces remaining city employees to become contract administrators.

Q: *How do you make a difference in people's lives?*

A: One of the unique things about Hendricks Park is that it is an urban forest—it is an oasis surrounded by the city. As such, it is quite accessible to the citizens of Eugene. I think of it as the relief valve for the stresses of everyday urban life. And, for many people, it is their first introduction and perhaps only connection to the natural world.

Q: *What advice do you have for someone preparing for a career in this field?*

A: You need to have good people skills. That will help you in just about every direction you might want to take your career in. Classes in public speaking, mediation, and facilitation, and relationship building would be very helpful. Learn everything you can about the ecosystem where you want to work, and have a vision for how to best serve the place and the people there.
(For further information about the City of Eugene's Parks and Open Space see www.eugene-or.gov and follow the link to Parks and Open Space).

THE WIDE, WILD WORLD OF OUTDOOR RECREATION AND PARKS

Every day in the U.S. National Park Service (NPS), over 40,000 people report for work in nearly 400 national park areas. Half of these are NPS employees in a wide variety of professional and trade careers. The other half is made up of concession employees working for private hospitality firms under contract to the NPS (operating lodges, restaurants, stores, and campgrounds). The U.S. also has 155 national forests, 20 national grasslands, and 222 research and experimental forests, as well as other special areas, covering more than 192 million acres and employing over 30,000 professionals (National Forest, n.d.).These numbers don't include the vast numbers of employees working to support outdoor recreation in the myriad other federal, state, and local, agencies, non-profit organizations, and businesses. There is one thing most of these employees have in common, however, and that is working in or near a great outdoor environment, with some spectacular scenery just over their shoulder.

Indeed, there are many employees whose job it is to provide and maintain space for outdoor recreation in North America. These careers offer some exciting and rewarding job experiences if you're passionate about open space and outdoor recreation.

Today, careers in the national and state parks, national forests, and other public lands are even more exciting than they were in 1880, when the first national park ranger, Harry Yount, rode his horse into the new Yellowstone National Park, and began "ranging."

At the federal level, there are nearly 400 national park areas, 545 fish and wildlife recreation areas, 200 million acres of national forests, and over 4,000 other public land recreation sites. Canada has 39 national parks and hundreds of provincial parks. In the U.S., all 50 states have similar areas, from the six million-acre Adirondacks State Park in New York (the largest publicly protected area in the contiguous United States), to a large variety of seashore, lakeshore, and forest parks in every state.

The nation's cities, too, offer unique park and recreation experiences and jobs. These areas include the 5,100-acre Forest Park in Portland, Oregon; the incomparable 840-acre Central Park in New York City; and countless city picnic sites, swimming beaches, and playground areas in virtually every area of the country.

A Brief History of Open-Space and Recreation in North America

Many volumes have been written about the history of North American open space and outdoor recreation, so we'll be covering just some of the highlights. Those who choose outdoor recreation as a career area should expect to learn a lot more history, because it's critical to understanding how to manage the outdoors today and for future generations. You'll also learn about a few key people whose passion and influence greatly shaped what we know and love today about recreation, including men like Fredrick Law Olmsted, Theodore Roosevelt, Stephen Mather, and John Muir, whose legacies live on today in a public land philosophy and in the open spaces they helped create, preserve and manage.

Open Space for Recreation in Urban Areas

From the earliest days of Western European Settlement of North America, the vast and forbidding American frontier seemed limitless, so there was little initial concern for setting aside land for recreation or resource management. Soon, however, problems arose with deforestation, overhunting, and crowding in populated urban areas, which resulted in the establishment of village greens and laws related to forests and game (McLean, Hurd, & Rodgers, 2008). The earliest parks were **village greens** that were established during the colonial period and which still exist throughout North Eastern states like Massachusetts, Connecticut, Vermont, and New Hampshire today (McLean et al., 2008). America's oldest municipal park is the **Boston Common**, which was set aside by residents of Boston in 1634 to serve as a piece of land for grazing cattle and public gatherings. Bostonians made a conscious decision to keep this open, green space in their city that no buildings could be constructed upon without the approval of all citizens (National Park Service, n.d.).

Central Park today seems such a natural part of the New York City landscape that many people don't realize that it's man made (Central Park Conservancy, n.d.). The design for Central Park by Olmsted and Calvert Vaux (a British architect) was

FREDERICK LAW OLMSTED
(APRIL 26, 1822-AUGUST 28, 1903)

FREDERICK LAW OLMSTED was an American journalist and landscape designer who was responsible for designing many well-known urban parks, including Central Park and Prospect Park in New York City and the Emerald Necklace in Boston, MA. Olmsted's unique way of designing urban parks was to make everything—paths, trees, and bushes—fixed in a particular place with a purpose—and that purpose was to bring the atmosphere of wildness to the urban dweller. Olmsted stated:

"We want a ground to which people may easily go after their day's work is done, and where they may stroll for an hour, seeing, hearing and feeling nothing of the bustle and jar of the streets, where they shall, in effect, find the city put far away from them. …We want, especially, the greatest possible contrast with the restraining and confining conditions which compel us to walk circumspectly, watchfully, jealously, which compel us to look closely upon others without sympathy" (www.nps.gov/history/nr/twhp/wwwlps/lessons/86b ostonparks/86bostonparks.htm).

When landscape architect Frederick Law Olmsted delivered his lecture, "Public Parks and the Enlargement of Towns in Cambridge, Massachusetts," in 1870, Boston was an overcrowded, noisy, and dirty city. Concerned with the health and happiness of Bostonians restricted to these unhealthy surroundings, the city hired Olmsted to design a park system. The series of parks he designed over the next several years is known as the Emerald Necklace. Each unique "jewel" in the Emerald Necklace—from lovely waterways to botanical gardens to peaceful meadows to tree museums—plays a vital role in linking the citizens of Boston together through nature.

selected from among 33 competitors in 1857, and it set the stage for a particularly American vision for urban park design that still stands in stark contrast to formal European gardens. Achieving Olmsted and Vaux's vision was not as easy as it appears: the area was rocky, swampy, and muddy, and 500,000 cubic feet of topsoil had to be brought in from New Jersey. This was only a start—more than 10 million cartloads of materials and debris were carted in and out on horse-drawn carts (Central Park Conservancy, n.d.).

In addition to providing vision for urban park design, **Frederick Law Olmsted** also recommended an innovative form of management that included an executive office, a skilled landscape architect, and an unpaid board of directors to oversee park decisions (Central Park Conservancy, n.d.). Olmsted is considered to be the founder of American **landscape architecture**, a profession that deals with arranging land and buildings for human use and enjoyment, as well as the launching of the urban parks movement in the 19th Century. According to Linda Flint McClelland (1998), author of *Building the National Parks*, "Of Olmsted's greatest parks, Franklin Park in Boston, designed in the 1880s, established the strongest precedent for the design of natural areas" (p. 39). McClelland continues, "The Olmsted firm's work at Franklin Park forged a design ethic for natural parks which would be carried into the twentieth century by landscape architects, be adopted and adapted by the National Park Service designers, and flourish in the park conservation work of the 1930s in national, state, and metropolitan parks" (p. 41).

National Parks and National Forests

When Congress decided to establish **Yellowstone National Park** in 1872 by reserving land "dedicated and set apart as a public park or pleasuring ground for the benefit and enjoyment of all the people" it sparked a series of unanticipated events. The National Park Service (2006) notes, "This idea of a national park was an American invention of historic consequences, marking the beginning of a worldwide [emphasis added] movement that has subsequently spread to more than 100 countries" (p. 8). Ken Burns, director of "National Parks: America's Best Idea" (2009) noted that the idea of the National Parks is just as uniquely American as the Declaration of Independence, and it's just as radical. Today, most people take for granted the idea "that the most special places in the nation should be preserved, not for royalty of the rich, but for everyone" (Public Broadcasting Service, n.d.), but at the time this was done, it was indeed a radical concept.

The newly established park led to a quarter-century of protracted struggle to define a code of policies to guide the administration, protection, and development within public parks (Cramton, 1932). Louis Cramton completed his report, *Early History of Yellowstone*, in which he described key policy decisions that crystallized over 25 years. As Cramton pointed out, "Some of these policies are so universally concurred that it does not occur to us now that they could have ever been questioned," and others were thoroughly established as national policy through the first 25 years of Yellowstone's administration (p. 1). Here are four of those policies that are of particular relevance to outdoor recreation professionals today:

(1) That the federal government may reserve and keep control of the management of land. Notably, the experiment of turning great scenic regions over to the state for management was not deemed successful.

(2) There are twin purposes to the land reserved: (a) the enjoyment and use of the area as a "pleasuring ground for the benefit and enjoyment of the people" and (b) at the same time this required "the preservation, from injury or spoliation of all timber, mineral deposits, natural curiosities or wonders within said park and their retention in their natural condition" (p. 1, emphasis added).

(3) The parks are to be administered primarily for the enjoyment of the people and leases and concessions in the park are decided on in accordance with "the welfare of the visitor" as the first consideration. (p. 2).

(4) Enjoyment of the areas shall be free to all the people—at first it was thought leases of utilities would provide needed monies for park management, but it was soon realized that the federal treasury would need to appropriate money for development and maintenance. (Today, however, you need to pay an entrance fee or purchase a National Parks and Federal Recreational Lands pass.)

Other policies describe how parks will be: under the control of the **Secretary of the Interior**, as opposed to the military, a game preserve and not a hunting reservation, and guided by national interests rather than those of local benefit. And, of obvious interest to our current topic on careers in outdoor recreation, "Recreation is an essential purpose of park use even though secondary or incidental" to preservation (p. 3). It's important to note, however, that recreational use *does not* take precedent over preservation. As stated in the National Park Service's Management Policies (2006), "The fundamental purpose of the national park system ... begins with a mandate to conserve park resources and values" (p. 10). Enjoyment of the parks is taken to mean not only the enjoyment of park visitors, but also those who enjoy the parks from afar. Clearly, the enjoyment of those distant can only be ensured "if the superb quality of park resources and values is left unimpaired [and] ... when there is a conflict between conserving resources and values and providing for the enjoyment of them, conservation is to be predominant" (p. 11).

John Muir (see break out box) would have been pleased with the National Park Service's current management policy that places preservation of park resources as the top priority. However, it has not always been clear that preservation would win out, because many other voices promoted uses such as timber, tourism, watershed, and range use and these uses are usually in conflict with preservation—especially when preservation is taken to mean "left unimpaired."

Preservation was ultimately balanced with the need for multiple use. As early as the late 1800s, it was noted that the national parks would not meet all the land management needs of future generations. Setting aside land for multiple uses first began with the **Forest Reserve Act of 1891**. Several early leaders and visionaries, including **President Teddy Roosevelt** and the first Chief of the Forest service, **Gifford Pinchot**, led the nation in efforts to retain and manage millions of acres of federal forest land for future generations (Forest Service, n.d.).

Roosevelt was known as the "conservation president." He not only impacted the national parks system by establishing five new parks, he was also the first president to invoke the Antiquities Act to use his executive authority to override controversy in order to preserve natural wonders before special interests could make such preservation impossible (National Park Service: History E-Library, n.d.). Interestingly, President Jimmy Carter was the final executive to use this remarkable power to set aside millions of acres of Alaskan wilderness at the same time they were being threatened by developers.

Roosevelt was able to find a way to balance his support of Muir's entreaty for preservation with Pinchot's philosophy of multiple use. When the management of the forest reserves was transferred from the Department of the Interior to the new **Forest Service** in 1905 as an agency of the **Department of Agriculture**, Roosevelt championed his friend Gifford Pinchot and his philosophy of multiple use. Pinchot was the chief of the new forest service and "...with Roosevelt's willing approval, restructured and professionalized the management of national forests, as well as greatly increased their area and number" (U.S. Forest History, n.d.).

Following much debate about appropriate use of federal forest land, the **Multiple Use-Sustained Yield Act** (more generally referred to its acronym **MUSY**) was passed in 1960, which directs the Secretary of Agriculture to develop and administer land for five renewable resources: 1) outdoor recreation, 2) range, 3) timber, 4) watershed, and 5) wildlife and fish values (Forest Service, n.d.).

Due to space limitations, it is not possible for us to go into the history of the numerous additional federal agencies that administer outdoor recreation, state parks or Canada's national and provincial parks system. Suffice it to say that there are numerous outdoor recreation opportunities and jobs at the state and local levels. If you understand the difference in national parks, which are set aside for preservation and enjoyment, and national forests, which are managed for multiple uses, you'll have a pretty good foundation to gain a deeper understanding of parks, forests, and other outdoor recreation management agencies in the location you are most interested in.

Outdoor Recreation and Non-Profit Organizations

The Sierra Club, founded by John Muir and other supporters in 1892, was one of the first **non-profits** to complement the missions of agencies responsible for outdoor recreation (see chapter on Recreation in Non-Profits for more information). There are many additional outdoor recreation-related non-profits today, and these will be listed later in the chapter, but a review of the Sierra Club's mission statement illustrates the connection between non-profits and outdoor recreation:

> To explore, enjoy, and protect the wild places of the earth; To practice and promote the responsible use of the earth's ecosystems and resources; To educate and enlist humanity to protect and restore the quality of the natural and human environment; and to use all lawful means to carry out these objectives (Sierra Club, n.d.)

Outdoor Recreation and For-Profit Concessions

Stephen T. Mather was the first park professional to articulate the policy that allowed the establishment of park concessionaires to provide basic visitor comforts and services in the then-undeveloped parks. One of his goals was to provide creature comforts in order to encourage the public to visit (*National Park*

JOHN MUIR (1838-1914) was America's most famous and influential naturalist and conservationist. He is one of California's most important historical personalities. He has been called "The Father of our National Parks," "Wilderness Prophet," and "Citizen of the Universe." He once described himself more humorously, and perhaps most accurately, as, a "poetico-trampo-geologist-botanist and ornithologist-naturalist etc." Legendary librarian and author Lawrence Clark Powell (1906-2001), (anticipating an event that was not to occur until 2006), said of him: "If I were to choose a single Californian to occupy the Hall of Fame, it would be this tenacious Scot who became a Californian during the final forty-six years of his life."

His words and deeds helped inspire President Theodore Roosevelt's innovative conservation programs, including establishing the first National Monuments by Presidential Proclamation, and Yosemite National Park by congressional action. In 1892, John Muir and other supporters formed the Sierra Club "to make the mountains glad." John Muir was the Club's first president, an office he held until his death in 1914. Muir's Sierra Club has gone on to promote and support the establishment of new National Park areas and a National Wilderness Preservation System.

Muir's last battle to save the second Yosemite, Hetch Hetchy Valley, failed. But that lost battle ultimately resulted in a widespread conviction that our national parks should be held inviolate. Many proposals to dam our national parks since that time have been stopped because of the efforts of citizens inspired by John Muir, and today there are legitimate proposals to restore Hetch Hetchy. John Muir remains today an inspiration for environmental activists everywhere.

John Muir's life reminds us of the important things that just one person can do:

"If you think about all the gains our society has made, from independence to now, it wasn't government. It was activism. People think, 'Oh, Teddy Roosevelt established Yosemite National Park, what a great president.' BS. It was John Muir who invited Roosevelt out and then convinced him to ditch his security and go camping. It was Muir, an activist, a single person," according to Patagonia founder and outdoor enthusiast Yvon Chouinard, in a recent *Sierra Magazine* interview. (Sierra Club, n.d.)

STEPHEN T. MATHER (1867-1930) recognized magnificent scenery as the primary criterion for establishment of national parks. He was very careful to evaluate choices for parks, wishing the parks to stand as a collection of unique monuments. He felt those areas that were duplicates might best be managed by others. Within the framework of "scenery," his preservation ethic covered such issues as the locations of park developments, provision of vistas along roadways, and the perpetuation of the natural scene. Mather always wished to have the parks supported by avid users who would then communicate their support to their elected representatives. His grasp of a grassroots support system encouraged the rise of "nature study" and modern interpretation, as well as other park services, and was followed by increases in NPS appropriations (*National Park Service: The First 75 Years, n.d.*).

Photo: AAPRA.org

Service: The First 75 Years, n.d.). Today, the National Park Service and other public outdoor recreation agencies create agreements or contracts with many **for-profit concessions** to provide amenities to park and public land visitors. At present, there are several large concessionaires and many mid-sized companies contracting with the National Park Service. In addition to lodging and food, concessionaires may provide event planning and other services (see more details on concessionaires later in this chapter as well as the three chapters on The Hospitality Industry, Travel and Tourism, and Commercial Recreation and Leisure Businesses).

Outdoor Recreation Today

Today, outdoor recreation opportunities are as important to Americans as they've ever been. What better way to de-stress, exercise, and connect with friends and family than spending time in the out of doors? Many people use local green spaces on a daily basis and they also take comfort knowing that National Parks, Forests, and Wilderness Areas are available for their personal use or that of future generations.

In the most general sense, outdoor recreation professionals need to know about managing outdoor resources, working with visitors, and techniques for ensuring the financial sustainably of outdoor areas. As you read about these topics, be aware that most jobs require specialized knowledge, skills, and abilities you'll be able to learn about later in the chapter.

Managing Outdoor Resources

With visitation to national park areas alone in 2008 nearing 300 million visits, not counting the other hundreds of millions of outdoor recreation visits to other public and park lands across the nation, the science and practice of outdoor recreation management provide a wide variety of job opportunities. How do we provide for the increasing use of recreational visitors today, while protecting park and recreational resources for future generations?

Public lands, whether local, state, or federal, encompass various purposes and recreational uses. Much land allows for a variety of multiple uses, including hiking, camping, climbing, mountain biking, horseback riding, off-road vehicle use, fishing, and even hunting. Local and regional parks also may include organized sporting opportunities, such as swimming, competitive field sports, and other uses. On the other end of the spectrum are lands set aside specifically for a predominate use, such as desginated wilderness areas. Here, one may hike, camp, and often fish. However, hunting or motorized uses are generally prohibited.

With such a wealth of recreational opportunities, job descriptions (if not always opportunities) remain abundant. Beyond the more obvious jobs of park ranger, recreation planner, or tour leader, is a whole field of opportunities from law enforcement, to education, to business and financial interests, and to science and research.

For example, enlightened public land management requires research and science about the possible impacts to park resources from recreational users, as well as the social impacts that increased use, particularly in wilderness areas, will have on the recreational user. Careers in both scientific and social research will continue to play a large role in public land management.

For example, most outdoor management agencies today reflect concerns of carrying capacity in making management determinations on increasing visitor and resource use. The concept of **carrying capacity**, while around from early in the 20th century, was given voice in management beginning in the 1960s. In an article in 1964 in the U.S. Forest Service publication *Forest Science*, "The Carrying Capacity of Wild Lands for Recreation," author J. Alan Wager wondered, "if these lands have maximum carrying capacities at which recreational use should be limited." In posing this question, he also recognized that carrying capacity determinations should be looked at both from the impacts on the resource, as well as impacts on human visitors to the area. (*Forest Science*, Monograph 7, supplement to Number 3, 1; September 1964; Society of American Foresters). (http://www.ingentaconnect. com/content/saf/fs/1964/00000010/A00703s7/art00001?crawler=true)

This is but one example of the skills needed in being able to provide for today's recreational user, while still preserving the resource for tomorrow.

Working with Park Visitors

Most jobs in outdoor recreation involve working with visitors and outdoor users. Even if the job entails indoor work, interaction with the people that visit the area is both inevitable and rewarding.

One key concern is providing the information and environmental education to allow visitors to have a safe and rewarding experience. Many people coming to a park area, particularly a wilderness area, may be facing environmental conditions that are alien to their everyday life. In addition, just by being away from home may make them less aware of the problems they could face. Giving them the tools to have a safe and rewarding visit are an important part of any recreational worker's job.

There are three key factors in providing protection and safety to visitors:

- *Protecting people from the resource:* Natural conditions, such as wild animals, rough trails, fast-flowing rivers, and other environmental conditions can pose dangers to people unaccustomed to open country.
- *Protecting the resource from people:* Similarly, some people can believe that taking fossils or plants, cutting trees, or even shooting wild animals is an acceptable use when there appears to be so much open land around. This, of course, is seldom the case.
- *Protecting people from people:* Unfortunately, even when on vacation in park lands, crime, and altercations between people still occur. Making people aware of these possibilities, even in a tranquil-looking campground, is important.

To provide this protection to people and the resource, education and interpretation are the first tools that outdoor recreation workers use. The term **interpretation** can mean different things. Although many people may think of it as language interpretation, in the environmental education context, the goal of all interpretive services is to increase each visitor's enjoyment and understanding of the parks and to allow visitors to care about the parks on their own terms (see National Park Service, http://www.nps.gov/learn/index.htm). With the large variety of multiple interests that people bring with them on vacations and outdoor visits, the ability of an outdoor recreation worker to relate to these interests is critical.

Such interpretation can take the form of providing basic information at an entrance station; preparing effective interpretive signing and other media; giving prepared talks or presentations about the human and natural history of the area; teaching organized environmental education classes through public and private schools; and assuring that websites and other remote services provide enough advance information for people planning trips to outdoor areas. Because of the key role that interpretation and education play, there is a large range of job careers specific to these professions. Nearly all outdoor land-management agencies provide opportunities for environmental educational and interpretive careers. This can be one of the most rewarding jobs that outdoor recreation can provide, and is the key tool of any park ranger.

Grand Teton National Park-Snowboarder Rescued From Backcountry

Park rangers and Jackson Hole Mountain Resort ski patrol rescued a backcountry snowboarder after he became stranded on a cliff. The snowboarder entered the park's backcountry with three companions. He became stranded on a cliff in the Northwest Passage area and was unable to climb back up or continue boarding down. He was in voice contact with his companions, who descended into Endless Couloir, and caught the attention of an off-duty ski patroller, who called for assistance on his cellphone. Jackson Hole ski patrollers picked up a rope and technical gear before skiing to help. One patrolman was lowered down to the snowboarder's position, and placed a climbing harness on him, then lowered him over a short cliff to a point where he could safely traverse back into Endless Couloir. The rope was then tied off and the patrolman rappelled off the same point to help the snowboarder exit the couloir. Everyone returned safely.

—"Morning Report" NPS, 3/5/07

Planning, Financial Sustainability, and Partnerships

We all generally help pay for outdoor recreation lands through our taxes and other means. Because of this, it is important that all outdoor recreation workers understand the financial components of working with public resources.

Funding for public land recreation programs comes from three main sources:

Taxes. Federal, state, and local taxes often help support a variety of park and recreational lands. Consequently, seeking and listening to public input into major land-management decisions is very important to a land manager.

Private donations. Many individuals and private institutions often provide supporting funds for park and recreation programs. This can range from the small personal donation of a frequent park user to a non-profit "Friends of the Parks" group, to the planned, corporate sponsorship of a visitor center, recreation center or other facility. Working with non-profit and for-profit entities is an important part of any recreational management activity.

User fees. Fees can make up an important part of a park or recreation area financial picture. Though seldom if ever able to cover all costs, some state park agencies are able to cover a large portion of their management costs. These fees range from visitor use fees such as park entrance fees, campground fees, and various recreation charges. They also may include fees from concessionaires or other private services contracted to work in park and recreation areas. In general, the public has historically supported these fees when they are seen as reasonable and fair.

Planning and Open Space in Eugene, Oregon

GINNY ALFRIEND, Park Specialist for the City of Eugene Parks and Open Spaces, tells us that planning helps to determine the course that her area takes over time. "As the City of Eugene grows and develops, land is bought and set aside for public use. The planning team, with input from the citizens of Eugene and City staff and consultants, determines how those lands will be used. Planning provides the vision for how our community will look and feel over time. Please see the City of Eugene's web page, www.eugene-or.gov, follow the links to Parks and Open Space and then Planning to have a more in-depth look at the role they have."

Because of the increasing costs agencies face in managing park areas and providing for recreational use, careful financial planning, in the context of overall planning activities, is essential. For example, over the past decade, the National Park Service began working with the non-profit National Parks and Conservation Association (NPCA) in providing jobs for recent MBA graduates. In exchange for scholarships from NPCA, the National Park Service provides positions in park areas related to financial planning, budget, or other careers. As a consequence, many national parks have developed business plans for their areas that clearly show the expected funding sources, private revenue opportunities, and costs to effectively manage the area for public use over a period of time.

Such financial management plans are just a part of the overall planning requirements that any public park or recreation land faces. For example, the National Park Service policy states:

> Park planning helps define the set of resource conditions, visitor experiences, and management actions that, taken as a whole, will best achieve the mandate to preserve resources unimpaired for the enjoyment of present and future generations. (NPS Management Polices, 2006; p. 21)

Most land-management agencies at all levels work with defined partners to reach shared recreational and land management goals. This can include both in-kind assistance (such as organizing volunteer or other project work assistance in a park), and helping to provide financial assistance for project or longer term management activities. These partners, often but not always non-governmental organizations, can provide key assistance to recreational managers through their ability to attract financial and other support. These range from local "friends" groups that provide volunteers to staff local visitor centers, provide interpretive programs, or assist visitors in campgrounds; organized associations that run educational bookstores and other facilities in park areas; or groups such as NPCA (mentioned above) that provide opportunities for students of outdoor recreation with career opportunities.

Another important example is universities that work on a cooperative basis with recreational agencies in providing scientific research, cooperative park study units, and other educational and management assistance.

Any career in recreational management will generally allow you to be involved with many similar support and educational groups without which the level of services in many areas would not be as easily possible. As public and private agencies will always face difficult financial decisions and planning issues, the importance of such partnerships will only grow in the future.

It's clear that the management of outdoor recreation resources and visitor services requires a dedicated and educated staff of permanent and seasonal employees as well as long-term planning efforts to ensure sustainability. Next, you'll find out how you can take your passion for the outdoors and match it with just about any type of job you can imagine.

CAREERS IN OUTDOOR RECREATION

Would you like a job in outdoor recreation? How can you get one?

When people hear about a career in outdoor recreation they typically think of a job like "park ranger," and in the past this would have been fairly accurate. Today, however, the need for financial and environmental sustainability combined with the potential of partnerships that enhance the scope of influence for outdoor recreation enthusiasts mean good careers can be found in the public sector with government agencies, in the non-profit sector with organizations dedicated to preservation and enjoyment, and with for-profit commercial organizations providing concessions and guiding others in outdoor recreation activities.We'll talk about outdoor recreation careers in all three sectors, and depending on your specific interests, you may want to read more about Recreation in Non-profit Organizations in chapter 4, The Hospitality Industry in chapter 11, and Commercial Recreation and Leisure Businesses in chapter 13.

Passions

Careers in outdoor recreation attract people with a keen interest in the environment, with the wide-range of activities that park visitors engage in (hiking, wildlife watching, climbing, white-water rafting, camping, etc.), or with an excitement to learn about the variety of specialized job duties that professionals do (fire-fighting, search and rescue, boating, skiing, first aid, resource protection, etc.). These careers encompass the broad world of natural and cultural resources management, forestry, land use planning and facility development, environmental education and other similar career fields. Depending on where you focus your interests, a career in outdoor recreation can encompass a very wide variety of jobs and career paths.

If your interest is in natural or cultural resources, you might want to look at careers such as park ranger, park recreation planner, resource manager, interpreter, environmental education, law enforcement, and other jobs. Jobs in these areas are found within governmental agencies at the federal, state, and local levels. For example, if you are more focused on a local community, a career as a recreation planner or city park worker may be for you. If you are interested in resource management on a broader scale, consider state and national government agencies.

If your passion is sharing the outdoors with youth, you may want to consider the non-profit sector with a career such as camp director or counselor, and even jobs working with at-risk youth through wilderness therapy (refer to chapter 7 on Therapeutic Recreation). The non-profit sector also includes opportunities in conversation with agencies like the Trust for Public Lands, a national nonprofit organization working to protect land as parks and open space who's mission it is to "conserve land for people to enjoy as parks, gardens, and other natural places, ensuring livable communities for generations to come" (The Trust for Public Land, 2009).

Finally, if you are more interested in the commercial aspect of recreation, the field of career opportunities in parks is even broader. Work in the outdoor concessions industry includes commercial campgrounds, hotels, restaurants, golf courses, swim centers, outdoor events centers, tour operator, and the large and vibrant world of tourism services that are located within many national, state and local parks. Jobs are available in all aspects of outdoor recreation and travel, and at all levels, from community-based to international in scope.

It's a Small, Large World!

Working in parks and recreation makes you a part of a unique close-knit group of people. Although a park ranger, a hotel manager, and an environmental advocate work in different jobs with different missions, they all usually have many similar interests and passions. If you share the underlying passion, but aren't yet sure of which career avenue fits you best, gaining work experience in any of the varied fields can often transfer to another field. Rangers have become business people have become advocates. Get out there and try it!

Pay and Perks

In choosing a career focus, it's always important to consider your financial goals and desires. If your main goal is to get rich, and you truly mean that, then you should probably consider a different career area. Unless you become a high-level manager of a large concession company, or start your own wildly successful outdoor business, then this is not a field in which large financial rewards are predominant. However, you can be financially comfortable, have job security, have access to excellent health care and retirement, as well as enjoy opportunities for promotion, all while doing a job you love and believe in.

If your goal is to work for a public agency, positions start at minimum wage and advance to around $150,000 for the few high-level positions. Full-time, permanent government jobs in outdoor recreation come with good insurance and retirement plan opportunities, and many agencies promote from within. Keep in mind that these permanent positions are competitive and may be difficult to get. If your goal is to work in a non-profit, you may start with zero pay as a volunteer, and salaries start at entry-level and advance to salaries that are comparable to corporate managers of smaller companies, especially when a person has a strong track record with fund-raising. For-profit companies also range from minimum wage to corporate management salaries. Like any other job with a corporation, education and experience are key.

Preparation

You can easily answer this question for yourself, at least on a broad, general basis. For instance, by answering the question, "What qualities do you want in a friend or companion?" Employers are looking for someone who can be trusted, someone who listens, and someone who respects the organization's values. If you are a person with these general qualities, you are more than halfway to making an employer happy.

A career, of course, will also demand some specific knowledge, skills, and abilities. These abilities begin with general experience and education, becoming more specific and targeted as you move forward in a career.

For instance, let's look at an entry-level park ranger job in a federal or state agency. These jobs will certainly require, at minimum, a high school diploma and some basic life experiences that show an ability to work effectively with people. As you develop your ranger skills, you may seek to move into another job with increased responsibilities and challenges, perhaps as a supervisor or technical specialist. This will often require a bachelor's or master's degree in areas such as recreation management, forestry, communications, law enforcement, education, planning, business administration, hotel management, forestry, or biology. It will also require more work experiences to go with your education. Consequently, to prepare for a career, you need to look beyond the specific job to the bigger picture of how you would like your career to advance. An employer is often not looking just for a person skilled in a particular job, but one who can someday move beyond that job and contribute to the larger goals and responsibilities of the agency.

Possibilities

Having a career versus having a job has changed over the years. For job security, a career was foremost in our grandparents' minds. Experiencing two world wars and a worldwide economic depression during the 20th century led most people to seek the financial security of a permanent job they would keep most of their working life. This attitude began to change during the last few decades of the 20th century. The country and world were more prosperous. Financial stability in the United States and other developed countries, along with the financial successes of earlier generations (those that chose careers over jobs), have given many young people entering the outdoor recreation job market unprecedented opportunities. As a result, sometimes it seems that having a job is more important than having a career.

Hiring and career trends in outdoor recreation, park management, and related fields will generally follow the trend of economic well-being or anxiety in the population. Outdoor recreation activities require a certain expenditure of time and money, often associated with a vacation and travel away from home. These activities will be adversely affected when the economy makes people feel they need to restrict their non-essential spending. Nonetheless, even in periods of economic unease, or national trauma, people often seek the outdoors for relief. After the tragic events of September 11, 2001, while international travel plummeted, travel to local park areas increased. Yosemite National Park noticed, at least anecdotally, an increase in day visitors to the park. The outdoors and park setting seemed to provide solace for some in a grieving nation.

In the field of outdoor recreation, we believe you can have both! Let's examine possibilities in each of the three major areas where outdoor recreation jobs are located today.

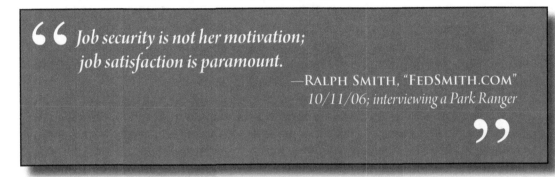

> **" "** *Job security is not her motivation; job satisfaction is paramount.*
>
> —RALPH SMITH, "FEDSMITH.COM"
> *10/11/06; interviewing a Park Ranger*
> **" "**

Government Land Management Agencies

Government land management agencies involved in outdoor recreation are managed based on specific legislated governmental purposes. These purposes may include the protection and preservation of particular resources, scientific research, or multiple uses that can include outdoor recreation. The purpose of many federal parks and public lands, as well as many state and local parks, is to conserve natural and cultural resources for long-term protection to allow them to be available for use over many generations. For instance, parks may have research, wilderness, or specific environmental protection objectives that may take precedence over recreation. In other instances, the primary purpose for some public lands may be resource extraction (mining, oil exploration, timber) or other resource uses (grazing, hydroelectric). On the other hand, many public recreation areas may also include a wide variety of recreational activities, including boating, hunting, hiking, camping, skiing, snowmobiling, off-road vehicle use, and other activities. In areas where there are multiple users, they may have conflicting interests and motivations, which result in some interesting challenges for employees!

Passions—Conservation/environmental ethics, natural resources, historic preservation, extreme activity (fire-fighting, smoke-jumping, law enforcement, search and rescue), wild open spaces, physical challenge, being part of a team, public service, working with outdoor resources as well as visitors.

Pay and Perks—Federal hourly wage pay scales apply to both seasonal/part-time and permanent, full-time jobs. However, permanent positions often begin at a higher scale than do seasonal positions, and are usually tied to a career track of progressively higher wages over a defined period of time. State pay varies according to prevailing wage, as do municipalities. Most agencies, at least for career positions, offer health coverage, pensions, and/or matching savings plans similar to 401(K) plans.

Preparation—For agency employment, although there are some professional jobs requiring a degree or other credentials (outdoor recreation, biologist, geologist, hydrologist, law enforcement, etc.), many entry-level jobs require no higher degree other than a high school diploma. However, most professional career employees with federal and state agencies usually have a college degree, in subject areas such as parks and recreation management, law enforcement, education, or one of the sciences.

Most entry-level jobs require a basic high school degree, and some related experience. That being said, having a four-year college degree will often provide the difference in competing for career positions, especially as you move up the career ladder. The U.S. government recommends the following degree fields for park and recreation management and natural resource management:

Fish and Wildlife Admin.	Outdoor Recreation Planning
Gen. Biological Science	Forestry
Program Analysis	Recreation Management
Wildlife Biology	Law Enforcement (Ranger)
Wildlife Refuge Management	

How to Prepare for a Government Land Management Agency Career

The key to most agency jobs, at the federal, state, or local level, is experience. Education, however, can substitute for experience and can get you in the door at a higher pay level. For example, many job announcements may require one of the following:

- One year of general experience OR two years of education above high school with six semester hours of related coursework. (Includes most entry-level jobs, such as park aid, information desk, or ranger aid).
- Level 5 requires one year of specialized experience equivalent to Level 4, or four years of college leading to a bachelor's degree with 24 semester hours of natural science, social sciences, or recreation management. (Includes more challenging jobs such as park ranger, education specialist, biological technician, or similar).
- In lieu of two years experience at Level 7, education at the graduate level in an accredited college or university meets the requirements for positions at Level 9. (Includes professional level jobs such as supervisory ranger, biologist, or site manager).

Possibilities—Most agency jobs, from municipality to state to federal, are open to everyone on a competitive basis. There are often broad opportunities for seasonal and part-time employment. However, gaining a permanent career job is more difficult, often requiring passing a written test, having previous governmental service (such as the military), or having relevant education (degrees or certifications).

At both federal and state agencies, many employees begin in a seasonal or temporary position, usually while attending school. At the federal level, although there are always jobs that are available to all qualified applicants, entry into many permanent positions is often restricted to those currently employed with the government. Jobs open to all are, therefore, often very competitive.

At the state and federal level, a career will often take one from an entry-level ranger or other field job, to a supervisory position in their field, and eventually to a management position in charge of park planning, maintenance, and finances. However, many successful careers can be and are based on staying at one level of expertise and enjoyment without moving into management. Examples might include a district ranger, a public affairs officer, a firefighter, or a field research biologist.

Progression through a career, at least at the federal level, often occurs more rapidly if one is able to move to different parks and areas of the country. For example, you may work for several years at a park or wildlife refuge in California, then transfer with a promotion to an area in Michigan or Alaska. While moving is certainly not required to progress with a career, promotions within one area may be harder to accomplish.

Right now 1.8 million people work for the government, not including the military or the postal service. The government will have to replace almost a million of them in the next few years — as many as already work at Ford, IBM, and Bank of America, combined.

—"UNCLE SAM WANTS YOU"
by Po Bronson and Ashley Merryman; Time, July 13, 2006
(as quoted by the Partnership for Public Service, www.ourpublicservice.org/).

Here are some examples of agencies where you could seek a job or career with a government conservation agency:

Federal Level

The Department of the Interior, as a cabinet level agency, oversees 500 million acres of the nation's public lands, many with outdoor recreation resources. Some of the main agencies involved specifically in outdoor recreation are: the National Park Service (NPS) with over 385 national park sites in all 50 states; the Bureau of Land Management, whose 261 million acres include many national recreation areas;

Expand Your Possibilities
Know Hiring Trends for Conservation Scientists and Foresters

- According to the U.S. Bureau of Labor Statistics (www.bls.gov), employment of conservation scientists and foresters is expected to increase more slowly than the average for all occupations through 2014. Growth should be strongest in private sector consulting firms. Overall employment of conservation scientists and foresters is expected to decline slightly in the federal government.

- More than one in three workers were employed by the federal government. Another 21 percent of conservation scientists and foresters worked for state governments, and about 11 percent worked for local governments. The remainder worked in private industry, mainly in support activities for agriculture and forestry or in wood product manufacturing. Some were self-employed as consultants for private landowners, federal and state governments, and forestry-related businesses.

- Demand will be spurred by a continuing emphasis on environmental protection, responsible land management, and water-related issues. Growing interest in developing private lands and forests for recreational purposes will generate additional jobs for foresters and conservation scientists. Fire prevention is another area of growth for these two occupations.

the U.S. Fish and Wildlife Service, whose wildlife refuges help protect America's wetlands, migratory bird flyways, and sport hunting opportunities; and the Bureau of Reclamation with over 300 outdoor recreational sites, many supporting water-based recreation. These agencies combined protect over 450 million acres of public lands for recreation and similar public purposes, and see an annual visitation at their 4,739 recreational sites of over 408 million (U.S. Department of the Interior. http://www.doi.gov/facts.html).

The Department of Agriculture, also a cabinet-level agency, includes the U.S. Forest Service. Although responsible for managing over 200 million acres of national forest for multiple use, the Forest Service also manages over seven million acres of outdoor recreation sites, including 400 wilderness areas and 35 other recreation sites that are available for recreation to its 205 million annual visitors (U.S. Department of Agriculture, U.S. Forest Service http://www.fs.fed.us/recreation/programs/facts/).

The U.S. Army Corp of Engineers also has a robust recreation responsibility at over 2,500 recreation sites, mostly water oriented, serving 360 million visitors a year (Department of Defense, Army Corp of Engineers. http://www.fs.fed.us/recreation/programs/facts/).

State Level

Every state has a department of natural resources, parks department, or similar agency. For the approximately 57,000 outdoor recreation jobs in all states, each state will have its own hiring procedures. Many of the jobs are similar to those in federal agencies. According to the National Association of State Park Directors, there are 5,842 state park areas comprising over 13 million acres, with over 826 million visitors annually, and employing 53,898 total personnel (including part-time and seasonal) in 2004 (http://isu1.indstate.edu/naspd/).

Local and Municipal Agencies

Most cities of any size maintain some form of a city recreation and parks department. County, municipal, and city parks provide a large operational base to begin a job and develop an outdoor recreation career. Most cities of any size support a city parks and recreation department. These important park programs provide urban families with a wide variety of recreational programs, often directed at youth. (The previous section covered many jobs in local agencies. Local agency outdoor recreation career opportunities are covered here because they are similar to opportunities found at the state and federal levels).

Non-Profit Outdoor Recreation Agencies

These organizations, often called **"NGOs"** for **"non-governmental organizations,"** are numerous in the world of parks and recreation, and have different objectives:

- Supporting conservation agency objectives: (National Park Foundation, Trust for Public Lands, Nature Conservancy, Association of National Park Rangers, etc.)
- Providing conservation and recreation employment or training: (Student Conservation Association, Outward Bound, etc.)
- Encouraging lifestyle choices using outdoor recreation: (Boy and Girl Scouts, YMCA/YWCA, church youth organizations and camps, etc.) (note that these human services non-profits are discussed in chapter 4, Recreation in Non-Profit Organizations).

These organizations hire both part-time and full-time help, from camp counselors, to recreational instructors, to professional careers in planning, legal, and scientific endeavors, as well as providing career opportunities in their own right. Work experience gained at NGOs often can serve as a springboard to careers with a government conservation agency or for-profit company with similar objectives. They should not be overlooked in considering a career in outdoor recreation and parks. Consider the following to determine if a career in an NGO is right for you.

Passions—Conservation/environmental ethics, natural and cultural resources, advocacy for a cause, politics, fund-raising, "change the world".

Pay and Perks—Beginning pay often is $0, as these organizations attract many volunteers for little or no compensation (other than stipends for cost of living). However, all but the smallest have some paid staff, which can be substantial for the largest organizations. Depending on the size of the NGO, full-time staff employees can be paid comparable to starting salaries at agencies; though high-level management positions for the larger NGOs can be negotiated for comparable, professional salaries similar to some for-profit companies. (Often salaries at these levels are based on fund-raising expertise and success). Many provide health and other financial benefits.

Preparation—Unless seeking particular business, legal, or scientific credentials —which many of the larger NGOs do seek—positions with most NGOs rely more on past experience than on positive educational requirements. There is often cross-over between for-profit and non-profit entities, so experiences gained in either can transfer. As with agency employees, most NGO volunteers and employees are well-educated, at least in their field of interest, with many working toward or already holding college degrees. Career fields with NGOs often require experience or training in fund-raising, business, and supervision.

How to Prepare for a Career with an NGO

As with government conservation agency careers, experience is as highly respected as education. Many entry-level positions at NGOs are at low, or even no, pay. NGOs often have volunteers providing much of the support work of a small or limited staff. Larger organizations that are national in scope may have regional offices with paid staff overseeing field projects.

Education is the key to higher-level paid positions at the larger non-profits. Because non-profits by necessity must seek funding, education and experience in business management or fundraising are important. A funding manager or regional manager for a larger non-profit may require a minimum of a bachelor's degree, five years of direct experience, and demonstrated success in foundation and corporate fundraising and/or marketing. Project leaders may require technical degrees in the sciences rather than business-related skills. As you move up the career ladder in non-profits, the requirements for education and experience increase. For example, a project supervisor or crew leader may require a BA/BS in Environmental Education/Science or related field, or equivalent field experience, and three years of progressively responsible program management experience.

Possibilities—Broad and varied, but also limited. They operate at international, national, and local levels. Although all non-profits have some staff to support their work, full-time positions are relatively limited and often volunteer in nature (except for the largest organizations). Also, be aware that positions are often office-based, indoor environments even for those NGOs with parks and recreation missions. Today, you can readily locate non-profits related to your area of interest is easy via the Internet. Once you locate the agency website, it is relatively easy to learn more about job and career options.

Here are some examples of agencies where you could seek a job or career with an NGO:

The National Park Foundation (NPF) was established by Congress to serve as the national charitable partner of the U.S. National Parks. Their mission "is to strengthen the connection between the American people and their National Parks by raising private funds, making strategic grants, creating innovative partnerships and increasing public awareness." You can learn more about NPF from their website at www.nationalparks.org

The Student Conservation Association (SCA) is a leading conservation service organization for young people. Founded in 1957, SCA hires over 3,000 "conservation volunteers" annually to work on park and conservation programs in all 50 states. Many, if not all, of the federal agencies, and many states, with recreational responsibilities use SCA's popular volunteer programs. Many SCA alumni go on to have careers with the National Park Service and other similar endeavors. You can learn more about the SCA from their website at www.thesca.org

The Trust for Public Lands (TPL) is a good example of an advocacy group that works to support the protection of lands for public recreational use and preservation. Working on a willing-buyer/willing-seller basis, they purchase properties of significant historical or natural qualities, and then hold them until they can find an entity, often an agency, that can manage them for these causes. You can learn more about the TPL from their website at www.tpl.org

The Nature Conservancy is a leading conservation organization that is committed to preservation and addressing threats to conservation. They work around the world to protect ecologically important lands and waters for nature and people. Their mission is "to preserve the plants, animals, and natural communities that represent the diversity of life on earth by protecting the lands and waters they need to survive." You can learn more about the Nature Conservancy from their Web site at www.nature.org

The Sierra Club, founded in 1892, is America's oldest grassroots environmental organization that is committed to working together to help people explore, enjoy and protect the planet. Each state has a local chapter, and they have numerous goals including safeguarding communities, clean energy solutions, green transportation and resilient habitats. You can learn more about the Sierra Club from their website at www.sierraclub.org.

The Rails to Trails Conservancy is a non-profit organization based in Washington, D.C., whose mission is to create a nationwide network of trails from former rail lines to connect corridors in order to build healthier places. You can learn more about the Rails to Trails Conservancy from their website at www.railstotrails.org.

The Truth About Career Possibilities in NGOs

Long careers in a single non-profit organization are not as common as those with government conservation agencies. There are some CEOs of non-profits who began with the organization when it was first formed, or were indeed involved in forming it, and stay with it through a feeling of ownership. However, advancement in a career of non-profit work will more than likely occur if you work with different organizations through your career, even in fields of interest in which you did not begin.

Many people with careers in agencies, or with for-profit companies, often will be active as volunteers with a related non-profit organization. Serving on the board of a related organization (if it's not a conflict of interest with your "day" job) can be tremendously rewarding for both personal satisfaction and career development.

For Profit, Commercial Outdoor Recreation Businesses

Few park or recreation areas operate without the support of or coexistence with businesses directly related to the recreation objective. One example familiar to all is food vendors at organized sports events. However, the world of park concession management provides great opportunities for those business-oriented careerists with an underlying support and love for recreation or conservation objectives.

Career opportunities exist in areas such as lodges, food and beverage services, campgrounds, guided backcountry trips, ski areas, extreme sports, climbing/rafting schools, etc. Some employees in these businesses either came to them initially because of a love for the outdoors and recreational aspects, or gravitated to them after a time spent working in other similar recreational endeavors. This is an excellent opportunity to mix a passion for business with a love of the outdoors and recreation. As mentioned earlier, you should check out chapter 11, The Hospitality Industry and chapter 13, Commercial Recreation and Leisure Businesses for more information, but we will also cover those industries that relate directly to outdoor recreation.

For-profit businesses are competitive by nature and intent. Consequently, they are always seeking talented, educated people to make a career with them. Within the outdoor recreation field, for-profits operate lodging, campgrounds, food services, and specialized tours such as white-water rafting, fishing, and camping. Is a career in a for-profit outdoor recreation related business for you?

Passions—Business, financial, entrepreneur, competition, reward/risk, unique work environment, customer service, "power of capitalism," in addition to your love of outdoor recreation.

Pay and Perks—Minimum wage to "name your price." Concession operations in park and recreation areas have job experiences similar to businesses in any small city (food and beverage, hotel, bookkeeping, computer technology, labor, management, etc.). Pay at most levels will reflect local community salaries in comparable positions. Lower-level management positions, such as hotel manager, campground manager, and the like, will also pay comparable salaries of similar non-recreation services. However, other benefits may include room/board compensation based on remote locations. Higher management level jobs are similar to any business, may be negotiable, and are often higher than a comparable management position in an agency.

Preparation—An MBA can be a gold-star education for these positions, and it will help support your quest for higher salaries. At the four-year college level, courses showing an interest in the particular business, or general business and financial degrees, can help provide an entrée to this world, although few entry-level positions have positive education requirements. Gaining education and experience in your particular interest in the parks and recreation field, then applying this to the corporate world of a recreation-oriented business can be useful in addition to pursuing general financial or business accreditation. Gaining experience through seasonal or part-time work can be very helpful in competing for permanent positions in companies.

Possibilities—Unlimited. With the growth of outdoor recreation and tourism, there are an expanding number of companies and concession operators catering to the parks and recreation environment. Here are some examples:

The Potential for Career Development in For-Profits

There are extensive opportunities in the hospitality industry, whether within or outside of the outdoor recreation field. Larger companies eagerly seek employees with career interest and potential.

If you enjoy the world of food and beverage, for instance, but would also like to apply it in a park or outdoor-oriented setting, you can begin to gain experience in innumerable locations. Some hospitality companies have divisions that specialize in park or recreational settings.

Career advancement opportunities are also vibrant. It is not too far fetched, for example, with hard work and skill, to move from a server, to a restaurant food and beverage manager, to general manager of the full facility. Most larger hospitality companies are eager to gain long-term employees dedicated to the company. To attract and retain such employees, a company will often offer good benefits and excellent opportunities for training. Because retention of trained and qualified employees is more efficient and cost-effective, finding a life-long career in a company that matches your interests can be rewarding.

How to Prepare for a Career with a For Profit, Commercial Outdoor Recreation Business

The key here is to understand that many permanent or management employees often started their careers with the company in entry-level positions and were then promoted from within. Fortunately, there is a large availability of seasonal and entry-level jobs, few requiring any positive education requirements other than a high-school education. These positions are often seasonal, but they can be a springboard for beginning a career or gaining permanent employment. Higher level permanent jobs almost always have educational requirements. Qualified candidates for food and beverage positions must have a minimum of two or three years of supervisory experience in a food and beverage environment. Most full-time positions will also require a degree in a related field.

Delaware North Companies Parks and Resorts, Xanterra Parks and Resorts, and Aramark are three major concessioners operating within many federal and state parks and outdoor recreation areas. They operate some of the largest concession operations in places such as Yellowstone, Grand Canyon, and Yosemite National Parks. These are but three examples of hundreds of similar concessioners, large and small, operating in public park and outdoor recreation areas.

Delaware North Companies Parks and Resorts   www.delawarenorth.com
Xanterra Parks and Resorts   www.xanterra.com
Aramark   www.aramark.com
See also www.concessions.nps.gov for a more complete listing.

Commercial Outfitters and Guides offer their clients guided experiences from camping, hiking, hunting, fishing, rafting, and a wide variety of other outdoor activities. While many of these companies are sole proprietorships with modest job potential, nearly all hire staff to carry out their often seasonal guide work. Working a season or two with one that meets your interests would be helpful if you were considering starting your own business, or weren't ready or interested in the formalities of a large agency, NGO, or business.

SUMMARY OF OUTDOOR RECREATION CAREER POSSIBILITIES

Career	Passions	Pay and Perks	Preparation	Possibilities
Conservation agency	Public service	Minimum wage to professional salary	Positive educational requirements in many jobs.	Competitive. Permanent positions are more difficult to get.
Non-profit organizations	Change the world	0 $ to ? professional and corporate comparable	Positive educational requirements in some jobs. Experience is most important.	Various opportunities at the lower levels. Permanent positions are relatively few.
For profit companies	Power of capitalism	Minimum wage to corporate management	Positive educational requirements in some jobs. Experience is most important.	Unlimited

FUTURE OPPORTUNITIES, ISSUES, AND CHALLENGES

There will probably always be a demand for outdoor recreational uses. Year to year visitation statistics may ebb and flow, but over the past 50 years have generally showed a steady trend upwards. While this trend could certainly shift in the future, in particular during stressful economic times, the human population will certainly continue to grow. Consequently, career opportunities in outdoor recreation will more than likely remain viable.

Several key factors will, as always, determine job opportunities:

Funding

Because public funds from taxes are a large part of financial support for public recreational land management and preservation, public financial status can have a significant impact on jobs. For example, during the recession that began in 2009, the state of California has looked at closing all state park lands until the financial picture improves. This obviously seriously impacts careers and jobs within the state parks. Similar financial problems can manifest themselves in any publicly supported endeavor. Following and understanding the political process in developing a public budget is important in looking at future career opportunities.

Population

The 2010 census will provide key data for predicting regional and national growth, financial status, and other important information to help chart where possible growth areas might come. Any career seeker, whether in outdoor recreation or not, should not discount the importance of trend predictions that such a census can provide. An increasing population, especially a population concentrated in larger and congested cities, will probably continue to seek relief from these conditions through open space or other outdoor recreational endeavor, if the past is any guide.

Environmental factors

As more is learned about global climate change, animal populations, pollution, and other environmental indicators, recreational patterns may change in the future. For example, off-road vehicle use, allowed in many areas, may change either by restricting such use in some areas, or evolving the use to less impacting technologies. Similarly, hunting or fishing patterns most likely will change as streams and watersheds are either further impacted or restored.

Education

Education about the environment and the outdoors, from grade school through college, and in the experiences of everyday life, will continue to play a critical role in how people relate to and use their environment. Keeping environmental and outdoor education topics alive in the classroom will be instrumental to providing the interest of future generations to take advantage of outdoor use and recreation. (This in itself offers possible education and teaching career opportunities, of course).

By keeping attuned to these issues you will gain a better understanding of how future outdoor recreation opportunities will evolve.

> ### Funding Challenges for Local Parks
>
> " Funding issues continue to be a challenge, and following the money usually shows where the employment opportunities lie. For example, Federal money to support storm water management has created several new jobs within parks to manage riparian and wetland areas. There has also been a shift in the public sector from relying solely on tax funding to pursuing grant monies and public/private partnerships. And, in other cities, routine maintenance duties (such as restroom maintenance and garbage/litter pick up) are now contracted out to the lowest bidder. While this may save money for the municipality, it creates a lower class of employees (and taxpayer!) and forces remaining City employees to be contract administrators.
>
> —GINNY ALFRIEND
> *Park Specialist IV*
> *for the City of Eugene Parks and*
> *Open Space in Oregon* "

RESOURCES AND GETTING INVOLVED

The Internet is a major tool for investigating career opportunities. Many key websites specifically related to parks and outdoor recreation have been cited earlier in the chapter under "possibilities." However, there are a few more organizations you should be aware of because these organizations can help you prepare for your future career.

Professional Organizations

Natural Resources Defense Council (International)
http://www.nrdc.org/
"NRDC is the nation's most effective environmental action organization. We use law, science, and the support of 1.2 million members and online activists to protect the planet's wildlife and wild places and to ensure a safe and healthy environment for all living things."

Conservation International (International)
http://www.conservation.org/xp/CIWEB/home
"A U.S.-based, international organization, Conservation International (CI) . . . applies innovations in science, economics, policy, and community participation to protect the Earth's richest regions of plant and animal diversity in the biodiversity

hotspots, high-biodiversity wilderness areas as well as important marine regions around the globe. With headquarters in Washington, D.C., CI works in more than 40 countries on four continents."

National Parks and Conservation Association (National)
http://www.npca.org/
This 85-year-old NGO is a key advocate for the national parks, and sometimes the strongest critic of the National Park Service. Headquarters in Washington, D.C., with regional offices throughout the country.

Bay Area Ridge Trail Council (Local)
http://www.ridgetrail.org/
This organization is attempting to complete a 300-mile public trail that circumnavigates the San Francisco Bay area. It works "in close partnership with local governments, public agencies, nonprofit land trusts, and local grassroots activists in the nine counties of the Bay Area to complete the Ridge Trail."

Association of National Park Rangers (National)
www.anpr.org
Organization founded by national park rangers, "created to communicate for, about and with National Park Service employees." Publishes quarterly magazine *Ranger* for all members.

International Ranger Federation (International)
http://www.int-ranger.net/
A federation of ranger associations from over 50 countries. Holds a World Ranger Congress every three years in a different country. Sixth Congress held in 2009 in Bolivia. Headquarters in the UK.

Washington [State] Outfitters and Guides Association
http://www.woga.org/
This association bills itself as the only industry organization in Washington that represents outfitters, sport-fishing guides, horse and llama packers, whitewater rafters, hunting guides, and other outdoor professionals who supply "outfitted services" to the recreational public in our state." It is an excellent source to seek out companies, who are members that provide these activities. New York, Oregon, and many other states have similar organizations that can provide an easy way to research similar opportunities across the country.

America Outdoors
http://www.americaoutdoors.org/
"America Outdoors is an international association representing the world's finest active travel outfitters, tour companies and outdoor educators."

Certifications/Licenses

There are not any particular certifications needed to work in the National Park Service or an other public lands agencies. However, the National Association for Interpretation (NAI) offers six certifications including: Certified Interpretive Manager, Certified Interpretive Planner, Certified Heritage Interpreter, Certified Interpretive Trainer, Certified Interpretive Guide, and Certified Interpretive Host. See their website at www.interpnet.com/about_nai/index.shtml for more information.

Within land management agencies, you can expect to find required training and certifications related to certain positions, such as fire fighting, law enforcement, park dispatch, and so on. Some companies may require, or recommend, certification or licenses for outdoor guides depending on regulations and training available in a particular region. Also, you may want to check out the Epply Institute for Parks and Public Lands at the Indiana University, which offers courses to members of the public for those interested in educational opportunities related to outdoor recreation and interpretation. Many of the courses are free of charge. See their website at www.eppley.org/ for more information.

Where to Get Experience

Because of the nature of park, recreation, or tourism work, there are many opportunities for seasonal (often summer) or part-time work. Working during the summer at a job that strikes your interest is an excellent way to see if you like what you think you are interested in and builds work experience that will be of significant help in getting a full-time job after school.

Students should always look for and consider opportunities to enter an internship program while attending school. Internships allow you to add experience and skills to a comparable filed of study. Some offer opportunities to enter into a full-time job after graduation. Federal agencies have several programs, including:

The Student Conservation Association (SCA) has postings for internships and employment, and their goal is to provide college and high-school aged members with hands-on conservation service opportunities in virtually every area of outdoor recreation. Their goal is to help prepare the next generation of conservation leaders. See the SCA website at www.thesca.org for more information.

USAJobs is the official job site for the U.S. Federal Government. The Student Educational Employment program offers access to work experiences directly related to your academic field of study, and you may be eligible for permanent employment after successfully completing your education and meeting work requirements. See their website at www.usajobs.gov/students.asp for more information.

You can apply for an internship through one of these programs, but you can also often apply directly to any agency or company where you are interested in working. Many state and local agencies and NGOs also have special internships that are supported by a grantee seeking a particular outcome, such as having underrepresented groups employed in outdoor recreation.

Many for-profit companies also seek students for entry-level positions in which they can groom qualified employees for careers with their company. See the concessionaires' websites earlier in the chapter under "possibilities."

Additional Online Resources

Confused about where to start looking for a job? Try a job-search agency such as Monster® (http://www.monster.com/), Net-Temps (http://www.net-temps. com/), or others. There are two additional companies that specialize exclusively in park and recreation oriented jobs and careers:

Coolworks
http://www.coolworks.com/
This "cool" website, which bills itself as helping to find "thousands of jobs in great places," can help you find a seasonal job or career in some of the greatest places on earth. Get a summer job in Yellowstone, Yosemite, or another national park.

OutdoorIndustryJobs.com
http://www.outdoorindustryjobs.com/
This website provides links to outdoor jobs and careers in the outdoors, bicycle, action sports, fitness, hunting and shooting, fishing, and snow sports industries.

CONCLUSION

This section has provided a brief introduction to the career opportunities in the field of parks and recreation. If you have read this far, you appear to have the prime requirement for any successful career—interest!

Go back to the start of the chapter and review the "Focus Questions." If you haven't spent much time in a park or recreation venue, go now. While there, watch some of the people working there who seem to match up with some of the jobs we've discussed in this chapter. Can you see yourself in that ranger uniform/guide raft/visitor center/lodge front desk? If so, talk to them. Ask them what they think about their jobs. Write down what they say, and give it serious thought.

Next, look around the location where they are working. Are there a lot of people around? How do they interact with these people? Would you like working with and talking to these tourists or co-workers on a daily basis?

More importantly, you can have the experiences of a lifetime, and live in some of the most unique real estate in the country. Old Faithful geyser in Yellowstone is fun to watch as you drive through on a two-week vacation. Living at Old Faithful in the winter, skiing along the Firehole River on a moon-lit night, and hearing wolves howl outside your cabin can't be matched.

Study, plan, and think about your career. It is your future. But at some point, you will just have to get out there. In the words of retired Yellowstone park superintendent Bob Barbee: "If you look too closely at a crystal ball, you wind up with glass in your mouth." Good luck! Hope to see you on the trail some day!

"
*Everybody needs beauty as well as bread,
places to play in and pray in, where
Nature may heal and cheer and give
strength to body and soul alike.*

– JOHN MUIR

"

FOR FURTHER INVESTIGATION

For More Research

1. **Implement:** Before the school year ends, you need to test your dreams. Is there a reasonable opportunity to get a job in your area of interest? Is the beginning (and future) pay enough?

    Choose one each from each type of organization covered under "Possibilities": (a) Government Conservation Agencies, (b) Non-Profit Organizations, and (c) For-Profit Companies. Through phone, e-mail, or preferably in person, contact each group. Ask about seasonal job opportunities, the types of job, locations, and salaries. Then apply for a job. Even if you aren't completely sure, or even if the chances appear slim, by applying for a job you will be forced to seriously think about the work and the pay. And if you succeed in getting a summer or part-time job, you will be provided with an easy way to seriously test your interests and passions for such a career.

2. **Investigate:** On the next rainy/snowy/windy day, when you really don't want to go outside, pick a website from the discussion of "Non-Profit Organizations." Spend a few minutes looking at the website, then contact the organization either by phone, e-mail, or preferably in person. (Note: You may also do the same thing for a local organization that interests you). Ask them:
    (a) How do you primarily fullfill your mission? Who do you primarily work with in doing this?
    (b) Do you advocate for change? Discuss what they advocate for and how they do it.
    (c) Explain your career interests or ideas. Do they have suggestions for you to follow up on?

(d) Ask if you can set up a meeting with the executive director or some other employee for a more in-depth informational interview. Buy him or her a cup of coffee and discuss what the job entails.

Active Investigation

Now that you have finished this chapter, make use of what you have learned. Take action and set goals. Here are a few suggestions:

1. **Explore:** Next month, take an overnight trip with a friend to a nearby park. Either camp or stay in a park lodge. Play like a tourist:
   - Take a guided tour.
   - Eat in a restaurant.
   - Take a hike.
   - Ask for information or directions.
   - Talk with a park or lodge employee about their job (see the informational interview activity in chapter 2 for suggestions)
   - Your choice. . .

When you return home, review the "Focus Questions" at the start of the chapter. Did your overnight stay help you to answer some of these questions? How? Write down your thoughts. Then write down brief answers to the following questions:

(a) Would you want to do what some of the people you met did? Why or why not?
(b) Think of what you and your friend did and how you interacted on your trip with the people you met. If you were an employee in the park or lodge you visited, would you have wanted to play host to yourself (e.g., answered your questions, helped you find the trail, served you dinner, etc.)? Why or why not?

Recommended Reading

Although the Web is powerful, do not disregard the written word. There are key environmental and conservation books that have had, and continue to have, a great impact on the establishment of parks, and the beginning of recreation.

Classic Texts. Most of these books are still in print or easily obtainable from libraries or used bookstores. Copyright dates are for the original publications.

Leopold, A. (1949). *A Sand Country almanac*. New York: Random House, Inc. Leopold's book contains a classic collection of conservation essays that greatly influenced the establishment of wilderness areas and modern game management.

Udall, S. L. (1963). *The quiet crisis*. New York: HarperCollins Publishers.
Ex-assistant Secretary for the U.S. Department of the Interior writes about the history of a conservation land ethic of the United States, and thoughts on the future (introduction by John F. Kennedy)

Albright, H. M., & Taylor, F. J. (1928). *Oh, ranger!* Vistabooks. (Reprinted by Stanford University Press, 2010, Stanford, California)
The second director of the National Park Service, Horace Albright, tells stories of the early days of the national parks in stories and vignettes of his work in Yellowstone and other places. The book was written with newspaper reporter Taylor.

Tilden, F. (1951). *The national parks: What they mean to you*. New York: Alfred A. Knoff.
The classic book on the national parks and what they mean to all of us. Also, by the same author, Interpreting our Heritage (1957) is the "bible" for environmental interpretation.

Sax, J. L. (1980). *Mountains without handrails*. Ann Arbor, MI: University of Michigan Press.
Professor of law, writer, and thinker, Sax focuses on the political and emotional battles regarding recreation, wilderness, and the preservation of America's parks.

Abbey, E. (1968). *Desert solitaire*. New York: Random House, Inc.
Gonzo journalism about the national parks and governmental policies in the management of the national parks and the western public lands, particularly in the desert and canyon country of Utah and Arizona.

Pinchot, G. (1947). *Breaking new ground*. Washington, D.C.: Island Press.
Autobiography of the founder of the U.S. Forest Service, and of forestry management in America, with a contemporary perspective of the conservation movement of the early 20th century.

Also, any books by John Muir.

Recent Writings. There has been much written since the beginning of the modern environmental movement in the late 1960s. Below are just a few of the thousands of appropriate readings.

Smith, J. F. (2006). *Nature noir: A park ranger's patrol in the High Sierra*. New York: Houghton Mifflin Publishing Company.
A California state park ranger reflects on his job and on the meaning of park lands to the American public.

Charles, R. F. (2003). *National park ranger: An American icon.* Lanham, MD: Roberts Rinehart Publishers.

A history of what it's like to be a park ranger by a career ranger with 30 years of experience.

Sellars, R. W. (1997). *Preserving nature in the national parks: A history.* Boston: Yale University Press.

Sellars, a historian with the Park Service, shows how the Park Service has, throughout its existence, allowed the preservation of endangered species and habitats to be governed by politics. His book discusses the NPS's conundrum between traditional tourism management and growing ecological concerns.

Recommended Viewing

There are many DVDs available in libraries and elsewhere that will help you learn about specific park areas and outdoor recreation pursuits. If you have access to cable television check out shows on "The Discovery Channel," "Animal Planet," and "National Geographic." Also, check out the six-DVD series, "The National Parks: America's Best Idea," a 2009 PBS Documentary by Ken Burns, www.pbs.org/nationalparks, which is sure to become a classic.

REFERENCES

Burns, K. (director). (2009). *The National Parks: America's Best Idea* [DVD]. Public Broadcasting Service.

Central Park Conservancy. (n.d.). Central Park History. Retrieved September 28, 2009 from www.centralparknyc.org/site/PageNavigator/aboutpark_history_cp_history_150yrs

Cramton, L. C. (1932). *Early History of Yellowstone National Park and Its Relation to National Policies.* Washington, D.C.: United States Printing Office. Retrieved September 28, 2009 from www.nps.gov/history/history/online_books/yell/policies/yell_history_policies.pdf

Delaware North Companies. (n.d.). Delaware North Hospitality & Management Services. Retrieved October 21, 2009 from http://www.delawarenorth.com/

Gaskill, P. L. (2001). *Introduction to leisure services in North Carolina* (4th ed.). Dubuque, IA: Kendall/Hunt Publishing Co.

McClelland, L. F. (1998). *Building the national parks: Historic landscape design and construction.* Baltimore, MD: The Johns Hopkins University Press.

McLean, D. D., Hurd, A. R., & Rodgers, N. B. (2008). *Kraus' recreation and leisure in modern society* (8th ed.). Sudbury, MA: Jones and Bartlett Publishers.

National Park Service. (2006). *Management Policies 2006.* Washington, D.C.: U.S. Government Printing Office.

National Park Service. (n.d.). *Teaching with Historic Places Lesson Plans: The Emerald Necklace: Boston's Green Connection.* Retrieved September 28, 2009 from www.nps.gov/history/nr/twhp/topic.htm#tourism

National Park Service: The First 75 Years. (n.d.). *Stephen T. Mather.* Retrieved October 6, 2009 from http://www.nps.gov/history/history/online_books/sontag/mather.htm

National Park Service: History E-Library. (n.d.). *Theodore Roosevelt and the National Park System*. Retrieved June 10, 2010 from http://www.nps.gov/history/history/hisnps/NPSHistory/teddy.htm

Public Broadcasting Service. (n.d.). *A Film by Ken Burns: The National Parks—America's Best Idea*. Retrieved October 2, 2009 from http://www.pbs.org/nationalparks/

U.S. Forest Service. (n.d.). *History*. Retrieved October 2, 2009 from http://www.fs.fed.us/aboutus/history/

U.S. Forest Service History (n.d.). *Gifford Pinchot (1865-1946)*. Retrieved June 10, 2010 from http://www.foresthistory.org/ASPNET/people/Pinchot/Pinchot.aspx

Sierra Club (n.d.). *John Muir Exhibit*. Retrieved October 6, 2009 from http://www.sierraclub.org/john_muir_exhibit/

Sierra Club. (n.d). *Sierra Club Policies: Mission Statement*. Retrieved October 9, 2009 from http://www.sierraclub.org/policy/

The Trust for Public Land. (2009). *The Trust for Public Land: Mission Statement*. Retrieved October 25, 2009 from http://www.tpl.org/tier2_kad.cfm?folder_id=1965

"

The master in the art of living makes little distinction between his work and his play, his labor and his leisure, his mind and his body, his information and his recreation, his love and his religion. He hardly knows which is which. He simply pursues his vision of excellence at whatever he does, leaving others to decide whether he is working or playing. To him he's always doing both.

—JAMES MICHENER

"

7

Recreational Therapy and Therapeutic Recreation

RICHARD WILLIAMS
East Carolina University

FOCUS QUESTIONS

Q: *Are you interested in devoting your professional life to using recreation to help improve the health and quality of life for people with disabilities?*

A: Students who choose to major in recreational therapy have often discovered in their own lives that recreational activities are not only fun but are also beneficial in many different ways. Having experienced these benefits, students often have a desire to use recreation as a means to help people with illnesses and disabilities improve their health and quality of life.

Q: *Do you have a passion for sports, art, music, dance, theater or some other recreation activity that you are eager to share with others?*

A: Recreational therapists use recreation-related skills they already have in order to develop and implement programs that have positive outcomes for people with illnesses and disabilities. For instance, if you are an accomplished skier or dancer, you can use that expertise to help others.

Q: *Are you interested in the challenge of being a part of continuous improvement in a young and growing allied health profession?*

A: Recreational therapy is a relatively new profession, and the field continues to grow and change in exciting ways. Young professionals entering the field have immediate opportunities to help shape the future of RT.

Q: *Which appeals to you more—treating clients in a clinical setting to improve their abilities or facilitating meaningful leisure and recreation participation to improve health and quality of life in a community setting?*

A: Recreational therapists can be found in a wide variety of settings that serve people with illnesses and disabilities. Some people prefer to provide clinical services in a medical setting such as a hospital, while others choose community-based settings such as group homes, schools, and public parks and recreation departments.

KEY TERMS

Recreational therapy
Leisure focused
Therapeutic recreation specialist (TRS)
Recreational therapist (RT)
Clinical outcomes
Leisure Ability Model
Health Protection/Health
    Promotion Model

Recreation Service Model
International Classification of
    Functioning, Disability, and
    Health (ICF)
Third parties
Evidence-based practice
Standards of practice

PROFILE 1: COULD THIS BE YOU?

CAMERON BARHAM is a recreational therapist who works at Pitt County Memorial Hospital in Greenville, NC. After graduating from East Carolina University, Cameron began working in PCMH's neuro-rehabilitation unit. PCMH is a regional teaching hospital with an award-winning recreational therapy department that offers services to clients with many different disabilities and illnesses. Most of Cameron's clients are older adults who have had strokes, but he also works with clients with other neurological disorders.

Q: *We spoke to Cameron at his job recently and asked him what goals he has for his clients and how he helps them achieve them.*

A: The most common goals we have are related to cognition, problem solving, depression, anxiety, social interaction skills, and fine motor skills. I use different activities as interventions, including games. One of the most effective things I use is dominoes. It works because the clients like to play it, and at the same time they gain fine motor skills by manipulating the tiles. They improve their cognitive skills through counting and problem solving, and they also gain social skills through their interactions with other clients as they play.

Q: *What's the most challenging aspect of your job?*

A: Sometimes it is difficult to motivate clients, particularly those who are depressed. I always tell my clients that can't is a four-letter word and that change doesn't happen overnight, but I expect them to try and not give up. I explain that while we're going to work on functional outcomes, I won't forget that the first part of the word 'functional' is 'fun,' so we try to have fun, too.

Q: *Can you tell me about a memorable experience you have had with a client?*

A: Most of my clients are older adults, but about a year ago, I had a client who was a young veteran who was injured by a roadside bomb in Iraq. He had diminished strength in the left half of his body that left him unable to walk or use his left arm. He also had post-traumatic stress disorder and was experiencing significant difficulty adjusting to life back home.

We were about the same age, and during the month he was in the hospital, I slowly built a strong rapport with him. Although he made great progress during treatment, he still had a way to go when he left the hospital.

Normally after clients are discharged, we don't see them again, but after a year away, this man came back for a surprise visit. I was in the rehab gym, and in he walked without the aid of the cane he used a year before. He walked up to me, shook my hand, and with his left hand (which had been nearly useless when I met him), he handed me his business card.

Since leaving the hospital, he had made great strides in his rehabilitation and had recently started making a living as a motivational speaker. He came back to thank me, and I'm not embarrassed to say that I got a big lump in my throat. Moments like that keep me motivated, and I am reminded why I chose recreational therapy in the first place. I get the chance to make a difference.

PROFILE 2: COULD THIS BE YOU
by Dr. Robert Barcelona

TOM CARR, CTRS, is a program coordinator in charge of Athlete Development at Northeast Passage, an organization that provides barrier-free sport and recreation opportunities for individuals with disabilities. Among his many duties, Tom is responsible for a program that provides opportunities for competitive athletes with disabilities to train and attend college as student athletes. Tom's job includes:

- Recruitment of athletes
- Coaching and physical training
- Equipment modification for athletes

- Sponsorship identification
- Sport policy and rules development
- League and tournament administration

Q: *How did you get involved working with athletes with disabilities?*

A: When I was in college, I ran on the track team and loved sports. But I also had a strong interest in health promotion. I wanted to work with sports and athletics, and I did some volunteer work in an adaptive skiing program as part of a class in therapeutic recreation. I knew right away that I wanted to work with this group of athletes, but I also knew that I wanted to do more than just adaptive skiing. I found out that there was vast array of opportunities to work with athletes with disabilities at all levels of the competitive spectrum.

Q: *What motivates you in your job today?*

A: Helping to make a difference was a big thing for me. I like to be involved with beginners and seeing the instant gratification when they are introduced to a sport and get a positive experience. But I do a lot of my work with high-level, competitive athletes. What is even more rewarding is seeing their long-term growth. Seeing them begin a sport, and then 10 years later, they are competing in the Paralympics on the national and international stage.

Q: *Can you give an example of this?*

A: We had one sled hockey player who, before his injury, was headed toward a career in professional hockey. He was injured at 16 and went through a rough transition. We introduced him to sled hockey, and he struggled at first. The thing is, just like in any sport, he worked hard, and dedicated himself to being better. He tried out for the U.S. national team and ended up scoring the game winning goal on TV at the Paralympics in Torino, Italy.

Q: *So what do you do in your job? What does a typical day look like?*

A: My job is never boring. I know that I couldn't sit around and do one thing all day. A typical day for me may involve physically training an athlete, adapting equipment, doing tournament design, engaging in a league conference call, coaching a sled hockey game, and watching or helping with some of our other programs. My job is somewhat unique in that I get to be directly involved with elite, high level athletes, but I also have the chance to be an administrator and a program leader.

Q: *Are there any challenges?*

A: Given the scope of our jobs, there is always something going on, so managing priorities can be tough. I can never seem to cross the last thing off my to-do list. It is also difficult to get the word out about all that we do and all of the opportunities that we provide. So many stories about disabled athletes are about the human interest element—overcoming the challenge of the disability. That's fine as far as it goes. But the real story needs to be about the athletic excellence that is on display with these athletes. That is what is impressive to me.

Q: *Any advice for students who are interested in this aspect of the sport industry?*

A: As a student, I tried to work as closely as I could with professionals in the field, so I could learn and make connections. Get active in the field early. It's never too soon—volunteer, observe, and try to find a mentor. The worst thing that can happen is that you realize that this isn't what you want to do. I'd also suggest getting a diversity of experiences. Doing an internship with an adaptive sports organization, like Northeast Passage or the Paralympic Games would definitely help.

For more information on Northeast Passage, visit http://www.nepassage.org.

WHAT IS RECREATIONAL THERAPY?

When asked, recreational therapists echo Cameron's and Tom's sentiments about why they became recreational therapists: they make positive differences in people's lives. These positive changes don't happen randomly. Rather, they are the result of systematic planning and implementation of a therapeutic process known as recreational therapy that takes advantage of the benefits of recreation.

One of the terrific things about recreation is that it is not only fun, but most of it is good for you physically, psychologically, and socially. Take soccer, for instance. Although you might never earn a penny playing soccer, you certainly receive physical benefits through cardiovascular health and endurance. Success can lead to improved self-confidence, and if you become an avid soccer player, you might start to identify as an athlete, thus promoting a healthy self-image. Soccer, which is normally played with others, leads to the development of friendships and social support.

If there were a pill that could be developed that could simultaneously lead to cardiovascular fitness, improved self-confidence and self-image, and improved social support, it would sell billions of units. People would line up around the block to get it, and they would pay a fortune for it. There is no such pill, but thank goodness there is recreation, or more to the point of this chapter, there is recreational therapy.

Simply put, **recreational therapy** is practiced by trained and certified (and in some states, licensed) professionals who use recreation and other activities to help people with illnesses and disabilities gain new skills and restore skills that have diminished due to injury or illness.

The Right to Recreation

It is important to recognize that everyone has activities he or she does for fun and socialization such as sports, hobbies, and games. Basketball, watercolor painting, shopping with friends, hiking, canoeing, and writing poetry might not sound like activities that have much in common, but they are all recreation. As long as an activity is meant to be fun and is both pro-social and healthy, then it can rightly be called recreation. For centuries, people have recognized that recreational activities are good for individuals and society. Recreational therapists tap into the physical, psychological, and social benefits inherent to recreation in order to help people with disabilities gain valuable skills.

Only relatively recently has much attention been paid to the rights of everyone to participate in recreation activities. Thanks in part to social movements and the passage of legislation such as the Americans with Disabilities Act (1990), people with illnesses and disabilities have gained increased access to inclusive recreation services. Additionally, the conception of disability has expanded beyond traditional notions that placed people with disabilities into subordinate social roles. Additionally, a new conception of disability, perhaps best expressed by the World Health Organization's **International Classification of Disability, Functioning, and Health** (widely-known by the acronym ICF), provides a more holistic view of disability than traditional conceptions. Instead of describing people with disabilities as a minority, the ICF frames disability as a part of life common to everyone at some point and to varying degrees. Instead of focusing on cause of disability, the ICF encourages people to focus on the impact of disability. Significantly for recreational therapists, life activities (including recreation) are a central component of the ICF model.

A Brief History of Recreational Therapy as a Profession

It is difficult to point to a specific moment when recreational therapy became a profession. Rather, over the course of decades in the 20th century, people with the understanding that recreation can be therapeutic began to organize themselves into a profession. The American Red Cross provided recreation to soldiers as early as the First World War and began to offer services deemed hospital recreation to wounded soldiers (Bedini, 1995; Dieser, 2008; James, 1998). By 1949, the Hospital Recreation Section of the American Recreation Society was formed, giving a central organization for the budding profession. However, a hallmark of the profession since the very beginning has been a philosophical debate among its members about the nature of recreational therapy that can be labeled **leisure-focused** and clinical-outcomes focused. In 1953, this philosophical difference led to the founding of a competing organization named the National Association of Recreation Therapists. Despite fundamental disagreements between members of these national organizations, they joined forces in 1966 to become the National Therapeutic Recreation Society, a branch of the National Recreation and Park Association.

Throughout the latter half of the 20th century, numerous academic programs began offering courses and degrees in therapeutic recreation and recreational therapy. However, there was little consensus about the type of training needed for practitioners, and there was no control over who could identify him- or herself as a therapist. So, after years of diligent efforts to lay the groundwork for an independent credentialing body, the National Council for Therapeutic Recreation Certification (NCTRC) was formed in 1981. Among its many roles, NCTRC determines who can use the title Certified Therapeutic Recreation Specialist and serves as a gate-keeper of the profession by administering a certification exam.

In the early 1980s, the familiar philosophical differences (leisure-focused vs. clinical outcomes-focused) between members of the profession led to the founding of the American Therapeutic Recreation Association in 1984. This new national organization provided a philosophical home to people who viewed RT as a health care profession best used to facilitate functional improvements rather than enhanced leisure. There remain two national organizations today, and the debate about the nature of the profession continues.

An Ongoing Discussion: Two Philosophical Views

Although Recreational Therapy is relatively new as professions go, recreational therapists have two national organizations, each with somewhat different philosophies. Similarly, there are two terms most often used to refer to the profession: therapeutic recreation and recreational therapy. These two terms reflect the different philosophies of the two national organizations.

Founded in 1966, the National Therapeutic Recreation Society is a branch of the National Recreation and Park Association. The American Therapeutic Recreation Association was founded in 1984 and is independent from NTRS. Although the philosophies of the two national organizations have tended to drift toward each other over the years, it is still safe to say that NTRS's philosophical position is more leisure focused, while ATRA's philosophy is more focused on clinical outcomes.

Leisure Focused (Therapeutic Recreation Specialists)

Those practitioners and scholars who have a leisure-focused philosophy of the profession generally believe that the purpose of recreational therapy services is the facilitation of leisure for people with illnesses and disabilities and refer to themselves as **Therapeutic Recreation Specialists (TRSs)**. Services are designed to facilitate knowledge, skills, and abilities that lead to satisfying leisure expression. The fullest expression of this philosophy is the Leisure Ability Model proposed by Peterson and Gunn (1984). A version of this model was adopted in 1979 by NTRS as its official model for delivery of services. Peterson and Gunn identified the development of an appropriate leisure lifestyle as the ultimate outcome of services.

Clinical-Outcomes Focused (Recreational Therapists)

Alternately, **recreational therapists (RTs)** have a **clinical-outcomes focus** and generally believe that services should be designed to increase the functional abilities of clients. Examples of functional abilities include strength, balance, endurance, memory, mood control, and stress management. While recreation activities likely play a large part in the development of these skills, recreational therapists with a clinical focus use other non-recreation activities in the promotion of functional outcomes as well.

Today, therapeutic recreation specialists (TRSs) and recreational therapists (RTs) work in a wide variety of health care and community settings, including acute care and rehabilitation hospitals, long-term care facilities, correctional facilities, schools, and public recreation and parks departments. Because professionals in the field work in such a wide variety of settings and with so many different sorts of people, models of practice have been important tools that have helped unify the field.

FOUR MODELS OF PRACTICE

Models of practice guide practitioners in the organization of their programs and service delivery. While many different models of practice have been proposed, the first three models presented in this section are widely cited and represent an evolution of practice models over time. They also illustrate the evolution from leisure-focused practice to a clinical outcomes focused practice. The fourth model is not specific to RT, but rather it is the ICF, a model endorsed by the World Health Organization that has been adopted worldwide by health care professions. This model can be applied to RT practice, and in the estimation of many professionals, it is critical that RT abandon its own practice models in favor of placing recreational therapy services within the comprehensive model that the majority of other health-care professions have embraced.

Leisure Ability Model

The **Leisure Ability Model** (Peterson & Gunn, 1984) is widely recognized as the field's first model. According to its adherents, the purpose of recreational therapy is the facilitation of a leisure lifestyle. The model has three main components: treatment, leisure education, and recreation participation. Within treatment services, clients gain knowledge, skills, and abilities needed for full leisure participation. In leisure education, participants engage in an educational process that is designed to help them gain an understanding of the value of leisure, gain social skills, and develop self-determination. Recreation participation services provide the opportunity for leisure expression, relaxation, fun, and a chance for clients to practice skills learned in treatment and leisure education. At any given time, participants might participate in any combination of services from all three components of the model.

Health Protection/Health Promotion Model

The Leisure Ability Model has been a lightning rod for controversy ever since it was introduced, so it didn't take long for alternative service delivery models to be proposed. One of the first alternatives was Austin's (2004) **Health Protection/Health Promotion Model**. Drawing on Mazlow's Hierarchy of Needs Theory, Austin designed a model with three components: (a) prescribed activities, (b) recreation, and (c) leisure. According to Austin, the purpose of RT services is to help clients move from a state of illness and dependence to a state of self-actualization and health. The ultimate goal is for RT clients to engage independently in leisure that promotes health.

Recreation Service Model

In an effort to provide RT with a model suitable for clinical practice in health care settings, burlingame (1998) proposed a service delivery model based on a World Health Organization (WHO) model. The WHO model was organized into levels of care and "provided a framework for the diagnosis, treatment, funding and outcome measurement of all health care services (including recreational therapy) worldwide" (burlingame, p. 95). The levels of care contained in the WHO model included: (a) disease, (b) impairment, (c) disability, and (d) handicap. Essentially, burlingame's model adapted the WHO model and described the nature of RT services within each level of care. In addition to the four levels of care provided by the WHO model, the Recreation Service Model includes three levels of care specific to RT: (a) education, (b) organized recreation programs, and (c) independent activities.

International Classification of Functioning, Disability, and Health

In 2001, the WHO adopted a new and comprehensive model for health care known as the International Classification of Functioning, Disability, and Health (ICF). More than 190 countries have endorsed the ICF model as the worldwide standard for the measurement and classification of disability and health. By taking the stance that all people face suboptimal health at some point in their lives, the ICF model discourages the conception of people with disabilities as a separate group. Instead, the model encourages practitioners to focus on the impact rather than the cause of a disability. In this light, health care practitioners and others account for not only medical and biological aspects of disability but also the social and environmental factors that impact and are impacted by disability.

Because the ICF model is a universal model for health care, many leaders in the field of RT have strongly encouraged practitioners to use it as the framework for organizing their clinical activities including assessment, planning, programming, and evaluation of programs and client progress. A primary advantage of adopting the ICF model in RT includes giving RT practitioners a common professional vocabulary and theoretical stance in their interactions with fellow health care providers.

CAREERS IN THERAPEUTIC RECREATION AND RECREATIONAL THERAPY

Because recreational therapists work with many different types of people with disabilities, they can choose among many different work environments, everything from hospitals to public recreation departments. In general, individual recreational therapists develop specialties related to certain disabilities and interventions. For instance, a recreational therapist in a community setting may develop into an expert at teaching and facilitating adaptive sports for people with physical disabilities.

Most recreational therapists are primarily responsible for providing direct services to people with illnesses and disabilities. With experience, front-line practitioners may be promoted to departmental and other management positions.

Passions

Motivations for becoming a recreational therapist differ from person to person, but common motivations include a passion for helping people with disabilities and a belief in the power of recreation and leisure to positively transform lives. Although the pay for well-trained recreational therapists continues to improve, no one goes into the field to become wealthy. The primary motivation for many recreational therapists is the passion they have for helping their clients. Recreational therapists are people who experience joy when watching clients gain valuable skills, confidence, and self-esteem while engaging in meaningful and fun activities. If you have any doubt about this, just re-read the profiles at the start of this chapter.

Many RTs report that having a family member or friend with a disability was the initial motivation they needed to pursue this profession. Others have experienced RT either directly or through observation and knew immediately that RT was a career they wanted to pursue. Although the author of this chapter had never heard of recreational therapy until he was 25 years old, he had invented it in his mind long before. When he met a recreational therapist and learned there was such a profession, he immediately began making plans to return to school.

Pay and Perks

As with many professions, resources tend to go to the most highly trained and highly skilled RT practitioners. Additionally, certain types of facilities typically pay their employees more than others. For instance, the national average pay of recreational therapists in rehabilitation hospitals is higher than for their colleagues in long-term care facilities. Other factors such as geography and education level play a part in determining practitioner salaries. The best sources for current salary information are the U.S. Bureau of Labor Statistics (www.bls.gov) and the National Council for Therapeutic Recreation Certification (www.nctrc.org). Both report regularly-updated salary trends of recreational therapists.

The perks are an attractive feature of RT jobs, because while RT lacks high pay, it makes up for it (at least in part) with perks that many find self-motivating. Practitioners in RT often experience extraordinary autonomy in their jobs. It is not uncommon for recreational therapists to have relatively flexible schedules and to have the freedom to design and revise interventions and assessments. While tasks such as documentation and staff meetings are more structured (and important parts of the job), recreational therapists also spend much of their time planning and facilitating interventions directly with clients. Facilitating recreation programs is challenging and invigorating and is often the part of the job that clinicians like most. Since interventions can take place in a pool, a gym, a classroom, or on an outing to the community, they provide welcome variety and excitement that is difficult to find in traditional office work.

Preparation

The National Council for Therapeutic Recreation Certification (NCTRC) specifies the minimum requirements for use of the title Certified Therapeutic Recreation Specialist (CTRS). These standards continue to become more stringent and include requirements related to amount and type of formal higher education, practical experiences in the field (e.g., internships), and the passage of a national standardized exam.

Once certified, recreational therapists must annually renew their certification and become recertified every five years. To qualify for recertification, recreational therapists must demonstrate that they have actively practiced RT and continued their professional education by attending professional conferences, taking college courses, receiving in-service training, and participating in other educational opportunities and scholarship.

Possibilities

Most recreational therapists are front-line clinicians who work directly with clients. With experience, training, and additional education, recreational therapists have taken on administrative duties, serving as managers of RT and other departments within health care settings. Many of those RTs who take on administrative duties also maintain a caseload of clients.

According to the National Council for Therapeutic Recreation Certification (NCTRC), most recreational therapists work in either a hospital (41.6%) or a skilled nursing facility (19.3%). The remainder work in settings such community parks and recreation departments and schools. As a recreational therapy student, you might already have strong ideas about the type of facility where you would like to work as a professional. However, it is worthwhile to consider the characteristics of many of the most common settings where recreational therapy is practiced.

Recreation Therapy in Hospital Settings

There are many different types of hospitals. Typically, recreational therapists work in acute care hospitals and rehabilitation hospitals. Acute care hospitals offer a wide variety of services to meet the immediate medical needs of many different types of illnesses and disabilities, including both physical and psychiatric conditions. Because of the expense of hospitalizations and medical treatment in general, the goal of acute care is to medically stabilize patients as quickly as possible. Whereas long-term hospitalizations used to be common, according to the Centers for Disease Control (2009), the average length of stay in U.S. hospitals is now less than five days. Once stable, patients can be treated long term through outpatient and other services.

After becoming medically stable, some patients are admitted to rehabilitation hospitals for long-term treatment. While many types of patients receive treatment in rehabilitation hospitals, some of the common diagnoses include spinal cord injuries, stroke, and brain injuries. Patients in rehabilitation receive treatments designed to restore physical and cognitive skills that have been lost or diminished and to develop new skills that will be needed for independent functioning in the community. RT programs in hospitals include fine and gross motor skills training using crafts and games, aquatic therapy, therapeutic exercise, community re-entry outings, and stress management. It is common for recreational therapists in hospital settings to work on treatment teams with other health care professionals such as occupational therapists, physical therapists, physicians, nurses, and social workers.

Passions—If you would like to work in a medical environment and be a member of a treatment team with professionals such as doctors, nurses, occupational therapists, physical therapists, and speech and language pathologists, then becoming a recreational therapist in an acute care hospital may be your best alternative. These fast-paced and demanding environments are not for the faint of heart. Only highly trained and highly skilled professional thrive in acute care settings. Recreational therapists who work in acute care hospitals tend to focus on clinical outcomes dictated by the needs of clients. A large recreational therapy department in an acute care hospital may offer services to patients in physical rehabilitation, behavioral health, acute pediatric care, cardio-vascular rehabilitation, and many other specialty areas.

Pay and Perks—Most recreational therapy jobs in acute care hospitals will be full time and will carry benefits such as health care insurance, retirement benefits, paid vacation, and sick leave. The NCTRC (2004) reports that hospitals offer among the best-paying jobs for recreational therapists.

Preparation—A student who would like to ultimately work in a hospital setting should begin preparing while in school by completing practica and an internship in an acute care hospital. Such experiences will help students gain skills that will be valued in the job market. These experiences will also help students gain valuable contacts in settings where they might ultimately work. Additionally, students should consider taking elective classes such as aquatic therapy that will help them develop specific and marketable skills valued in hospital settings.

Possibilities—The best advice for young professionals and students who would like to work in a hospital setting is to steer clear of geographic limitations. In other words, to get the sort of job you want, you may have to consider moving to a city or region with a highly desirable recreational therapy position. Students who steadfastly insist on staying in a limited geographical area may struggle to find the perfect job simply because there are relatively few recreational therapy positions in any given location that match an individual's professional interests.

The Shepherd Center in Atlanta is a world-renowned rehabilitation hospital with a large and very active recreational therapy program. Programs at the Shepherd Center include adaptive sports, adaptive art and music, horticulture therapy, community outings, and leisure skills development. These services are designed to help patients develop skills so that they can be independent, active, and healthy when they return to the community.

Recreation Therapy in Skilled Nursing Facilities

As the U.S. population continues to age, it is anticipated that more and more people will receive services from skilled nursing facilities. Clients who receive treatment from a skilled nursing facility are usually not unhealthy enough to require hospitalization in an acute care hospital, but they have health limitations that prevent them from living safely at home.

Skilled nursing facilities are not nursing or retirement homes meant for custodial care. Rather, clients in skilled nursing facilities receive active treatment designed to promote improved functioning. Recreational therapists in these settings help clients develop and restore fine and gross motor skills, balance, strength, and cardiovascular health. Additionally, recreational therapists may work with clients to alleviate depression, to learn to cope with stress, and to remain socially integrated. As in acute care and rehabilitation hospitals, recreational therapists in skilled nursing facilities often serve on treatment teams with other professionals and often co-treat with physical therapists, social workers, and occupational therapists.

Passions—Many students know immediately that they want to work with older adults. Perhaps they had influential experiences caring for an older relative or neighbor, or perhaps they have had meaningful volunteer or professional experiences that have sparked their professional interests. Even if it has never occurred to you to work with older adults, you might consider exploring the possibilities of working in a skilled-nursing facility as many professionals find this work to be extremely rewarding. Older adults have accumulated decades of wisdom, skills, and knowledge that they are often eager to share.

Perks—The pay for recreational therapists in skilled-nursing facilities is among the highest of all in the profession. Additionally, unlike the relatively short lengths of stay in hospital settings, patients in skilled-nursing facilities may receive services for weeks, months, or longer. These extended stays facilitate meaningful therapeutic relationships and permit therapists time to make significant impacts on their patients' health over time.

Preparation—Students who would like to work in skilled-nursing facilities should consider completing practica and an internship in a skilled nursing facility. Additionally, students might consider taking courses in gerontology to gain knowledge and skills that will be both marketable to employers and helpful once employed. Some schools may offer gerontology certificates or similar concentrations. Finally, students should consider building their resumes and their abilities by taking advantage of the numerous volunteer opportunities at skilled-nursing facilities.

Possibilities—By all accounts, the U.S. population is aging, and it is anticipated that more and more recreational therapists will be needed to meet the demands for services for older adults. Although it is hard to predict employment trends, well-trained students with volunteer experiences, practica, and internships in skilled-nursing facilities may expect to be in high demand in the future.

Recreation Therapy in Community Settings

States and all but the smallest municipalities provide parks and recreation services for their citizens. Since the passage of the Americans with Disabilities Act in 1990, these services must be accessible to people with disabilities. Ideally, parks and recreation programs and facilities are designed to be inclusive, meaning that people with and without disabilities participate in the programs together. While many parks and recreation professionals strive to make all of their services inclusive, many still provide separate programs designed exclusively for people with disabilities. Examples of two well-known programs include Challenger League Baseball and Special Olympics. Often, recreational therapists are hired by parks and recreation departments to coordinate, plan, and facilitate recreation services for people with disabilities (see the chapter on Community Recreation for more details).

Recreational therapy programs in community recreation and parks departments are as varied as people's recreation interests. Therefore, cultural arts programs, adaptive sport programs, and outings to local sites of interest are commonplace and popular. Other communities hire recreational therapists to work as community support personnel for people with psychiatric and cognitive disorders living in the community. The support often comes in the form of the facilitation of social interaction and helping people learn activities of daily living and to use community resources (such as public transportation).

Although there are not many recreational therapists currently working in schools, federal legislation (IDEA) has identified RT as a service that can be requested as part of a student's Individual Education Plan. Recreational therapists have worked in public schools as support personnel for children with disabilities, as leisure educators, and as community transition specialists. Considering the important role recreation and leisure play in the development of children, schools are logical places for expanded involvement of recreational therapy in the future.

Some of the standards typical of clinical recreational therapy settings are a little more relaxed in community settings. For instance, recreational therapists working in the community may not document client progress as thoroughly as their counterparts in an acute care hospital. One benefit to working as a recreational therapist in the community is the ability to interact with clients and those around them for long spans of time. Thus, community-based recreational therapists often get to know the family and friends of their clients and have the potential to make lasting and deep impacts on the quality of life of their clients.

Passions—Recreational therapists in community settings often become deeply involved with their clients, their families, and communities. Often, these therapeutic relationships can last years, and community-based recreational therapists are often in the enviable position of contributing to (and witnessing) significant development of their clients over time.

Some people can never imagine themselves being "tied to a desk" and hope to find a job that gets them up and moving. Most recreational therapy jobs fit that description, but perhaps none more so than community-based jobs. Depending on the nature of the agency, recreational therapists can expect to spend much of their time outdoors, on community outings, in residences, in recreation centers, and in schools.

Pay and Perks—The pay in community settings varies widely depending on the size and nature of the employing agency. Parks and recreation departments in large municipalities can have large budgets, but too often these services are underfunded. Recreational therapists have become experts over time at learning to accomplish much with relatively few resources and to form collaborative relationships that provide support.

The hours of recreational therapists in community-based settings can be irregular when there are special events to be planned and delivered, and many services are offered in the evenings and during weekends. Such flex scheduling can be frustrating to some, but for others, it is a valuable perk.

Preparation—It is particularly important for community-based recreational therapists to have a wide range of recreation knowledge and skills related to sports, arts and crafts, and games. Cultivating a large repertoire of such skills will help in the planning and provision of services to people with individual interests. Additionally, recreational therapists in these settings must be particularly familiar with their communities to help connect their clients with resources and to serve as advocate for their clients and agencies.

Possibilities—The passage of the Americans with Disabilities Act led to a sea change in the delivery of many services for people with disabilities. Specifically, large state-operated residential facilities have become decentralized, and clients who formerly lived in often-locked and sub-standard large institutions have now been placed in community settings such as group homes. The shift to least-restrictive environments has created many opportunities for recreational therapists. Additionally, although the numbers of recreational therapists working in public schools is very low, legislation such as IDEA opened the door for recreational therapists in schools.

To help reduce the ever-increasing cost of health care, many have suggested providing fewer services in hospitals and other medical facilities in favor of less-expensive community-based settings. As long as clients are medically stable, adaptive sports, community living skills, healthy living, exercise, and many other programs can be just as easily offered in the community as in hospitals and often at a fraction of the expense. Such a reform will create additional opportunities for recreational therapists interested in working in the community.

Summary of Career Options

There are many different types of career opportunities for recreational therapists in addition to the ones discussed here. Most commonly, recreational therapists work in hospital and long-term care settings, but there are other alternatives. Working in parks and recreation departments, schools, and other community settings can lead to rewarding careers that provide practitioners the chance to have long-lasting therapeutic relationships with their clients. The choice of a career is an individual one, and RT students are encouraged to seek out a variety of volunteer, practicum, and internship experiences while in school to determine the work setting that fits their goals and skills the best.

SUMMARY OF RECREATIONAL THERAPY (RT) CAREER POSSIBILITIES

Career	Passions	Pay and Perks	Preparation	Possibilities
Recreational therapy in hospital settings	Strong desire to work in a fast-paced, demanding medical environment. Desire to be part of a treatment team made up of other medical professionals, including MDs, PTS, OTs, social workers, nurses, and others.	Full-time, professional-level pay with benefits. Hospital settings tend to offer the highest RT salaries.	Only the best prepared, most highly trained RTs work in hospital settings. BS in RT or BS in recreation with an RT concentration. Obtain CTRS certification and state licensure. RT internship in a hospital setting.	Acute care hospitals where patients with illnesses and injuries, both physical and psychiatric, come to be stabilized. Rehabilitation hospitals where patients go for longer term treatment.
Recreational therapy in skilled nursing facilities	Strong desire to work with older adults. Desire to develop a therapeutic relationship and contribute to clients' health and quality of life over time. Desire to be part of a treatment team.	Full-time, professional-level pay with benefits. Skilled nursing facilities offer very good RT salaries. Clients in skilled nursing facilities have longer stays so you can develop more meaningful therapeutic relationships.	BS in RT, or BS in recreation with an RT concentration. Obtain CTRS certification and state licensure. Coursework or minor in gerontology. Volunteer experiences with older adults. RT internship in a skilled nursing facility.	Highest area of demand. Skilled nursing facilities providing active treatment, similar to rehabilitation hospitals. Nursing facilities providing long-term care for elderly patients who can no longer live at home.
Recreational therapy in community settings	Desire to work in a more relaxed, community-based setting. Desire to work with clients, their families, and the community over time. Desire to be involved in many activities and settings, such as community arts, outdoors, and sports programs.	Pay and benefits will vary widely with the size of the community and employing agency. Desire to work a flexible work schedule—many events will be evenings and weekends. Desire to form partnerships with others to make things happen.	BS in RT, or BS in Recreation with an RT concentration. Obtain CTRS certification and state licensure. Get very involved in the community so you connect your clients to resources and serve as an advocate.	Recreation and parks departments. Public schools and out-of-school-time programs. Any agency providing adaptive sports programs.

FUTURE OPPORTUNITIES, ISSUES, CHALLENGES

The debate about the essential nature of recreational therapy is ongoing. Many professionals contend that the field should be primarily aligned with parks and recreation, focusing on leisure-related outcomes. Critics of this vision of the profession advocate abandoning leisure-related outcomes and associations with parks and recreation in favor of the alignment of the field with allied therapies such as occupational therapy and physical therapy. As stated earlier, this young profession has a bright future that is still being shaped by its practitioners.

A primary argument against the leisure-focused RT goals is that **third parties** will not usually pay for the leisure-related outcomes type of RT services. These third parties include private insurance companies, Medicare, Medicaid, workman's compensation, and other entities in the business of providing funding for health care. However, recreational therapists who provide (and document) health-related outcomes for their clients often are considered covered services by third parties. In fact, in health care settings such as hospitals and skilled nursing facilities, recreational therapy has been practiced for decades as a clinical intervention, and it is widely recognized as an effective treatment option for a range of illnesses and disabilities. Medicare and many private insurance companies cover recreational therapy services via mechanisms similar to other health care services.

In the past several years, the American Therapeutic Recreation Association has been promoting the ATRA Medicare Project to lobby federal policy-makers to further clarify Medicare's coverage of recreational therapy. Medicare is such a large source of health care funds that it often sets the tone for private insurance companies and their willingness to cover specific services. While RT has long been included in the budget for Medicare, the regulations governing Medicare are inconsistent and often confusing. As a result, money earmarked for RT services in health care settings has often been spent in other ways. Financial considerations are only one of the hurdles that recreational therapy faces in the coming decades.

Most RT practitioners work in a highly competitive health care arena. Such an environment requires both efficiency and effectiveness, and recreational therapists must develop several features to secure the future of the profession. Among the most important priorities for the profession is the continued development of a body of knowledge that will allow practitioners to provide **evidence-based practice.** Additionally, systematic adherence to **standards of practice** and the development of and adherence to standard treatment protocols must be insured. Having valid and reliable research documenting outcomes will enable practitioners to provide efficient, effective, and standardized services and to justify their services to health care administrators, colleagues in allied professions, clients, and the public.

RESOURCES AND GETTING INVOLVED

Recreational therapy is a relatively small profession, and it is important to establish and maintain professional relationships within and outside of the profession. With the advent of new technology, networking has never been easier. Students and others are encouraged to join and participate in RT and health care email listservs and Facebook and Myspace pages. One of the best ways to meet other professionals and students in RT is to attend RT conferences, and students routinely pay significantly less than others for conference registration fees. Finally, volunteering at agencies that provide services to people with disabilities is a great way to give back to the community, to explore professional options, and to create important professional ties.

Professional Organizations

American Therapeutic Recreation Association
http://www.atra-online.com/

National Therapeutic Recreation Society
http://www.nrpa.org/ntrs

Certifications and Licenses

All recreational therapists must attain and maintain certification through the National Council for Therapeutic Recreation Certification. More information can be obtained by visiting the homepage for the National Council for Therapeutic Recreation Certification, http://www.nctrc.org.

Currently, only a handful of states require a license to practice RT, but there are several movements underway in states to require licenses to practice RT. To find out more information, contact your state or regional recreational therapy organization. A simple Internet search will help you find the contact information for your state or regional organization.

Where to Get Experience

Prior to practicing recreational therapy, individuals must gain certification by the National Council for Therapeutic Recreation Certification. However, there are plenty of job opportunities working with people with disabilities in recreation contexts. For instance, many public park and recreation agencies hire people to manage programs designed for people with disabilities such as camps, adaptive sports, and Special Olympics. While these are not RT positions, they do provide an opportunity for people to get a taste of what it's like to work in the field.

One of the best ways to gain experience in recreational therapy is to find a dedicated recreational therapist and ask to volunteer. Almost all recreational therapists were required to volunteer in community and health care agencies when they were students, and it is likely that they will be very accepting and willing to accommodate enthusiastic volunteers.

It is important to remember that recreational therapists work in agencies that have very strict rules related to client confidentiality, infection control, and safety. Volunteers in RT settings often usually required to complete extensive training, a background check, and will be expected to follow certain rules of conduct.

CONCLUSION

If you are an energetic and creative person interested in working with people with disabilities and illnesses, then recreational therapy very well may be the profession for you. Most people have an intuitive sense that recreational activities are good for people, and recreational therapists use the inherent enjoyment in recreation to help people gain these valuable benefits. As a relatively young and growing profession, recreational therapy has made great strides in recent decades, yet work remains to be done as the profession continues to evolve and improve. If you choose to become a recreational therapist, you are encouraged to gain all of the experience and technical skills you can while you are in school. These experiences and skills will not only help you attain a job you will like when you graduate, but you will become a better therapist. Recreational therapists do not earn the same living as investment bankers, but a serious case can be made for a career that daily provides the opportunity to make real and positive differences in the lives of others.

FOR FURTHER INVESTIGATION

For More Research

1. Visit the websites for both ATRA and NTRS (listed under professional organizations above). Compare and contrast the information about the RT/TR profession you discover there (e.g., mission, vision, standards of practice). Also, check out membership requirements and see when and where the next regional and national conferences will be taking place.
2. Visit the website for U.S. Department of Labor statistics (bls.gov) and conduct a search using the term "recreational therapists." The Bureau of Labor Statistics tracks employment and salary trends for most professions.
3. Visit your school's library and find bound volumes of NTRS's *Therapeutic Recreation Journal* and ATRA's *Annual in Therapeutic Recreation*. Then, catalogue the types of research studies that have been published about recreational therapy.

Active Investigation

1. *Benefits of Recreation Activity*

On a piece of paper, write down three recreation activities that have been meaningful to you during your life. Then, list all of the physical, psychological, and social benefits that you have received from each activity (or that could reasonably be received). Finally, consider what sort of people with disabilities might benefit most from the activities your chose. Would the activities need to be adapted in any way for people with disabilities?

2. *Disability in Perspective*

This activity may not apply to you if you have already experienced a disabling condition, but for others, it can be eye-opening. Sit quietly for one minute and consider how your life would change if this afternoon you were in a car accident and acquired a spinal cord injury. Write down 10 ways that your life would be impacted. Consider your involvement in school, work, recreation, and other life activities, and be sure to consider how your family and friends will be impacted. How will your relationships be impacted?

Recommended Reading

Austin, D.R. (2004). *Therapeutic recreation: Processes and techniques* (5th ed.). Champaign, IL: Sagamore Publishing.
This text covers a broad array of information and offers a strong foundation that therapeutic recreation professionals can utilize to improve quality of their services.

Long, T., & Roberstson, T. (2008). *Foundations of therapeutic recreation.* Champaign, IL: Human Kinetics.
This text showcases how therapeutic recreation professionals can address various clients' needs throughout the life span through the use of therapeutic programs, modalities, and activities

Porter, H.R., & burlingame, j. (2006). *Recreational therapy handbook of practice: ICF-based diagnosis and treatment.* Enumclaw, WA: Idyll Arbor
This handbook of recreational therapy clinical applications is designed to implement the ICF. The authors' goals are to standardize communication, research, and therapy within RT and facilitate clearer communication with other disciplines.

REFERENCES

Austin, D.R. (2004). *Therapeutic recreation: Processes and techniques* (5th ed.). Champaign, IL: Sagamore.
Bedini, L. (1995). The 'play ladies'—the first therapeutic recreation specialists. *Journal of Physical Education, Recreation & Dance, 66,* 32-35.
burlingame, j. (1998). Clinical practice models. In F.M. Brasile, T. Skalko, & j. burlingame (Eds.), *Perspectives in recreational therapy* (pp. 83-106). Ravensdale, WA: Idyll Arbor.
Centers for Disease Control and Prevention. (2009). *Hospital utilization.* Retrieved December 31, 2009 from http://www.cdc.gov/nchs/fastats/hospital.htm
Dieser, R. (2008). History of therapeutic recreation. In T. Robinson, & T. Long (Eds.), *Foundations of therapeutic recreation.* Champaign, IL: Human Kinetics.
James, A. (1998). The conceptual development of recreational therapy. In F. M. Brasile, T. Skalko, & j. burlingame (Eds.), *Perspectives in recreational therapy* (pp. 7-38). Ravensdale, WA: Idyll Arbor.

National Council for Therapeutic Recreation Certification. (2004). *NCTRC newsletter*, Fall. 5.

Peterson, C.A., & Gunn, S.L. (1984) *Therapeutic recreation program design: Principles and procedures* (2nd ed.). Englewood Cliff, NJ: Prentice-Hall.

“

I've been looking forward to this with my friends since I first came to school. I'd love to do this for a living.

—ANDY LANE, SENIOR
Whitewater rafting participant

”

8

Campus Recreation, Leisure, and Intramurals

DOUG KENNEDY

Virginia Wesleyan College

FOCUS QUESTIONS

Q. *What is campus recreation?*

A: **Campus recreation** is the intentional effort by schools to provide leisure time programs that contribute to enhancing the well-being of the campus community. These programs may include formal sport leagues and special events as well as informal opportunities to use a school's recreation facilities. Campus recreation often includes co-curricular and diversional activities provided by a student activities office.

Q: *Why choose a career in campus recreation?*

A: Campus recreation professionals are passionate about working around young, college-age students and the chance to have a positive impact on their lives. Many students have never had a fitness program before, attended a particular cultural event, or tried a sport like SCUBA or kayaking, and campus recreation staff help them develop interests and skills that last a life-time.

Q: *Is campus recreation mostly about sports?*

A: Sports and intramurals are a big part of campus recreation but it's about a whole lot more. Campus recreation programs not only provide an opportunity to balance the hard work of being a college student, they may also be co-curricular and relate to a specific class. Programs may include camping, wellness, entertainment, clubs, and other ways students, faculty, and staff spend their leisure time. The slogan "work hard, play hard" describes a number of campus recreation programs.

Q: *What kind of things would a campus recreation professional expect to do on a day-to-day basis?*

A: Most campus recreation professionals oversee one or more program areas. They enjoy managing both people and facilities because life in campus recreation is about both. College students are often looking for creative recreation programs that at times might be very serious but are also just plain fun. For example, the popularity of the Harry Potter novels and movies has caused over 200 colleges and universities to create Quidditch teams. There's even an International Quidditch Association with its own world cup! Starting such a program at any school would require a great deal of creativity and excellent management skills to be successful.

Q: *How do you see technology changing campus recreation?*

A: Like many areas in higher education, campus recreation has embraced technology to provide an enhanced experience. Today many schools have gone paperless. That means students can register for programs online. Personal electronic devices like the IPod are being integrated into exercise equipment so you can listen to music or watch movies of your choice. Even traditional activities like backpacking have been changed by technology like GPS receivers. The integration of technology will undoubtedly continue as will some challenges that come with it.

KEY TERMS

Campus recreation   Extramural sports
Student learning imperative   Recreational sports
Co-curricular programs   Club sports
Intramural sports   Student activities

PROFILE 1: COULD THIS BE YOU?

KEVIN MARBURY is the Director of the Department of Recreational Sports at Old Dominion University. On a daily basis he oversees intramural sport programs, sport clubs, informal recreation opportunities, fitness programs, and aquatic programs.

Along with these areas, he also has responsibility for personnel management, problem solving, planning, and financial management.

Kevin got his start in municipal recreation, but his love for working with college students led him to start his career in campus recreation. Now, after 22 years in the profession, he's received the Award of Merit from the Virginia Recreational Sports Association for his exceptional performance and is busy managing Old Dominion's new $25 million student recreation center.

Q: *How important is campus recreation?*

A: I realize every day that what we do in campus recreation makes a positive impact on students now, and that impact will carry over for the rest of their lives. Everyone in my department is committed to the programs we provide and realizes that being involved in something like a sport club is not only fun for our students but also offers them an opportunity to learn leadership skills, develop new friends, improve their communication, and develop other areas they'll use in their work and personal lives.

Q: *Do most staff and participants come from similar backgrounds?*

A: No, they don't. Campus recreation is very diverse. What makes a huge difference is having a real variety of staff and participants. As a matter of fact, we recently had a student come to us for a part-time job who knew nothing about recreation; her major was accounting. She started as a scorekeeper for our intramural leagues and over time, as she developed management skills, she's taken on more and more responsibilities. The same is true for our participants. Very often in our fitness programs, we'll get participants who have never worked out. It's so exciting then to see them make huge gains in their health and develop lifestyles that will help them for the rest of their life.

Q: *What recommendations would you have for anyone who is considering campus recreation as a career?*

A: There are a few things I think are critical. You have to like working with young people. Some schools have more non-traditionally aged students, but at the core of most schools are 18- to 22-year-old students. It's a great group to work with and they'll keep you young! You should also develop two or three mentors who have been in the profession for a while. Challenges will come up on a daily basis, and the advice of others who have been in campus recreation longer than you will help you make good decisions. Your mentors will also be incredibly valuable in helping you develop as a professional and finding other positions. Lastly, you have to enjoy managing people and facilities. Both can be a challenge at times, but nothing's more rewarding than watching your staff develop and your facilities serve your participants.

Q: *Where do you see campus recreation going in the next 20 years?*

A: Right now we're in a tremendous building phase across the country. At some point, that will slow down. When it does, we'll really need to focus on providing programs when people want them. We're moving away from things like group exercise programs and developing individual fitness programs that will allow participants to complete them on their timetable and get immediate feedback. As technology becomes more a part of our lives we'll increasingly have to make use of that or down the road our programs will seem too "old fashioned!" The next 20 years are going to be an exciting time! (For further information about Old Dominion University's Department of Recreational Sports see http://studentaffairs.odu.edu/recsports/about/index.shtml).

Profile 2: Could This Be You?

Willie Harrell and Jason Seward are on the other end of the spectrum from Kevin Marbury. Both are just starting their careers and each directs half of the campus recreation program at Virginia Wesleyan College.

Willie is the Director of Aquatics and Fitness, and he oversees the college's indoor pool, fitness center, and racquetball courts. The total operation of these areas includes programs, staff, and facilities. Willie's counterpart, Jason, is the Director of Recreational Sports and Outdoor Activities. His office plans and oversees all the intramural leagues, sports clubs, and sport tournaments in addition to planning the year-round outdoor recreation activities and running the climbing wall. By working together and contributing to the college's campus recreation program called "RecX," they have seen participation in their programs quadruple over the past three years.

Q: *Do you need any specialized education and training in these positions?*

A: (Jason) My degree in recreation and leisure studies has been important in my being able to provide the right programs. Beyond that, I'm a certified park and recreation professional, I've completed a course in wilderness first aid, and I continue to attend educational sessions at conferences to keep up-to-date.

(Willie): I'm a certified aquatic facility operator as well as a certified personal trainer and certified park and recreation professional. I believe it's mandatory for someone in my position to have these certifications from a reputable agency.

Q: *What do you two like most about your jobs?*

A: (Willie) Working with students. This is a great group that really appreciates everything you do for them. We follow the principles of what's called the **"student learning imperative."** Specifically, we really believe that we contribute to one of the main principles, which says that experiences in and out of the class contribute to learning and personal development. So whether you are a participant in one of our programs or working in our department as a lifeguard, you're developing skills that you can use in the classroom and will help you after graduation. I also love the fact that I get to teach students to kayak, scuba dive, become triathletes, and even train for marathons.

(Jason): Willie's right. At this school (and others) you have the opportunity to expose students to experiences outside the classroom that carry over into their studies and will stay with them long after they graduate. We call what we do in campus recreation "serious fun" and that's just what it is. We get to plan fun programs but what the students get from them can make a serious difference in how happy they are to be in college and how well they'll do in their classes. When I take a group to the Florida Keys to kayak and snorkel, or to West Virginia for some whitewater rafting, they not only enjoy the activity but they learn how to be independent, communicate with others, deal with adversity, and develop new interests.

Q: *What's helped you get started in your campus recreation career?*

A: (Jason) I'm just finishing my third year in this position. Before that I worked in resort recreation for a year. What I've really discovered is how important it is to get involved with professional organizations and try new programs. Students don't want to do the same old thing. Sharing new ideas with others and not being afraid to try some crazy ideas can really make a difference in how well you do your job.

(Willie): I'm finishing my seventh year in this position. Before that, I worked for a few years as an aquatics director with the YMCA. I agree with what Jason said and would only add that trying new things will not only keep your students, faculty, and staff happy but will make you look forward to your job every day!

Q: *You both mentioned new programs as being very important. Can you give some examples?*

A: (Willie) Some programs we do are just plain fun, and some might be a little more serious. Last year we tried a Belly Flop Contest and invited schools from around the state. It was a ton of fun and great competition for participants and spectators. On the other hand, we recognized that many people couldn't find the time to participate in our fitness programs. So, we partnered with an on-line fitness program called MobileFit. As soon as we did that, our fitness participation skyrocketed.

(Jason): I guess the one thing that comes to mind was something we started this year at the end of the fall semester when everyone needed to blow off some steam. We wanted to also get our dedicated runners out with some people who didn't run much, if at all. So one night at 11:00 we had an Underpants Run, where students, faculty and staff ran around campus in their underwear! It raised some eyebrows but everyone had a great time and now it will become an annual event.

(For further information about Virginia Wesleyan College's Campus Recreation program see http://www.vwc.edu/student_life/recreation/)

WHAT IS CAMPUS RECREATION?

Odds are you have come into contact with a campus recreation professional. Campus recreation professionals take on the challenge of providing fun and beneficial recreation programs for their target populations in ways that are similar to community recreation professionals. Community recreation is responsible for the leisure-time activities of the general public, but campus recreation's clients are predominately college or university students, faculty, and staff. Right now, over 11 million college students use their campus recreation facilities. More than two million students are part of college sport clubs and over a million intramural events are held every year (NIRSA, 2009). The National Intramural-Recreational Sports Association (NIRSA) has identified several goals for campus recreation programs. These include the provision of programs that enhance recruitment and retention, attract diverse groups such faculty, staff and students, serve personal needs that aid good mental and physical health, and assist academic units preparing students for a career in campus recreation.

How Did Campus Recreation Get Its Start?

Campus recreation traces its roots back to the earliest colleges in the United States. Phi Beta Kappa, now an honor society, was the first Greek-letter social organization with its founding at the College of William and Mary in 1776. The early 1800s then saw an increase of other fraternities with sororities following suit in the mid 1800s. This same period saw the first extramural event in 1852, when Harvard met Yale in a rowing race that is still held every year. Other events became formal intercollegiate competitions with baseball taking place in 1859 and football in 1869. During the same period, intramural events were held with the first recorded track meets appearing in 1870. As time progressed, and the value of student recreational activities was seen, both athletic and social programs continued their growth.

The early 20th century then saw the first campus recreation professionals hired as valued members of higher education communities. As World War I and II unfolded, and the value of rigorous physical training was better understood, physically active campus recreation programs increased in number. The post-war growth in student enrollment seen in the 1950s also produced a large increase in campus recreation programs (Mittelstaedt, et. al., 2006). At the same time, the first professional organization was formed. The 1970s and '80s saw this continued growth as coeducational participation increased as a result of Title IX and enhanced opportunities for women (McLean, Hurd, & Rogers, 2005). More recently, campus recreation has seen a boom period as schools rushed to complete increasingly elaborate recreation centers. This trend developed as schools found themselves facing increasing for students coupled with recognition of the value of recreation facilities not only in recruitment of students, faculty, and staff, but also in their being able to retain them. For the campus recreation professional, the start of a new century has seen unprecedented opportunities for professional employment and participation by all members of the college community.

Campus Recreation Today

Today we are witnessing an emphasis on campus recreation like never before. All areas of campus recreation are becoming fully integrated within the strategic plans of colleges and universities. The incredible investment in recreation facilities on many campuses is proof that schools have discovered the benefits of this career area. As campus recreation's value is better understood through on-going assessment of students its continued growth should continue for quite some time.

Goals and Roles: Before, During and After

Kevin Marbury, Director of Recreational Sports at Old Dominion University emphasizes the importance of campus recreation's accomplishments: "I realize every day that what we do in campus recreation is make a positive impact on students now and that impact will carry over for the rest of their lives" (personal communication, February 2, 2007).

Campus recreation is much more than unlocking the doors to the pool or posting a sign saying a softball league is forming. It's a comprehensive set of programs and facilities with goals designed to help the school, its students, employees, and alumni. Campus recreation works hand in hand with all areas on campus such as academic programs. Many professors will encourage participation in out-of-class activities that complement the in-class instruction. For example, a debate provided by your Student Activities Office between two candidates for your local mayoral election office might be tied to a political science class. Or perhaps a clinic on strength training provided by a Fitness Coordinator would be scheduled at a time when an exercise science class is studying that topic. These **co-curricular programs** help demonstrate how learning in the classroom applies to life now and later in the real world.

The following table illustrates the role campus recreation takes over the course of a student's life at a college or university. Campus recreation helps achieve some important goals before a student chooses what school to attend, after the first day of classes, and after graduation, campus recreation helps to achieve important goals.

TIME PERIOD	BENEFITS OF CAMPUS RECREATION
Before: High School	Increases attractiveness of college or university to prospective students. Promotes a sense of joining a community. Enhances a sense of inclusion for all types of students.
During: New Student	Aids in assimilation to the college community. Reinforces the decision to enroll. Aids retention during the critical first semester. Develops bonds within residence halls and between residents and commuters.
During: Established Student	Helps balance work/leisure needs. Helps with stress management and other wellness. Provides ongoing social opportunities. Allows students to socialize with faculty and staff. Increases academic performance by enhancing quality of life.
After: Alumni	Provides opportunities for alumni to return to campus. Some facilities, like fitness centers, may be used by alumni and generate revenue for school. Participation in campus recreation enhances alumni appreciation for the school and may lead to increased financial support.

Facilities

Recently, over a billion dollars was spent to build new campus recreation facilities (NIRSA 2006). The following schools completed new, award-winning recreation facilities:

RECENTLY COMPLETED CAMPUS RECREATION FACILITIES

School	Facility	Cost	Features
California State University Fullerton	Titan Recreation Center	$32 Million	Gymnasium, indoor running track, climbing and bouldering walls, fitness and multipurpose studios, racquetball courts, outdoor leisure pool

Springfield College	Fieldhouse and Wellness Center	$21.5 million	Four multiuse courts and a 200-meter track, 15,000-square-foot fitness center, campus recreation offices, climbing wall
Colorado School of Mines	Student Recreation Center	$21.1 million	Competition gymnasium, recreation gymnasium, multiple fitness areas, climbing wall, indoor pool, outdoor recreation program headquarters
Eastern Washington University	University Recreation Center	$20.4 million	Ice rink, sports pub, fitness center, indoor track, climbing wall
	Athletic and Recreation Center		Fitness center, racquetball courts, multipurpose court, elevated 1/8-mile track, poolside wet classroom

Management of these facilities will be the job of a campus recreation professional. Since any facility is only as good as the staff that supports it, an effective facility manager will need to address many aspects of facilities management, including: human resources, budget, maintenance, scheduling, and risk management. Looking more closely at just one of these, human resources, shows that the manager will need to recruit both full- and part-time staff and develop an annual training program. Since many recreation centers are staffed by student workers, a plan must also be in place to ensure that employees are available during breaks and the summer when most schools see fewer students on campus. Now, consider that students returning from one year to the next may expect a raise in pay or increased responsibility, and the manager will need a good performance appraisal system in place. Then, there are the day-to-day challenges that will pop up. The campus recreation professional needs to be flexible and love a challenge when the local high school comes to use the pool for a meet and minutes before a lifeguard has called in sick. Or, suppose a storm has produced a leak right over the basketball court hours before the intramural championship is scheduled to be played! Above all else, recreation center management takes a love of challenge, the ability to be flexible, and a desire to balance all the needs of participants, staff, and the facility.

CAREERS IN CAMPUS RECREATION

You'll find a number of professionals dedicated to enhancing the college experience for students inside all campus recreation facilities. Their life's work is to add something meaningful to the life satisfaction of students, faculty, and staff alike. A quick look at bluefishjobs.com, the online home of the National Intramural-Recreational Sports Association's career center, usually reveals openings in campus recreation in every state as well as international schools. Professionals from all levels of experience, be they graduate assistants just getting started or seasoned professionals ready to lead the biggest departments, are always needed. What makes this especially important to a student interested in campus recreation is the ability to start a career right out of college. Or it's also possible to pursue a master's degree while gaining experience as a graduate assistant in campus recreation. Students and new professionals can often gain specialized training in their specific area of campus recreation while working and become involved early in professional associations that further their career.

Passions

If you asked most campus recreation professionals what they liked most about their career, they'd probably share the same feelings as the professionals profiled at the beginning of this chapter. Each recognized their love for working with students, the role of recreation in making their campus a wonderful place to work, study, and live, and the impact their work has on student development. College students bring a constant feeling of energy, inquisitiveness, independence, determination, creativity, and passion to their leisure time activities. Campus recreation professionals love the college atmosphere, and working with students, faculty, and staff at their school. They like the pace of planning activities according to the school calendar, working long hours, and looking forward to school breaks when they can recharge! They also have a great deal of creativity and desire to give new ideas a try. Above all else, campus recreation professionals love working with students, get their satisfaction from seeing student growth, and know that their work is critical to making their school one that students want to attend, be a part of until graduation, and value as alumni.

To understand the work of professionals within all the varied areas of campus recreation, it's important to recognize what makes campus recreation professionals tick. College and university campuses are communities where a great deal of diversity typically is found. Students make friends from different parts of the country, different religions, different races, all of whom come to campus with a love for a variety of recreation and leisure interests. Campus recreation professionals accept the challenge of this great diversity and are driven by the desire to improve their campus so it's a fun place to study, work, and live. Critical to being successful at this is the ability to partner with people from across the campus. Campus recreation professionals understand that their jobs may have them partnering with the campus health service one day to provide a wellness program and then working with music majors next to co-host a concert. In fact, embracing a co-curricular philosophy means the campus recreation professional believes in the value of providing programs that complement classroom learning to drive home the importance of what a professor is teaching.

Campus Recreation Creativity

Bringing together groups from across campus is often the goal of campus recreation. Many schools including Notre Dame, Central Michigan, and Southern Illinois now hold cardboard boat regattas where clubs, dorms, and organizations compete to see whose cardboard boat can be navigated around a course before sinking (with students in it)! In fact, this activity was named one of the "101 things to do before you graduate" by *Sports Illustrated*. http://sportsillustrated.cnn.com/2007/sioncampus/05/09/graduate.midwest/index.html

---

Pay and Perks

There are some pay and perks that are similar for all campus recreation career areas. Entry-level salaries depend upon responsibilities, education, experience, region, and school budgets. Perks include flexible work hours and schedules that follow the academic year. You may work long hours during the fall and spring semesters, but you'll usually get a break after each semester is over. So, if the schedule you lived on when you were in college appeals to you, that's a plus. Reimbursed travel to professional conferences and workshops is often available. In addition, many schools will support you to obtain specific certifications that will help you do your job better as well as make you more marketable. Also, campus recreation facilities are normally available for use by employees and often their families as well.

Entry-level salaries in campus recreation are similar to those in public and commercial recreation and they will be roughly comparable to those entering the teaching profession in any particular region. Of course, assistant director and director positions have higher pay levels, which are commensurate with education and experience. Educational requirements vary slightly depending on the area of campus recreation. We'll discuss some specifics in the possibilities section.

Preparation

At a minimum, to be well prepared for a career in campus recreation, you will need a bachelor's degree with a major in an area of recreation and leisure services. This degree is critical in understanding how to determine participant needs, plan and conduct programs, manage your facility and human resources, and market your programs effectively. Key to preparing for a career in campus recreation is the experience you earn. Campus recreation offers many opportunities for student workers to serve as referees, assistants with promoting events, or perhaps belaying people on a climbing wall. At many schools, the campus recreation staff is filled with students! After gaining some experience through part-time work, the next step would be to complete an internship. These internships are intensive, typically semester-long experiences are an excellent way to gain a deeper understanding of the field and complete work that will show potential employers your value. Because the field is so diverse, you can intern at a school of your choice. For example, if you attend a large school, consider complementing your experience by interning at a small one. If you aren't sure what area of campus recreation to pursue, think about interning where your experience will allow you to rotate among many areas. Lastly, it's always a good idea to earn as many certifications as possible. Some such as First aid and CPR are useful in all areas. Others such as the Aquatic Facility Operator certification offered through the National Recreation and Park Association, or the Certified Personal Trainer offered by the American Council on Exercise or another certifying agency will increase your qualifications to work in specific areas of campus recreation.

Consider Graduate Assistantships

An excellent way to start your career in campus recreation is by continuing on with a graduate assistantship while earning your master's degree. Many schools use graduate assistants to work in campus recreation. In return for working 20-30 hours a week, you will receive a monthly stipend and often a waiver for your tuition. Graduate assistantships are listed at www.bluefishjobs.com and on each school's website. Don't wait too long, though. Most schools fill their assistantships early in the spring for the upcoming fall semester.

Discovery and Getting Experience

The best way to better understand what campus recreation is all about is to get a part-time job in campus recreation while you're in school. Most campus recreation programs are happy to employ students as office assistants, referees, instructors, and other positions. It's a great way to learn more about this area and earn a few extra dollars doing something you enjoy. Check with your campus recreation staff as well as your financial aid office.

Possibilities

There has probably never been a better time to be a campus recreation professional. More than ever before, schools view campus recreation as a critical element in making the college experience a satisfying one. This is evident through an increase in hiring as well as an increase in the variety of positions within campus recreation. While some schools, predominantly smaller ones, may still employ the "jack of all trades," many have turned to a staffing model that requires specialists to be responsible for the wide variety of recreation programs. Also, higher education has seen a dramatic escalation in the number of campus recreation facilities that have been built or are in the planning stages (Hignite 2006). With the competition for students increasing, schools are constructing ever more elaborate student centers, recreation centers, outdoor recreation areas, and similar facilities in an effort to attract and retain students.

As new facilities are created, it is the campus recreation professional who is responsible for facility operations. This provides an excellent opportunity for career growth. At the entry level, you may be expected to plan and implement recreation programs. As your career develops, there could be opportunities to become more involved with the highest levels of management. The figure below might help to illustrate a typical career progression.

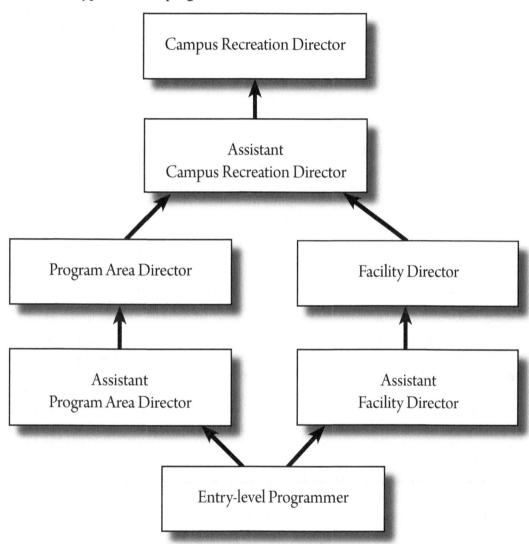

When professionals start a campus recreation career, they might be responsible for direct program development such as intramural sports. As a programmer, success will be judged on the number of participants in programs as well as participant satisfaction reports. Entry-level professionals design programs, market them, manage their budget, hire and train student assistants such as referees, oversee scheduling and field preparation, and basically complete all the steps required of any recreation programmer. If the professional's passion is for intramural sports, the next step may be to serve as an assistant director of intramural sports, eventually leading to a position as the director of intramural sports. In either of these higher level positions, the employee will take on increasing responsibility for oversight of programs, facilities, and staff. An alternative path for advancement is facility management. A professional may become interested in managing facilities, such as a student recreation center and its associated facilities (e.g., pool, intramural fields, ropes course, etc). Eventually, a campus recreation career path can continue until it reaches a position with responsibility for overseeing a complete campus recreation division or facility.

Campus Recreation is a broad career area, and there are several specialties you may want to consider. A few are described below, along with the passions, preparation, and possibilities for each area.

Intramural and Recreational Sports

It's the end of a long day in the classroom. You've worked hard all day and answered many questions when called upon. You were prepared for today's classes, and now you've got to start preparing for tomorrow. Assignments are coming due, and the end of the semester is coming quickly. You feel your stress building, but you know you've got an opportunity to blow off a little steam with friends. In a couple of hours, your intramural volleyball team will meet and take on . . . who knows? The preceding scenario might describe you, your professor, or someone else who attends your school. Intramural and recreational sports break down barriers to bring everyone together. Behind the scenes making this possible are the intramural or recreational sports staff.

While many schools are known for their intercollegiate sports teams, and have a great number of students who are intercollegiate athletes, intramural sports serve many more students than incollegiate sports every year. **Intramural sports** include all those activities where students compete against other students at their school. Sometimes they may even compete against intramural teams from other schools. In that case, the event is known as an **extramural sports**. Some schools use the classic term intramural sports, while others see their role as being broader and use **recreational sports**.

Regardless of the term used, let's go back to our example of the intramural volleyball league. Before this intramural league can begin its first game, the intramural sports professional must complete many steps, including:

- Determine start and end of the season.
- Market the league to develop interest.
- Recruit teams to play.
- Reserve volleyball courts.
- Schedule all games.
- Ensure that equipment is available.
- Recruit, train, schedule and handle payroll for officials.
- Record results, update standings, and oversee league progress.
- Re-schedule games that are cancelled.
- Repeat most of the steps above for playoffs!
- Award prizes.

Of course, within each step above, there are many smaller tasks to be completed. These campus recreation professionals must pay a great deal of attention to detail and have an infectious enthusiasm that will help recruit participants to team and individual events. For every sport that can be played by a college student, there's a league, tournament, or contest waiting to be organized.

Passions—Recreation programming, organization, fun, creativity, teamwork, sports, communication, competition, student and community development.

Pay and Perks—The national average for a Director of Campus Recreation is $61,670. (Chronicle, 2009). However, the value of this career field is much greater than any salary. The perks of working in campus recreation include the great availability of starting positions around the country, the excitement of ever-changing programs, following a school calendar, and plentiful opportunities to get involved with professional organizations such as the National Intramural Recreational Sports Association.

Preparation—Bachelor's degree in recreation or a related recreational sports field. Experience in intramural programming and management of sport clubs is essential. Becoming a Certified Park and Recreation Professional (CPRP) as defined by the National Recreation and Park Association is an excellent way to demonstrate entry-level knowledge of the profession.

Possibilities—There are excellent opportunities for mobility within campus recreation from this area. With colleges in every state, the number of potential employers is great. Additionally, this area provides many opportunities to gain experience in related fields and offices within higher education.

> ### Don't Forget Clubs!
>
> Schools are also increasingly emphasizing their club sport programs. These clubs range from the competitive and formal that will compete against other schools (extramural) to the fun and casual that will get together to share their common interest in an activity. A good example is Sam Houston State University, which offers the following **club sports:** martial arts, cycling, volleyball, paintball, dodgeball, bowling, baseball, inline hockey, hapkido, outdoor adventure, powerlifting, racquetball, rugby, soccer, tennis, ultimate frisbee, and wrestling (http://www.shsu.edu/~rca_www/club_sports/).

Student Activities

Keeping students happy outside of the classroom has been an increasing goal for every school because it aids in retention. **Student activities** are a part of campus recreation and include activities such as concerts, celebrations, cultural events, and assisting student clubs and organizations. Student activities are a critically important area because they have the capacity to reach such a broad cross-section of students. Also student activities are often co-curricular in nature; thus, the programs and activities are connected to material being covered in an academic course. The opportunities that co-curricular programs provide are not only supporting the academic mission but also the overall student development mission of the institution.

The student activities director is a very challenging but exciting position, because of the wide range of activities schools provide. One day the student activities director might be planning a homecoming parade, overseeing the details of a state or U.S. Senator speaking to political science students and members of the student government association, and before the day ends works on promoting a major rock concert to be held the next weekend. Clearly, if you work in student activities, you'll have plenty of variety.

Passions—Working with students and faculty, organizing special events, utilizing creativity, marketing programs, working with performers and agents.

Pay and Perks—For a director of student activities, the average salary is $54,931 (Chronicle 2009). Perks include working closely with faculty on co-curricular programs, exposure to the entertainment industry, and following a school calendar. There are also opportunities to be involved with professional organizations such as the National Association for Campus Activities.

Preparation—Bachelor's degree in recreation, student personnel, or higher education administration.

Possibilities—This position is often at the center of campus life, so the opportunity to make a significant impact on campus life is excellent. In doing so, you'd have the chance to partner with local performers and explore your creative interests. If your dream career includes producing events like concerts and festivals then the possibilities are endless (as long as your budget holds out)!

It's All About Variety!

Darton College in Georgia is one example of a school that offers a variety of programs through its student activities office. Here are a few: Welcome Back Party, Fun Flicks—Make your own video, Honors Day, Hypnotists, Magicians/Comedians/Ventriloquists, Fall Fling, Blizzard of Bucks Wild and Crazy Game Show, Darton Beach Party, Bring Your Own Banana Day—Free banana splits, One Hit Wonder—Make your own CD, Munch-a-Mania, Old Tyme Photos, Art Fairs, Distinguished Lectures Series, Cartoon Portraits, Peanut Boil, Fall Convocation (http://www.darton.edu/current/stu_aff/activites.php).

Fitness and Wellness

Campus recreation professionals often specialize in the area of fitness and wellness. This might include personal training, supervision of a fitness facility, or even providing wellness programs such as weight loss and smoking cessation. This area also requires specialized training and certification beyond a bachelor's degree. For the safety of participants, it is critical that fitness professionals hold recognized certifications in the areas they teach. The campus recreation professional overseeing fitness and wellness programs must have an outgoing personality with an endless sense of enthusiasm if he/she is going to attract and retain participants who might be out of shape. It's that person with the smiling face that students expect and want to see every day as they head for a workout.

Passions—Fitness, health promotion, working with participants of all fitness levels, desire to improve the health of others.

Pay and Perks—Salaries for full-time fitness and wellness coordinators are usually in the $30,000 range but of course depend on the size of the program. The main perk of this position is the ability to gain great satisfaction from aiding people in meeting their fitness and wellness goals. If you have an interest in wellness areas such as yoga, Pilates, weight loss, and the newest forms of fitness, then this area lets you explore all of those. Opportunities may also exist to work with a school's sports teams.

Preparation—Bachelor's degree in recreation, exercise science/physiology, health promotion. Fitness trainer certification through a recognized organization such as the American Council on Exercise or the American College of Sports Medicine.

Possibilities—This position has responsibility for impacting the health and wellness of all members of the college community. Of all the positions within campus recreation this one has the greatest potential for showing the direct impact of the services offered. In addition, services can be offered to employee family members so the reach of the fitness staff can extend well beyond students only.

Fitness: Beyond Lifting Weights

The University of Delaware is an excellent example of a school whose fitness opportunities extend well beyond traditional weightlifting. Some of the creative programs offered there include: kickboxing, power Pilates, UD step, weight training for women, yogilates, butts and guts, and cardio muscle (http://www.udel.edu/fitness/classes/index.html).

Aquatics

Like the campus recreation professional who specializes in fitness and wellness, aquatics staff working within campus recreation are also highly specialized. Beyond teaching aquatics-related skills, this professional might also work with outside groups, host events such as swim meets, be responsible for the maintenance and operation of an aquatic facility, and oversee a staff of lifeguards. Because of this, aquatic specialists also require training and certification beyond a bachelor's degree. More and more, aquatic facilities that mirror small waterparks are being added to schools. It isn't uncommon now to see waterslides and lazy rivers turning up on campus.

Passions—Teaching others to swim, aquatic fitness, management of aquatic facilities, working with intercollegiate and outside swim teams.

Pay and Perks—Salaries for full-time aquatics directors are usually in the $30,000 range, but of course depend on the size of the program and are often higher when there are more facilities to oversee. Besides the opportunity to work with a school's intercollegiate swimming team, another perk is the chance to assist local public and private swimming programs that may use your facility.

Preparation—Bachelor's degree in recreation, physical education, management. Specific training and certification related to aquatic facility management is also required. This includes the Aquatic Facility Operator's certification provided by the National Recreation and Park Association and the Certified Pool Operator provided by the National Swimming Pool Foundation; as well as training offered by the Red Cross covering lifeguarding and swimming and water safety certifications.

Possibilities—Aquatics can be a lifetime leisure pursuit. Aquatic professionals have the opportunity to provide programs for all age and fitness levels. As innovative facilities are added to schools, the aquatic professional has the opportunity to network with aquatic professionals from commercial waterparks and explore their practices through such organizations as the World Waterpark Association.

Swimming: Continued Popularity

According to the National Sporting Goods Association, in 2006, 56.5 million Americans went swimming two or more times. This places swimming as the second highest activity after "exercise walking" and has been the case for over a decade (http://www.nsga.org/public/pages/index.cfm?pageid=153).

Campus Aquatic Facilities: The Next Generation

Recent trends point to the continued growth of non-traditional aquatic facilities on campus. Schools are now adding features often seen at waterparks. Southern Methodist University's Dedman Center features an area called "The Falls," where students may sunbathe in and around an outdoor pool that doubles as a fountain.

Georgia Tech University's Crawford Pool complex includes not only a traditional 25-yard pool but also a current channel, free-form play area, 16-person spa, and 184-foot water slide! (http://www.campusrecreation.gatech.edu/facilities/aquaticscenter.php)

Outdoor Recreation

Many schools recognize the importance of promoting outdoor recreation opportunities so students can gain an appreciation for everything the local environment can provide. Whether students come from nearby or from around the country or world, outdoor recreation can open their eyes to activities they may have never known existed. A look at the outdoor recreation programs offered by colleges and universities shows a broad variety that includes camping, hiking, snowboarding, triathlon, wakeboarding, mountain biking, kayaking, rock climbing, ultimate Frisbee, rodeo, sailing, and scuba diving. With an increasing concern for the environment on a national level, outdoor recreation on campus is seeing a great resurgence of interest. Professionals offering outdoor recreation opportunities may outsource their leadership to companies with the technical expertise required. If not, this specialty requires both proficiency in leading a program and also requires training in first aid and risk management specific to activities that take place in remote settings.

Passions—Camping, outdoor leadership, travel, climbing, mountain biking, canoeing, skiing, backpacking, sailing, surfing, and other outdoor pursuits.

Pay and Perks—Full-time positions in outdoor recreation aren't as numerous as others in campus recreation. Full-time salaries may be comparable to those in fitness and wellness. The main perk to this position is the chance to make your work what other people consider their recreation!

Preparation—Bachelor's degree in recreation, outdoor leadership or recreation, environmental education. Specific training and certification related to outdoor pursuits and safety are required. This may include wilderness first aid certification, canoe and kayak instructor training provided by the American Canoe Association, and various instructor courses offered by the National Outdoor Leadership School.

Possibilities—Outdoor recreation continues to grow. According to the National Sporting Goods Association, participation in 2006 activities such as backpacking, boating, hiking, and skiing all increased from the year before. Schools also recognize the importance of outdoor recreation and see it as a way to better connect students with the community and to enhance retention (http://www.nsga.org/public/pages/index.cfm?pageid=149).

First-year Orientation Programs and Outdoor Recreation

For over 20 years, Harvard University has offered a First-year Orientation Program (FOP). This voluntary program includes six day trips to Maine, New Hampshire, and Vermont. It's described as an "introduction to Harvard that takes place in the woods" (http://www.fas.harvard.edu/~fop/).

The Outdoor Program, run by recent Everest summiter Brien Sheedy, takes 25 percent of freshmen on orientation adventures such as nine-day canoe trips. Trips like kayaking and ice climbing are offered most weekends. Water and avalanche rescue are among the clinics offered.

At the University of the Puget Sound, nine-day freshman orientation programs are offered that take students hiking, snorkeling, swimming, and sailing. This program also was cited in the *Chronicle of Higher Education* along with programs at Bemidji State University, University of California at Santa Cruz, and Reed College that include outdoor recreation opportunities

(http://chronicle.com/che-data/articles.dir/articles-36.dir/issue-02.dir/02a03701.htm).

Double-Dipping

If you have an interest in an area of outdoor recreation, you should speak to your campus recreation director. It isn't unusual for schools to hire students as assistants during programs and on trips. This is a great way to participate in your activity, gain experience, and perhaps be paid as well.

Facility Management

The start of the 21st Century has shown a significant growth in the renovation of existing campus recreation facilities as well as the construction of new ones. This includes a trend toward integrated campus recreation facilities that include elements of a student center, athletic facility, food service area, library, and wellness center (*Recreation Management*, 2006). These mega-centers seek to unite many student service areas on campus. As the importance of recreation facilities on a campus is increasingly recognized as a factor related to school selection and retention, so too, has the importance of facility managers increased. Campus recreation professionals also specialize in the management of their facilities so they can be used by students, faculty, staff, families, and even members of the local community. In some areas, the campus recreation facility also doubles as a community recreation center when it hosts swim meets, basketball leagues, or even softball tournaments. The significance of allowing local agencies to use a campus recreation facility is that doing so may generate revenue to offset the cost of operating the facility and aid in the town and gown relationship between a school and its local community. Facility managers must understand budgeting, personnel management, risk management, maintenance, scheduling, and the other functions related to managing a complex organization.

Passions—Budgeting, personnel management, risk management, maintenance, scheduling, complex organizations, planning, marketing.

Pay and Perks—Salaries for facility managers depend upon the size and number of facilities and range from $40,000 to $60,000 for experienced managers.

Preparation—Bachelor's degree in recreation, or a management-related field. Specific training and aptitude in personnel management and facility maintenance are essential.

Possibilities—As the number of campus recreation centers being constructed grows, so too, do the opportunities for employment in this area. Because college campuses have a diverse variety of facilities, there's an excellent opportunity to gain experience in managing other types of facilities such as athletic and educational facilities.

Facility Management: More than Buildings at East Carolina University

When you think of recreation facilities, you might think only of buildings. East Carolina University is a great example of a school that is moving beyond the traditional recreation center. Its student recreation center already houses aquatic facilities, racquetball/squash courts, fitness and aerobic areas, and gymnasium areas. In order to expand its offerings to students, the University is developing the North Recreational Complex.

Located 10 minutes from the center of campus, it will include eight multipurpose fields that can be set up for soccer, flag football, lacrosse, ultimate frisbee and rugby. The complex also includes a six-acre lake for fishing and boating, a field house, and a beach area (http://www.ecu.edu/cs-studentlife/crw/facilities/north_complex/images/Close_up.jpg).

Moving Over to Move Up

Working within higher education provides excellent opportunities to become involved with the work of a variety of different campus divisions. As an intramural sports director you might work on a retention project with the admissions and residence life offices encouraging first-year students to join an intramural team as soon as they get to campus. That will help them feel a part of the community right away. This will also give you an idea of how schools operate and what other areas might interest you. It isn't unusual for a career progression to look like this:

Graduate Assistant ->Intramural Programmer-> Assistant Director of Recreational Sports -> Director of Campus Recreation-> Associate Dean-> Dean!

SUMMARY OF CAMPUS RECREATION, LEISURE, AND INTRAMURAL CAREER POSSIBILITIES

Career	Passions	Pay and Perks	Preparation	Possibilities
Intramural and recreational sports	Recreation programming organization, fun, creativity, teamwork, sports, communication, competition, student and community development	Entry-level salaries are typical of new grads but may rise significantly according to size of campus/ recreation program.	Bachelor's degree in recreation or a related sports field. Experience in intramural programming and management of sport clubs is essential.	Excellent opportunities for mobility as schools continue to increase their intramural and recreational sports offerings.
Student activities	Working with students and faculty, organizing special events, utilizing creativity, marketing programs, working with performers and agents	Salaries tend to be average to below average for new grads. Salary depends on program size and budget.	Bachelor's degree in recreation, student, personnel, or higher education administration	Because this area usually partners with other campus departments as well as off-campus agencies, there are good opportunities to move up into other positions in higher education and entertainment.

Career	Passions	Pay and Perks	Preparation	Possibilities
Fitness and wellness	Fitness, health promotion, working with participants of all fitness levels, desire to improve the health of others	Typical of new grad salaries. Opportunities for private practice may also be available.	Bachelor's degree recreation, exercise science/physiology, health promotion. Certification through recognized organization such as the American Council on Exercise or the American College of Sports Medicine.	Increasing concerns for student wellness will provide increasing employment opportunities.
Aquatics	Teaching others to swim, aquatic fitness, management of aquatic facilities, working with intercollegiate and outside swim teams	Typical of new grad salaries but will increase or decrease depending on the size of facility and amount of revenue generated.	Bachelor's degree and specific training related to aquatic facility management and instruction	At present, somewhat limited, but higher level management opportunities are increasing as aquatic facilities are added domestically and internationally.
Outdoor recreation	Camping, outdoor leadership, travel, climbing, mountain biking, canoeing, skiing, backpacking, sailing, surfing, and other outdoor pursuits	Typically low at the entry level.	High school diploma to bachelor's degree. Training and certification related to an outdoor specialty is necessary as is experience in outdoor leadership	Entry-level opportunities are plentiful, as are internships. Higher level management positions are limited and sought after
Facility management	Budgeting, personnel management, risk management, maintenance, scheduling, complex organizations, planning, marketing	Entry-level Salaries are typical of new grads but may increase according to facility size and budget.	Bachelor's degree and experience working within recreation facilities as well as an ability to manage multiple tasks	An ongoing increase in campus recreation facilities has created an increased demand for facility managers at all levels.

FUTURE OPPORTUNITIES, ISSUES, AND CHALLENGES

The field of campus recreation has changed over time to meet the changing needs of college students. While the future of campus recreation is especially bright with the increased understanding in how it aids in the recruitment, retention, and long-term growth of students, there are still challenges that must be met. If you choose a career in campus recreation, expect the seven topics described below to garner increasing attention:

1) **Technology:** Technological development occurs at such a brisk pace that equipment seen as state of the art one year may be seen as old very quickly. Schools will be challenged to provide the budget necessary to continually keep up with technological developments.

2) **Risk Management:** The growth in adventure sports such as snowboarding, mountain biking, rock climbing, and white water kayaking is occurring at a time when schools want to minimize their exposure to costly personal injury lawsuits. Campus recreation professionals will be challenged to provide exciting programs with an element of risk while ensuring the safety for their participants.

3) **24-7:** While campus recreation has never taken place strictly between 9-5, there's an increasing need for programs early in the morning and late at night. As is true in other recreation professions, other people's leisure time is the campus recreation professional's work time. This means that evening and weekend work can often be the norm.

4) **Non-traditional aged students:** As the country ages so too do our campuses. Many schools have seen an increasing number of students outside of the traditional 18-22 year old age range. This will place an emphasis on providing programs for specific age groups as well as creating new guidelines that encourage participation across the lifespan.

5) **Innovation:** Within every area of campus recreation is a never-ending stream of new products, programs, and practices. The area of fitness alone has seen the popularity of strength machinery that complements free weights explode until the equipment choices are now staggering. A decade ago, Pilates classes were unheard of. Today they continue to grow and have evolved into Pilates Fusion, which adds the use of free weights. As innovation continues, campus recreation professionals will need to be diligent to keep abreast of the newest opportunities.

6) **Obesity and Sedentary Living:** The national trends are alarming. Childhood obesity and a lack of exercise have increased dramatically. With much of campus recreation focused upon activity, it will be an increasing challenge to motivate participants to try to continue activities that may be perceived as causing some discomfort.

7) **Assessment:** Schools are under increasing pressure to demonstrate what students are learning. Regional accrediting agencies have moved schools into an era of outcome-based assessment to document how both academic and non-academic areas of campus are functioning. For campus recreation, this means measuring not only the number of participants but also the benefits they,

and the school, receive from programs. This has provided campus recreation professionals with an opportunity to make clear the tremendous benefits of their work to recruitment, retention, and alumni loyalty.

RESOURCES AND GETTING INVOLVED

Professional Organizations

Association for College Unions International
www.acui.org
An organization of campus union/center and student activities professionals

Association for Experiential Education
www.aee.org
Promotes and develops experiential education with a focus upon outdoor education

Association for Outdoor Recreation and Education
www.aore.org
Provides networking and advocacy opportunities for both students and professionals in the field of outdoor recreation/education as it relates to not-for-profit agencies.

National Intramural-Recreational Sports Association
www.nirsa.org/
An organization of professionals and students that promotes quality intramural and recreational sports opportunities through education and the networking.

National Swimming Pool Foundation
www.nspf.com/
Provides research, education, and certification opportunities for aquatics professionals.

National Association for Campus Activities
www.naca.org
Assists student activities professionals through education and opportunities to discover and develop new programs.

National Association of Sports Officials
www.naso.org/
The largest sports officials organization that addresses education and training of officials at all educational levels.

National Recreation and Park Association
www.nrpa.org
Dedicated to the advancement of public parks and recreation opportunities, this organization provides numerous educational and professional development opportunities.

Wheelchair Sports USA
www.wsusa.org
Assists in the development of sproting opportunities for athletes 7-21 with physical disabilities.

Certifications, Licenses

Certified Park and Recreation Professional (CPRP)
http://www.nrpa.org/Content.aspx?id=412
The CPRP demonstrates entry-level knowledge within the broad field of parks and recreation with a focus upon programming, management, and facilities operation.

Fitness Certifications
http://www.acefitness.org/ American Council on Exercise
http://www.nasm.org/ National Academy of Sports Medicine
http://www.acsm.org/ American College of Sports Medicine
There are many certifications within the area of fitness. It is important to select those from recognized agencies with a quality history. The three listed here are well-regarded.

Aquatic Facility Operator
http://www.nrpa.org/afo/
This certification demonstrates knowledge of pool operations to include areas such as safety, risk reduction, sanitation, and overall management.

Certified Pool Operator
http://www.nspf.org/FAQ.html
This certification also focuses upon pool operations. On-line learning opportunities are available.

Wilderness First Aid
http://wfa.net/
This certification focuses on providing first aid beyond the trail-head, and it is an excellent addition for anyone pursuing a position in outdoor recreation and trip leadership.

Continuing Education
http://www.nirsa.org/Content/NavigationMenu/Education/
NationalSchoolofRecreationalSportsManagement/NSRSM.htm
This is one example of continuing education opportunities led by recognized professionals working in the field that will help you further develop skills in intramural and recreational sports.

Where to Get Experience

The best way to get involved with campus recreation is to meet the professionals and students that work in campus recreation now. Your school may list part-time job opportunities in campus recreation in the student employment office. Another great way to become involved besides networking on your own campus is to check the excellent online resources at the National Intramural-Recreational Sports Association. Just go to www.nirsa.org and click on "students" to find scholarship information, student newsletters, resume and interview tips and more.

CONCLUSION

If you like the atmosphere of the college campus, want a flexible work schedule that just might alternate between frenzied and relaxed, enjoy serving students, faculty, and staff, and have a creative side that is willing to give new ideas a try, then campus recreation might be a good career choice. While there are challenges present, the future certainly looks bright for this area, and there is every reason to believe that the start of the 21st century is seen as an era where campus recreation is valued more than ever before.

FOR FURTHER INVESTIGATION

For More Research

1. Check the website of three colleges or universities of similar size to your school. Now check the website of a school with more students, and one with fewer students. How do their campus recreation programs and facilities compare to your school?
2. Pick one certification that would help you be better qualified for a career in campus recreation. What's required to earn that certification?
3. Go to the websites for the National Association for Campus Activities and National Intramural-Recreational Sports Association. What events do they sponsor that would help you as you started your career in campus recreation?

Active Investigation

1. Pick a campus recreation program at your school. What benefits does it provide? What campus recreation programs are offered at your school?
2. Interview 10 students and determine the following:
   - Do they participate in campus recreation programs?
   - If so, what types of programs?
   - If not, why not?
   - What are some campus recreation programs they would like to see offered at your school?

3. Volunteer to assist with a special event offered by your student activities office. What tasks were completed by the staff to provide this event?
4. Interview Activity: Select a campus recreation professional at your school. Use the questions below to discover more about what they do. Refer to the Informational Interview instructions under "Active Investigation" in chapter 2 for more information before conducting your interview.

   1. What is the title of your position?
   2. What are your responsibilities?
   3. What responsibilities do you like most and least?
   4. What type of personality is needed to be effective in campus recreation?
   5. What are your work hours? Does this change during the year?
   6. Does your job have a set routine or does it change frequently?
   7. If you could add one campus recreation facility on your campus, what would it be and who would work there?
   8. What advice would you have for someone preparing for a career in campus recreation?

Recommended Reading

Each of the following book chapters and articles provides an understanding of the role of campus recreation within higher education, skills needed, programs offered, and the benefits provided.

Barcelona, B., & Ross, C. (2004). An analysis of the perceived competencies of recreational sport administrators. *Journal of Park and Recreation Administration, 22*(54), pp. 25-42.

Fred Leafgren, & Elsenrath, Dennis E. (Eds.). (1986). The role of campus recreation programs in institutions of higher education. *New Directions for Student Services*, Volume, Issue 34, pages 3-17.

Belch, H., Gebel, M., & Mass, G. (2001). Relationship between student recreation complex use, academic performance, and persistence of first-time freshmen. *NASPA Journal*, Volume 32, Issue 2, pp. 254-268.

Haynes, D., & Fortman, T. (2008). *The College Recreational Sports Learning Environment. Recreational Sports Journal,* Volume 32, Issue 1, pp. 52-61.

NIRSA. (2008). *Campus recreation: Essentials for the professional.* Champaign, IL: Human Kinetics.

Recreational Sports Journal: http://hk.humankinetics.com/rsj/journalAbout.cfm

These two websites contain up-to-date information related to student activities and recreational sports:

NIRSA Know
http://www.nirsa.info/know/2009/07/index.html

Campus Activities Programming Magazine
http://www.naca.org/MediaCenter/PagesCampusActivitiesProgrammingMagazine.
aspx
This website contains the latest job listings in campus recreation. It provides an excellent look at the knowledge, skills and abilities employers seek.

Current Job Opportunities in Campus Recreation
http://www.bluefishjobs.com/

REFERENCES

Chronicle of Higher Education. *Median Salaries of College Administrators by Job Category and Type of Institution, 2008-9* Retrieved August 29, 2009, from http://chronicle.com/article/Median-Salaries-of-College/47062/

Hignite, K. (2006). Sweat Equity. *Business Officer 40,* 29-33.

Larson, D. (2006) State of the Industry. *Recreation Management 7,* 32-45.

McLean, D.D., Hurd, A.R., & Rogers, N.B. (2005) Kraus' Recreation and Leisure in Modern Society. Sudbury, MA: Jones and Bartlett.

Mittelstaedt, R., Roberston, B., Russell, K., Byl, J., Temple, J., & Ogilvie, L. (2006). Unique Groups. In Human Kinetics (Ed.), Introduction to Recreation and Leisure (pp. 197-228). Champaign, IL: Human Kinetics.

NIRSA (2009). *NIRSA's Rich History.* Retrieved August 30, 2009 from http://www.nirsa.org/Content/NavigationMenu/AboutUs/History/History.htm

"

Sport is the focus of what we do—but what we do is about more than just sports. We use sport to make a difference in the lives of the people we serve.

— **KEVIN CUMMINGS**
Executive Director
Massachusetts Amateur Sports Foundation

"

9

Sport Management and Sports Teams

ROBERT J. BARCELONA
Clemson University

FOCUS QUESTIONS

Q: *I really love to play sports, does that mean I would like a sports management career?*

A: Students who are interested in sport management need to be interested in both sport and management. Loving sports isn't enough. Sport management is a career that requires professional preparation and a specific set of competencies. Read the following questions as well as the rest of the chapter and see if a career in sport management might appeal to you!

Q: *Does the business side of sport appeal to you? Are you interested in sales, marketing, promotions, and events?*

A: If the business side of sport appeals to you then you may want to seek a job on the business and sport performance side of sport management. Most entry-level positions in professional sports tend to be in sales, corporate relations/sponsorships, or community relations and marketing.

Q: *Does working directly with people participating in sports activities appeal to you? Do you enjoy programming, scheduling tournaments and policy implementation?*

A: Most positions in recreational sports, interscholastic sports, and youth sports, are focused on program development and leadership. If you work in this aspect of sport management you will be hands on with the actual sport activity.

Q: *Are you okay with working long hours?*

A: In professional sports and intercollegiate athletics, it's not unusual to arrive in the office at 8:00 a.m. and not leave until 11:00 p.m. or later during a home game. In recreational sports, contests often take place at non-traditional times, such as at night or on weekends, to accommodate participants. This means sport managers are working while others are playing.

Q: *Would you like change and diversity in your job?*

A: While sport management has core competencies that are fairly specific, most professionals are asked to wear many different hats. The constant change of duties is one of the things sport managers really like about their jobs! Read the profiles below to see what professionals in the field think!

KEY TERMS

Sport management   Commercial sector
Sport participation   Sport business
Sport performance   Sport programming
Management skills   Resources/venues
Public sector   Athlete/player development
Not for profit sector   Youth sport

PROFILE 1: COULD THIS BE YOU?

KEVIN CUMMINGS is the Executive Director of the Massachusetts Amateur Sports Foundation. Kevin oversees two multisport festivals, as well as five sport and educational programs. As Executive Director, he is responsible for all aspects of this amateur sport organization, including the following:

- staffing
- funding
- marketing and promotions
- sport and program operations
- policy development

Kevin began working full time in the field of sport management in 1984. He is passionate about his job, and took the time to tell us what he does.

Q: *Kevin, can you tell about what you do in your job?*

A: I oversee a large sport organization, one of the largest amateur, multisport athletic events in Massachusetts. I'm ultimately responsible for staffing, funding, promotion, operations, bookkeeping, kicking the copier, dropping mail off—you name it. I can tell you that each day is different, and the end of the day usually looks different than I thought it would when the day began.

Q: *That sounds exciting—but what does this have to do with sports?*

A: Sport is the focus of what we do, but what we do is about more than just sports. We use sport to make a difference in the lives of the people we serve—whether that means providing opportunities to showcase talented athletes, promoting good sports through our sportsmanship program, providing fitness and physical activity opportunities, offering scholarship and education programs, or enhancing the careers of our staff and volunteers. In this job, it's good to love sports, but the job is about more than just that.

Q: *What advice could you give someone thinking about a career in sport management?*

A: Get experience. Start now—go out and volunteer with a sport organization, build your resume. It's about more than just being a former athlete. You need to learn how to manage events, work with people, multi-task. Do what is required to make it happen, and don't wait. It's not too early—my best interns are the ones who have volunteered for me for four years, and our interns have gone on to jobs in professional football, college athletics, minor league baseball, and amateur sport. They got where they wanted to go because they got experience working in the sport industry while they were in school.

Q: *Great advice! Last question – what do you love most about your career?*

A: I love telling people about what I do. When I tell them that I run the MASF/ Bay State Games, their response always is, "Is that really a job? You actually get paid to do that?" People are always amazed that I am able to work in this job and make a living doing it. I like making a difference in people's lives. I'm proud of our success stories. Like one of our former baseball players who played in the Bay State Games. The exposure he received from our program got him a scholarship to play in college, and that opened up doors. He was recently drafted by the Washington Nationals. There are literally thousands of stories like that from former participants, volunteers, and interns.

For more information on the Massachusetts Amateur Sports Foundation and Bay State Games, go to http://www.baystategames.org.

PROFILE 2: COULD THIS BE YOU?

AMBER RADZEVICH is the Assistant Athletic Diector for Marketing and Communications in the Department of Intercollegiate Athletics at the University of New Hampshire (UNH). She is primarily responsible for the marketing and promotion of seven ticketed NCAA Division I sports, as well as game day promotions, themed events, and managing corporate partnership contracts. Amber works closely with students. She is responsible for the Cat Crew Internship program, and is the liaison for cheerleading, the mascot, and athletic bands.

Amber has worked professionally in intercollegiate athletics since 2004. She recently gave us the inside scoop on her job and what it takes to work in this segment of the sport industry.

Q: *It sounds like you have a lot of responsibility in your job, Amber. Is that a good thing?*

A: Definitely! It is what I love about this career. No two days are exactly the same, and there is always something to be excited about. In this job, I get to wear a lot of hats, and do different things, like marketing, game day promotions, and working with our alumni and corporate partners. I even sing the National Anthem before games sometimes!

Q: *That is a lot of hats! Are there any challenges that come with so much responsibility?*

A: It's hard to stay balanced sometimes. We work hard all year, but between September and March, I'm busy during the day, most weekends, and late at night. But I love coming to work, and this doesn't feel like a job. We're a smaller department, so we have a real family environment and a feeling of connectedness.

Q: *How did you get interested in a career doing sports marketing and promotions?*

A: I was student athlete (women's soccer), and I was really active outside of my team, too. I also had a lot of writing experience with the school newspaper. I became co-president of the student athlete advisory committee (SAAC), and that leadership role allowed me to practice many of the skills that I need for this job.

Q: *So there was a natural connection between your out-of-class experiences and sports marketing?*

A: Absolutely. Being a student athlete was helpful, but it was my writing experience and my leadership role with SAAC that allowed me to develop the skills needed for this job.

Q: *You also oversee the Cat Crew Internship program, which provides opportunities for college students to get real-world experience in intercollegiate athletics. What advice would you give to prospective students who are interested in this career setting?*

A: Take every opportunity to get involved, whether the opportunities are paid or unpaid. I'm looking for students who are creative, confident, and well-spoken. Be able to sell yourself; if you can't sell yourself, how are you going to be able to sell a team? I like to see interns have a foundation or some experience with sports, but I also want to see students expose themselves to new and different experiences, too. I like students who have a willingness to learn.

Q: *Great advice, Amber. One last question: how do you make a difference through your job?*

A: By helping students have positive experiences. Cat Crew gives that to students who want to learn about the sport industry, and get involved in sport marketing. But my job also helps create positive experiences for student athletes. Helping increase our attendance rate by 40% for women's hockey, for example, makes the game-day experience better for both the players and fans. Working with our corporate partners to design promotions that achieve their marketing objectives and improve the fan experience also makes a difference.

For more information on the University of New Hampshire Wildcats, visit http://www.unhwildcats.com. Job and internship opportunities in intercollegiate athletics are often posted at http://ncaa.thetask.com/market/jobs/browse.php.

THE WIDE WORLD OF SPORT MANAGEMENT

Sport is a significant component of our social fabric. Hundreds of thousands—and in many cases, millions—of people involve themselves in sport activities, either through active participation in recreational sports, or through watching or following the athletic exploits of others. Sport is a multibillion dollar industry that is global in scope. It is connected to many of our social systems, including education, the economy, public health, the media, domestic and international politics, and community development.

Consider the following statistics, and think about what is involved in providing and managing these sport experiences for the hundreds of thousands (and millions) of people who are taking part in them:

- Over 17 million spectators attended a game at a National Football League stadium in 2005 (Sports Business Research Network, 2007);
- Approximately 40 million children and adolescents in the United States (Petitpas, Cornelius, Van Raalte, & Jones, 2005) and 2.2 million in Canada (Kremarik, 2000) participate in organized youth sports programs each year;
- Over seven million high school students participated in an interscholastic sport in the United States in 2004-05 (National Federation of State High School Associations, 2007);
- 385,000 college students participated in an NCAA-sponsored sport in 2004-05 (National Collegiate Athletic Association, 2007);
- Approximately 25 million people played one or more rounds of golf in 2006 (National Sporting Goods Association, 2007);
- Over 15 million people attended a Minor League baseball game in 2005 (Sports Business Research Network, 2007);
- Over 500,000 Americans of all ages participate in State Games (National Congress of State Games, 2007);
- 42.7 million Americans held memberships in sport and fitness clubs in 2007 (IHRSA, 2007)

Sport management refers to the professional career of planning, organizing, leading, and controlling sport events, programs, personnel, and facilities. Sport management is incredibly wide in scope—consider all the various images presented in the break-out box below.

Images of Sport Management

When you think of sport management, which of the following images come to mind?

- Professional sports played by high-paid, talented athletes for the entertainment of spectators
- Grassroots sport programs that help to build interest in a particular sport activity
- Big-time college athletics events, like the NCAA basketball tournament or the football Bowl Championship Series
- After-school intramural sport programs and sport clubs
- Multimillion dollar stadiums and arenas
- Community-based sport and fitness facilities
- Sport programs that are designed to develop and showcase athletic talent
- Sport programs that are designed to build confidence, increase fitness levels, and expose participants to a range of positive outcomes
- Major international sport competitions, like the Olympics or the Pan-American Games

- Sport opportunities for disabled athletes, like the Paralympics or Northeast Passage's Athlete Development Center
- Sport-related businesses that are profit-focused
- Sport programs and facilities, which are available to the widest array of participants, regardless of their ability to pay

All of these images are associated with careers in sport management. It is important to recognize that the sport industry is a wide and complex career landscape.

History of Sport Management

The roots of sport management can be traced all the way back to the days of Roman sports. Even in ancient times, people were responsible for planning and presenting large-scale sporting events for the entertainment of the populace. In the modern era, sport management as we know it can be traced back to England, with the popularity of thoroughbred racing and the development of governance structures designed to organize and manage the growth of the sport (Masteralexis, Barr, & Hums, 2005). The staging of the modern Olympic Games, beginning in the late 19th century, the growth of professional sports leagues and tournaments around the same time, and the increasing popularity of intercollegiate athletics (particularly college football) laid the foundation for the professionalization of sport management. In addition, the growth of organized youth sports, intramural sports in colleges and universities, and a growing concern with physical fitness helped to illuminate the importance of participation-based sport. As a response to the growing need for educated sport professionals, the first academic program in sport management was started at Ohio University in 1964. Since then, the popularity of sport management as an academic discipline and as a viable profession has continued to grow.

Sport Management Today

Today, hundreds of colleges and universities offer academic preparation and degree programs in sport and/or recreation management at both the undergraduate and graduate levels. The body of knowledge in sport management draws on a variety of academic disciplines, including kinesiology and sport sciences, business and management, and recreation and leisure studies (Jamieson & Toh, 2000). This makes sport management an interdisciplinary profession. One of the strengths of sport management is that professionals can work in a variety of career settings. The sections that follow will help you understand the job settings that are most interesting to you.

Sport Management Philosophies

Chances are good that if you have read this far, you probably have a passion for sport. Having a passion for sport is important, and it is a good first step toward a career in sport management. However, it's important to carefully consider what your interests in sport are, because not all sport management positions are the same.

Sport management professionals are involved in managing a wide range of sport programs, services, and venues. These opportunities exist along a continuum that focuses on sport participation on one end and sport performance on the other (Coakley, 2004). Think about your interests in sport, and consider your passions and talents. If you are interested in designing and managing sport programs for the primary purpose of encouraging active participation in sport, then career settings such as youth and amateur sport, sport and fitness clubs, resorts, interscholastic sport, or intramural sport may be right for you. If, on the other hand, your interest is in managing and marketing sport opportunities primarily focused on elite athletes, or staging sport events for the purposes of entertaining spectators, then career settings such as professional sport, intercollegiate athletics, sport management and marketing agencies, or National Governing Bodies/National Sport Organizations might be a good fit (see Figure 9.1).

FIGURE 9.1: PARTICIPATION-PERFORMANCE CONTINUUM

Participation
Focus: designing and managing sport programs for the primary purpose of encouraging active participation in sport

Performance
Focus: managing and marketing sport opportunities primarily for elite athletes or staging sport events for the purpose of entertaining spectators

Youth sport
Intramural sport
Sport and fitness clubs

Interscholastic sport
State Games

Professional sport
Intercollegiate sport
Sport Management and
  Marketing Firms
National Governing
  Bodies/National Sport
  Organizations

This continuum concept can help provide sport managers with different philosophical frameworks to work from. Providing opportunities for sport participation includes developing programs that encourage **sport participation** regardless of ability, age, sex, or other characteristics and is based on the idea that sport has the potential to yield a variety of benefits to individual participants and their wider communities. Well-developed programs and facilities that enable wide participation in sport are justified based on their ability to improve health and well-being, reduce disease, contribute to cognitive learning, enhance social integration, and stimulate economic development, among others. In many ways, increasing opportunities for sport participation is not an end in itself, but it is a means for a sport manager to work toward achieving broader individual and societal goals.

Sport managers who are concerned with **sport performance** are generally focused on skill development and talent identification. The primary emphasis in this case is on developing skill, assembling talent, achieving elite performances, and entertaining spectators. The ends in this case could be winning championships, creating national pride, building fan loyalty, and/or enhancing revenue streams.

Regardless of where your interests lie, it is important to realize that careers in the sport industry combine both sport and management. The concept that people may gloss over is **management skills**, meaning that sport managers must be passionate about the business and management-related tasks that are associated with staging or providing the sport experience. While sport serves as the backdrop for the industry, it should be no surprise that most of the day-to-day job responsibilities of sport managers focus on critical knowledge areas such as management, financing, event planning, marketing, legality, governance, and research, among others (Barcelona & Ross, 2005).

Sport Management Sectors

Sport management career settings are located within all three major sectors of the economy, including the public sector, not-for-profit sector, and commercial sector.

Generally speaking, sports management jobs in the **public sector** refer to government-provided or -sponsored sport opportunities, such as municipal parks and recreation departments, school athletic departments, municipal sport councils or sport tourism bureaus, or Armed Forces sport and fitness programs in the United States. Governments may also fund or subsidize sport stadium or arena construction, maintenance, and operations (refer to the chapters on Community-Based Recreation and Armed Forces Leisure Services for more details).

Sport management jobs in the **not-for-profit sector** and in private sport organizations operate in the public's interest, yet do so outside the direct control of government. Many not-for-profit sport organizations exist to provide services to members, or to serve particular constituencies, such as sport National Governing Bodies (in the United States), Ys, grassroots youth sport organizations, or State Games (in some States) (refer to the chapter on Recreation in Non-Profit Organizations for more details).

The **commercial sector** consists of sport organizations that exist to make a profit for their owners or shareholders. Commercial sport enterprises can include professional sport organizations, commercial sport and fitness clubs, resorts, sporting goods manufacturers, or sport management and marketing firms. Table 9.1 shows the relationship between sport management career settings and the management sectors that they generally fall under.

TABLE 9.1
SELECTED SPORT MANAGEMENT OPPORTUNITIES BY MANAGEMENT SECTOR

Public Sector	Not-for-Profit Sector	Commercial Sector
Definition:	Definition:	Definition:
Government-sponsored sport and recreation services, primarily at the federal, state/provincial, and local levels in the United States and Canada.	Sport and reccreation organizations that generally operate in the public's interest, but do so outside the direct control of the government.	Sport organizations that exist to make a profit for their owners or shareholders.
Municipal parks and recreation agencies	Private, not-for-profit community organizations	Professional sport
Armed Forces MWR programs	Local community sport organizations	Commercial sport and fitness organizations
State games (in selected states)	State games (in selected states)	Sport management and marketing firms
School-based intra-mural sports and sport clubs	National governing bodies	Sport merchandising
Intercollegiate athletics	Sport advocacy organizations	Resorts
Campus recreational sports	National/international youth sport organizations	

Sport management jobs are varied in terms of their career setting, organizational philosophy, management sector, and job emphasis. Opportunities for employment in the sport industry depend on individual interests, talents, and the realities of the job market. Sport management graduates may find employment in a wide variety of career settings, including:

- Professional sport organizations
- Intercollegiate or interscholastic athletic departments
- Youth and amateur sport
- National governing bodies/national sport federations
- Sport management and marketing companies
- School and college intramural sports
- Resorts
- Sport facilities and venues
- Lifestyle and recreational sports
- Sport councils and sport tourism
- Sporting goods and merchandising
- Sport and fitness clubs

Sport Management: Four Major Job Emphases

The jobs that sport management graduates perform in these settings are as varied as the settings themselves. When people use the term sport management, it is sometimes difficult to decipher what it is that they are referring to. By saying that you want a job in sport management, you are suggesting not only a career setting (professional sport, college athletics, recreational sport, youth sport), but you are also referring to the nature of the specific job—or the job emphasis—that you are doing within the setting.

There are four major job emphases in sport management: a) sport business, b) sport programming, c) resources/venues, and d) athlete/player development. **Sport business** refers to the business side of the sport industry. Most positions in professional sport are focused on sport business. These include sales, sponsorship/corporate relations, marketing and promotions, media/communication, ticketing, financing, and athlete representation. **Sport programming** refers to positions that focus on the design and delivery of programs and events targeting sport participation. Sport programming positions include many jobs in recreational sports, youth sports, or sport event management. **Resources/Venues** includes those jobs that focus on managing the physical places where sport happens, including stadiums, arenas, multisport complexes, and sport-specific venues, such as golf courses or ski areas. Finally, **athlete/player development** refers to those positions that focus specifically on talent or skill development in sport, and can also refer to positions that focus on assembling sport talent. Jobs in this area include coaching, scouting, strength and conditioning, and sport operations positions within the professional sport industry.

Many Sport Management Jobs have Multiple Responsibilities

Many sport management jobs have responsibilities that cut across multiple areas. For example, Mike Gamache, the program director for the Oyster River Youth Association (ORYA), an organization that provides recreational sports for youth and adolescents, has a position that is primarily sport programming, yet he also has responsibilities that include aspects of sport business, venue management, and athlete/player development.

OYRA's mission states that they "meet the changing needs of the children and families in our community for sports and recreational activities by acquiring and maintaining facilities, promoting volunteerism and seeking collaborative and strategic partnerships" (http://www.oryarec.org).

Mike tells us that, as program director, he handles a lot of things: "I'm pretty much responsible for everything that the organization does. I supervise over 100 sports programs for youth ranging in age from preschool to high school. Some of the programs require me to be very hands on. I handle budgeting and fees, player evaluation, supervision of volunteer coaches, equipment and uniforms, scheduling practices and games, coordinating meetings, communications, payroll, and organizing game officials. For other programs, I'm more hands-off, as they have strong and active volunteer boards that handle most of the day-to day responsibilities."

Can you imagine yourself as a sport management professional? Could you see yourself working in a setting that provides and manages these varied types of experiences? If so, you may be interested in a career in sport management. The next part of this chapter covers some specifics about working in the port industry.

CAREERS IN SPORT MANAGEMENT

By now, you may be wondering about how you can determine if sport management is the right direction for you, and if so, how you should best prepare for a career in the sport industry. In other words, what knowledge, skills, and abilities will you need to be competitive in the job market, and what does the overall job market for sport management careers actually look like? The following sections will provide the answers to these questions..

Passions

For those who truly love sports and are passionate about management, careers in the sport industry are exciting and rewarding. Remember, sport management is, first and foremost, about applying management skills in a sports-related setting. Many of the day-to-day duties of sport managers have little to do with sports, per se. Sport managers are much more likely to be working with budgets, developing marketing ideas, or selling advertisements then they are to be hobnobbing with professional athletes or media elites. In recreational sport settings, sport managers are likely to be communicating with parents, training coaches and volunteers, developing new programs to target participation, or developing policies that govern sport contests in relative anonymity.

That said, sport settings can be fun places to work. Most sport management jobs are highly sought after, and the public is generally impressed with the fact that sport management professionals make a living doing something that they truly love. Through their jobs, sport managers have the chance to make an impact on the lives of athletes, fans, spectators, and their overall community. Think about it—in professional sports, you are usually selling a product (like a team, league, or event) that evokes community pride and good will. Likewise, in recreational sport settings, you may know that you have helped young athletes develop their talents and abilities both inside and outside of sport.

Pay and Perks

Starting salaries in the sport industry do not differ greatly from other entry-level positions in fields like education, general sales, marketing, or the various social sciences. In fact, they are generally similar across sport settings. It is a misconception that professional sports jobs pay significantly more than jobs in recreational sports or that jobs in the commercial sector pay more than jobs in the public sector. Variability in salary is more a function of the hiring organization and the specific sport management job than in the sector or setting. Ultimately, a good starting salary is wholly dependent upon the individual needs and lifestyle of the job seeker.

Geography, benefits packages, and experience all play a large role in starting salary. Jobs in areas with higher costs of living will often pay more to offset high living expenses. It is also important to consider the value of fringe benefits when considering total compensation. A good benefits package, including health and life insurance and retirement options can add up to 30% in value to a starting salary, making a $30,000 per year job worth close to $40,000. Opportunities to increase earning potential will grow as your sport management career advances. Top-level administrators can earn close to (or in some cases, well into) six-figure salaries with good benefits packages.

Preparation

As we mentioned before, sport management is a multidisciplinary field, meaning it draws from a variety of academic disciplines to build its body of knowledge, including business and management, kinesiology and the sport sciences, and recreation and leisure studies, among others. Jobs in the sport industry also cover a wide variety of career settings, so it is important to consider both academic preparation and the development of core sport management competencies.

Academic Preparation

Students interested in careers in sport management can begin by obtaining an undergraduate degree in any number of academically related disciplines. Job seekers may find that different sport management positions require specific degrees. For example, an entry-level position as a youth sports coordinator for a local parks and recreation district might find that the job requires a bachelor's degree in recreation, sport management, physical education, or a related field, while an events management position with a sports marketing and management firm might require a bachelor's degree in any number of fields, including marketing, advertising, business administration, or sport management.

Because there are so many varied career settings in sport management, completing an academic minor or emphasis can help provide depth and direction to a sport management degree. For example, a minor in youth development or education can be useful for students who have interest in youth sports or interscholastic athletics. A minor in business administration, or a strong business foundation, including courses in accounting, economics, sport finance, sales, and marketing, can help support any number of sport management careers.

Graduate degrees are usually not required for entry-level jobs in sport management. In fact, sport organizations may prefer a candidate with an undergraduate degree and relevant work (or volunteer) experience over a candidate with an advanced degree but limited experience. There are notable exceptions, however. Positions in higher education settings, such as campus recreational sports or college athletics, often require a master's degree in sport management, recreation, higher education administration, marketing, or similar fields. Sport agents often have graduate degrees in law, business, economics, or accounting. Master's or other professional-level degrees may also be helpful for career advancement.

It is important to find a university program that closely fits your desired career preference. For example, a sport management program that focuses primarily on sport business and sport marketing might not be the best program for a student who has an interest in recreational sports. Similarly, academic programs that do not offer exposure to sport business management principles may not be the best choice for students who have an interest in professional sport or other sport business settings. Before choosing a program, speak with faculty about their program's philosophy and curriculum requirements. Find out about the faculty's experience and contacts in the sport industry and the kinds of jobs that their students get when they graduate. It is also a good idea to talk with students in the program to get their perspective.

Develop Sport Management Competencies

Sport management has a distinct body of knowledge, exemplified by its core competencies. Research on professional development in sport management (Barcelona, 2001; Toh, 1997) shows that the following competency areas are important for sport management professionals to possess:

- Business procedures
- Marketing, promotions, and communications
- Technology applications and computer skills
- Facilities and equipment management
- Governance
- Legality and risk management
- Management techniques
- Philosophy and sport sciences

- Programming and Event Management
- Research and Evaluation

While there is a general core set of competencies that are important for sport management professionals, different career settings and jobs will place more or less emphasis on specific competency areas (Barcelona & Ross, 2005). For example, jobs in professional sports may emphasize business procedures and marketing, while jobs in recreational sports may emphasize programming and facilities management.

Also, sport management organizations can be incredibly diverse. Some professional sports front offices, intercollegiate athletics departments, or sport management and marketing firms are extremely large operations, with hundreds of employees, while some are much smaller. The same is true for recreational sport organizations. Generally speaking, in larger organizations, employees may have more narrow sets of job responsibilities, and positions may be more focused. In smaller organizations, employees need to be more competent in more areas and job functions may be broad (Barcelona, 2004). Aspiring sport management professionals should focus on selecting a combination of academic preparation and hands-on experience whereby they can develop a broad base of professional competencies to better position themselves for a variety of jobs within the sport industry.

Possibilities

One of the positives of the sport management job market is its vast scope. Think about the job search process as if you were fishing with a net. Just like in fishing, the wider you cast your job search net, the better chance you have of landing a job in the sport industry. Consider this for a moment. Suppose you are interested in working in a sales and marketing capacity for a Major League Baseball team. There are 30 Major League Baseball teams, and a quick search of the employment pages on each team's website yields a small number of actual jobs. Given the popularity of Major League Baseball as an ideal employment setting, available positions often attract hundreds of applicants.

Casting your job search net a bit wider so that it includes positions in the National Association of Professional Baseball Leagues (the "Minor Leagues") or in Independent Baseball will increase the job opportunities available. There are hundreds of these professional baseball teams in the United States and Canada. However, even the most obscure professional baseball team is likely to have an extremely competitive pool of applicants for whatever jobs they have available. Considering sales and marketing jobs with other professional sport leagues or teams outside of baseball will also increase your job search opportunities, although the same competitive employment marketplace still exists. If this sounds discouraging, it also highlights the realities of a competitive job market in certain segments of the sport industry.

There is hope for potential job seekers, however. If you love sports, there are career positions available in sport management. While job opportunities in certain industry segments, like professional sports, are limited, there are good jobs available in other aspects of the industry, including recreational sport, youth sport, disabled sport, amateur sport, State Games, and venue management, among others. For example, according to the United States Department of Labor, jobs in the recreation industry are expected to grow faster than average through the year 2010, with jobs in the fitness and physical activity industry expected to grow even more rapidly through the same time period (U.S. Department of Labor, 2002). Many of these settings are profiled in the pages that follow, and are designed to give students a broader view of what the sport industry encompasses.

By now, it should be apparent that sport management is a broad and complex field encompassing many different career settings and job types. Sport management careers run the gamut from grassroots, recreational sports to elite sport and athletic endeavors. The following section attempts to provide insight into some of the most popular sport management career areas. Remember, the sport industry is so diverse, it is impossible to cover many aspects of the sport management job market. Use these career possibilities to get acquainted with some sport management career options, then use the resources provided in this chapter to gather more information.

Interscholastic and Intercollegiate Athletics

School and college athletics are popular sport settings for participants, spectators, and job seekers. The unifying theme of interscholastic and intercollegiate athletics is the notion that sport participation enhances the educational experience of students, and that athletics participation is an important extension of the school and college curriculum.

Passions—Leadership and supervision, budgeting, scheduling, fundraising, marketing, policy development, networking, risk management, planning, student development

Pay and Perks—Full-time salaries are consistent with other sport management settings. Interscholastic athletic director salaries are similar to the salaries of department heads, and are generally considered to be administrative-level positions. Entry-level salaries in intercollegiate athletics tend to be modest, yet strong benefits packages are often part of the total compensation package. Athletic directors at large colleges and universities are generally well paid, with salaries that are often well into the six-figure range.

Preparation—Career paths are varied and often have different requirements for entry into the profession. Depending on the state or province, middle and high school coaches and athletic directors may be required to possess a valid teacher certification, especially in the public school system. Secondary school athletic directors should have strong coaching backgrounds, in addition to experience with league and tournament scheduling, personnel management, governance and compliance, equipment procurement, finance and budgeting, marketing and promotions, and strong leadership ability in working with parents, businesses, and other program stakeholders.

Preparation for jobs in intercollegiate athletics depends on the nature of the position. It is always wise to focus on acquiring the generally recommended sport management competencies, and then focusing on the specific skills needed for particular jobs. For example, sports information directors (SIDs) must have strong writing and communication skills, a journalism background, an interest in statistics, and experience working with the media. Compliance officers usually have a strong legal background (many are law school graduates) and an interest in policy and rules enforcement. Marketing and promotions staff must be creative, have a background and interest in events planning and program design, and have the ability to sell marketing and sponsorship ideas to corporate clients. The job of the athletic director, especially at Division I institutions, is in many ways like that of a chief executive officer (CEO) in a corporation. Much of the athletic director's job is spent outside of sport. Athletic directors tend to focus on business administration principles, including fundraising, revenue generation, governance, long-range and strategic planning, personnel management, and alumni and corporate relations.

Possibilities—Jobs in interscholastic and intercollegiate athletics are varied. In general, jobs in this setting can be found in: a) individual schools and colleges; b) leagues or conferences; and c) state and national professional organizations, such as state high school associations, the National Federation of State High School Associations (NFHS), the National Collegiate Athletic Association (NCAA), the National Association for Intercollegiate Athletics, and the National Junior College Athletic Association (NJCAA). Besides athletic director positions, full-time jobs in interscholastic athletics in middle and high schools are rare. Coaching positions are generally part time. Careers in intercollegiate athletics are more varied, and tend to fall into the following categories: a) marketing and promotions; b) ticket management; c) sports information and media relations; d) compliance; e) athlete-academic affairs; f) fundraising and development; g) facilities and events management; h) athletic administration (athletic director).

Interested in a Career in Intercollegiate Athletics?

Seek out opportunities to do service learning, field work, part-time employment, or internships with the athletic department at your college or university. Many athletic departments offer part-time job or volunteer opportunities for students in marketing and promotions, ticket sales, events management, or other areas in intercollegiate athletics (See "Cat Crew Internship"). This is a good way for students to get to know the various subsets of athletic administration, get a good sense of the opportunities and skill sets required of the various jobs, and develop a network of contacts to assist with the future job search!

Sporting Organizations

Sporting organizations are concerned with the growth, administration, and development of particular sport activities and/or multisport events. In general, sporting organizations are categorized in three ways: a) sport specific organizations, including National Governing Bodies and National Youth Sporting Organizations; b) multi-sport organizations; c) education and advocacy organizations.

Passions—Love of a particular sport or sport-related cause, interest in the growth and development of sports and sport programs, policy development, marketing and promotions, event management, planning and organizational development, fundraising.

Pay and Perks—Compensation varies by position and organization. In many cases, salaries and benefits packages are consistent with other sport management settings. In small, not-for-profit organizations, jobs may be short term and tied to specific funding sources, like grants. Many national governing bodies/national sport federations have a relatively stable number of full-time professional staff members fulfilling various job roles.

Preparation—Preparation for jobs in sporting organizations are similar to other sport management settings. In most cases, an undergraduate degree in sport management, recreation management, business administration, marketing, or a related field, plus relevant work experience in the sport and recreation industry and demonstrated experience in the general sport management competencies will help prepare a job seeker for positions in these organizations.

Possibilities—Job opportunities in this area are varied. Many sporting organizations offer internships and full-time positions focusing on sport programming, events management, marketing and communications, sponsorship, and sales. These positions are generally found in the following types of sporting organizations: a) sport-specific organizations focus on the growth and development of a particular sport. National governing bodies (NGBs) (called national sports organizations in Canada) are one type of sport-specific organization. NGBs such as USA Hockey or NSFs such as Skate Canada are recognized as the governing organization by the sport's International Federation (IF). NGBs and NSFs are charged with both grassroots and elite sport development; b) national youth sporting organizations are also generally sport specific and serve to promote participation and development in a variety of sporting activities. Examples of national youth sporting organizations include Little League Baseball, Pop Warner Football, or the American Youth Soccer Organization. In many cases, the national organization provides tools, resources, and a governance structure to guide local affiliated leagues in the operation of their youth sport programs; c) multi-sport organizations promote both recreational and competitive opportunities in a variety of sporting activities. State Games in the United States and Provincial Games in Canada are examples of multisport organizations; d) education and advocacy organizations exist primarily to promote a sport-related cause or to provide education and resources related to a particular sport issue, such as coaching and parent education, character building, sportsmanship, and sport safety. Organizations such as the National Alliance for Youth Sports (NAYS), the American Sport Education Program, and the Positive Coaching Alliance (PCA) are examples of these types of organizations. In some cases, sport specific and multisport organizations also include education and advocacy as a component of their mission and goals.

THE NATIONAL CONGRESS OF STATE GAMES is a membership organization that represents 37 Summer State Games and 14 Winter State Games in the United States. Over 500,000 participants of all ages compete in State Games annually in the U.S. (http://www.stategames.org). For example, the Bay State Summer Games attracts over 9,000 athletes representing more than 300 cities in Massachusetts. The Bay State Games Mission is, "To promote personal development, education, fitness, teamwork and sportsmanship through athletic competitions and scholarship programs for the people of Massachusetts." (http://www.baystategames.com)

Professional Sport

The popularity of professional sports is evidenced by stadium and arena attendance, television viewership, and a marriage of sports and entertainment that has led to a 24-hour media cycle of sports-related coverage, stories, and live programming. The high-profile nature of professional sports and the perceived excitement of working in this aspect of the industry has made professional sport a popular career choice for sport management graduates.

Passions—Specific sport settings, sales, advertising and promotion, general marketing, operations, facility and event management, sponsorship development, media relations, community development, corporate relations

Pay and Perks—Salaries for entry-level professional sports employees may be lower than other sport management settings, especially for positions with franchises in minor professional leagues. Some positions may be seasonal or part-time. Some entry-level positions, especially sales, marketing, or corporate relations jobs, offer a base salary and commission structure. Perks include event attendance, the opportunity to affiliate with a high profile organization, and the networking opportunities that occur through experience and getting involved within the industry.

Preparation—Sport management students interested in professional sports should ideally complete a full-time internship with a professional sports franchise or league prior to graduation. Internships are highly sought after, usually require long hours (50 or 60 hours per week), and are mostly unpaid. Typically, internships with professional sports teams will last throughout the season—up to six months, in some cases. The internship experience is critical in building a network of contacts in the industry. Networking is extremely important in all job searches, but particularly so for positions in professional sports. Because jobs are so competitive, job seekers often rely on their network of contacts to help their applications stand out. In addition, most professional franchises and leagues post internship and full-time positions on their websites. Many professional leagues also have their own recruiting methods. For example, attending the Winter Meetings with a resume in hand and a list of contacts in the industry is still considered to be one of the best methods for seeking employment in professional baseball.

Possibilities—Jobs in professional sports are highly sought after. Students interested in professional sports as a career option need to work hard to find and identify opportunities for employment. There are few public listings for professional sports jobs, and jobs that are publicly listed can attract hundreds of resumes. Most professional sport franchises are split between the business side and the player development side of the organization. The business side of the organization includes positions such as stadium operations, media relations, ticket sales, finance, corporate relations and sponsorships, and marketing and community relations. In some cases, these positions might be combined, or they might be labeled slightly differently. Player development positions include scouting, talent identification, coaching, equipment management, and athletic training. Almost all entry-level positions in professional sports are on the business side of the organization, typically in sales or community relations. There are generally few entry-level player development jobs available for the typical sport management graduate. The good news is that for those dedicated, hard-working, and opportunistic students, careers in professional sports are possible and available, and once in the door, career advancement and new job opportunities can become more readily available.

THE FOCUS FOR STUDENTS interested in careers in professional sports should be getting in the door; opportunities for career advancement and finding alternative employment tracks (player development or other more competitive positions) become easier when working within the industry than when trying to break in from the outside.

Sport Marketing and Management Firms/Sport Agency

Sport agents represent athletes and handle contract negotiations. In addition to contract negotiations, many sport agents may handle athletes' endorsement contracts, financial planning, legal services, post-career counseling, and provide a variety of personal care services. Full-service sport marketing and management agencies are fast becoming the industry standard. Some sport agency firms still focus primarily on athlete representation, yet others offer a diverse array of services such as sport marketing and branding, media consultation, and events management. Some firms have even expanded their reach into the broader entertainment industry.

Passions—Customer service, sales, law, negotiation and mediation, event management, corporate relations

Pay and Perks—Compensation and benefit structures will depend greatly on the size of the sport management firm, the clients that the firm represents, and the nature of the job. Sport management and marketing firms are competitive businesses. Compensation packages in the largest, best known firms can be quite lucrative, especially for representatives of high profile athletes or events.

Preparation—The best way to prepare for a career in a sport management and marketing firm depends on the type of job that you are seeking. For example, in addition to general sport management competencies, sport agents need to have significant knowledge of sports law, accounting, and financial planning. In addition to a suitable undergraduate degree with a strong business and management orientation, it is usually recommended that sport agents attend a law school that specializes in sport and entertainment law. Some sport agents pursue masters of business administration (MBA) or masters of accountancy degrees. On the other hand, event managers need to focus on concerns such as event structure, facilities, sponsorship, financing, policy development, program control, personnel, publicity, risk management, media coverage, hospitality, and event evaluation, among others. Entry-level positions generally require a bachelor's degree in sport management, business administration, marketing, or a related field. Many full-service sport management and marketing firms, such as Octagon and IMG, offer significant internship programs designed to provide exposure to the industry.

Possibilities—Jobs with sport management and marketing firms are highly competitive. Job categories tend to focus on two major tracks—athlete representation and events management. Many sport management and marketing agencies are full-service firms that include both perspectives. Sport agents are in the business of taking care of the many needs of professional athletes. Event managers do not generally involve athlete representation, but are focused on the planning, coordination, and management of sports events. These might be large scale, elite events such as the Gravity Games, or they might be large scale grassroots events such as the NBA Hoop-it-Up. Notable full-service sport management and marketing firms include IMG and Octagon.

OCTAGON, a major sport management and marketing firm, offers students the "Octagon Experience," an in-depth 10 week internship designed to provide students with experience in their "athletes and personalities" division. Another major sport management and marketing firm, IMG, offers internships in various divisions based on the organization's needs and the candidate's preference.

Additional Sport Management Career Possibilities

Sport management covers such a vast array of career opportunities, it's not possible to go into depth on all of them. Here are three important sport management career areas that are discussed in more detail in other chapters.

Youth and amateur sport. Participation in organized community youth sport programs outside of school is estimated to be in the range of 30-40 million in the United States and approximately 2.2 million in Canada (Kremarik, 2000; Petitpas, et al., 2005). **Youth sport** can be defined as the provision of organized sport opportunities for children and adolescents outside of the school setting. The philosophical orientation of youth sport organizations vary from primarily recreational opportunities designed to maximize participation to competitively oriented programs designed to develop and showcase athletic talent. See chapter 3 on Community Recreation, which covers youth development, for helpful information.

One of the big challenges for youth sport administrators is articulating and enacting a positive philosophy for youth sports in an environment where there are often different and conflicting goals!

Intramural sports. The term intramural translates literally to "within the walls." Traditionally, intramural sport programs have been associated with school or college-based recreational sport pursuits offered for the benefit of all students. Intramural sport programs can also be found in military settings and are offered to the military personnel (and their dependents) assigned to a specific location, such as a military base. See the chapters on Campus Recreation, Leisure and Intramurals and Morale, Welfare, and Recreation for more details on sport-related career possibilities in these settings.

Intramural sport programs differ from interscholastic or intercollegiate athletics in several ways: a) intramural activities are based in the school or college; b) activities are provided for the benefit of the students (or perhaps faculty-staff) of the school or college; c) they operate on a "sport for everyone" philosophy—there are usually no try-outs or cuts based on ability; d) they operate with minimal or no formal coaching or supervision and are generally participant-led.

Venue management. Facilities have always been a critical component of the sport enterprise. Without access to a suitable physical space to play or perform, sport cannot take place. Similarly, as sport and entertainment have become more intertwined, designing sport facilities to accommodate the needs of both athletes and spectators has become increasingly important. With the opening of each new sports venue, new levels of athlete and spectator comfort are being reached. Clearly, sport facilities and venues are critical components of the sport management industry. Refer to the chapter on Event Management, Meeting Planning, Entertainment and Conference/Exposition Services for more details sport venue management career possibilities.

> The $250 million Fed Ex Forum, home of the NBA's Memphis Grizzlies and college basketball's University of Memphis Tigers, offers fans in premium seating a variety of amenities, including access to special dining and beverage options, in-seat service, and personal televisions. (http://www.fedexforum.com)

SUMMARY OF SPORT MANAGEMENT CAREER POSSIBILITIES

Career	Passions	Pay and Perks	Preparation	Possibilities
Interscholastic or intercollegiate athletics	Leadership and supervision, budgeting, scheduling, fundraising, marketing, policy development, networking, risk management, planning, student development	Consistent with other sport management settings. Starting salaries may be modest but generally there are very good benefits packages. Potentially high salaries for intercollegiate athletic directors.	Varies with the position. Demonstrated job competencies, teacher certification required for many interscholastic jobs. Practical experience and academic preparation in sport management or related field.	Interscholastic athletics=athletic director positions in schools. Intercollegiate athletics =marketing and promotions, ticket management, sports information and media relations, relations, compliance, athletic-academic affairs, fundraising, and development, facility and events management, athletic administration
Sporting organizations	Love of particular sport-related cause, interested in growth and development of sport and sport programs, policy and organizational development, event management.	Varies by position and organization	Similar to other sport management settings. Practical experience and academic preparation in sport management or related field.	Jobs with sport-specific organizations (NGBs) and (NSFs), national youth sporting organizations, multisport organizations (state/provincial games, Olympics), education or advocacy organizations.
Professional sports	Sport-specific settings, sales, advertising and promotions, marketing, facility and events management, media and communication, corporate relations, community decvelopment	Varies by position and organization.	Similar to other sport management settings. Practical experience through internships and academic preparation in sport management or related field. Networking is particularly important because jobs are so competitive.	Jobs in stadium operations, media relations, ticket sales, finance, corporate relations and sponsorships, marketing, and community relations. Fewer opportunities in player development, such as scouting.

Career	Passions	Pay and Perks	Preparation	Possibilities
Sport marketing and management	Customer service, sales, law, negotiation, event management, and corporate relations	Varies by position, and organization, but compensation packages with large firms can be very lucrative.	Focus on developing business and management competencies, sports law, accounting, financial planning, and event management. Practical experience through internships and academic preparation in sport management, business, law, marketing, or related fields.	Jobs in athlete representation and events management

Future Opportunities, Issues, and Challenges

As sport management continues to grow as a popular academic major, it is becoming more and important for students to be exposed the depth and breadth of the sport industry within their coursework. Sport is about more than fun, games, and entertainment. While sport is part of our understanding of leisure, it is also a major industry segment tied to key areas of our society, such as education, law, the economy, health, community development, and the media. Students of sport management must be interested in these larger systems, especially when understanding how sport fits into the fabric of a community. To say that one loves sport but isn't interested in how sport intersects with economic stimulus, educational outcomes, health, or community development demonstrates a lack of depth and limits the ability of sport management to be taken seriously as a viable academic area of study.

As you've seen, sport management is a field that encompasses much more than careers in professional sports or collegiate athletics. To have the best chance of landing a sport-related job, it is best to explore all of the potential career areas within the field and to remain open minded about the broad range of job opportunities within the sport industry. It is also important to keep abreast of growth areas within sport management. Examples of growth areas include: the popularity of action sports among youth, the push for active and healthy lifestyles, and the increasing numbers of active older adults who are interested in continuing sports participation. These trends, as well as future directions we cannot yet predict, represent growing opportunities for sport management professionals.

A major challenge for the field of sport management is to continue to present an integrated perspective even as the profession embraces more specialized opportunities in instructional, recreational, performance-focused, and elite sport. To some extent, these divisions can be seen within academic preparation programs, as sport management is often located in various departments/academic units. Sport management may be found within business schools, kinesiology or physical education departments, or in recreation and leisure studies programs. While sport management requires a strong business and management foundation, it nevertheless remains an interdisciplinary profession. This means that sport management needs to consider perspectives of sport that continue to draw upon a range of professional disciplines (including all of those listed above). In addition, sport management must continue to incorporate the social sciences, such as psychology, sociology, economics, history and political science, which can all be used to frame our understanding of sport management and its place in our social systems.

RESOURCES AND GETTING INVOLVED

Perhaps by now you have a sense that a career in the sport industry is for you. You may have even identified a career setting and a job emphasis that interests you. In addition to choosing the right academic major and understanding the professional competencies necessary for a career in sport management, it is time to get involved in your new career in a deeper way. Consider the following sections on professional organizations, certifications, and tips for getting experience. This information will be useful to you as you build your qualifications for a sport management career.

Professional Organizations

In addition to finding the right academic preparation program and completing an internship, students are encouraged to seek out additional professional development opportunities. Many of the various subfields in sport management have professional associations that provide opportunities for knowledge dissemination and professional development for their members. For example, the National Intramural-Recreational Sports Association (NIRSA), National Recreation and Park Association (NRPA), American Alliance for Health, Physical Education, Recreation, and Dance (AAHPERD), International Association of Assembly Managers (IAAM), International Health, Racquet and Sportsclubs Association (IHRSA), Resort and Commercial Recreation Association (RCRA), Sport Marketing Association (SMA), and North American Society for Sport Management (NASSM) are all professional associations that are designed to further various aspects of the sport management field. Other organizations such as Athletic Business (AB) focus on providing resources and materials for sport management professionals.

Many professional associations hold annual conferences, and most offer student membership options. A number of professional associations offer career and internship fairs, or post available jobs on their websites. Student involvement in relevant professional associations provides another pathway into the sport management field.

Following is a list of professional organizations that are relevant to sport management. Each of these organizations represents different facets of the sport management profession, and will be more or less relevant depending on your career interests. Check them all out to see which ones appeal to you most.

American Alliance Health, Physical Education, Recreation, and Dance
AAHPERD www.aahperd.org

North American Society for Sport Management
NASSM – www.nassm.org

Sport Marketing Association
SMA – www.sportmarketingassociation.com

National Intramural-Recreational Sports Association
NIRSA – www.nirsa.org

National Recreation and Park Association
NRPA- www.nrpa.org

International Health, Racquet, and Sports Club Association
IHRSA – www.ihrsa.org

College Sports Information Directors of America
CoSIDA – www.cosida.com

International Association of Assembly Managers
IAAM – www.iaam.org

National Collegiate Athletic Association
NCAA – www.ncaa.org

National Association for Intercollegiate Athletics
NAIA – www.naia.org

National Junior College Athletic Association
NJCAA – www.njcaa.org

National Federation of State High School Associations
NFHS – www.nfhs.org

Disabled Sports USA
DSUSA – www.dsusa.org

Women's Sports Foundation
www.womenssportsfoundation.org

U.S. Golf Association
USGA – www.usga.org

Young Men's Christian Association
Y – www.ymca.net

Certifications, Licenses

Many professional associations also offer the opportunity for professional certification. Some notable professional certifications in the field include the Certified Recreational Sports Specialist (CRSS), Certified Park and Recreation Professional (CPRP), Certified Youth Sports Administrator (CYSA), and Certified Facility Executive (CFE), among others. Pursuing a certification helps to demonstrate commitment to professional development in the sport management field. In some cases, depending on the sport management career setting and particular job, professional certification is required or strongly recommended for employment.

Where to Get Experience

Preparing for a career in the sport industry is serious business. While good jobs exist, most are highly sought after. Obtaining a career in sport management means more than doing well in your academic classes (although this is important too!). It means gaining experience, building competence, demonstrating commitment, and making contacts. Consider the following tips to help you get involved and prepare for a career in the sport industry.

Enroll in an undergraduate academic program related to your career area of interest. If your college or university does not have a sport or recreation management undergraduate program, consider majoring in business administration, marketing, journalism, communications, education, or other academic programs that will help you build your competencies in the critical areas for sport management.

Get to know your professors outside the classroom. Many professors have contacts in the sport industry and can be valuable resources for helping you get started in the field. Some professors may allow undergraduates to assist with their research. These experiences can build competence in critical areas (like research, evaluation, and communication) and can provide networking opportunities within the sport industry.

Do an independent study. If your academic program allows it, go to your professors and request to do an independent study that focuses on your area of interest. Good independent studies can help build critical competencies in the field. Marketing and communication plans, program design, sponsorship development, or research and evaluation projects can help to show off your abilities, develop skills, and help you get to know your professors better outside of the classroom.

Take advantage of service and experiential learning opportunities. Many sport and recreation management programs (as well as other fields) offer classes that incorporate field-based experiences within their curriculums. Take these classes, get a variety of experiences in a wide-range of sport settings, and put these experiences on your resume. Be a leader and showcase your talents when you have the opportunity. This is a great opportunity to get to know your professors.

Do volunteer or part-time work in the field early and often. The experiences that you receive outside of the classroom are as important as what you learn inside the classroom. You can start by volunteering to work in your college's athletic department, or working part time in the intramural sports office. Spend your summers working with youth in a summer sports camp, or working with a professional sports organization. The more relevant work experience you have on your resume, the better chance you will have of standing out in a competitive job market. Here's a list of settings you can look for a part-time or volunteer opportunity:

- College/university athletic department
- Campus recreation/intramural sports
- Community recreation department programs
- Sports officiating/umpiring
- Local running events
- Youth sports coaching
- State Games
- Local professional sports franchise (major or minor league)
- Sport/recreation management major's club or association

Join a professional organization (or two, or three!). Many areas of sport management have professional organizations that represent them. Find out from your professors which associations they belong to. Get a student membership to one, attend a meeting, and see what it has to offer. Many professional organizations offer low-cost memberships to students and provide access to internship and full-time job opportunities. Some associations encourage student leadership. Take advantage of these leadership opportunities by volunteering to help out at conferences, sitting on committees, or standing for office. These are great places to develop your leadership abilities and begin building your professional networks.

Do a full-time internship. There are a wide variety of internship opportunities in the sport management field. Internships provide students with real-world, practical experience. They also help to develop contacts. To re-phrase the old saying— "it's what you know AND who you know" that helps open career doors in sport management. Quality sport and recreation management programs will require an internship as a component of their curriculums. Other academic programs may offer credits for internship experiences. Take advantage of these opportunities! In many cases, the internship experience is the key that unlocks the door to your first full-time job.

Develop a network of working professionals in the field. Through all of your experiences, both inside and outside the classroom, continue to develop a list of professional contacts in the field. Don't be afraid to ask your contacts for career advice, information on the profession, and job search assistance. Most will be glad to help. Remember that these relationships need to be nourished. Keep in contact with your mentors even when you aren't asking them for something, and always remember to follow up with a thank you!

CONCLUSION

Sport management is a demanding profession. The popularity of sport has created tremendous opportunities for careers that do not involve playing the game. It is important to remember that sport management is both a profession and a career. Many sport management jobs demand long hours and are rarely as glamorous as they might otherwise appear to be. Students who are interested in sport management need to be interested in both sport and management. Being a great athlete or loving sports is not enough. Rigorous academic preparation, meaningful internship or field work experiences, professional contacts, and a desire to work extremely hard are prerequisites to an entry level position in sport management.

FOR FURTHER INVESTIGATION

The following resources have been assembled to help you find out more about careers in sport management. Websites for professional associations, relevant sport management organizations, and other information that may help you investigate sport management careers are listed here.

For More Research

1. Go back to the extensive list of professional organizations listed in the previous section. Choose five that seem to be the most relevant to your area of interest. Go to each website and review and report on: mission, educational opportunities, up-coming conferences, educational opportunities, and job postings.

2. Below you will find organizations that are related to four particular areas of interest within sport management. Choose one area that interests you and go to those websites. Review and report on: mission, educational opportunities, up-coming conferences, educational opportunities, and job postings.

Sport Management and Marketing Firms
Octagon (www.octagon.com)
SMG (www.smgworld.com)
IMG (www.imgworld.com)

Olympics and Paralympics
International Olympic Committee
United States Olympic Committee
International Paralympic Committee

National Youth Sport Organizations and Advocacy
Little League Baseball (www.littleleague.org)
American Youth Soccer Association (www.ayso.org)
Pop Warner Football (www.popwarner.org)
National Alliance for Youth Sports (NAYS – www.nays.org)
American Sport Education Program (ASEP – www.asep.org)

Professional Sports
Major League Baseball (www.mlb.com)
Minor League Baseball (www.minorleaguebaseball.com)
National Football League (www.nfl.com)
National Basketball Association (www.nba.com)
Women's National Basketball Association (www.wnba.com)
National Hockey League (www.nhl.com)
American Hockey League (www.theahl.com)
East Coast Hockey League (www.echl.com)
NASCAR (www.nascar.com)
Indy Racing League (www.indycar.com.com)
Major League Soccer (www.mlsnet.com)
United Soccer Leagues (www.uslsoccer.com)
Professional Golf Association (www.pga.com)
Ladies Professional Golf Association (www.lpga.com)

3. Examine some of the jobs, qualifications, and salaries in the sport management field. This particular exercise is limited to certain sport management positions, but you can do your own research and expand your search beyond the sources listed here.
    *   Check out the following websites:
        —NCAA jobs:
        http://ncaa.thetask.com/market/jobs/browse.php
        —Sport venues and Facilities jobs: http://www.iaam.org/IAAM_News/Pages/NLcareerlist.htm
        —Intramural-Recreational Sports jobs: http://nirsa.jobcontrolcenter.com/search/results/

Active Investigation

1. Sport Management Case Study: To get more in-depth information on a particular sport organization, conduct a short case study of an actual organization in the career setting of your choice. Collect information from websites, professional/trade associations, research journals, statistical information, personal interviews, and other relevant sources. Use a diversity of sources! Research and analyze the following information:

    *   Introduction of the agency/organization, including a discussion of its management sector (public, not-for-profit, commercial), and funding structure (taxes, fees, grants, fundraising, sponsorships, some combination)
    *   Organizational mission and goals
    *   Description of the general range and types of services, programs, and facilities offered
    *   Description of the clientele/customers/users of the service – who does the agency target or try to attract to its services/programs?
    *   Description of employee positions, types of jobs, qualifications, etc. Discuss full-time, part-time, and volunteer positions, if applicable

- Several issues or trends impacting the agency/organization or the wider sport management career setting
- Additional information—include any additional information related to the industry segment. Include information taken from personal interviews, key statistics/indicators, or other information that will enable you to obtain a better understanding of this organization and/or sport management career setting
- Expand your search by looking at the websites of professional sport teams and leagues (major and minor) and national governing bodies/national sport federations. Take a look at the positions and salaries listed.
- Get a sense of the job types, duties, qualifications, and starting salaries for these various positions.
- What themes do you see? Do any of these jobs or career settings interest you?

Recommended Reading

Martens, R. (2001). *Directing youth sports programs.* Champaign, IL: Human Kinetics.
This book offers the best collection of administrative resources available to youth sport directors. It contains a wealth of hands-on, practical information that will help you develop a sound program philosophy and compatible policies.

Masteralexis, L.P., Barr, C.A., & Hums, M.A. (2009). *Principles and practices of sport management* (3rd edition). Sudberry, MA: Jones and Bartlett Publishers.
This text offers a comprehensive introduction to the sport management industry, and it covers a variety of sport management careers.

Mull, R.F., Bayless, K.G., & Jamieson, L.M. (2005). *Recreational sport management* (4th edition). Champaign, IL: Human Kinetics.
This book is designed to prepare students in sport management for solid careers and it is also a practical tool for professionals working in the field, with more than 60 forms and checklists to ensure smooth day-to-day operations.

REFERENCES

Barcelona, R.J., & Ross, C.M. (2005). An analysis of the perceived competencies of recreational sport administrators. *Journal of Park and Recreation Administration, 22*(4), 25-42.

Barcelona, R.J. (2001). *An analysis of the perceived competencies of recreational sport managers: Toward a competence-based model for academic and professional development.* Unpublished doctoral dissertation, Indiana University.

Barcelona, R.J. (2004). Examining the importance of recreational sport management competencies based on management level, agency type, and organizational size. *Recreational Sports Journal, 28*(1), 45-63.

Coakley, J. J. (2004). *Sport in society issues and controversies* (8th ed.). Boston, MA: McGraw Hill.

International Health, Racquet, and Sportsclub Association (2007). About the industry. Retrieved June 28, 2007 from http://www.ihrsa.org

Jamieson. L.M., & Toh, K.L. (2000). Professional preparation in sport management: A narrative meta-analysis. *NIRSA Journal, 24*(1), 31-43.

Kremarik, F. (2000, Autumn). A family affair: Children's participation in sports. *Canadian Social Trends.*

Masteralexis, L.P., Barr, C.A., & Hums, M.A. (2005). *Principles and practices of sport management.* Sudberry, MA: Jones and Bartlett Publishers.

National Collegiate Athletic Association (2007). College sports statistics and records. Retrieved June 28, 2007 from http://www.ncaa.org.

National Congress of State Games (2007). About us. Retrieved June 28, 2007 from http://www.stategames.org.

National Federation of State High School Associations. (2007). Participation data. Retrieved June 28, 2007 from http://www.nfhs.org.

National Sporting Goods Association. (2007). Sports participation. Retrieved June 28, 2007 from http://www.nsga.org.

Petitpas, A. J., Cornelius, A. E., Van Raalte, J. L., & Jones, T. J. (2005). A framework for planning youth sport programs that foster psychosocial development. *The Sport Psychologist, 19*, 63-80.

Sport Business Research Network. (2007). Sports participation summary. Retrieved June 28, 2007 from http://www.sbrnet.com.

Toh, K.L. (1997). *Constructing and validating the competencies of sport managers (COSM) instrument: A model development.* Unpublished doctoral dissertation, Indiana University.

United States Department of Labor. (n.d.). Occupational outlook handbook 2002-2003 edition. Retrieved February 19, 2003, from http://www.bls.gov/oco/ocos058.htm.

“

For as long as anyone can remember, people have celebrated. Celebration itself is perhaps the most common denominator that we have, crossing all barriers of race, religion, ethnicity, age, politics, economics, education, and geography. ...The need to celebrate seems inherent in everything we do and touches virtually every life on the planet.

— SOURCE: INTERNATIONAL FESTIVALS
AND EVENTS WEBSITE
(Overview) URL: http://www. ifea.com

”

10

Special Event Management:
Meeting Planning, Conference/Exposition Services, and Entertainment Events

EMILYN SHEFFIELD
California State University, Chico

POLLY CRABTREE
California State University, Chico

FOCUS QUESTIONS

Q: *Do you love seeing an event coming together?*

A: Without a doubt, seeing results from all your efforts is one of the most gratifying aspects of becoming an event planner. Sometimes it might take a year or more to make an event happen, but you will see how all your planning and organization come together to make an event. You will be able to gauge the outcome of the event against its purpose and objectives. Successful event planners demonstrate patience, so if you are looking for instant gratification, then you may want to explore other professional options.

Q: *Do you have the organizational skills to be successful as an event planner?*

A: The ability to multitask is a necessity for an event planner. The successful planner needs to know where in the event planning process he or she is for all events scheduled for the coming year, or sometimes even two years. Some venues, caterers, and musicians must be booked more than a year in advance, and the successful event planner will anticipate these needs and exercise appropriate advance planning. Organizational skills help the event planner deliver a great event on time and on (or, hopefully under) budget.

Q: *Can you deal with stressful situations?*

A: Stress in the form of demanding clients, unrealistic expectations, and unanticipated problems or conditions can occur at any time. The successful event planner will use creativity and problem-solving skills to resolve challenges with a minimum of drama and fuss. When it is necessary to take the issue to the client, the event planner should take the problem and at least one, but preferably two, workable solutions. The most important thing for the event planner to remember is to appear calm and confident at all times.

Q: *Are you prepared to put your client in the limelight?*

A: Although there is the potential for your career in event management to put you in the spotlight, the primary credit will go to your client. You have to be prepared for your client to take all the credit for your success and you must deflect the credit your client's way. It is your job as an event planning professional to help your client achieve the event's objectives and to make your client look good.

KEY TERMS

Event professional
Special event
ROI
Multi-tasking
Venues
Vendors
Incentive travel
Destination management company
   (DMC)

Independents
Specialized entertainment venues
Certified Meeting Professional
   (CMP)
Accepted Practices Exchange
   (APEX)
Convention and Visitor Bureau
   (CVB)

PROFILE 1: COULD THIS BE YOU?

ROBI TSE works for the Golden Gate National Parks Conservancy, the official nonprofit partner for one of the nation's most visited national parks. "Anything we can celebrate, we will," stated Robi Tsi shortly after our interview got underway. Robi helps plan and execute dozens of events each year for the Conservancy's members, sponsors, donors and visitors to the Golden Gate National Recreation Area in California.

Q: *How did you come to work for the Golden Gate National Parks?*

A: After working in New York for seven years, I found myself missing the parks and open spaces of the Bay Area. So, I returned to San Francisco and learned about the Golden Gate National Parks Conservancy through a family friend. As part of the Conservancy's development division, I work with other Conservancy colleagues to plan and execute a year-round calendar of events.

Q: *What do you love most about your career?*

A: Our team does more than plan parties for a good cause. Conservancy events show people new things about their parks and inspire them to want to do more to protect the parks. What I like best is working with people who are passionate about parks and who share and celebrate our common purpose—to ensure parks for all forever.

Q: *Parks For All Forever. ... That sounds like a great mission statement. Is it?*

A: Well, it certainly summarizes the goal to which we aspire and direct our efforts. Wallace Stegner said, "The national parks [were] America's best idea." We support the National Park Service and its mission to preserve America's special places and share them with visitors.

Q: *What are some of your favorite Golden Gate National Parks Conservancy events?*

A: Two of our larger events—the Trails Forever Dinner and Turning the Tide—are representative of how events support our mission. Every fall, we host the Trails Forever Dinner to raise funds to create a world-class trail experience for park visitors. A committee comprised of Conservancy members and staff planners selects a different theme and park venue each year. Nearly 500 guests, attired in "trail chic," enjoy an evening of food and fun. The highlight of the evening is a fabulous auction of one-of-a-kind park experiences. Since 2001, we've raised millions to support Trails Forever and programs to bring area youth into the parks. In the spring, the Institute at the Golden Gate, another initiative of the Conservancy, sponsors a program called Turning the Tide. Environmentalists gather at Fort Baker, the newest park destination, to develop proactive responses to the most critical global environmental issues of the day.

Q: *Well, that certainly sounds like more than planning parties for a good cause. Do you have any advice for an aspiring event planner?*

A: Sure. The work is exciting and creative, but you'll also find yourself working lots of nights, weekends, and holidays. A successful event planner must have a "plan

B" for every contingency. Keep the day before any big event completely open–that way when something comes up you'll have time to implement your "plan B" and bring off another great special event!

For further information about the Golden Gate National Parks Conservancy see http://www.parksconservancy.org. Check out the "Our Work" tab for more on Trails Forever and the Institute at the Golden Gate, peruse the Conservancy's on-line Calendar, or use the search feature to learn more about the parks.

PROFILE 2: COULD THIS BE YOU?

DAN VICINI started his own company, Dakota Events, LLC, after working for more than a decade in the incentive travel industry. His is the classic entrepreneurial strategy of finding a need and filling it well. Even better, Dakota Events, LLC provides time for him to accompany corporate groups to hallmark sporting around the world. I caught up with Dan as he was headed out to the Winter Olympics and here's what he had to say…

Q: *Tell me about Dakota Events, LLC. Why did you decide to create your own company?*

A: Dakota Events, LLC is a hospitality and event staffing company. We offer high-caliber staff to corporate meetings and incentive programs. We can provide local staff or independent contractors who travel around the country and internationally to fulfill my clients' on-site needs. On-site services include registration, food and beverage management, activities, meeting services, transportation, and executive services. Dakota Events was created because the service I was receiving from other third-party vendors was not up to standard when I was working for a former employer. Since I knew and understood what my client was looking for, I formed Dakota Events, LLC to fulfill that need.

Q: *Why did you set up Dakota Events as an LLC?*

A: In order to do business with corporate America, you have to adhere to many laws, insurance guidelines, and company policies. When you start a company that has employees, you should always form your company as an LLC (limited liability corporation), LLP (limited liability partnership), S-Corp or corporation. Incorporating provides an extra layer of protection if an employee, independent contractor, or company takes legal action against your firm. It also enables you to set up the mandatory insurance policies that are required to do business in any of the 50 states. Most of your clients will require that you have at least a $1 million umbrella policy that would cover anything from workers compensation to negligence. Dakota Events is an LLC because it gives me the flexibility, tax benefits, and the legal format required by the state of Nevada. Plus that extra layer of protection for my assets should anyone take legal action against the company is really important.

Q: *What do you love about your career?*

A: I've had a nice run in the event and hospitality industry. I've had a chance to see the world, stay in 5-star hotels around the globe, and dine in some of the best restaurants out there. Most of my friends can't believe what I do and where I go for an occupation. Most people go into an office five days a week, day in and day out. My day is different every single day. Now that I own Dakota Events, I have even more flexibility with my schedule, the jobs that I choose, and the companies I want to associate with.

Q: *How does your work make a difference to your clients?*

A: I would have to say that over the past 15 years of working with different clients, staff, and companies, I have developed a great sense of what my clients are looking for and the service levels that should be standard today. I can anticipate their on-site needs and make the proper recommendations enhancing their attendees' experiences. In today's market, you also have to be very budget savvy, know the clients' budgets, and always stay within their guidelines. If you can anticipate change and have the dollar amount with those changes, you will be even a greater asset to your clients.

Q: *What special challenges confront you and your current company?*

A: The economy runs the show in the incentive and hospitality industry. When the economy is doing well, companies spend money on meetings and incentives. In today's market, we are having one of the worst economies since the '80s (from what I'm told); companies are being strategic in their spending. The good news is that meetings have to take place, employees need to be recognized, and companies are required to invest in ideas and training.

Q: *How did you get into this profession?*

A: I graduated with a degree from California State University, Chico. In my opinion, resort and lodging management is one of the best programs offered there. When I graduated, it was mandatory to complete a full-time, four-month internship. Rather than taking the path in the hotel industry, I completed my internship with a meeting and incentive company in the Bay Area. When my internship was over, I was hired full time and started my career in this industry.

Q: *You still find time to accompany corporate groups to big-time sporting events around the United States and in other counties. How do you swing that?*

A: I've handled such sporting events as the Final Four, Super Bowl, World Series, Winter and Summer Olympics and the PGA Tour. Honestly, these events refuel my passion for what I do. They also allow me to work closely with some of my clients in exclusive settings with their top executives. I make time for these events because they allow me to network with the decision makers and build the trust and relationships that lead to future business for Dakota Events. I also get to see some of the greatest athletic contests on earth!

Q: *What career advice do you have for professionals just getting started?*

A: Always treat your work or your projects like they are the most important program or event you will ever do. Do what is asked, ask questions, and take notes. Be honest and build relationships inside and outside of work. Decision makers want to know they can trust you. Trust will win business time and time again. By networking and keeping in touch with fellow students from your academic degree program, you find doors opening for you. My best advice, though, is to never burn a bridge. You never know whom you will work with next or, more importantly, whom you will be working for.

You can learn more about Dakota Events on-line at http://www.dakotaeventsllc. com/.

Pursue Your Passion for Events–And Get Paid!

Is there anyone who hasn't been to a special event? Professional events like meetings and conferences and social events like festivals and concerts permeate contemporary society. Colorful fliers capture your eye and imagination as you walk down the street. People tweet" or forward links to friends about headliners at entertainment venues. Professional associations offer conferences to help their members keep up on industry trends. Membership associations and special interest associations sponsor events to raise funds, serve members, and increase their visibility. If it seems like events are absolutely everywhere, it is because they are!

A sampler of recent graduates from the authors' university illustrates the range of job settings for qualified special event professionals to practice their superb skills. Each person completed an undergraduate degree in recreation and parks management (gender neutral names or initials have been used here), and is now employed in the exciting world of special events:

- Taylor plans tradeshows for a large, high-tech online auction firm.
- Jamie manages a four-day festival for a convention and visitors bureau.
- Sam coordinates international tradeshows for a software vendor.
- Alex organizes habitat restoration events volunteers at a national recreation area.

- Sun coordinates alumni events for a mid-size university.
- Dana coordinates a downtown market for a business development association.
- Ryan is a trainer for a professional association.
- AJ staffs large conferences and tradeshows in convention destinations.

History and Growth of Professional Event Management

For eons, people have gathered to celebrate the seasons and cycles of nature and life. In pre-agricultural eras, groups met to trade and celebrate seasonal changes. Markets anchored celebratory and commercial activity in the agricultural era and athletic contests increased as settlements and towns emerged. With the rising affluence that accompanied the industrial revolution, the stage was set for festivals, celebrations, and special events to increase in number and frequency. For years, the event planning function was embedded as part of a broader job or position, but as events grew in importance, the need for specialized professionals emerged, too.

The industrial revolution created prosperous middle classes with the income and leisure time to support entertainment events. Ironically, this new leisure time in the form of weekends and paid vacations and holidays for the average employee led to a new industry with common professional practices, codes of ethics, and career tracks for others. Business events are still important and have evolved over time to support economic eras centered on manufacturing, services, and information.

We may be thousands of years past the early seasonal gathering of trading nomads, the athletic spectacles of early civilizations, or the first farmers' markets, but these events continue to flourish along with dozens of other types of business and social events. The **event professional**, or person paid to plan and implement the event, evolved right along with society, and now we see specialization and thousands of local, regional, state, national and global events.

Event Management Today

Most segments of the event and entertainment industry are expanding, although regional growth patterns and priorities do exert an influence. A **special event** is exactly what the name suggests. The "special" refers to the non-routine nature of the event. While a special event may occur at the same time each year, it is special by virtue of its infrequent scheduling, its novelty, or some other non-routine feature. The term "event" suggests structure and planning. So, a special event is a non-routine, but structured, activity designed and implemented to achieve the sponsor's (or client's) objectives.

Destination areas look to stellar events to help draw visitors when capacity is available, to position or reposition the destination, or to add value to the visitor experience. Civic celebrations are back in vogue. Nonprofit organizations use special events to raise resources or to advance their missions. New products are being launched constantly and everyone is courting the conference and meetings market.

Special events are designed for many purposes. For example:

- A community special event may be a seasonal or holiday event, or a tournament, or a festival.
- A nonprofit organization special event may be the primary fund-raiser for the organization, a valued member service, or a way to express appreciation to volunteers, donors, and other supporters.
- A university special event may be part of a community outreach strategy, or a way to encourage alumni to return to campus.
- A business special event may be part of a sales campaign or a way to draw attention to a new product, service, or location, to secure customer loyalty, or to accomplish other strategic objectives.

Trends in Event Management

A solid understanding of societal and economic conditions will prepare you to seek opportunities in periods of change. Keeping an eye on demographic and lifestyle trends is essential to event and meeting planning. Scanning a wide range of sources will help you separate trends that will last from the merely trendy. When you notice the same themes in many sectors, you may have a trend on its way to becoming a basic business practice. Keep a sharp eye, and you will soon become known as a trend-spotter, or better yet, a trendsetter in your chosen sector of this industry.

As the new century enters its second decade, five things are changing the shape of the event and meeting industry and they are likely to continue doing so for some time.

- Creativity continues to be highly prized in the event and meeting industry. Event professionals who can combine classic elements in innovative ways are always in demand. Unique and authentic events resonate strongly with sponsors and participants. Even a firm with an established portfolio of popular themes and venues can utilize new entertainers, new color schemes, and new lighting techniques to delight clients and guests.
- Accountability has increased as the visibility and importance of the event and meeting industry has grown. Fiscal responsibility and **ROI (return on investment)** as well as clearly defined and measured objectives and outcomes are becoming more prevalent throughout all industry sectors. This emphasis on accountability has increased the professionalism of the industry and encouraged the growth of continuing education, professional certifications, and research and evaluation protocols.
- Sustainability has expanded to include more than just "greening" events. Environmental awareness has expanded to include social, cultural, and economic measures along with the environmental ones. Wholesome, positive events and meetings now pursue triple-bottom-line goals on-site and back through the supply chain. Experienced professionals work to incorporate sustainability from planning to implementation.
- Inclusion has increased as event participants have become more diverse. People are living longer, there is a new global baby boom underway, and societies are becoming more racially and ethnically diverse. Global economic and communication networks are bringing people from far-flung corners of the

world together. The savvy planner draws from this international well to craft creative and culturally inclusive events for all.

- Technology has transformed all aspects of society, including the event and meeting industry. Social networking and other computer-aided communications help increase interest in events and increase communication before, during and after the event or meeting. Virtual and hybrid meetings are on the rise along with other technological innovations.

Sound interesting? What is the nature of the work and how do you get started?

CAREERS IN EVENT MANAGEMENT

Jobs for event and meeting professionals exist in every sector of society. Better yet, since event-planning skills are highly transferable, good planners are able to move effortlessly between industry and organizational sectors. Skills valued in all sectors include time management, the capacity to work on multiple events with cascading deadlines (**multi-tasking**), the ability to remain calm when things are chaotic, and the resourcefulness to deliver memorable experiences while staying within the available financial and human resources. Successful event planners also possess a solid working knowledge of the fundamental concepts, current trends, and emerging issues of their chosen professional setting.

The business of events is contractual, so good planners must be able to review binding documents and work within their established parameters. No discussion is complete without mentioning the importance of fiscal responsibility and return on investment (ROI). As meeting and event planning has professionalized, there has been a corresponding increase in outcome accountability. Sponsors and clients want to know that they are getting a good return on their investment in the form of visibilities, sales leads, employee skill development, or similar outcomes. On the festival and entertainment side of the industry, owners and sponsors are interested in similar accountability, albeit with different measures.

Event planning occurs months, and sometimes years, prior to the actual event and often across long distances. Consequently, written and oral communication skills and a firm grasp of business technology (e.g., PDAs, fax machines, various web-based planning and communication devices) enable an event planner to work seamlessly with a wide range of colleagues. Finally, event planners work with and through a wide range of clients, co-workers, and contractors, so excellent communication skills and an ability to work with all types of talent are essential.

Like in any profession, there is specialized language. Some common terms are included in this chapter, but if you encounter unfamiliar terms in job descriptions or professional publications, you can find an extensive online glossary sponsored by the member organizations of the Convention Industry Council. Go to the well-organized CIC website (http://www.conventionindustry.org/glossary/) for a glossary of more than 3,800 industry terms and for links to member organizations.

Passions

If you like variety, creativity, and high-energy work settings, you may find yourself drawn to a career as an event or meeting professional. If you are attentive to detail and find satisfaction from helping others achieve their business or mission objectives, this could be the career field for you! If you can remain calm and resolve problems quickly and well as events unfold, then you can be very successful and enjoy a long and rewarding career.

Preparation

Education and experience in event planning will provide a good foundation for building a career in the professional event-planning field. A quality education will help students learn how to function in loose, fluid team situations. Event professionals must work with employees, contractors, vendors, volunteers and the client's representatives to design and deliver superb events for their clients.

The events industry values experience. Fortunately, universities tend to provide many opportunities for event planning experience as part of academic programs. Recreation programming knowledge and experience provides a solid background for the organizational, communication, and management skills that a good event manager requires.

Whichever degree program you select, make sure you gain the knowledge and hands-on experience to become a proficient event management professional. Strong written and oral communication skills are required because event professionals need to communicate well with their clients, contractors, management, event audiences, and members of the media. Interpersonal skills are also an asset; successful planners have a knack for handling the most difficult clients and situations with apparent ease and confidence.

> " Regardless of their title, all meeting professionals need to have certain qualities. Freeman (a large tradeshow and event management company) looks for project managers or account executives who are resourceful, responsive, tenacious, ambitious, and principled. It helps if a candidate has the ability to read and understand diagrams and floor plans, as well as calculate figures such as proportions, percentages, area, circumference, and volume.
>
> — JACKSON, L.A. (2005)
> *Want to be an event planner?*
> *Black Enterprise. Vol 36(4) p. 132-136.*
> "

Possibilities

Event and meeting professionals possess a specialized skill set that transcends any single setting. Event planning is widespread and growing so rapidly that you will find opportunities in all industries and sectors. As your skill set grows through experience, and your professional network expands, you may find there is no limit to your success and effectiveness as an event or meeting professional.

There are dozens of organizational schemes to categorize the meeting and events industry. Snodgrass (2001) and Kilkenny (2006) offer industry frameworks organized by work setting. Their pragmatic approach is useful for students contemplating an event management career since it shows the range of work settings. Their framework is adapted here to describe career opportunities in specialized firms, in corporate and organizational settings, and in hospitality and entertainment venues. Lucky you, soon-to-be event planner, an incredibly wide range of opportunities await you in the fast-growing career field.

Special Event and Meeting Planning Firms

Event and meeting planning firms exist to serve the event and meeting planning needs of their clients. They work with a network of **venues** (e.g., facilities) and **vendors**, specialized service providers such as florists, caterers, rental companies, and entertainers, to ensure that a client's objectives for an event or meeting are met. Firm size varies to reflect the available opportunities. Some firms are national in scope with offices in most destination cities; other companies are smaller with just a few employees that focus on a single industry sector or area.

Is working in an event or meeting planning firm for you? It might be if you love organizing events and activities and can work as part of a team to help clients or sponsors achieve their objectives.

Passions—If you like event planning and lots of it, then an event or meeting planning firm may be for you. Most firms have an operations division that actually organizes and implements events and meetings as well as a sales division that secures business for the firm.

Pay and Perks—The pay ranges from hourly to career-level salaries. Perks can be very creative and include travel, gift/product samples, and invitations to experience the destination, venue, or product first-hand. Many event and meeting firms are sole proprietorships or partnerships. This means with experience, you may be able to enjoy the rewards of owning your own business. A well-established firm often maintains enduring relationships with a cadre of core clients, so long-term relationships and friendships with like-minded clients are also job perks.

Preparation—In event and meeting planning, there are simply no substitutes for attention to detail and the ability to multi-task. Event planning experience is always a plus, and fortunately, you can get lots of experience by planning events and activities for your social groups, clubs, and organizations. Resourcefulness and creative problem solving are valued skills to bring to the organization or firm. Many beginning positions include lots of clerical work, so good customer service etiquette, an ability to use standard office equipment, and strong computer technology skills are a plus.

Possibilities—If planning is your passion, this is the place to be. Event planners are hired for hallmark sporting and entertainment events (e.g., Olympics, Superbowl, concert tours), well-known festivals and seasonal events, and smaller, community-focused events like Farmer's Markets and festivals. Add meetings and conventions and social events, like weddings and fund-raisers, to this list and your options are almost limitless. Specialized types of event and meeting planning firms have evolved, including:

- Incentive Travel Firms: These firms create unique and memorable travel programs to reward performance in a variety of sales and technology fields. They have event planners and travel directors who accompany incentive groups to exciting destinations. Large incentive travel firms sometimes have an in-house travel agency providing more employment opportunities.
- Destination Management Companies (DMCs): These firms are experts in a single destination city or region. They typically work with incentive travel firms, conference and meeting planners, and corporate travel professionals to handle all the destination-specific details necessary to ensure a successful group gathering.
- Independent Event Firms: Independent event firms, also known as **independents**, can operate anywhere and range in size from one-person small businesses operating in home to large, full-service event and meeting planning firms. Depending on size and experience, an event firm may specialize in milestone celebrations like weddings or coordinate complex national or international concert tours. Other event firms manage hallmark special events and festivals. Still others specialize in meetings and conferences. From entertainment to education, event firms handle all aspects of an event, meeting, or conference.
- Festival Management Firms: Large festivals have expanded to require full-time professional staff, especially in the areas of sponsorships and vendor relations. Even smaller festival-style events such as farmers' markets and special events in downtown entertainment districts keep a couple of folks busy planning the festivities.
- Public Relations and Advertising Firms: Meeting and event planning is often included in a well-conceived public relations or advertising campaign. Some PR firms have in-house events divisions with career opportunities for event planners while others partner with an event planning firm to meet client needs.

MARITZ TRAVEL is a global corporation with more than 1,500 locations in sixty countries. They combine advanced technology and a vast network of suppliers to help companies achieve results through special events, incentive travel programs, and corporate meetings. The company manages more than 2,000 meetings and incentive travel programs each serving more than 400,000 travel program participants. Go to their website (www. maritz.com) and search their wide assortment of case studies to learn how they combine industry knowledge and technology to help their clients achieve results and attain goals.

You can also read about current employees (http://www.maritz.com/maritz-people. html) and their jobs. Some travel-related job titles with a large incentive travel company like Maritz might include travel account manager, project manager, and travel director.

Event Planning in Corporate or Organizational Settings

Need more ways to envision your future in event and meeting planning? Do you want to combine your planning skills with a cause? Are you drawn to public service but cannot quite see yourself as a teacher or youth leader? Do you like the structure of a corporate setting? If so, you will be delighted with the range of opportunities that await you as an event or meeting planner in a corporate or organizational setting.

A review of the specifics related to events in corporate and organizational settings can help you determine if this setting is for you.

Passions—Do you want to save the world or an important little part of it? Do you long to improve the human condition, support social or environmental causes, or improve society? If so, association and organizational settings provide some of your very best event planning opportunities. You can use your event planning skills to support or improve something you care about. Working in a corporate setting showcasing innovation or training a workforce also has rewards.

Pay and Perks—Pay covers a wide range and tends to be higher in corporate and government settings, but people working in the nonprofit sector often report the highest levels of job satisfaction. Job perks often include travel, lots of hospitality-related functions, and cutting edge industry knowledge.

Preparation—In addition to event and meeting management skills, industry knowledge is always a plus. In some sectors, experience in fund-raising and sponsor development is a valued skill. In others, a solid background in adult education or specialized content expertise is highly prized. Since many events and meetings help to raise operational funds, solid negotiation skills can help distinguish you from the competition.

To learn more about event planning opportunities in corporate and organizational settings, ask your campus advisor for introductions to alumni working in the sector you are interested in learning more about. Or, contact a professional association that supports your interests to see if they can identify an affiliated professional located near you. You can also check around your hometown or campus location to see who you can "cold call" for an informational interview.

Possibilities—One of the most attractive aspects of corporate and organizational settings for meeting and event professionals is the vast array of opportunities available in a large, robust economy like the United States. Professionals working in organizational, governmental, and corporate settings support every sector of society. Check out this list of organizations where event planners are needed:

Corporations. Most corporations produce a product or provide a service and this ensures they have a need to introduce that product or service to the marketplace. Tradeshows and conventions provide customers and clients with a first-hand opportunity to see new products, test services, or compare product and service features in a high-energy environment. Corporations also invest in their employees with meeting professionals attending to the training and development needed to maintain a cutting-edge workforce.

Trade and Professional Associations. Trade and professional associations have grown in number and importance in the past fifty years. Since many rely on annual conferences and other training functions to raise operating revenue for the sponsoring organization, association staff members are often responsible for organizing these important revenue events.

Nonprofit and Nongovernmental Organizations. Nonprofit organizations are devoted to member or societal benefits and enjoy a special place in society. Many nonprofit organizations hold special events to raise visibility and funding. Event planners have a unique opportunity to design creative and entertaining events while generating funds for the cause. Positions range depending on the size of the organization but often the event planning duties are embedded as parts of several colleagues' jobs and make extensive use of volunteers.

Educational. Educational institutions provide additional opportunities for event planners. Most campuses have a full calendar of festivals, meetings, and entertainment events for community residents and campus audiences. Dozens of students clubs and organizations are offering events, activities, and meetings throughout the academic year.

Governmental Organizations. Many local parks and recreation departments host festivals and special events as part of a comprehensive community recreation and tourism program. In many cities and communities, some of the more important and interesting meeting and event venues are managed by governmental organizations. Governmental organizations also invest in workforce development and training and some maintain campuses to ensure adequate training opportunities.

Event Planning in Hospitality and Venue Settings

In the past fifty years, the hospitality sector has expanded to support special events, meetings, tradeshows, and conferences. From large cities to small communities, public infrastructure investments like conference centers, arenas, and other specialized venues support the industry as well as the communities where they are located. Other private sector gathering places such as theme parks, attractions, private clubs, and cruise lines often target the meeting and event market to help diversify their customer bases and increase business during shoulder seasons.

Check out these specifics to help you determine is a career in a hospitality setting or entertainment venue might be for you.

Passions—This sector provides opportunities to plan special events and meetings within the structure of a special "built" environment. In these settings, special events and meetings are often sought to help increase profitability and/or use during slower periods or shoulder seasons.

Pay and Perks—Entry-level employees receive hourly wages, often without benefits. Opportunities for advancement occur early and often, especially in hotels and resorts. Mobility within a company can often provide opportunities to move around the United States or other countries. The hours are often long, but the perks are great if you love to travel. Frequent networking events provide outstanding opportunities because industry partners strive to showcase their services to impress potential clients.

Preparation—Superb organizational skills combined with a solid understanding of marketing will help you excel. Creativity and the ability to work as part of a team will help ensure success.

Possibilities—You will find your best opportunities in large cities and destination areas. In smaller communities or venues, though, you can sometimes combine event planning with other job tasks. Here is a list of locations/organizations you should consider if you want to oversee events and entertainment in the hospitality sector:

Attractions. Theme parks, museums, art galleries, and similar attractions are adding meeting and event planners to their staff rosters. Hosting special events can increase the visibility of the attraction as well as support the bottom line through increased revenue.

Clubs. Country clubs, fitness facilities, and other membership-based clubs are offering more special events, often as part of the marketing and positioning strategy for the property. Generally, the event planning function is only part of someone's job. Some clubs with large food and beverage operations will have event planners on staff to assist with weddings and other, similar family milestone events.

Cruise Lines. Cruise lines use events to create a sense of excitement and energy onboard. For general cruises, events help entertain guests. In recent years, themed cruises have become more popular; music cruises, sci-fi cruises, and wine and chocolate-lovers cruises attract new passengers to cruise ships. Cruise lines have also targeted the corporate meeting and incentive market.

Hotels and Resorts. Most hotels and resorts have some type of function space for groups and gatherings. In smaller properties, the meeting and event organizers are generally located in sales and marketing or catering. In larger properties, a convention services department provides a complete range of meeting services. (See the chapter on The Hospitality Industry for more detailed information.)

Specialized Entertainment Venues. Stadiums, auditoriums, concert halls, and theaters are merely four types of specialized entertainment venues. Professionals in these settings generally work with outside meeting and event planners, but house managers and other specialists require many of the same skills to be effective. (See the chapter on Sports Management for more detailed information on sports venues).

Tourism Organizations. Destination marketing organizations have found festivals and special events to be a great strategy to increase the visibility of the destination and help position it in the competitive market place. Volunteers often plan these festivals and special events, but professionals are increasingly involved as contractors or employees to manage the large-scale special events sponsored by tourism organizations (See the chapter on Travel and Tourism for more information).

Venue Management

Facilities have always been a critical component of the sport enterprise. Without access to a suitable physical space to play or perform, sports cannot take place. Sport venues and facilities are located in both large and small markets, and can be either publicly or privately financed. They can be used for professional sports, collegiate athletics, elite level high school events, international sports competitions, or other forms of top level sport contests. These facilities are primarily focused on creating environments conducive to producing high-quality sport events, both for athletes and spectators. In addition, sport facilities can include those that are primarily focused on providing opportunities for sport participation, including multisport athletic complexes and sport-specific facilities. While the focus of these facilities is on promoting opportunities for sport participation, attention to amenities that enhance the sport experience such as locker rooms, food service, equipment rentals, relaxation space, and some opportunity for spectator accommodations is also important.

Similarly, as sport and entertainment have become more intertwined, designing sport facilities to accommodate the needs of both athletes and spectators has become increasingly important. With the opening of each new sports venue, new levels of athlete and spectator comfort are being reached. Clearly, sport facilities and venues are critical components of the sport management industry. For example, the $250 million Fed Ex Forum, home of the NBA's Memphis Grizzlies and college basketball's University of Memphis Tigers, offers fans in premium seating a variety of amenities, including access to special dining and beverage options, in-seat service, and personal televisions. (http://www.fedexforum.com)

FUTURE OPPORTUNITIES, ISSUES, AND CHALLENGES

Event and meeting planning has grown and professionalized in the past fifty or sixty years, and it appears to be poised for increased visibility and expansion. When consumer confidence is high and the economy is growing, meeting and events flourish, budgets are generous, and opportunities for planners abound. Conversely, when the economy contracts, the events industry shifts as well. In-house planning divisions get smaller or, sometimes, get outsourced, and the smaller, independent firms often report an upswing in business during the same period.

Natural disasters can negatively impact the events industry for years, adding further economic disruption to nature's first-round destruction. Seemingly unrelated scandals can have far-reaching and negative consequences as the financial sector excesses of 2008 and 2009 led to a reduction in corporate travel through all industries.

Taking a slightly longer view, though, helps the event professional stay positive, proactive, and employed. They keep in mind that events have served human needs for thousands of years and that resourceful event professionals will always be in demand. But they also get into the habit of saving a portion of their earnings to tide them over during the lean times.

SUMMARY OF OUTDOOR RECREATION CAREER POSSIBILITIES

Career Sector	Passions	Pay and Perks	Preparation	Possibilities
Special event or meeting planning firms	Lots of event planning, cause-related fundraising, travel, entrepreneurship	Hourly to executive. Creativity and solid budgeting skills help you advance quickly.	Experience required; degree preferred. Programming, customer service, budgeting, and strong oral and written communication skills will help you succeed.	Sales or operations. Coordinate event teams. Plan hallmark events. Own your own business or work as part of a global firm.
Corporate or organization event planner	Corporate work environments, tradeshows and product launches, cause-related marketing	Hourly to executive. Sector knowledge and an ability to translate event outcomes to organizational goals will help you advance.	Degree preferred; sector knowledge required. Experience with large events and documenting outcomes are valued skills.	Positions are often located in the marketing or human resources departments.
Event planner in hospitality or venue setting	Onsite meetings, celebrations, sports, entertainment	Hourly to executive. Hospitality or facility management experience helps you get ahead.	Experience required, degree preferred. Personal network or internship often gains access. Supervisory experience is a plus.	Catering, event/convention services, seasonal or cyclical schedules provide "break-in" opportunities if you are available.

Industry veterans are excited about the role of festivals and special events in the life of a community, regardless of how "community" is defined. Nonprofit organizations raise funds to pursue their missions through special events. Festivals and events contribute to people's happiness and enjoyment as well as the host community's identity and financial viability. Planners and sponsors are delighted to showcase new and different talent from around the community or the world.

Similarly, conference, tradeshow, and business meeting professionals are excited about the growing stature of their contributions to the strategic direction of the business or association. They are pleased to be adding value through professional development and training or to be introducing new products and services to the marketplace.

RESOURCES AND GETTING INVOLVED

The Internet has become a major tool for investigating career opportunities. Key websites specifically related to parks and recreation associations and resources related to specific areas such as non-profits, sports management, hospitality, and travel and tourism have been identified in other chapters. In addition to those resources, you should also become aware of these organizations and resources to prepare for your future career. Use the Internet for information and research but do not forget that meeting and event planning is a highly customer-service oriented endeavor that runs on personal relationships.

Professional Organizations

As the event and meeting industry has expanded and become more specialized, many organizations have emerged to support industry and professionals' needs. Several leading organizations are listed in alphabetical order and each has its niche in the industry. The Convention Industry Council (CIC) is particularly noteworthy. This "federation of leading national and international organizations involved in meetings, conventions, and exhibitions" represents more than 30 professional organizations with more than 100,000 professionals. CIC sponsors the **Certified Meeting Professional** (CMP) designation, a prestigious professional certification. CIC also sponsors APEX, the **Accepted Practices Exchange**, a collection of best industry practices. The CIC website includes links to all members' websites. In addition to the CIC website, interested readers can check out various websites for industry news, research, and career opportunities, including internships. Many associations have chapters located in major cities and destination areas so you can check to see if a chapter is located near you.

American Society of Association Executives
http://www.asaecenter.org/
ASAE and the Center for Association Leadership believe associations have the power to transform society for the better, and their passion is to help association professionals achieve previously unimaginable levels of performance.

Association for Convention Operations Management

http://www.acomonline.org/

ACOM members learn to be more effective service managers, gain a better understanding of the breadth of their roles, and learn about planners' expectations.

Convention Industry Council (CIC)

http://www.conventionindustry.org

CIC facilitates the exchange of information; develops programs to promote professionalism within the industry (including Certified Meeting Professional, CMP, industry certification programming); and educates the public on the economic impact of the industry.

Corporate Event Marketing Association

http://www.cemaonline.com

CEMA considers itself the premier community for technology event marketing professionals and an industry hub promoting professional networking opportunities, industry education, and peer-to-peer knowledge sharing.

Hospitality Sales and Marketing Association International

http://www.hsmai.org

HSMAI is a global organization of sales and marketing professionals representing all segments of the hospitality industry and an industry leader in identifying and communicating trends in the hospitality industry.

International Association of Conference Centers

http://www.iacconline.com

IACC's members operate conference centers that comply with association standards to provide the most productive meeting facilities around the world.

International Association of Assembly Managers (IAAM)

http://www.iaam.org

IAAM is an organization committed to the professional operation of amphitheaters, arenas, auditoriums, convention centers/exhibit halls, performing arts venues, race tracks, stadiums, and university complexes.

International Festivals and Events Association

http://www.ifea.com

The IFEA's mission is to serve the needs of the festival and event industry members who produce and support quality celebrations for the benefit of their respective communities.

International Special Events Society

http://www.ises.com

ISES provides professional development and networking so special event professionals can successfully compete in today's challenging market.

Meeting Professionals International
http://www.mpiweb.org
MPI is a global community of meeting and event professionals that connects members to the worldwide support, industry knowledge, and business opportunities needed to be successful in the meeting planning industry.

Professional Convention Management Association
http://www.pcma.org/
PCMA is an organization of professionals who organize and manage meetings, conventions, exhibits, and seminars and suppliers who support the industry.

Where to Get Experience

The key to success for event professionals is experience. Professional event planning is an ever-changing and demanding field that requires upbeat and flexible creative problem solvers. For most event professionals, the ability to be a creative problem solver only comes with experience. Take advantage of the event planning opportunities presented in college: join a social organization that holds events with other organizations, volunteer to help with student government events, or volunteer to work with campus departments that host events for students, parents, or alumni.

When you have some basic event planning experience under your belt, approach the community or regional recreation department, a local non-profit organization, or the Chamber of Commerce to see if you can assist with an upcoming event. Often these investments lead to an internship, summer job opportunity or a referral to a similar setting in another area closer to home.

So you are ready to work hard and you have some great experiences in college. Be persistent and demonstrate your desire to succeed by your determination to find a place in this exciting world. Be resourceful and levelheaded; everyone values capable, personable, and resourceful co-workers.

Finding a Dream Job in a Dream Destination

How do you find job leads in a new area? A good starting place, when you have a geographic location in mind, is to go to the destination's **convention and visitor bureau (CVB)** and/or Chamber website to see if they have a member's directory online. Use keywords like special events, wedding planner, party planner, corporate events, destination management, incentive travel, or receptive operator to find firms that are working in the geographic area. Another route is the alumni connection. Check with your campus alumni association to see if event professionals are working in your desired geographic area. If they are, try to arrange an information interview. A third option is to locate the local chapter of one of the professional societies to see what they can provide. Their websites are generally full of local news and contacts. Another, more time intensive, but tried and true approach is to: 1) identify the elected leadership, 2) do some background research on them and their companies/firms, 3) contact one or more for an information interview, and 4) follow up with a letter of thanks and a resume that you encourage them to circulate. Face time (e.g., interviewing in person) is the key.

CONCLUSION

If you are organized, creative, patient, able to multitask, and problem solve, then this may be the career for you. Reread the questions at the beginning of the chapter, and if you have negative feelings about any of them, then you might want to look into a different career path. If you have positive feelings, a career as a special event professional provides a terrific way to pursue your passions. If, for example, you love organizing trips and are passionate about vintage movies, you may find a perfect career organizing consumer shows for movie buffs. If you like the idea of working in the music industry but not as a performer or music industry executive, working at an entertainment venue or in a trade association allows you to pursue your passion from a paid perspective.

Connections help you advance, and many people propel their careers by moving between companies within the same industry or geographic area, or move upward within the company. But it is a small tribe in constant motion. Be honest, be ethical, and be nice to everyone; today's competitor is tomorrow's colleague. Now get out there and make your passion pay out through endless possibilities!

FOR FURTHER INVESTIGATION

Now that you have finished this chapter, make use of what you have learned. Take action and set goals. Here are a few suggestions.

For More Research

1. Investigate: Research the event planning field online by checking out the websites for the professional organizations listed in the chapter.
   • Research job listings for future ideas of jobs that are available in the field
   • Look for professional development opportunities—conferences and meetings might be held close to you
   • Search for student programming available including scholarships and internships
   • Be creative and look at websites in a field that interests you (i.e., professional sports, music, theatre, literature)
2. Contact an organization directly and conduct an informational interview with a professional in the field. Talking to a field professional can give you key insights to the field that are missed in publications and on the web. You will most likely find that if you speak to three field professionals, you will find three very different backgrounds leading to careers in the event planning field. It will be helpful to review the informational interview instructions in chapter 2 as you plan for your interview.
   Some specific questions to ask include:
   • What is the educational background of the field professional?
   • What previous work experience do they have?
   • What recommendations do they have for breaking into the event planning field?

3. Pick an area where you are interested in living. Go to their destination marketing organization (DMO) website and look for the online membership directory. There you will find listings of meeting planners, incentive travel planners, and other industry professionals. Sometimes the DMO will offer an event planners guide. After you check out the professional opportunities in the meeting and conference area, review their special event calendar to learn about the range and scope of the festival and event scene.

Active Investigation

1. Explore: In the next month, experience events from the perspective of a spectator:

Attend an industry event
- Trade show
- Non-profit charity fundraising event
- Organized social event
- Large-scale concert or sporting event

2. Host your own small-scale event

- Host a gathering for a nonprofit or cause for which you are sympathetic
- Host a direct-sales gathering for friends and family (i.e., Mary Kay, Juice Plus, Pampered Chef, etc.)
- Host a milestone celebratory event for family and friends (i.e., anniversary, birthday, or graduation party)

After the event, ask yourself these questions. Can you see yourself working as an event planner? Which aspects of your event planning experience did you most enjoy? Which did you least enjoy?

3. Implement: Before the school year ends:

Work with an event planning professional to see if this field might be your calling
- Interview an event planner to get a better idea of the demands of the job
- Job shadow an event planner during an event

Take an active role in the event planning field
- Volunteer to help with a university event
- Join a campus organization that hosts events
- Take an event planning class at your university

Work in the field
- Get an event planning internship for the summer
- Get a part-time job in the event planning field

Recommended Reading

Trade Publications and Association Magazines

The need for planners, vendors, and suppliers to exchange information has created a strong market for trade-oriented publications. Links to online versions of some of these trade publications and association magazines enable you to find contacts, ideas, and applied information about meeting and event planning.

Convene http://www.pcma.org/Convene.htm
The online version of the Professional Convention Management Association's award-winning magazine, a leading meeting industry trade publication. Past issues are archived.

Event Solutions http://www.event-solutions.com/
Print and online publication from Event Solutions, an events industry trade publication. Check out "Event Profiles" for ideas and search the "Black Book" for contacts.

Meetings and Conventions Magazine http://www.mcmag.com/
Published since 1965, the trade publication helps planners manage events and careers. See "Destinations" for suppliers at various convention destinations.

One+ Magazine http://www.mpiweb.org/Magazine/Archive.aspx
Sponsored by Meeting Professionals International, One+ archives features, columns, and case studies. Print, on-line, and Spanish language versions of One+ are available.

Special Events Magazine http://specialevents.com/
Print and digital versions of this publication target planners who produce events in large-scale hospitality venues.

Successful Meetings Magazine http://www.successfulmeetings.com
Two on-line publications provide meeting professionals with educational content, ideas, and resources for all types of planners.

Books on Meeting/Conference Planning

Convention Industry Council. (2008). *The convention industry council manual* (8th Ed.). Convention Industry Council.
Comprehensive resource for managing meetings successfully with forms, lists, and industry glossary. A study reference for the CMP exam.

Craven, R. E., & Golabowski, L. J. (2006). *The complete idiot's guide to meeting and event planning* (2nd ed.). Indianapolis, IN: Alpha Books.
Part of the popular "Idiot's Guide" series available at most bookstores.

Fenich, George, G. (2007). *Meetings, expositions, events, and conventions: An introduction to the industry* (2nd ed.). New Jersey: Pearson Education, Inc/Prentice-Hall.
This second edition textbook has updated content and a revised chapter on technology.

McLaurin, D., & Wykes, T. (2010). *MPI's planning guide: A source for meetings and conventions* (3rd ed.). Dallas, TX: Meeting Professionals International.
Sponsored by MPI, this recently updated guide is an industry standard.

PCMA. (2006.) *Professional meeting management: Comprehensive strategies for meetings, conventions and events.* Professional Convention Management Association in partnership with Kendall/Hunt Publishing.
PCMA calls PMM5 "the most complete meetings management, meeting planning and conference planning textbook in the industry" and a "life-long resource." The book is recommended reading for the CMP Exam.

Books on Event and Festival Planning/Management

Allen, J. (2005). *Time management for event planners: Expert techniques and time saving tips for organizing your workload, prioritizing your day, and taking control of your schedule.* Hoboken, NJ: John Wiley & Sons.
A book filled with industry-tested techniques to improve your time management skills.

Allen, J. (2009). *Event planning: The ultimate guide to successful meetings, corporate events, fundraising galas, conferences, conventions, incentives, and other special events* (2nd ed.). Hoboken, NJ: John Wiley & Sons.
The book is an updated and expanded version of a popular sourcebook that expanded into a series of planning guides. Forms and checklists are included in the text with additional content at the publisher's website.

Getz, D. (2005). *Event management and event tourism* (2nd ed.). New York: Cognizant Communication.
This textbook presents event planning and management within a tourism framework.

Goldblatt, J. (2007). *Special events: The roots and wings of celebrations* (5th ed.). Hoboken, NJ: John Wiley & Sons.
This text connects the growing special events industry to an "ancient human need to celebrate with ceremony and ritual" and new, global opportunities. Case studies, best practices, and web resources are included in the book.

Kilkenny, S. (2007). *The complete guide to successful event planning.* Ocala, FL: Atlantic Publishing Group.
This book provides a step-by-step guide for planning events of any size. It also includes a companion CD of additional material.

Silvers, J. R. (2004). *Professional event coordination.* Hoboken, NJ: John Wiley & Sons.
Silvers presents event planning as a production with special attention to audience and infrastructure. Additional content available on the publisher's website.

Van Der Wagen, L., & Carlos, B.R. (2005). *Event management for tourism, cultural, business and sporting events.* Upper Saddle River, NJ: Pearson.
A resource that sets event planning within the larger context of tourism, sports, and culture and includes an emphasis on career options.

Recommended Viewing

About.com—Career Profile: Event Planner
http://video.about.com/careerplanning/Career-Provile--Event-Planner.htm
This three-minute video captures the life of a DJ turned meeting planner. Watch his firm "turn" a room between back-to-back weddings while he describes essential attributes for success.

Education-Portal.com—Event Planning Professions overview
http://education-portal.com/videos/Event_Planning_Professions_Video_How_to_Become_an_Event_Planner.html
Learn about the background, aptitudes, and skills required by event planners as well as industry certifications and tips for gaining experience. Additional information on the website.

REFERENCES

Kilkenny, S. (2006). *The complete guide to successful event planning.* Ocala, FL: Atlantic Publishing Group.
Snodgrass, J. (2002). *Become an event planner.* FabJob.com.
Wolgemuth, L. (2009, December 28.) The 50 best careers of 2010. *U.S. News and World Report.* (On-line) URL: http://www.usnews.com/money/careers/articles/2009/12/28/the-50-best-careers-of-2010.html

"

Success seems to be connected with action. Successful people keep moving. They make mistakes, but they don't quit.

— CONRAD N. HIILTON
Founder of Hilton Hotel Corporation

"

11 | The Hospitality Industry

Morgan W. Geddie
California State University, Chico

Yao-Yi Fu
Indiana University at Indianapolis

Focus Questions

Q: *Do you consider yourself to be a people person?*

A: Working with all different kinds of personalities, and liking it, is all part of a job in hospitality. Different guests have different needs and co-workers come from all over the world. However, there is much more to a hospitality job than being a "people person," and after working with guests on a day-to-day basis, you might find that you do not like people quite as much as you thought. A truly successful hospitality professional views the unhappy guest an opportunity to serve and to improve his/her people skills.

Q: *Are you okay having a job that involves a variety of activities and can involve change at any moment?*

A: Anytime you are dealing with the public, you have to be ready for the unexpected. You can never say to a guest "that is not my job" even if it is not your responsibility. You must rise to the challenge to correct the situation and make the guest happy.

Q: *Teamwork is usually needed in the hospitality industry. Do you really enjoy working on teams?*

A: You cannot do everything on your own or you will quickly burn out. You must learn to delegate responsibility so become an excellent trainer with confidence in the abilities of your employees to make the correct decisions.

Q: *Would you be willing to work in the evenings, on weekends, and on holidays?*

A: The hospitality industry runs twenty-four hours a day, seven days a week, and does not stop for holidays. You will probably work nights, weekends, and holidays. This is especially true at the beginning of your career.

Q: *Are you willing to relocate?*

A: A career in hospitality can take you to all parts of the world, and if you want to move up in a company you need to be willing to relocate. This is an opportunity for you to explore different parts of the U.S. and beyond. You may not want to leave home, but you can always make it your goal to eventually return to your hometown.

Q: *Do you enjoy organizing a party or arranging an activity for your friends or family?*

A: People in the hospitality industry are social. A hospitality manager must have an eye for details. You need to be able to visualize an event and be able to see it through to completion.

KEY TERMS

Hospitality industry
Interval ownership
Gratuities
Culinary
Lodging industry
Full-service hotels
Concierge
Restaurant industry
Certified Hotel Administrator (CHA)

Certified Lodging Manager (CLM)
Certified Food and Beverage Executive
  (CFBE)
Certified Hospitality Technology
Professional (CHTP)
Certified Hospitality Accountant
  Executive (CHAE)
ServSafe

PROFILE 1: COULD THIS BE YOU?

MARCIA SCHAEFER is the Event and Dining Room Supervisor for Buca di Beppo, a restaurant in Greenwood, Indiana. She's a Certified Server Trainer and sometimes works as a bartender at the establishment. Marcia generates new event and party business for Buca di Beppo. She negotiates contracts and guides clients through specialty ordering. She is also responsible for all front-of-house management duties including floorplans, reports, and deposits, and she often trains new servers in their duties. As one of Buca di Beppo's most valued employees, Marcia handles large groups and provides excellent service to all guests, giving a history of the restaurant and an introduction to the unique dining experience at Buca di Beppo.

Q: *How do you make a difference through your work?*

A: I hope that I add a little joy to the lives of the guests who visit Buca. I am reminded of a specific guest's visit that always makes me smile. It was prom night and I was serving a table of young people who were on their way to prom. As the host brought them to their table, one of the girls snagged her dress on a piece of carpet transition strip and tore a section of the dress. She was very distraught. I got her and the others to order so they could maintain the evening's schedule. As I was talking to them another guest at the next table announced that she had a travel sewing kit. What are the odds in this day and age? While I was doing this, I also had a table that was doing a tasting for their rehearsal dinner. The tables were fairly closely located so I pulled up a chair and worked on the dress as I continued to describe the food and wine to the future bride and groom. I was able to repair the dress well enough to get her through the evening and she once again was smiling and excited about the prom. I have calmed mothers of the grooms and helped with surprise birthday parties for people from eight to eighty. I also have regulars that have all but adopted me into their families. I have the joy of making someone's evening a "night to remember."

Q: *What challenges you on your job?*

A: Every day brings new challenges of all types and levels. I have to remain calm when I deal with customer service problems. In this industry, you do not always have the privilege to deal with someone at their best. I have also gotten to a location and had to "make do" with what was on hand when things were forgotten, broken, or just different from what was promised. In this industry, "making do" also means never letting the guest know that anything is wrong or was ever wrong.

Q: *How did you get into this profession?*

A: I have always been the one in my family and with my friends who took care of things. I organize, construct, get donations, and just make sure everything is taken care of. I also have been accused of being a "mother hen." I have had a variety of jobs, and I always go back to the service industry where I can help to create life-long memories.

Q: *If you could give a young professional interested in this career area one piece of advice, what would it be?*

A: I would tell them not to go into this industry unless they love it. It is hard work and time consuming. It takes you away from your family on weekends and holidays, so that others can spend time with their families. But it can be some the most rewarding time as well as the most frustrating times you may have.

PROFILE 2: COULD THIS BE YOU?

KEITH JOHNSON is the Recreation Manager at Marriott Dessert Springs Villas in Palm Desert, California. Desert Spring Villas is a Marriott Vacation Club property. **MARGO TIGHE** is the Director of Recreation at Marriott's Timber Lodge and Grand Residence Club in South Lake Tahoe, California.

Q: *How do you make a difference through your work?*

A: (Keith) I truly feel that what we do has a huge impact on the guest experience. If you think back on any of your own personal vacations, you probably remember fun experiences you spent with your family. It's usually centered around some kind structured or unstructured activity. Rarely do you remember the lightbulb that wasn't working, the remote that had batteries that stopped working, or the two washcloths your room was missing. If the recreation department does its job and provides a fun way for people to spend time together, then everything else fades into the distance.

(Margo): In my personal make-up is the desire to make a difference in the lives of others and those in need, so working for a company like Marriott with their "spirit to serve" philosophy is a natural fit. Marriott International is a corporate sponsor for Children's Miracle Network, and in my job I have had the privilege of creating and organizing a fundraising event called "Chip in for Children," raising thousands of dollars for children's hospitals.

Q: *What do you love about your career?*

A: (Keith) I love the fact that I get to mix my personal enjoyment with my work enjoyment. Often I'm out doing various activities with my wife and am thinking about how I can tweak things around to make it into an activity at our resort. It also allows me to see how things work in the recreation world at various levels whether it's as a shop mechanic, someone marketing a creative idea, or being the "visionary" trying to put together a long-term recreation plan.

(Margo): I'm fortunate to be working in a career that utilizes my strengths of creativity, strategizing, and interacting with people. I come to work every day excited by the opportunity to share my enthusiasm for recreation with others. No two days are alike. I am working in an ever-changing, evolving field, and I am always challenged, changing, and growing. My job allows me to meet new people and to create, develop, and implement new programs to enhance the vacation experience for our guests. What's not to love about that?!

Q: *Do you have a story about how you transformed a client's life through your services?*

A: (Keith) One of my fond memories was from a Mrs. Jacobson in Park City, Utah, who signed up for my mountain biking class. It was one of the first activities that I created, and it included learning how to use the gears/brakes while going down a small switchback. She hadn't been on a mountain bike before but wanted to learn so she could ride with her daughter. Mrs. Jacobson couldn't quite get it at first but was very persistent and got to the point where she could do the entire bike trail with switchbacks and all. Her excitement after we were done and debriefing with one another was infectious. All of the guests were extremely jazzed at that point. Being with someone who accomplishes something for the first time is very rewarding. Those are the moments that make everything else so worthwhile.

(Margo): I actually have many stories, but this one in particular is memorable and bittersweet. In my job, I have daily opportunities to transform lives in little ways and big ways. During one week in particular, our department was able to provide a week of happy memories for a family that included a dad, mom, and three children. A relative of this family had called our property to inform us that this particular family was on what would be their last family vacation, because the mother was terminally ill and was not expected to live much beyond this final trip. My department was able to plan some extra fun activities geared toward this mom and her family, allowing them to set aside their sadness for a while and just enjoy themselves. As a staff, we had to make an effort to focus on the positive in this situation and not dwell on the fact that these children only had a short time left with their mother. It was a rewarding and challenging week.

Q: *What challenges you on your job?*

A: (Keith) I like trying to accomplish something that I've never done before. Learning new angles to the recreation world is always fascinating to me. Currently I'm learning contract preparation, architecture/interior decorating for a new activities center, and Stargazing. It's as if I'm trying to learn everything I can so that some day I'm ready to open "Keith's FunLand." Whether that actually happens is irrelevant. What is relevant is that I find an enjoyable way to keep that zest for life alive with my wife and my work.

Q: *How did you get into this profession?*

A: (Keith) I grew up snow skiing as a kid and got into mountain biking when it became popular in the late '80s. My family was always outdoorsy. We went camping and fishing to many areas on the East coast as well as Eastern Canada. I moved out West after College and lived in many outdoorsy towns, including Lake Tahoe, CA, The Grand Canyon, AZ, Gunnison, CO, Park City, UT as well as spending a summer in SE Alaska. I enjoy traveling and seeing what different people do in their free time for entertainment. Traveling throughout the U.S. and overseas helps you to understand what life is all about.

(Margo): In high school, I worked summers as a camp counselor. It was as a counselor that I found I loved making a difference in people's lives in a recreational setting. In college, I pursued a degree in recreation with an emphasis in therapeutic recreation and a minor in adventure travel and tourism. Following graduation, I began working for Marriott Vacation Club as a front desk agent at a Colorado property, learning first hand about the hospitality industry. From the front desk, I moved to the activities department and eventually worked my way up to recreation manager. I transferred to South Lake Tahoe, CA, a few years ago and worked my way up to director of recreation. Along the way, Marriott has provided me with excellent management training programs. I have also had very supportive and encouraging property managers and mentors who have taken an interest in me personally and in my career development.

Q: *If you could give a young professional interested in this career area one piece of advice, what would it be?*

A: (Keith) Be smart, have fun, don't take yourself too seriously, laugh as much as possible, and be courteous when showing others how to do this as well!

(Margo): Know what you are good at. Do what you are good at. And do something good every day!

THE BIG WORLD OF HOSPITALITY

The **hospitality industry** is comprised of businesses such as hotels, resorts, cruise ships, theme parks, clubs and restaurants that provide food, beverages, and accommodation to guests. Hospitality is one of the largest industries in the world and is expected to continue growing.

There are an enormous number of hotel and restaurant establishments just about everywhere. Therefore, the opportunity for choosing where you want to work and live is great. The opportunity for career advancement in the hospitality industry is also excellent. Industry growth has allowed managers to advance more rapidly than in many other industries.

The hospitality industry provides exciting opportunities for people with a variety of backgrounds, experiences, skills, talents, and personalities. Many skills and experiences are transferable between different types of hospitality businesses. For instance, if you have restaurant experience, you can also work for a food and beverage department or catering department in a hotel.

Origins of the Hospitality Industry

The hospitality industry has been around for thousands of years. In Roman times, people would open their homes to travelers in hopes that they would be given a place to stay when they traveled. The story of Joseph and Mary traveling to Bethlehem in the Bible is a perfect example of early hospitality. The innkeeper had no rooms available but gave Joseph and Mary the use of his stable.

Over time, as travel and commerce expanded, business-minded individuals created dedicated restaurant and lodging facilities to meet the needs of growing numbers of travelers.

Changing economic systems led to greater industrialization, and that, in turn, led to more people having more disposable income. Advances in transportation enabled more people to travel greater distances. As people traveled more, the hospitality industry grew. The Ford Model-T made car ownership possible for average people and allowed them the luxury of travel when they wanted, where they wanted. After World War II, the interstate highway system was developed, increasing the ease of travel. The end of World War II was also the beginning of the airline industry, allowing for distant travel in a short period of time.

The hospitality industry has continued to evolve and expand as states and nations have emerged. New hospitality products and new destinations continue to add adventure and excitement to this vibrant industry segment.

The Hospitality Industry Today

The hospitality industry has become a part of day-to-day life in America. Nearly a third of all meals consumed by Americans are eaten away from home. This is mainly because most Americans are working and do not have time to cook a meal.

Lodging is available to fit the demands of all types of travelers. Whether it is the budget-minded family or the luxury a top executive expects and demands, a lodging option is available to satisfy.

Interval ownership (also known as a "timeshare" is an example of how lodging has evolved. Interval ownership allows the guest to purchase a week or more at a resort for as long as the resort is in operation and can even be passed down to their children.

The cruise line industry is also growing, as only around five percent of the American population has taken a cruise. This has spawned the growth of cruise lines to expand their offerings and entice more and more people to cruise.

As the hospitality industry has grown, so has the savvy of the consumer. Today's consumers eat out on a regular basis, are well traveled, and have high expectations for their hospitality experiences. This means the hospitality industry must continuously be evolving to meet these expectations.

CAREERS IN THE HOSPITALITY INDUSTRY

Many hospitality jobs may look glamorous, especially those with upscale restaurants or in luxurious resorts. It is true that many jobs are in beautiful, clean, and comfortable settings, but there is a lot of behind-the-scenes hard work that most people do not see. Whether they are entry-level or managerial positions, many jobs require long hours, and work in the evenings, on weekends and on holidays. The work can be stressful, hectic, and unpredictable. You may have to deal with guests who are demanding, irate, or unpleasant. Or, you might encounter a customer service problem that can be difficult to solve. In addition, hospitality employees are expected to provide friendly and prompt service even when they are tired or under stress. It takes patience when you are faced with those difficult or challenging situations. However, if you have a good deal of energy, like to meet and work with people, and enjoying helping people and making them feel welcome and comfortable, this could be an the right industry for you.

Passions

The hospitality industry offers a wide variety of career options. Therefore, if you really like the idea of working in this business, you can probably find a position in the industry that fits your interest, talents, and personality.

The hospitality industry is a people business. Not only will you interact with different kinds of guests, but it is also likely that you will work with people from a variety of backgrounds and cultures. If you enjoy meeting and helping people, this is the right industry for you. You may even meet a few celebrities!

The work is constantly different and challenging, because you help with customers who have different needs, preferences, and expectations. Anytime you deal with the public, you have to be prepared for the unexpected.

Many positions offer flexible work hours that can fit your preferences. However, when beginning your career you might not work the hours you would like.

Not only will you possibly live in wonderful places, but you may also work in fabulous facilities that most only dream of visiting! A career in hospitality can be your ticket to the world of luxury.

Pay and Perks

Salaries vary greatly in the hospitality industry, because there are an enormous variety of jobs. Entry-level employees frequently start working at minimum wage. However, many greatly increase their income with **gratuities** (tips), so the salary may not truly reflect the real income. Compensation for mid-level managers differs depending on the types, sizes, and locations of hospitality businesses. Generally, the higher salaries are found in larger businesses due to more complex work responsibilities. Many upper-level managers make six-digit salaries. Performance bonuses can add another 25% to the base salary.

If you love to travel, many hospitality jobs provide opportunities for traveling or living in different parts of the U.S. or in different countries. Some locations are more exotic than others, but all offer the opportunity to experience a different part of the country or the world.

Pay and perks vary a great deal. Some hospitality businesses offer compensation, such as free meals, lodging, use of recreation facilities, and bonus programs. Others assist employees with tuition for continuing education. It helps to be aware of the possible benefits so you can negotiate the best possible package for yourself.

Preparation

Although there are many jobs in the industry that do not require a college degree, most of those jobs are lower paying frontline positions. If you plan to establish a long-term career in the hospitality industry, college education or special training is needed for advancing to managerial positions. Moreover, an increasing number of hospitality businesses are hiring people with college degrees, and many companies give preference to people with a degree in hospitality management. Regardless of degree title, hospitality or recreation, a college degree will generally help you to advance more quickly in the industry.

There are many schools in the U. S. that offer two-year or four-year degrees in hospitality management or commercial recreation. The best programs combine strong leaderships and management skills with excellent customer service and fiscal accountability offerings.

Many hotel, resorts, and cruise ships have recreation departments. These departments oversee the vast array of activities that are offered to their guests. Conference centers also quite often have recreation departments directed more toward team-building activities. Students from commercial recreation programs often find excellent opportunities in hospitality settings where guests stay longer or conduct business on-site.

Some academic programs may focus on certain areas, such as hotel management, restaurant management, or **culinary** preparation, while other programs offer education in all those areas. The largest programs may offer specialized coursework for those planning to work in casinos, conference facilities, golf courses, destination resorts, and cruise lines.

Many schools require an internship in the industry before graduation. The internship requirement is beneficial because it helps you to gain valuable industry experience outside of the classroom. Many hospitality students are able to get managerial positions right after graduation because of the experience they gain through their internships.

Many hospitality students caters work part time while attending school. Hotels and restaurants offer a lot of part-time jobs such as servers, kitchen helper, front desk clerk, bell person, and housekeeper that can fit around a school schedule. Many students start building their careers in the hospitality industry with those part-time jobs, and this helps them determine if it is the right industry for them.

There is a good chance that you will interact with customers and coworkers of different nationalities and languages. In addition, many American companies expand their businesses in different parts of the world and send their employees to work in different countries. You might have a chance to work in a different country that uses a different language. Therefore, it would be helpful if you become proficient in a foreign language.

Possibilities

Like many other recreation-related careers, the possibilities in the hospitality industry are almost unlimited. It is very important that you start with entry-level jobs of different kinds so you can learn about different aspects of operations and become a well-rounded employee. Find good mentors and good companies that are willing to teach you and help you grow. Networking is vital in this industry. The more people you know, the more opportunities you will have for advancement. Being willing to relocate to different geographical areas is important because opportunities often happen somewhere else.

The more hospitality experience you have, the better your job possibilities will be when you graduate. Many companies offer paid summer internship programs and strongly promote students working each summer during their college career. These opportunities give the student a taste of what it will be like when they graduate as well as opportunities for employers to observe and develop potential managers. We will discuss career options within the lodging and restaurant industries. If these areas interest you, make sure you cross-check information in other chapters such as Outdoor Recreation, Travel and Tourism, Events Management, and Commercial Recreation to help you locate the niches of most interest to you.

Lodging Industry

The **lodging industry** caters to tourists, corporate travelers who need a place to stay for just a few days, and people who need extended stays due to relocation or long-term work assignments. There are a wide-range of different lodging properties, from small bed-and-breakfast inns that have a few guest rooms to large hotels that have a more than a thousand rooms. Many hotels provide basic accommodations, while **full-service hotels** provide restaurants, meeting rooms, exhibit halls, and ballrooms for conventions, wedding receptions, and social events. In addition, many hotels also offer recreational facilities for guests to enjoy, such as tennis courts, swimming pools, spa services, fitness centers, golf courses, and planned recreation activities. Since the lodging industry offers a great variety of facilities and services, a wide range of jobs in different areas can be found.

Every hotel organizes its jobs in a different way. Larger hotels tend to have more divisions, and jobs are more specialized. A large full-service hotel may have positions in front office, food and beverage, sales and marketing, accounting and finance, and human resources.

While a great number of career opportunities can be found from large hotels, a small lodging business can also offer a great learning environment for essential experience in hotel operations. Consider the following areas of lodging operations to learn more.

Passions—If your interests lie in travel and luxury, you should consider a career in lodging. You need to enjoy finding ways to make people happy whom you don't know and may likely never see again. Recreation majors can find success and satisfaction in any division but most often gravitate to front-of-house positions with strong customer contact, into marketing and sales, or into employee training and development positions in Human Resources.

Pay and Perks—The salaries vary within the lodging industry based on position, size of property, and service level. Traditionally a larger hotel will pay more, but this is not always true. The exception is that higher end luxury hotels are usually not as large but have higher levels of service, and they can pay very well for the right employee.

Hotels that have food service will often give meals to their employees during their shifts. This will reduce your grocery budget significantly, giving you more discretionary income.

Many lodging companies give free nights or reduced rates in hotels to their employees. This can be quite a savings when traveling and allows you the opportunity to experience other properties.

Preparation—Get a job in the lodging industry! Whether it be during the summer or during the school year, you will need experience within the industry. Recruiters like to see that a student has some related hands-on experience.

The job could be working as a front desk clerk, as a bellperson, as a housekeeper, or as a waitperson in the hotel coffee shop. This may require that you leave your job at the grocery store where you've sacked groceries for three years and are making a decent wage but think of this as an investment in your future.

Possibilities—There is a large range of lodging opportunities. From the 4,000-room casino hotels in Las Vegas, Nevada, to the four-room bed and breakfast in Buford, North Carolina—they are all possible employers.

You can move up in management in a large hotel chain with never ending opportunities for advancement. At some point you may want to start your own small independent hotel and grow that into something large (if that is your desire). People like Conrad Hilton and William Marriott started off with one property and built their businesses into multi-national corporations.

Front Office. The functions of the front office include processing reservations, registering and checking out guests, monitoring arrivals and departures, receiving and forwarding mail, providing local or other information to guests, and handling guest complaints. Since hotels are open around the clock, it is common to have three work shifts throughout the day. Front-office employees deal with guests constantly. Employees should be friendly, understanding, and willing to help guests. For people who plan to build a career in the lodging industry, the front office is a great department to learn about the lodging management toward advancing to managerial positions later on.

Uniformed Service. Positions in this department include bellhops, door attendants, and baggage porters. They carry bags, usher guests to their rooms, and assist guests in and out of their vehicles. Many full-service hotels also have **concierges** who provide information on local attractions and events, make travel arrangements and restaurant reservations, provide concert tickets, and assist with other special requests. Some hotels cross-train uniformed personnel in front office operations in case extra help is needed at the front desk.

Food and Beverage. Full-service hotels provide a variety of food and beverage outlets or services such as restaurants, coffee shops, bars, banquets, and room service. Many positions in the department are similar to those in the **restaurant industry**, as are the skills required. Many hotels outsource part of their food and beverage operations to restaurant chains. Having a chain restaurant in a hotel not only helps to promote brand-recognition for its business, but it also attracts more business from local residents.

Recreation Programming. Many hotels and resorts offer extensive on-site recreational amenities for their guests. Golf courses, aquatic facilities, recreation centers, and spas are four specialized facilities that are often staffed by professionals from parks and recreation programs. Some properties have large resort recreation divisions that operate year-round to ensure high levels of guest satisfaction.

Marketing and Sales. Employees in this department are responsible for selling guest rooms, meeting space or other space for weddings, banquets, and special events. The organization of this department can vary a lot depending on the size and type of markets that a hotel targets. Positions may include director of marketing, sales manager, banquet manger, convention service manager, and sales representative. Sales personnel may receive bonuses in addition to their salaries. When a conference or special event is taking place in the hotel, sales personnel need to be there with the clients to ensure the event is going well. Some sales people may travel frequently to meet with clients. Therefore, work hours can be irregular and long.

Housekeeping. This department is responsible for providing a clean and comfortable environment for guests' stays. Housekeepers clean guest rooms, lobbies, halls, and other public rooms and areas in a hotel. In larger hotels, this department may include executive housekeepers, assistant housekeepers, and floor supervisors.

Accounting Management. The responsibilities of this department include recording sales records, preparing financial reports and so on. Accounting personnel maintain fiscal records, ensuring income and expense are properly allocated between the cost centers, and they also respond to guest billing inquiries. Accounting employees should be detail oriented and have good written and verbal communication skills. Some hotels prefer employees with prior hotel experience.

Revenue Management. Positions in revenue management are relatively new in the lodging industry. There is a growing trend that increasing number of hotels are hiring revenue managers who help them to maximize their sales. Revenue managers must have knowledge with the hotel business and be familiar with their market segments. They work closely with the front office, marketing and sales department, and catering service department to develop sales strategies that meet a hotel's revenue goals. They monitor and evaluate past pricing strategies and reservation data, analyze markets, forecast future demands, and set pricing strategies for different market segments. Thus, revenue managers must have good analytical and communication skills.

Human Resources Management. This department is responsible for hiring employees, employee training, employee relations, compensation and benefits administration, legal compliance, and payroll and benefits administration. Job opportunities are available for people who have hotel experience or have a degree in human resources.

Restaurant Industry

Restaurant industry jobs are found everywhere across the U.S. and the world. There are various types of restaurants, from cafeterias, coffee shops, fast-food restaurants, casual theme restaurants, to fine dining restaurants. Even in difficult financial times, today's busy lifestyles encourage many people to dine away from home. The growth of this industry is predicted to continue. Therefore, job opportunities are abundant.

Passions—If you love food–preparing it or sharing it–then the food and beverage sector is for you. You'll get to serve at one of life's most essential levels and use your specialized skills to create welcoming settings for guests and clients. For some, food and beverage is a lifelong adventure. For others, it provides a way to learn, on the job, about the importance of customer service and the role of fine dining as a tool to enable any group of people to bond over the time-honored communal table.

Pay and Perks—Like most areas of hospitality, the pay range varies with the size of the operation and your position within it. But there are few economic sectors that offer such rapid opportunities for advancement. Your creativity and business acumen may be the only limits to your advancement. Perks range from complimentary meals to great industry events where professionals compete to "out host" one another and highlight their best features.

Preparation—In addition to your campus coursework, you will need to gain industry experience. Look for opportunities to supervise others, manage some aspect of the operation, or get involved in ordering and inventory. If you want to pursue a career in food preparation, look for opportunities to attend a reputable culinary academy and broaden your expertise to include food science and costing. If wine and/or spirits are your forté, seek specialized expertise and knowledge in those areas as well.

Possibilities—Large or small, at home or abroad, the food and beverage sector is so varied that you will find many options to locate your niche within it. If you want to provide down-home community for residents of your hometown, consider a cozy café. If you want to travel the world, consider a career with a national brand seeking to increase its international presence. This sector is broad, so get experience, finish your university degree, secure the best industry certifications and explore your opportunities.

Hosts and Hostesses. They greet and seat guests, offer guests menus, schedule dining reservations, answer questions, and inform guests about wait times. In some restaurants, they also work as cashiers. Hosts and hostesses are expected to make a great first and last impression on guests. Most restaurants prefer hiring people with friendly and positive attitudes.

Waiters and Waitresses/Servers. They take orders, serve food and beverages, prepare itemized checks, and accept payments. They should be able to answer questions about how menu items are prepared and make recommendations based on guests' needs and interests. They should also anticipate and react to guests' needs in order to provide prompt service. Depending on the type of restaurant, servers are expected to prepare salads or certain dishes at the tables. They may also clean and set up tables and run the cash register. The work can be very physically demanding. They are on their feet most of the time, bringing hot dishes to tables and carrying heavy trays of food, dishes, and glassware. Waiters and waitresses need good memories in order to accurately convey guests' orders. Being able to do quick arithmetic is helpful at some restaurants in order to total bills manually.

Dining Room Attendants. They assist waiters and waitresses with removing dirty dishes and soiled linens from tables, as well as cleaning and setting tables. They also keep the dining room stocked with a supply of silverware, glasses, dishes, and linens.

Chefs, Cooks, and Kitchen Workers. Chefs and cooks are responsible for creating menus and preparing food. Chefs usually have more skills and experience than cooks. While some restaurants have standardized menus, may restaurants offer tasty and unique foods that provide chefs opportunities to be creative and to experiment with new ideas. Some chefs are responsible for supervising kitchen operations and purchasing food supplies. Kitchen workers perform routine and repetitive tasks. They measure ingredients, cut meat and vegetables, prepare salads and cold items, and stir and strain soups and sauces. They also clean equipment, utensils, dishes, and silverware.

These employees need to be able to prepare food quickly under pressure, especially during peak dining hours. They stand on their feet for hours at a time and work near hot ovens and ranges.

Many people start their culinary careers as kitchen workers and work their way up to becoming chefs after years of training and experience in the kitchen. More and more people obtain training through high schools, two- or four-year colleges or culinary schools.

Cruise Industry

The cruise line industry offers career opportunities at sea and on land. The land-based jobs range from reservationists assisting customers in planning vacations to purchasing agents who place gigantic orders that are loaded on ships in their homeports each week and sales and marketing professionals who work with travel agents and meeting planners to fill the ships year round.

Cruise ships are actually made up of two components. The first is transportation, which the Captain oversees with the aid of the crew, which ensures that the ship reaches each port in a timely and safe manner. The second component is the lodging aspect. A cruise ship is basically a floating resort. Cruise ships have hotel rooms called cabins, as well as restaurants, bars, shops, spas, fitness centers, theaters, child care facilities, swimming pools, and an elaborate array of recreational facilities. The positions are similar to those offered in hotels, some of the positions might have different names.

Passions—A cruise, for many guests, is a once-in-a-lifetime adventure to celebrate a milestone event. If you like being part of a multinational group of hospitality professionals who work together to create memorable experiences for guests, this could be just the sector for you. Intrigued by exotic ports of call? Working on a cruise ship is an excellent way to see the world.

Pay and Perks—Most cruise ships are not registered as American Ships and thus are not subject to American labor laws and regulations. Consequently, pay and perks vary widely. Hours are long, but accommodations and meals are included, so you can save most of your pay if you are disciplined. All cruise ships have doctors and nurses onboard who provide free medical care for the crew.

It is not uncommon for cruise employees to work six or even seven days a week for three months. However, when you are off, you are flown home or to another destination of your choice for a month or more before returning to work on the same ship or another ship in the fleet.

Most cruise ships have many services just for the employees, such as a dining room, bar, gym, convenience store, and even a pool. Think of it as a "village" for the local inhabitants who work on the floating resort.

Preparation—Working in a restaurant or hotel is a good way to gain experience that will prepare you for a job in the cruise industry. The cruise industry does not expect you to join their crew with years of cruise experience in an entry-level position and will provide training to prepare you for a life on the seas. Cruise lines do not offer internships due to the required training before you step foot on the ship.

Possibilities—Many people work in the cruise sector for several years before moving on to more traditional hospitality careers. Career paths do exist, however, for experienced and excellent personnel.

Purser. This position is similar to a front desk agent with the front office manager being called the Chief Purser.

Steward. This position is similar to a housekeeper in a hotel. The head of housekeeping on a cruise ship is called Chief Steward.

Cruise Director. This position can vary from cruise line to cruise line but typically overseas the activities and entertainment aspect of the cruise.

Shore Excursion Desk Agent. These employees are in charge of booking and marketing tours and activities for guests when the ship is in ports of call.

Additional Career Possibilities
Whenever people have to be fed and sheltered, opportunities exist for people with a passion for hospitality. That means that you do not have to live in an urban area or resort setting to find solid career opportunities. You may find additional career possibilities in campus settings such as colleges, universities, and corporate training facilities. You may find career options in hospitals, senior care facilities, the military, or corrections. Some folks combine another passion with their hospitality training and find careers in residential camps or disaster relief.

SUMMARY OF HOSPITALITY CAREER POSSIBILITIES

Career	Passions	Pay and Perks	Preparation	Possibilities
Lodging industry	Travel and luxury	Minimum wage to executive levels	Four-year college degree in hospitality management	General manager, front office manager, director of sales, food and beverage manager, human resources manager
Restaurant industry	Creating, preparing, and sharing food	Minimum wage to executive levels	Four-year college degree in hospitality management	Owner, manager, chef
Cruise industry	Travel, guest service, and luxury	Minimum wage to executive levels	Four-year college degree in hospitality management	Sales and marketing, hotel manager, cruise director, chief purser, food and beverage manager

FUTURE OPPORTUNITIES, ISSUES, AND CHALLENGES

The hospitality industry grew rapidly in the United States during the twentieth century. The U.S. hospitality companies are still expanding, but many have entered international markets to continue their growth. The hospitality industry is always evolving. Whether it be a hot, new quick-service restaurant chain with meals under $5.00 that is sweeping the country or an ultra-luxury resort on a secluded beach with rooms selling for $1,000 per night. The hospitality industry will continue to grow.

Cruise ships are getting larger with some being large enough to have parks in the atrium with trees and grass as well as rooms on the interior of the ship with balconies overlooking the activities below. At the same time, there are much smaller ships being built with marinas that lower off the back of the ship for water activities.

Changes in lifestyle and legislation have spawned the growth of the gaming industry. This is a heavily government-controlled industry with great potential for growth. Whether you work on the casino floor, in the hotel, or in one of the restaurants, there are many career opportunities.

A career in hospitality can involve exploring opportunities in new places to respond to the needs of adventurers and novelty seekers. An underwater resort is proposed for Dubai, and Virgin Atlantic has established itself as a pioneer in space tourism, accepting reservations for commercial space flights for a one-of-a-kind vacation experience (Virgin, 2010).

Coffee shops, tea bars, and other small, trendy cafes continue to open at intersections, near churches, fitness centers, and commercial retail strips, and in neighborhoods. These "third places" (Oldenburg, 2000) are neat additions to livable community efforts by providing a space for regular interactions between friends and coworkers.

Finally, branded and franchise operations are finding new ways to enter new and smaller markets. Starbucks stores are ubiquitous to the point of twin locations on opposite street corners in major metropolitan areas. At the other end of the scale, national quick-service brands and franchisees are entering smaller communities with the modular and smaller scale operations that can be profitable in smaller markets while expanding the brand/franchise into new markets.

As long as people continue to travel or dine away from home, the hospitality industry will be continue to evolve to meet the needs of people away from their homes. From international destinations to "on-the-corner" nooks, hospitality providers will find unlimited opportunities to serve guests.

RESOURCES AND GETTING INVOLVED

There is simply no substitute for industry-specific experience. If you think you want a career in hospitality, you must get job experience early and often. Look to local opportunities, your own network of contacts, and professional organizations to secure that all important industry knowledge, expertise, and experience.

Professional Organizations

There are many associations in the hospitality industry. Those associations offer workshops, conferences, certificates, and training programs to help you learn about the industry. Many of the associations also post news articles on their websites so you can get current information about trends and industry issues. Most associations are actively seeking young professionals and offer special, deeply discounted rates for students. Joining one or more associations will provide you many networking and job-searching opportunities.

If you are interested in lodging you might want to join:

American Hotel and Lodging Association
http://www.ahla.com/

American Resort Development Association
http://www.arda.org//AM/Template.cfm?Section=Home

If your interests lie in hospitality accounting and technology, you might want to join:

Hospitality Financial and Technology Professionals
http://www.hftp.org/

If you think you might want to be a chef, you should join:

American Culinary Federation
http://www.acfchefs.org/

International Association of Culinary Professionals
http://www.iacp.com/

If you are considering a career in hospitality education, you should join:

International Council on Hotel, Restaurant, and Institutional Education
http://www.chrie.org/i4a/pages/index.cfm?pageid=1

If you think you want a career in restaurants, food service, or catering, you should join:

National Restaurant Association
http://www.restaurant.org/careers/

Society for Foodservice Management
http://www.sfm-online.org/

National Association of Catering Executives
http://www.nace.net/

Certifications, Licenses

Some associations sponsor certification programs designed to ensure a level of professionalism and currency. Three of many certification programs available to planners are identified here. Information interviews and online research will reveal additional certification programs for specialized aspects of the industry.

Hotel manager certifications
Certified Hotel Administrator (CHA) or **Certified Lodging Manager (CLM)** (American Hotel & Lodging Association Educational Institute, 2010).

Food and Beverage
Certified Food and Beverage Executive (CFBE)
(American Hotel & Lodging Association Educational Institute, 2010).

In addition there are other specialized certification programs for specific aspects of hospitality. Two of the many specialized certifications are **Certified Hospitality Technology Professional (CHTP)** and **Certified Hospitality Accountant Executive (CHAE)** (American Hotel & Lodging Association Educational Institute, 2010). Check with the various industry associations to learn more about their certification programs.

Certifications you should pursue during your college career that will increase your employability are:

Sanitation certification, this can come from through the National Restaurant Association **ServSafe** food Safety Training Program or from a state board or regulatory agency (ServSafe, 2010).

Alcohol Safety certification which is offered through the National Restaurant Association ServSafe Alcohol Program and helps servers of spirits learn how to safely provide alcoholic beverages (ServSafe, 2010).

Where to Get Experience

It is never too soon to begin working on your resume, and a good place to get started is by getting involved in the hospitality associations you can join on your own university campus. You need to be active in these clubs and become an officer. Employers like to hire graduates who have taken leadership roles.

The next step is to join national hospitality organizations and attend the regional meetings. These meetings are often held during lunch and are a perfect opportunity to network with managers. Force yourself to get out there and meet people, and before long they'll be talking to you about a summer internship or coming to work for them when you graduate!

Many national organizations also have student memberships, which means you can join for very little money. You can also attend their annual conventions at a reduced price, and most have special sessions and activities for college students. It is not uncommon for internship/career interviews to be scheduled during a convention, which allows you to look for job away from home without having to travel across the country at your own expense.

CONCLUSION

There are plenty of opportunities for your career development. The hospitality industry is one of the largest employers in the U.S. and in many other countries. There is always a need for skilled and experienced managers. Many people worked their way up from bellpersons or waiters to become top executives in the industry. Others have taken "a little restaurant" and built it into a franchise empire. Few industry sectors offer the advancement opportunities of hospitality. As long as you are willing to work hard and continue to learn, your future will be bright.

FOR FURTHER INVESTIGATION

The world of hospitality is timeless and contemporary. You will find nearly limitless opportunities if you gain the requisite skills, remain flexible, and are willing to relocate. Fortunately for you, most hospitality businesses have a good online presence (after all, they exist to be found by folks who are needing shelter, food, and community away from home) so you'll be able to find a lot of information without leaving the comfort of your chair. Also, even the smallest communities typically have accommodations, restaurants, and nightspots, so you will be able to expand and apply your new knowledge without leaving the local area.

For More Research

1. There are many job search websites for hospitality careers. You can explore them to see what kinds of jobs there are. By reading job descriptions on these websites, you will gain ideas about work activities and required skills and knowledge. Based on your particular interests—accommodations or food and beverage—select three websites and explore them thoroughly.

American Hotel and Lodging Association Career Center
http://www.ahla.com/careers/index.asp

Hcareers
http://www.hcareers.com/

Hospitality Link
http://www.hospitalitylink.com/

HospitalityJobsOnline
http://www.hospitalityonline.com/

Hospitality Resource Network
http://www.hospitalityresourcenetwork.com/

Hospitality Career Network
http://www.hospitalitycareernetwork.com/

Hotel Job Resource
http://www.hoteljobresource.com/

Hotel Jobs Network
http://www.hoteljobsnetwork.com/

HotelJobs
http://www.hoteljobs.com/

HOTELCareers
http://www.hotelscareers.com/

Foodservice.com
http://www.foodservice.com/employment/index.cfm

National Restaurant Association Job Bank
http://restaurant-org.new-jobs.com/

StarChefs
http://www.starchefsjobfinder.com/

2. Marriott and Outback Steakhouse are two well-regarded hospitality companies well known for their employee training and development. Visit their websites and investigate the "career" sections. Identify career opportunities that interest you within these two companies.
   http://marriott.com/
   http://www.outback.com/
3. What is your favorite fast-food restaurant or hotel? Go to their website and find information about franchise opportunities.

Active Investigation

1. Find people who are working for hotels and/or restaurants. Complete informational interviews by asking them what they like about the job and what the challenges of their work are. See the instructions in chapter 2 on how to conduct an informational interview.
2. Corporate properties offer mobility and lots of jobs, but many people have pursued their entrepreneurial dreams in the hospitality sector. Check with the local convention and visitors bureau, or chamber of commerce, and ask for leads to local boutique hotels/bed and breakfast inns or family-owned restaurants. Arrange an information interview with the owners to see how they established their enterprise.
3. Keep an eye open to see when a new hotel, restaurant, or nightclub opens in your community. If possible, locate the owners and see if you can meet them at

the establishment. It will be a great opportunity to learn something about how the owner/entrepreneur selected the type of establishment, its location, and the proprietor's motivations in opening the business.

4. Contact the conference hotel whenever you are attending a professional meeting to see if you can meet with someone at the property while you are on-site. It is one of the most cost-effective and less stressful ways to prepare for job interviews.

5. Get a part-time job in a hotel or restaurant where you are going to school or find work in a different destination resort each summer.

Recommended Reading

Hailey, A. (2000) *Hotel.* **Berkley.**
A bestselling novel about the guest and employees of an exclusive hotel.

Hilton, C. N. (1984). *Be my guest.* **Upper Saddle River, NJ:Prentice-Hall.**
The autobiography by the founder of Hilton Hotel Corporation.

Klein, R. A. (2002). *Cruise ship blues.* **Gabriola Island, BC, Canada:New Society Publishers.**
An expose on the darker side of the cruise industry.

Kroc, R. (1992). *Grinding it out:The making of McDonald's.* **St. Martin's. New York, NY.**
An autobiography by the founder of McDonald's Corporation.

Marriott, J. W. (1995). *Marriott:The J. Willard Marriott story.* **Deseret Book Co. Salt Lake City, UT.**
An autobiography by the founder of Marriott Hotels Corporation.

Mitchelli, J. A. (2009). *The new gold standard: Five leadership principles for creating a legendary customer experience courtesy of the Ritz-Carlton Hotel Company.* **McGraw-Hill. Columbus, OH.**
A glance inside the operations of Ritz-Carlton and why the company has twice won the Malcolm Baldrige National Quality Award.

Plank, G. (2005). *Saving the St. George.* **Lansing, MI: American Hotel and Lodging Institute.**
A novel on the running of a boutique hotel.

Sharp, I. (2009). *Four Seasons: The story of a business philosophy.* **Portfolio Hardcover.**
An autobiography by the founder of Four Seasons Hotels.

REFERENCES

American Hotel and Lodging Association Educational Institute. (2010). Retrieved from   http://www.ei-ahla.org/

Farner, B. (2005). Your Heath and You. Retrieved from http://urbanext.illinois.edu/yourhealth/default.cfm?IssueID=24

Oldenburg, R. (2000) *Celebrating the Third Place: Inspiring stories about the "Great Good Places" at the heart of our communities.* Marlowe & Company,

ServSafe. (2010). Retrieved from http://www.servsafe.com/

Virgin Galactic. (2010). Retrieved from http://www.virgingalactic.com/.

❝

The greatest part about my job is to hear from guests about how we have added value to others' lives. Travel positively affects people personally and socially, and our world benefits economically as well. Meeting people and connecting people from all over the world is pure joy.

— SANDY DHUYVETTER
founder, executive producer and host of TravelTalk MEDIA

❞

12

Travel and Tourism

VINOD SASIDHARAN
San Diego State University

FOCUS QUESTIONS

While deciding whether or not to pursue a career in travel and tourism, the reader is encouraged to consider the following questions:

Q: *Do I want travel to be a routine part of my job? Am I comfortable being in new places?*

A: If you have an urge to see the world and work in many different places, then travel and tourism is your business.

Q: *Am I willing to interact regularly with new people with different viewpoints/ ideas, varying knowledge levels, and diverse backgrounds?*

A: As an ambassador of travel, you will be extending your hand in friendship, revering the environment and celebrating the diversity of cultures while on your journeys.

Q: *Do I have the passion to adopt my job (and responsibilities) as a lifestyle?*

A: This profession is about spending your professional time in beautiful places and working with interesting people who want to change the world. It is not a career or a profession; it is a lifestyle and life.

Q: *Do I have the patience to invest my time, energy, and resources in helping others, as a major part of my job, without having complete control over the final outcome of my efforts?*

A: You will have to dedicate your life to tourism and guest services, to help people learn through travel and to get to know each other better, to foster peace, and to discover themselves once again.

Q: *Are long-term personal (including social and financial) rewards more important to me than short-term monetary gains?*

A: You have to be willing to work in this field because you will be doing what you love doing. You cannot expect to enter this field to become rich or even paid a high salary, even though that may evolve over time.

KEY TERMS

Tourism organizations
Cultural tourism
Ecotourism
Tourism industry sectors
Destination Management Organizations
   (DMOs)

Theme and amusement parks
Adventure tourism
Green travel and tourism
Sustainable tourism
Heritage tourism

PROFILE 1: COULD THIS BE YOU?

DAVID WILLIAMS is the Deputy Director for the Utah Office of Tourism (UOT). As the person in charge of market research for the office, David's responsibilities include:

- Gathering of travel and tourism statistics
- Generating travel-related economic forecasts
- Coordinating marketing programs
- Allocating funds for destination marketing
- Guiding political groups

Q: *What does your work involve?*

A: I am in charge of the market research for the office. This includes gathering statistics—visitation at parks, the airport, welcome centers, occupancy statistics, and attractions in Utah. I also purchase visitor profiles including who is coming, demographic and psychographic information, how much people spend, and how they found out about Utah. We have around $2 million to distribute to non-profit and destination marketing organizations in Utah for promotion.

Q: *How do you make a difference through your work?*

A: When I was hired, the UOT marketing budget was very small and we weren't able to get our message out to as many people as we would have liked due to lack of funding. I was able to research how other states fund their tourism offices, provided economic impact figures, and was very involved in an effort to convince the legislature to provide more marketing dollars so our office could compete in the marketplace. The legislature increased the UOT budget, so it is 10 times higher than it was previously. Now we are promoting Utah more aggressively than ever before.

Q: *If you could give a young professional interested in this career area one piece of advice, what would it be?*

A: I enjoy my career because I am passionate about Utah and enjoy marketing. If I didn't love living in Utah, it would be hard to come to work every day to promote it. You'll find your career much more rewarding if you believe in whatever you are doing.

PROFILE 2: COULD THIS BE YOU?

SERGE DEDINA is the Executive Director of WiLDCOAST, an international organization that utilizes tourism to protect and preserve coastal ecosystems and wildlife in Latin America and the Californias. As the person who runs WiLDCOAST, Serge has an array of responsibilities, including:
- Raising funds for ecotourism projects
- Coordinating ecotourism projects
- Building grassroots ecotourism support
- Conducting medias campaigns to promote ecotourism projects
- Carrying out coastal conservation efforts

Q: *What do you do during the week, as part of your work?*

A: We spent a week in Laguna San Ignacio, a gray whale sanctuary, and UNESCO World Heritage site in Mexico talking with ecotourism outfitters and filming a documentary with Phillipe Cousteau and Animal Planet on our efforts to protect the lagoon and gray whales and how ecotourism/whale watching is important for conservation efforts.

Q: *Do you have an example illustrating how you transformed your organization (or a client) through your services?*

A: One of my projects, Laguna San Ignacio Conservation Alliance, resulted in the permanent protection of a UNESCO World Heritage site that helped build the capacity of local landowners and ecotour operators to manage complex land management projects. We helped develop a local outfitters association, get them a bank account, launched an ecoloan program to buy four-stroke engines and replace polluting two-stroke outboard engines. We worked a deal to carry out conservation easements on the land owned by the ecooutfitters, protecting 140,000 acres.

Q: *What challenges you on your job?*

A: The challenges include: 1) working with fragile coalitions to preserve areas; 2) obtaining funding to do our work; 3) staying focused on strategic goals and not getting sidetracked; 5) focusing on business end of WiLDCOAST instead of just project management; 6) building new programs and projects and making decisions to discard old projects.

WISH YOU WERE HERE: GOING PLACES IN TRAVEL AND TOURISM

While all tourism jobs focus on the creation and provision of travel products and experiences, ranging from goods to services, the most unique aspect of these careers is that tourism professionals are often working at the crossroads of business, environment, culture, and government. Before we go into more depth about potential careers, we'll review how tourism has become a profession in its own right.

How Did Tourism Come to Be a Profession?

Due to the increasing propensity among people to travel, both domestically and internationally, destinations with specialized services and products that cater to the experiential needs of the traveler/tourist have emerged (and continue to emerge) all around the world. In the past, travel and tourism careers were seen as jobs in private-sector hospitality services, including hotels and restaurants. Recent years have seen an upsurge in specialized forms of tourism and tourism destinations, creating a variety of new tourism organizations and job opportunities across the globe.

Tourism organizations are responsible for planning and creating travel experiences for tourists. Tourism organizations consist of both for-profit and non-profit enterprises and provide specialized amenities such as: recreation resources (including parks and campgrounds, forests, protected areas, ski areas, beaches, etc.), sporting venues, theme parks, museums, cultural centers, historic sites, performance centers and theaters, convention centers, galleries and exhibition centers, zoos and aquaria, airlines/airports, stagecoaches, railways/stations, rental cars, transit systems, cruise ships/terminals, shopping centers, tourism information, tour companies, travel agencies, Web-based reservation systems, resorts, golf courses, hotels, and restaurants.

The significant contribution of travel and tourism to economic development combined with the central focus on tourist satisfaction has made it its own specialized professional area and study discipline. In addition to the travel opportunities combined with financial rewards offered by careers in tourism, professionals in the travel and tourism industry find their jobs to be exciting and fulfilling due to the variety involved in their work.

Travel and Tourism Today

What makes tourism a specialized discipline and professional area is the delivery of products and services geared toward satisfying the unique needs of travelers. Today, travel and tourism consists of the provision of experiences that are customized based on the specific interests of tourists. For example, **cultural tourism** refers to tourism opportunities that provide experiences to travelers who are motivated to travel for cultural enrichment purposes, **ecotourism** services provide environmental education opportunities, and business tourism offers products, services and amenities to people traveling for business-related purposes. As the needs of travelers become more sophisticated, professionals in the industry continue to develop and offer innovative tourism experiences and opportunities.

The main reason the tourism industry is appealing for people with a degree in recreation, parks, and tourism is the opportunity to apply their knowledge and strengths in sectors of the tourism industry that most suit their passions. **Tourism industry sectors** include hospitality establishments (hotels, restaurants), theme parks, cultural attractions, environmental attractions, nature parks, zoos/aquaria, destination management organizations, government agencies, sporting venues, specialty tour companies, travel supply stores, etc. (also see chapters on Outdoor Recreation, Sports Management, and The Hospitality Industry for more specifics about tourism-related areas).

To be successful in the multidimensional tourism industry, it is important for tourism professionals to have an in-depth knowledge of the various components of tourism and to be creative while developing new tourism opportunities for travelers. Tourism jobs can also be highly meaningful, mainly when the professional's work involves the creation of economic, community, and environmental benefits. The next section will help you determine if travel and tourism should be your career choice, and if so, what options would be meaningful for you.

TRENDY YET MEANINGFUL: WHAT ARE THE CAREER OPTIONS IN TRAVEL AND TOURISM?

Most tourism professionals are involved in jobs and projects that combine technological, economic, environmental, and cultural dimensions. Tourism jobs require collaborations with people from sectors such as attractions, hospitality services, transportation, visitor information, tourism marketing, governance, and non-governmental groups. The tourism industry offers professional opportunities for individuals from almost all academic backgrounds. For example, individuals interested in business-oriented jobs would find management careers in tourism to be the best match, whereas those interested in culture would be suitable for cultural interpretation and exhibition careers with cultural attractions, and those interested in environmental issues would find conservation-related careers with ecologically oriented tourism sectors to be most rewarding.

Passions

As discussed earlier, travel and tourism professionals have the privilege of working at the crossroads of business, environment, culture, and government. This means that these careers will appeal to those who enjoy getting and keeping current with a very broad array of knowledge. Different sectors within travel and tourism allow the person to focus more on business skills, cultural knowledge or environmental conservation.

Keep in mind that the opportunity to travel, as part of the job, is the most significant benefit, especially for those who enjoy visiting places and meeting new people. As you consider this benefit, keep in mind also that you need to be willing to embrace travel as a part of your work as well.

> **" Opportunities to Travel and Work Internationally…**
>
> I have had the pleasure of working in many cities in both Canada and the U.S. and have traveled extensively throughout a large part of the globe. Most importantly, I have found that the majority of people in tourism are delightful. They are people who have dedicated their lives to helping other people travel safely and enjoyably."
>
> —JOHN HOPE-JOHNSTONE, CEO
> *Corvallis Tourism*
> **"**

Pay and Perks

Wages and salaries for employees in the travel and tourism industry depend on the following main factors: academic qualifications, prior work experience, and professional certifications. Entry-level full-time employees usually start at around the pay grade for a four-year college graduate in an entry-level job and advanced-level staff can earn a good executive salary.

With regard to benefits, travel and tourism professionals in the public-sector tend to receive a wide range of health benefits; health-coverage and insurance in the private sector tends to vary depending on level of employment and size of the organization. Travel and tourism jobs frequently come with work-related travel allowances and funded opportunities for professional development.

Preparation

Permanent positions in the travel and tourism industry have traditionally been filled by people with degrees from a variety of academic disciplines. With the growing need for employees with specialized tourism knowledge, travel and tourism employers are increasingly seeking and hiring individuals with formal education and training in the tourism discipline.

A bachelor's degree in tourism or hospitality management, or a related discipline such as recreation management, is essential for acquiring an entry-level, full-time job with any reputable tourism organization. Graduates with this academic qualification, combined with 250 to 500 hours of internship and/or work experience, are seen favorably for filling permanent positions by travel and tourism employers.

Depending on an individual's specific career interests, an academic minor in business management, economics, environmental sciences, or social psychology enhances the likelihood of recruitment into the travel and tourism industry. It is typical for "new" tourism employees, especially those with bachelor's degrees, to start at entry level, and then progress on to mid- and advanced-level jobs within any tourism sector. Specifics about preparation will be discussed in more detail within the career possibilities section.

Broad Knowledge Yields Success

To be a success in tourism, you must have a working knowledge of its many components and how they interact. You must understand how the various sectors within the tourism industry help to move people from one place to another not just physically but emotionally.

TIP: Career Advancement in Travel and Tourism

While opportunities for career advancement are plentiful within the travel and tourism industry, formal education in the tourism field coupled with adequate professional experience is a must for a quick and steady career progression from entry-level to advanced-level jobs.

Possibilities

Tourism is the world's largest industry. In the United States, it is among the top three industries in almost every state, thereby providing diverse job opportunities for individuals from all academic and professional backgrounds and with varying skill levels. With growing investment in tourism development across the globe and proliferation of new, innovative tourism products and services, professional opportunities in the travel and tourism industry are going to continue to grow.

Organizations involved in the provision of tourism attractions, products, and services include those within the private sector, public sector, private-public partnerships, and non-governmental organizations. The three major sectors that provide job opportunities within the travel and tourism industry are:

1.   Destination management organizations
2.   Theme and amusement parks and local attractions
3.   Ecotourism and cultural tourism industries

The following information is intended to familiarize the reader with the functions of each of these three sectors, along with the passions, pays and perks, preparation and job possibilities within each. You will find additional information related to travel and tourism careers in several other chapters, including Recreation in Non-Profit Organizations, Outdoor Recreation, Event Management, The Hospitality Industry and Commercial Recreation.

Destination Management Organizations

Destination management organizations, often referred to as DMOs, may fall within the category of local-, regional-, or national-level agencies responsible for coordinating the growth of travel and tourism within their designated areas. Some examples of DMOs include national and state tourism offices, convention and visitors bureaus, chambers of commerce, economic development corporations, tourism information bureaus, visitor information offices, Port Authorities, etc. Although organizations represent the tourism needs and interests of both public- and private-sector businesses and are membership-based, they are usually funded by the government, and individuals working in DMOs are government employees. The functions of DMOs and mission will vary depending on the economic significance of tourism for the area. DMOs are usually involved in marketing the destination to tourists and media campaigns; providing information regarding travel opportunities, tourism attractions and businesses in the area; coordinating the services of tourism enterprises at the destination; conducting tourism research and compiling travel statistics; providing technical know how to tourism enterprises; facilitating the creation of new tourism opportunities; assisting in tourism policy making; and creating a general appreciation for tourism.

Passions—Tourism marketing, tourism economics, travel trends analysis, travel research, travel and tourism innovation, coalition-building among diverse groups and partnerships, working with people, and work-related travel.

Pay and Perks—Entry-level, full-time employees usually start at around the pay grade for a four-year college graduate in an entry-level job and advanced-level staff can earn a good executive salary. Being government employees, DMO job benefits tend to include full medical, dental, vision, and prescription drug coverage, along with a minimum of two-week paid vacation time, life insurance, disability compensation, and 401(K) plans. DMOs also offer a variety of professional development opportunities, which may include tuition reimbursement and funding for continuing education and conference attendance.

Preparation—A bachelor's degree in tourism or hospitality management, or a closely related discipline such a recreation management coupled with adequate professional experience is a must for a quick and steady career progression from entry-level to advanced-level jobs. Individuals with master's level degree in tourism, hospitality, or related areas and meeting and convention industry professional certifications are also highly favored by DMO employers.

Possibilities—Examples of job titles for positions available with DMOs are: director of convention and visitors bureau, convention services manager, sales and services coordinator, sales manager, tourism manager, destination management specialist, and visitor information officer. Refer to the chapters on Recreation in Non-Profits and Community-Based Recreation for information to complement travel and tourism jobs in these settings.

Tourism Manager, County Tourism Office

Responsibilities: Ability to assemble informative news releases, pamphlets, and brochures. Ability to coordinate a multitude of activities at one time. Ability to establish and maintain effective working relationships with Tourist Development Council, County staff, and outside agencies.

Qualifications: Bachelor's degree in marketing, public relations, journalism, communications, business or public administration, or hospitality management, and five years of progressively responsible experience in advertising or marketing in a public or quasi-public agency. Extensive knowledge of the principles, practices, and procedures of marketing and public relations.

Theme and Amusement Parks and Local Attractions

Theme and amusement parks and local attractions vary in scope from being significant at the local, regional, or national level and even international level. Some examples of national-level attractions include SeaWorld, the Walt Disney Company, Six Flags, and Universal Studios. Attractions of regional/local significance include Lego Land, CA, Idlewild, PA, Kennywood, PA, and Cedar Point, OH. Art, science, and natural history museums, performing centers and opera houses, and aquariums, zoos, and zoological gardens also fall within the category of tourism attractions. Events, festivals, and fairs showcasing arts, film, music and dance, comedy, and technology are increasingly becoming vital attractions drawing large numbers of tourists to destinations. Although theme parks and local attractions differ greatly in their respective functions and operations, the central goal of these tourism enterprises is to create entertaining experiences that have significant potential to attract and host visitors. The success of these enterprises depends on strategic partnerships with other sectors such as transportation, travel agencies, tour operators, DMOs, and hospitality services.

Passions—Working with people, guest service, guest entertainment, service innovation, new technology, partnerships, marketing, and economics are passions specific to this area.

Pay and Perks—While these tourism enterprises rely heavily on part-time or season employees hired at minimum wage and higher, entry-level, full-time employees usually start at around the pay grade for a four-year college graduate in an entry-level job. Advanced-level staff can earn a good executive salary. Employees may receive a multitude of benefits, including medical, prescription, vision, dental, life and disability insurance, 401(K) and Section 529 plan, performance bonuses, profit sharing, flexible job hours, paid time off/personal/holidays, and opportunities to earn awards.

Preparation—A high-school diploma is adequate for most part-time or seasonal jobs in theme parks, attractions and events. Most full-time jobs require a bachelor's degree in tourism or hospitality management, or a related discipline such as recreation management, coupled with adequate professional experience.

Possibilities—Some examples of job titles available in theme parks and working with local attractions include event manager, visitor information officer, rides manager, operations manager, media relations manager, project manager, promotions manager, and hospitality manager. Refer to the chapter on Event Management for more information about careers in this specific area.

Event Manager, Amusement Park

Responsibilities: Direct the concept, development, and implementation of internal and external events supporting marketing, sales, recruiting and/or synergy efforts through creativity, communication, collaboration, and commitment, negotiate and manage all logistics associated with outside vendors, interface with all levels of management and business units to ensure project objectives are achieved, manage internal and external creative resources to develop creative content, ensure high-quality throughout the pre-planning and onsite stages by overseeing the following (as applicable): accommodations, food and beverage, branding, audio-visual, lighting, entertainment and staffing, maintain strong working knowledge of event-day logistics and operations to ensure a high level of guest satisfaction, anticipate issues of concern and develop thorough contingency plans, manage event budgets, and manage and prioritize multiple projects.

Qualifications: BA in hospitality, communications or related field preferred. Two to five years event and meeting planning, cross platform knowledge (MAC/PC), ability to travel, ability to communicate effectively and efficiently across all departments/business units, demonstrate strong relationship building skills, proven ability to work in a demanding environment, self-starter.

Ecotourism and Cultural Tourism Industries

Ecotourism and cultural tourism industries are based on the principle of **sustainable tourism**, whereby the ecological and cultural resources of destinations are conserved, protected, and enhanced, tourism as well as other business opportunities are created to generate jobs for the local population, and low-impact forms of tourism are adopted. Ecotourism and cultural tourism, together referred to as sustainable tourism, promote experiential education for visitors by integrating and interpreting natural, social, and cultural themes at the destination. The enterprises that offer sustainable tourism products and services promote conservation through socially responsible (corporate social responsibility) and ecologically sound (environmentally friendly) business practices. While some DMOs as well as theme parks, attractions, and events may adopt sustainable tourism as their business model, other sectors that offer ecotourism and cultural tourism products and services include tour operations and expeditions, **adventure tourism**, nature parks and centers, cultural/heritage centers and museums, conservation organizations, resorts and hotels, restaurants, and transportation.

Passions—Conservation, environmental ethics, social ethics, cultural diversity, biodiversity, languages, economics, business, fund-raising, technology, innovations, education, training, working with people, regular travel as a major part of work, collaborating with other professionals.

Pay and Perks—Salaries will be based on skills and experience, ranging from entry level to full time. Employees usually start at around the pay grade for a four-year college graduate in an entry-level job and advanced-level staff can earn a good executive salary. Comprehensive benefits plans are usually provided, including health insurance, tax-deferred retirement plan, vacation leave, and holiday leave. Compensatory time is often awarded for weekend work.

Preparation—Most full-time jobs require a bachelor's degree in natural resources or sustainable tourism management, or a related discipline such as outdoor recreation management. A minor in environmental sciences or related disciplines such as geography is highly recommended, along with adequate professional field experience.

Possibilities—Some of the jobs available in the ecotourism and cultural tourism industries are cultural interpretation specialist, environmental interpretation specialist, conservation manager, museums and historical/cultural sites exhibit developer, museum director, tour and tourism director, zoos and aquariums exhibit developer, nature tourism coordinator, and environment and culture program coordinator. Refer to the chapters on Outdoor Recreation and Commercial Recreation for more details on travel and tourism careers that overlap with these areas.

Project Coordinator, International Environment and Culture Program

Responsibilities: The Project Coordinator will report directly to the two project managers and be located within the Program. The position's responsibilities may include: develop and manage annual budgets and quarterly budget revisions; support the development and assembly of project funding proposals; compose and coordinate funder reports; establish and manage contracts with partner organizations, consultants, and researchers; plan and organize workshop and conference logistics; update webpage and develop new outreach materials; support staff in annual project planning, meeting institutional deadlines, and completing general administrative tasks.

Qualifications: Successful applicants must have a bachelor's degree in a related field (political science, environmental science, international development, etc.) and be passionately committed to issues of environment and development. This position requires a highly motivated individual with exceptional organizational, communication, and interpersonal skills as well as the ability to handle and prioritize competing demands. This position is full time. Knowledge of another language is a plus.

Career	Passions	Pay and Perks	Preparation	Opportunity
Destination management organizations	Marketing, tourism economics, travel trends analysis	Entry-level salaries will be those of a typical four-year college grad up to executive levels	Bachelor's degree in tourism or hospitality management	Director, manager, coordinator, officer, seasonal jobs
Theme and amusement parks and local attractions	Service, guest entertainment service innovation, new technology partnerships, marketing, and economics	Entry-level salaries will be those of a typical four-year college grad up to executive levels	High school diploma to four-year college degree	Director, manager, officer, seasonal jobs
Ecotourism and cultural tourism industries	Conservation, environmental ethics, cultural diversity, bio-diversity	Entry-level salaries will be those of a typical four-year college grad up to executive levels	Bachelor's degree in natural resources or sustainable tourism management, minor in environmental sciences	Interpretation specialist, conservation exhibit developer, director, coordinator, seasonal jobs

FUTURE OPPORTUNITIES, ISSUES, AND CHALLENGES

Considering the growing global economic significance of tourism and the widespread prevalence of tourism resources, several new employment opportunities have continuously become available, especially as result of technological innovations, integrated travel infrastructure, new tourism products and services, and increasing traveler interest in travel and tourism industry have been aligning their efforts and strategies to address ecological (environmental) concerns, in response to changing/evolving societal priorities and awareness. Social concern for responsible practices has resulted in the emergence of a plethora of **"green" travel and tourism** products, industry alliances, and organizations, which attempt to make a difference in the industry by encouraging positive environmental changes in the business landscape.

Tourism is a business, and a community development tool with significant economic, environmental, sociocultural and political ramifications. Tourism businesses face the growing challenge of balancing profitability with quality of life in host communities. Issues at the intersection of the tourism industry and communities include transportation, migration, communication, unemployment, education, natural resources, and economic development. In this wider sense, sustainable tourism management is a comprehensive and inclusive approach, and an ongoing process. Sustainable tourism management underlines the interdependence of the environment with economy and society—the "triple bottom-line." The triple bottom-line framework encompasses a broad spectrum of issues that include, for example, natural, economic, social and cultural diversity, equity and human rights, corporate and individual responsibility and citizenship, globalization, and localization issues in travel and tourism.

Passion For Innovations....

I love my work since the travel and tourism industry is nearly always on the cutting edge. Today, you'll find hotels offering cutting-edge business tools, plus your favorite selection of tunes to be downloaded to your I-Pod. You'll sleep on the latest memory-foam mattresses from a hotel that will even sell you the product. Your aircraft is a miracle of modern technology, more glue than rivets and the miracle of the modern Global Distribution System (GDS) allows you to make the airline and all other reservations easily and safely. The cruise ships of today offer amenities never dreamt of ten years ago, and all of these things are brought together by a network of amazing technologies.

— JOHN HOPE-JOHNSTONE, CEO,
Corvallis Tourism

Resources and Getting Involved

The information presented in the following sections is intended to provide the reader with a starting point to get acquainted with various key for-profit and non-profit organizations in the travel and tourism industry, including their respective functions. Additionally, the main professional certifications and licenses recommended for those pursuing entry-level and advanced careers in the travel and tourism field have been listed for the reader's perusal.

Professional Organizations

ADME, Association of Destination Management Executives
www.adme.org
ADME is a global non-profit association dedicated to increasing the professionalism and effectiveness of destination management through education, promotion of ethical practices, and availability of information to the meetings, convention, and incentive travel industries, as well as the general public.

Cultural Heritage Tourism
www.culturalheritagetourism.org
This electronic clearinghouse includes information provided by many different members of Partners in Tourism, a coalition of the national organizations and agencies with an interest in cultural heritage tourism. This site is a resource for organizations and individuals who are developing, marketing or managing cultural heritage tourism attractions or programs. For those just getting started, there are guiding principles and how-to steps for launching a new effort. The website features success stories and the resources section includes key contacts in virtually every state as well as national resources for funding, technical assistance and other programs.

DMAI, Destination Marketing Association International
www.iacvb.org
As the world's largest and most reliable resource for official destination marketing organizations (DMOs), DMAI is dedicated to improving the effectiveness of over 1,300 professionals from 600+ destination marketing organizations in more than 25 countries. DMAI provides members—professionals, industry partners, students and educators—the most cutting-edge educational resources, networking opportunities, and marketing benefits available worldwide.

ECOTOUR at CI, Ecotourism at Conservation International
www.ecotour.org
CI is a U.S.-based, international nonprofit organization that applies innovations in science, economics, policy, and community participation to protect the Earth's richest regions of plant and animal diversity in the biodiversity hotspots, high-biodiversity wilderness areas as well as important marine regions around the globe. CI has supported the development of exemplary ecotourism products by providing technical assistance, capacity building, and funding to communities, entrepreneurs,

and partners as follows: development of viable ecotourism products and services; improvement of business management skills; design of marketing strategies and creation of market links; and development of associations, networks, and clusters that strengthen destinations.

IAAPA, International Association of Amusement Parks and Attractions
www.iaapa.org

IAAPA is a non-profit association that works behind the scenes to help attraction owners run their business smoothly and profitably. From increasing earnings and discovering new sources of revenue to improving operations and employee performance, IAAPA resources and programs are designed to ensure that attractions succeed.

PATA, Pacific Asia Travel Association
www.pata.org

PATA's advantage is that it continues to influence the direction the industry takes through its unique membership structure of public-sector tourism organizations; air, land, and sea carriers; and organizations engaged in the production, distribution, financing, consulting, educating and other technical aspects of the travel industry.

TIES, The International Ecotourism Society
www.ecotourism.org

TIES promotes responsible travel to natural areas that conserves the environment and improves the well-being of local people by: creating an international network of individuals, institutions and the tourism industry; educating tourists and tourism professionals; and influencing the tourism industry, public institutions, and donors to integrate the principles of ecotourism into their operations and policies.

UNWTO, World Tourism Organization
www.unwto.org

The UNWTO, a specialized agency of the United Nations, is the leading international organization in the field of tourism. It serves as a global forum for tourism policy issues and practical source of tourism know how. The UNWTO plays a central and decisive role in promoting the development of responsible, sustainable and universally accessible tourism, with the aim of contributing to economic development, international understanding, peace, prosperity and universal respect for, and observance of, human rights and fundamental freedoms. In pursuing this aim, the UNWTA pays particular attention to the interests of developing countries in the field of tourism.

USTOA, United States Tour Operators Association
www.ustoa.com

USTOA is a professional association representing the tour operator industry. The organization is composed of companies whose tours and packages encompass the entire globe and who conduct business in the U.S. The association has established some of the highest standards in the industry. Among these is the principle of ethical conduct, which requires members to conduct business according to a set of professional standards. Additionally, members must represent all facts, conditions and requirements relating to tours and vacation packages truthfully and accurately.

WAZA, World Association of Zoos and Aquariums
www.waza.org

WAZA's mission is to guide, encourage, and support the zoos, aquariums, and like-minded organizations of the world in animal care and welfare, environmental education and global conservation. WAZA is the "umbrella" organization for the world zoo and aquarium community. Its members include leading zoos and aquariums, and regional and national Associations of Zoos and Aquariums, as well as some affiliate organizations, such as zoo veterinarians or zoo educators, from all around the world.

WTTC, World Travel and Tourism Council
www.wttc.org

Raising awareness of the importance of travel and tourism, promoting synergies between the public and private sector, generating profit as well as protecting natural, social, and cultural environment, are the fundamental components of WTTC's mission. The WTTC is the forum for business leaders in the travel and tourism industry. With chief executives of some one hundred of the world's leading travel and tourism companies as its members, WTTC has a unique mandate and overview on all matters related to travel and tourism.

Certifications/Licenses

Professional certification/credentials are becoming increasingly popular among working professionals interested in fast-tracking their career progression. Some of these certifications include:

Destination management and marketing industry certification:
Professional in Destination Management (PDM)
www.destinationmarketing.org

Certified Destination Management Executive (CDME)
www.destinationmarketing.org

Destination Management Certified Professional (DMCP)
www.adme.org

Ecotourism and Sustainable Tourism certification:
University Consortium Field Certificate (UCFC) in Sustainable Tourism
www.ecotourism.org

Tour operators and wholesalers certification:
Travel Trade Supplier Certification (TTSC)
www.traveltradesmart.com

Cruiseline industry certification:
Accredited Cruise Counsellor (ACC)
www.cruising.org

Master Cruise Counsellor (MCC)
www.cruising.org

Elite Cruise Counsellor (ECC)
www.cruising.org

Elite Cruise Counsellor Scholar (ECCS)
www.cruising.org

Luxury Cruise Specialist (LCS)
www.cruising.org

Cultural and environmental attractions industry certification:
Certified Interpretive Manager (CIM)
www.interpnet.com

Certified Interpretive Planner (CIP)
www.interpnet.com

Certified Heritage Interpreter (CHI)
www.interpnet.com

Certified Interpretive Trainer (CIT)
www.interpnet.com

Certified Interpretive Guide (CIG)
www.interpnet.com

Certified Interpretive Host (CIH) www.interpnet.com

Where to Get Experience

Travel and tourism organizations are increasingly seeking and hiring individuals with formal education and training in the tourism discipline. For acquiring an entry-level, full-time job with any reputable tourism organization, it is essential to have between 250 to 500 hours of volunteering, internship and/or work experience, in addition to a formal degree in tourism or hospitality management, or a related discipline such a recreation management. While in college, students may find internship and volunteer opportunities at local convention and visitor bureaus, theme parks, cultural and environmental attractions, tour companies, etc. Some ecotourism and cultural tourism work opportunities may even be available through intramural programs at local colleges and universities.

Where to Get Experience

Jobs in food, hospitality and travel
http://www.quintcareers.com/hospitality_jobs.ht

Hospitality, recreation, and tourism career guide
http://www.khake.com/page61.html

Travel, transportation and tourism jobs
http://jobsearch.monster.com/Travel-Transportation-Tourism/get-jobs-3.aspx
Ecotourism Job Center. http://www.ecoclub.com/jobs/

Tourism jobs
http://www.smarthunt.com/Smart-jobs.cfm?CatID=28

Travel and tourism jobs
http://www.careerbuilder.com/ Key search terms: travel, tourism, attraction, park, hospitality, etc.

CONCLUSION

It vital for job seekers, especially those aspiring for entry-, mid-, and advanced-level careers within the travel and tourism industry to realize that in order to be successful in this field, one will need to incorporate travel as a routine part of the job and regularly interact with new people with different viewpoints/ideas.

The travel and tourism industry is dynamic and trend-oriented. The industry is unique in that it offers career options for individuals of all skill levels and from all academic backgrounds.

The travel and tourism professional has:

- Varying knowledge levels and passion to adopt the job (and responsibilities) as a lifestyle
- Patience to invest time, energy, and resources in helping others, as a major part of the job, without having complete control over the final outcome of efforts. If you want to work in this profession, you need to have the ability to prioritize long-term personal (including social and financial) over short-term monetary gains.
- Commitment to broaden knowledge every day regarding how other sectors within the tourism industry function and operate.

If these factors are compatible with an individual's job expectations, then a career in the travel and tourism industry is likely to be highly satisfying and personally meaningful.

For Further Investigation

For More Research

1. *Career Exploration:* Visit the websites of any five professional organizations from the previous section. From each website, identify a job/career that suits your professional goals and aspirations in travel and tourism.
2. *Occupational Certification:* From the list of professional certifications/ licenses, identify two certifications/licenses that would help you move towards an advanced-level career in travel and tourism. Create an action plan with a timeline for the steps you could take to earn these certificates.

Active Investigation

1. *Informational Interviews:* Contact a travel and tourism professional and set up an interview. During the interview, ask questions regarding qualifications, competencies, and experiences required to be a successful leader in the field. Review the informational interview instructions in chapter 2 as you are planning your interview.
2. *Field Observations:* Take a break and be a tourist for a week in your hometown. What are your needs? Which of your needs were fulfilled? Which were not? Why? How can your hometown make changes to satisfy the tourist?
3. *Journal Logs:* Maintain a journal for a month. In the journal, record what the media has to say about tourism, locally, nationally, and internationally. In your entries, examine if any of the international tourism trends are likely to change the way in which travel and tourism is being managed at the local and national levels.
4. *Local Action:* Write a letter or publication piece to your local newspaper, radio station, or website about the positives and negatives of tourism in your area. What can be done to improve visitor knowledge about your area? How will your ideas help the area economically, environmentally, socially?

Recommended Reading

Biederman, P. S. (2008). *Travel and tourism: An industry primer.* New Jersey: Prentice Hall.
Written by a former chief economist at Trans World Airlines, this book explores travel and tourism comprehensively, including travel sectors, promotional strategies, economic influences and business principles that govern the industry.

Boniface, B., & Cooper, C. (2009). *Worldwide destinations: The geography of travel and tourism* (5th ed.). Oxford: Butterworth-Heinemann.
This unique text provides an up-to-date, global perspective that explores the demand, supply, organizational aspects and resources of every tourism destination in the world. Current issues such as climate change, economic capacity, "grey" tourism and social impacts are discussed.

Cook, R. A., Yale, L. J., & Marqua J. J. (2010). *Tourism: The business of travel* (4th ed.). New Jersey: Prentice Hall.

This text presents an integrated model of tourism and addresses consumer behavior, service quality and personal selling. The authors cover the industry from a business perspective, including management, marketing, and finance.

Eberts, M., Brothers, L., & Gisler, A. (2006). *Careers in travel, tourism, and hospitality* (2nd ed.). New York: McGraw Hill and Companies

If you think a career in travel and tourism is your thing, read this book and the authors will help you hone in on the specialty area most suited to your passions, interests and abilities.

Goeldner, C. R., & Ritchie, J. R. (2009). *Tourism: Principles, practices, philosophies.* New Jersey: John Wiley and Sons.

This book, written by well-known consultants in the travel industry, provides useful information and guidance for tourism promotion and development organizations, chambers of commerce, and the many other organizations involved in the travel and tourism business.

REFERENCES

Biederman, P. S. (2007). *Travel and tourism: An industry primer.* New Jersey: Prentice Hall.

Eberts. M., Brothers, L., & Gisler, A. (2006). *Careers in travel, tourism, and hospitality* (2nd ed.). New York: McGraw Hill and Companies

Goeldner, C. R., & Ritchie, B. J. (2009). *Tourism: Principles, practices, philosophies.* New Jersey: John Wiley and Sons.

“

There are two major reasons I love doing what I do: First, there is the satisfaction of seeing our guests have a really great time and feeling the enrichment they are receiving from the experience. The second is being a part of helping our community economically, socially, and environmentally by bringing in visitors who are eco-sensitive, and sharing the beauty and wonder of this wilderness area with them. We do all this while creating jobs and tourist revenue that supports the community.

—MATT POLSTEIN
New England Outdoor Center

”

13

Commercial Recreation and Leisure Businesses

JIM GREINER
Wildwater Ltd. Rafting and
Starfish Exuma Adventures in the Bahamas

PAIGE SCHNEIDER
East Carolina University

FOCUS QUESTIONS

Q: *Since many jobs in commercial recreation are seasonal in nature, are salaries also seasonal? How can I compensate for off-season unemployment?*

A: Many jobs in this field are seasonal in nature, so it is important that you develop skills that can make you indispensable in the off-season. For instance, the kayak instructor who develops skills in repairing kayaks and kayaking gear can stay employed for most of the off-season getting gear ready for next season. Another example of this is the ski instructor who leads hiking trips in the summer, or takes employment with a rafting outfitter. Also, almost all commercial recreation businesses have a core of one or more key people who work for all or most of the year. Your goal should be to grow yourself into becoming that indispensable person.

Q. *When I graduate, I want to take some personal time to enjoy traveling and experiencing different cultures before I settle down. Is this possible?*

A. Those who live frugally can enjoy an outdoor adventure life where each year brings new experiences and different challenges and enjoy traveling and new experiences until they decide to settle down. Opportunities for seasonal jobs abound in the leisure industry. Use this time to build up a resume and experience by taking jobs that will prepare you for the future.

Q. *What qualities do I need to possess to operate my own business successfully?*

A. A great starting place includes good people skills, an entrepreneurial spirit, a good work ethic, and adequate working capital.

Q. *How can I get the working knowledge necessary to operate a successful recreational business*

A. The best way to learn a business is to involve yourself with an existing successful business. Get a part-time or summer job with a company that has a good reputation while you are still in school. Do this at several companies over the four to five years you are in school, and you will learn how to make your business a success.

Q. *What academic courses would help me succeed in a private recreation business?*

A. I took a minor in economics. Consider accounting, business, marketing, finance, group dynamics, computer skills, and public speaking as some of the important subjects to supplement your recreation career courses.

KEY TERMS

Leisure entrepreneur
Enterprises
Income
Expenses
Profit
Commercial recreation and leisure business

PROFILE 1: COULD THIS BE YOU?

JACK WISE is the CEO of Wildwater Rafting, an outdoor adventure firm located in the Southeastern United States. (www.wildwaterrafting.com). He has been with the company for over 20 years, starting as a river guide, then becoming a river manager, and finally serving as the chief executive officer of a $3.5 million company that takes over 60,000 people down whitewater rivers annually. During his tenure, the company has grown to four times it size. Since he arrived, the company has added a sailing and kayaking operation in the Bahamas, lodging, food service, and ropes courses. Jack is the perfect example of a person who started at an entry-level position and worked his way up to the company's most important position through hard work and experience. He built his skill set along the way.

His responsibilities include the following:

- Supervising the operation of four separate rafting centers.
- Overseeing the hiring and training of more than 200 employees annually.
- Managing budget and spending and keeping accurate records.
- Coordinating logistics, staffing, and equipment use between locations.
- Overseeing relationships with government agencies that administer business permits.
- Managing the business office and trip reservations

In an interview with Jack, we asked him about his career in the private sector of the recreation industry.

Q. *What are the most rewarding aspects of your job?*

A. There are a lot of exciting things, but I would have to say that the most rewarding is providing people with the opportunity to try new and exciting experiences in a special environment. It's also a bonus to be able to be involved in all these fun experiences myself.

Q. *There must be some parts of your job that are difficult or frustrating. What are some of those areas?*

A: In a phrase: Human resources. My main challenge is finding highly motivated employees and then training and keeping them. Since we are a seasonal business, we can rely somewhat on students and teachers to do the face-to-face leadership of operating trips, but separating those who do it as a pleasant pastime from those who are looking for a career opportunity is difficult at best.

Q: *So what personal characteristics do you look for when you're hiring new employees in the adventure business?*

A: Key qualities I look for are integrity, an interest in standards, good communication skills, a positive first impression, a willingness to learn, and reliability. The willingness to go the extra mile when needed is a critical asset. When hiring, it is important to realize that as an organization, you are only as good as the weakest link, so you need to make sure you hire quality people.

Q: *So what advice would you give to someone who wants to pursue a career in an outdoor adventure business?*

A: A college education is important to give you the basis from which to operate, plus personal experience, and the willingness to attempt anything and everything. In short: an entrepreneurial profile. Since a career-oriented person will necessarily need to have business skills to advance to a management position, I would recommend a minor in business, marketing, or economics. Strong computer skills are also very helpful. If you can't get the minor, at least take some courses to learn how to operate a successful business.

Q: *What misconceptions do you find new employees have about the adventure business?*

A: Some people come into this business thinking it's all fun with no work or responsibility. They have unrealistic expectations.

PROFILE 2: COULD THIS BE YOU?

GARRETT GRAHAM, manager of Camp Ton-A-Wandah, is a young man on a mission. He is the director of one of the most prestigious and most successful girls camps in the Great Smoky Mountain area of North Carolina. The camp was started in 1933, and accommodates three sessions each summer of over 200 campers. This area has over 60 other summer camps competing against each other for the camping dollar. Each summer, campers flock to Ton-A-Wandah (Cherokee for "Where the Waters Fall,") and it is Garrett's job to operate the program and please the campers and their parents. It is also his job to recruit campers to choose Ton-A-Wandah over other camps.

In his fifth year as director, Garrett oversees the maintenance, recruits the staff, and operates three sessions of over 200 campers each during the summer. To generate additional revenues, the camp also rents their facilities to church groups, family reunions, and weddings in the off-season. He supervises a full-time staff of seven. In a conversation with Garrett, we probed his mind about this job.

Q. *What are the most rewarding aspects of your job?*

A. Relationships with staff, families, and clients. We build relationships with families based on trust, and we are, in fact, the parents of each camper during the three weeks they are at camp. Every day is different. The job requires a great deal of flexibility, so I need to be good at a number of things. Other pluses are I don't have to wear a tie, and I'm being paid for something I love to do.

Q. *There must be some parts of your job that are difficult or frustrating. What are some of those areas?*

A: When things don't go as planned; like dealing with the H1N1 virus. We have to have almost instant alternatives for each problem as it occurs. Also, I am on the road a lot and away from my family. Each winter, I spend many days on the road recruiting campers and interviewing potential staff members. It can get old very quickly.

Q: *So what personal characteristics do you look for when you're hiring new employees in the adventure business?*

A: I hire staff who are willing to work in a group, self-starters, people who take personal pride in their job, and the people who value personal integrity.

Q: *So what advice would you give to someone who wants to pursue a career in the private camp business?*

A: Be flexible, be willing to work hard without complaining, and hone personal relationship skills. Get a job in summer working at a camp, and then work for another camp. Get involved in as many different perspectives as possible. Join the American Camping Association and the Association of Experiential Education (see professional organizations at the end of this chapter).

Q: *What misconceptions do you find new employees have about the summer camp business?*

A: They don't understand how long the day can be, they think it is all fun and excitement, and they forget that you don't go home at the end of the day. This is a 24-hour-a-day commitment, with only 24 hours off every three weeks.

Q: *What should I expect in the way of salary and benefits?*

A: The salary for a summer camp counselor is only $200-$300 per week plus room and board. Year-round program staff and management make a salary equivalent to teachers and other entry-level social workers. The salary range for Camp Directors varies, but it's closer to what a school administrator makes.

Q: *In retrospect, what are some of the things you wish you had known but didn't when you first joined Camp Ton-A-Wandah?*

A: I wish I had experienced more of budgeting, selling, and record keeping. But mostly, I wish I had known how much fun and how rewarding this work could be earlier in my career. I would have saved myself a lot of time and trouble searching for the perfect job.

For more on Camp Ton-A-Wandah, see their Web site at www.camptonawandah. com. Email: garrett@camptonawandah.com

WHAT YOU SHOULD KNOW ABOUT COMMERCIAL RECREATION AS A PROFESSION

Traditionally, many tend to think of recreation, parks and leisure services as a public service. If you ask the general public to describe the profession, they normally speak of National Parks, Little League baseball, the local tennis courts, neighborhood parks and open space, or morning fitness classes.

But if people voted with their pocketbooks, an entirely different picture would emerge, because the public's actual consumption of leisure services tends to validate private, for-profit recreation activities as the leader of the pack. Expenditures for professional athletics, movies concerts, entertainment, amusement parks, outdoor and adventure recreation and travel, and hundreds of hobbies, crafts, and cultural pursuits easily outspend the public sector. While other chapters of this book will cover many of these "for-profit" recreation pursuits, this chapter will concentrate on opportunities for leisure entrepreneurs, particularly in the outdoor adventure and retail recreation areas. The **leisure entrepreneur** is the person who is willing to take the chance that he or she can generate enough revenue from the leisure activity to sustain financial existence.

The Background of Leisure Entrepreneurship in America

In a country whose national philosophy is based upon a market economy and free enterprise as well as individual initiative, it is no surprise that recreational enterprises have flourished here. **Enterprises** can be described as businesses that generate income from their clients that is adequate to pay for all expenses, and still produce a profit. **Income** is the total dollar amount that the business generates, **expenses** are the total dollar amount of all payments made to support the business, and **profit** is amount by which income generated exceeds all expenses of the business.

Early in our history, much of this was fostered by the extravagant pastimes of the ultra wealthy, such as hunting clubs, country clubs, horseback stables, and so on. But as the middle class expanded, they too, wanted outlets for their leisure, so activity and interest-based clubs began to flourish. Theodore Roosevelt opened the door to the general population by championing our national parks and monuments and encouraging the general population to visit them and participate in outdoor activities. Guides and outdoorsmen who provided the expertise and equipment for the general population to enjoy these pursuits operated most of these activities. Of course, they charged for their services, and the private sector of recreation services was born.

Even today, the lodges, restaurants, and activities at national parks are still typically provided by the private sector (see the chapter on outdoor recreation for more information). In the meantime, America has embraced the private provision of recreation services to supplement what the public sector provides.

The Ups and Downs of Commercial Recreation Businesses

While the for-profit segment of the leisure profession is arguably one of the fastest growing categories in the field, at the same time it can also be one of the most transient and unstable. New business starts in the recreation and leisure area fail more than 60% of the time.

There are several reasons for this. First, be aware that specific activities can peak and slump rather quickly. Some leisure activities fall in the category of "fads," and may produce a great short-term gain, but fade quickly as time goes on. For example, slot car racing, indoor tennis centers, and drive-in movies are mostly things of the past. There has not been a major ski area built in the U.S. for more than 20 years. Tennis peaked in the 1980s, as did tent camping. So it is important that you don't confine your recreation enterprise to a single activity area that may be subject to becoming a fad and fade away as quickly as it appeared.

Another reason is that so many choose this type of business because they have a personal interest for a particular activity or pastime, but often they lack the knowledge and requisite dedication, skills or experience necessary to turn it into a desirable business. There is a big difference between loving to hunt and fish and supporting yourself (and maybe your family) as a professional hunting or fishing guide.

On the other hand, there a plus side that may appeal to you: individuals can usually start up an activity-based business with a minimum of capital, and the seasonality of many leisure businesses allows entrepreneurs the opportunity to work another job either part time or seasonally to support the recreation business until it grows enough to support them full time.

As you can see from the interviews at the start of this chapter, it is great to be in a job that allows you to follow your own personal interests and to be able to make a living doing what you really enjoy. For some, this personal joy is enough, and many highly educated persons who cherish their lifestyles so much they are willing to eat peanut butter and share a small apartment with three friends in the off-season to enjoy the benefits of doing what they love.

> There is a saying in the outfitter industry that goes like this:
>
> *Question:* "If an outfitter were given a million dollars, what would they do with it?"
>
> *Answer:* "Keep on outfitting until it is gone."

Careers in Commercial Recreation and Leisure Businesses

For this chapter, the phrases **commercial recreation and leisure business** are being somewhat narrowly defined. While one could include movie theatres, game arcades, resorts, cruise ships, and a wide variety of commercial sports, fitness and cultural activities as commercial recreation, our definition will be restricted to privately funded businesses that offer instruction and participation in outdoor adventure and other recreational activities. For the purpose of organization, we have grouped commercial recreation and leisure businesses into four categories, including: Campgrounds and Camps, Water-Related Businesses, Specialty Recreation Activities, and Retail and Hobbies. When selecting a career path, there are many things to consider in terms of passions, pay and perks, preparation, and possibilities.

Passions

Passions are the intrinsic values of the work experience that would complement your personal values and life goals.

Personal excitement for the major activity (or activities) involved, love of learning and doing, risk taking, entrepreneurship, physical challenges, analysis, love of teaching, problem solving, personal relationships, and communication are all prerequisites for success in this very tough and challenging (but enjoyable) vocation.

As a matter of fact, the opportunity to do very well financially in the private sector is significantly better than in the public sector, where job security and a highly structured, bureaucratic environment are the norm. People who crave great creative freedom and flexibility and are risk takers tend to thrive in private enterprise. On the other hand, these same folks must have discipline, organization, a nose for business, and strong people skills to ultimately be financially successful. A bit of luck also can help, or you can make your own luck if you analyze the situation thoroughly before you make a commitment. Let me offer a personal story to illustrate this point:

In 1970, I was invited by a friend to canoe the Chattooga River on a trip sponsored by Clemson University and the Sierra Club. I was awed by the beauty and wildness of the river, and the fact that it was totally undeveloped and government owned. I had previously rafted the Youghigheny River in Pennsylvania with a private outfitter and had a blast. It occurred to me that the Chattooga River had the potential to match or even surpass that fine river. I started researching the Chattooga, its launch and retrieval points, its rapids, and whether or not I could convince the Forest Service to grant me a permit to operate guided trips.

On one of my research trips, I crossed the river on a highway bridge and noticed a group of rafters preparing to launch. On a whim, my wife and I decided to chat with the group. Imagine our surprise when we discovered that the group was from Warner Brothers, and they were there filming scenes for the movie *Deliverance*, which was to debut the next winter.

On the spot, we decided that we would start our business here. With the help of a friend who was the local bank president, and all the cash value of my life insurance policy, we bought six rafts, wooden paddles and kapok life jackets, rented an abandoned schoolhouse, and founded Wildwater Ltd. Wildwater Ltd today is a three million-plus-dollar enterprise with 200 employees and almost 60,000 river trips each year. In addition to rafting, Wildwater conducts kayak and canoe clinics and trips, operates Jeep tours and canopy zipcourses, conducts corporate retreats, provides lodging and food service, and operates four stores.

We often think, "What would have happened if we had been at the bridge 30 minutes earlier or 30 minutes later, and had missed the film crew. Would we have still taken the chance?" We will never know, but the story does illustrate the need for some luck or divine intervention in becoming an entrepreneur.

Recreation businesses are not for the fainthearted, because recreational business failures are common. The successful business operator must be willing to work long hours at odd times, sometimes for little evident immediate reward. They must be willing and able to take risks, accept the consequences of their successes and failures, and be willing and able to get up again each time they get knocked down. If you enter this area of the profession, go into it knowing that the percentage of failures in private business ventures is much greater than in other sectors, and job security is not assured. It can be a great ride, but it is not for the timid or lazy.

While there are risks, the potential rewards of financial and personal satisfaction can be significant. There is something about making your living doing the things you most enjoy that transcends the profit motive. Loving what you do, and doing what you love, more than makes up in satisfaction and contentment for smaller financial rewards. Living your particular lifestyle and the freedom to make your own decisions and guide your own destiny are in themselves reward enough for experience-oriented individuals.

Pay and Perks

Monetary compensation varies tremendously in this segment of the leisure job market. Beginning pay starts at minimum wage and increases with experience and skill level. Full-time professionals in this area earn the equivalent of teachers and others in the human services field. Many jobs in this field include discounts or free use of personal equipment and gear, opportunities to live in areas of great scenic or recreational opportunities, and sometimes lodging and meals are included as an additional benefit. Mostly, guides and instructors start at minimum wage, and can double that amount with experience and tips. Often, particularly in wilderness areas, employees also receive room and board as well.

Those owning their own successful business can become financially independent, or they can lose everything, depending upon their business acumen, willingness to work, knowledge, ability to relate to others, and to solve problems.

Country singer Dolly Parton took a broken-down amusement park in her native Sevier County, Tennessee, and through innovation, cultural education, music, and good business practices turned it into the area's largest employer and a solid moneymaker with gross revenues of more than $100 million annually. In addition, she provided training and employment to many poor mountain people who otherwise would be destitute, and as part of the bargain, preserved many classic mountain crafts, music, and heritages.

Among the perks of working for or operating a for-profit recreation business is the joy of being able to participate in your favorite pastimes and get paid for it. Most employers have free or reduced prices for family, and it is common in the industry for companies to have reciprocal agreements allowing employees to enjoy free or reduced prices at other similar enterprises.

For instance, Wildwater Rafting provides complimentary raft trips for Dollywood, The Biltmore House, and the Great Smoky Mountain Railway employees, and in return these attractions provide comp tickets to Wildwater employees. Wildwater also has a co-op program with manufacturers of outdoor gear and clothing for employees to received discounted or free merchandise. These manufacturers believe that guests seeing their guides wearing a particular style or brand of clothing or gear will influence the guest to purchase that brand, and they are willing to provide free or wholesale goods to the outfitter and their staff for that benefit.

Finally, through trade associations and industry groups, employees and owners get to meet and know others in their particular field from across the country, which often results in complimentary reciprocal experiences and job opportunities for both employees and business owners.

Preparation

If you want to work in, or someday own, a recreation-related business, you'll need to prepare yourself and gain the education and experiences necessary in the specific industry you are considering.

First, you'll want a college degree in a professional discipline such as Leisure Services, Recreation Management, or in a Parks, Recreation, and Tourism curricula. Many of the classes you take with include hands-on projects to help you gain necessary skills. In addition, plan to take courses or a minor in business and/or marketing. While you're in school you'll want to build your resume by getting quality work experiences during the summer with successful companies in your chosen field.

All of the recreation-related businesses discussed in the next section have summer and part-time job opportunities that you should consider while attending college. Having completed these summer (or part-time positions) gives an applicant for a full-time job a big advantage in the process of finding a good internship and the job search that will follow.

The smart student will begin summer and/or part-time work at the end of his or her freshman year. Some will choose to experience different jobs each summer until they find the one that offers them the opportunity and experiences they wish to pursue on a career basis. Supervisory-level hiring in the for-profit sector is very often done in house or from competing companies. Therefore, if a student finds a good fit during summers or internships at a good company, he or she may wish to explore job options with that employer for post graduation full-time employment.

Some companies have guide schools or training sessions for potential employees. This is an important consideration if you are trying to choose between job offers. Attending these workshops or schools will increase your job placement opportunities significantly. If the management staff of a company gets to know you and your abilities through their school or training sessions, they will be more likely to select you when jobs are available.

Here's another good tip. Once you have the job, go to the boss and tell him or her that you have prepared for a career in this type of business and are interested in learning as much as you can about how it works and what opportunities for advancement are available in the company. It is typical for front-line employees in this type of job to take a short-term look at their employment, or concentrate on the experience itself, rather than the analysis of what makes the business successful. Let the boss know that your education prepares you for management and responsibility, and he or she will likely develop a new respect for you and open the gate to experiences that will lead to future advancement.

Possibilities

There are multitudes of opportunities in commercial recreation with potential for great personal rewards. Some may even find fortune and fame. While the seasonal nature of most for-profit recreation enterprises make becoming a millionaire less likely than other pursuits, you have only to look around your home community or your favorite vacation area to see literally hundreds who have made significant business successes by building on their personal talents and passions. As stated earlier, the businesses we discuss will be restricted to privately funded businesses that offer instruction and participation in outdoor adventure and other recreational activities, including some of the retail aspects of those businesses. For your convenience, we've grouped commercial recreation possibilities into four categories:

* Campgrounds and camps
* Water-related businesses,
* Specialty recreation activities
* Recreation Retail and hobbies

While there are hundreds of categories of private leisure businesses, we can summarize most of these into the four major areas listed below.

Making a Living and Loving Your Life

Most for-profit recreation ventures start out small, and many remain small. The wilderness areas of the American west are heavily populated with wilderness fishing, hunting, and backpacking guides who run one- or two-person family businesses. To many of these entrepreneurs, lifestyle is their most important value. Many of these businesses are passed down from father and mother to son and daughter for generations.

For these folks, lifestyle, nature, and simplicity are values to be treasured. Many sailboat charter captains live by the same creed. By and large, these people care little about amassing fortunes and possessing material items. Their idea of paradise is living their life simply, enjoying the sharing of a special place or experience with others, and having their "hobby" provide just enough cash to provide for the basics.

Significantly less than half of the 20+ whitewater rafting companies on Tennessee's Ocoee river are operating under the same ownership as when the river first granted permits for rafting some 25 years ago. The Ocoee is a dam-controlled river, so operators can only count on about 100 days a year when the Tennessee Valley Authority releases enough water from the dam to allow rafting. Many have found making a living in those circumstances to be difficult at best, impossible at worst.

One of the inevitable pitfalls of the commercial sector is the seasonality of many businesses. Snow skiing, rafting, sailing, and most watersports operate in restricted time frames when the weather allows participants to comfortably participate. Unless you are located in Florida, southern California, or other temperate areas, leisure businesses are required to earn their profits over a very short period. As a result, many jobs with these firms do not provide year-round employment. This presents a challenge for the business owner and his or her employees, and it presents a challenge for business owners who never know if the employees they trained this year will be back the next year. The other issue brought about by a restricted season is that employees typically work very long and hard hours during the peak season.

Campgrounds and Camps

These are two separate areas that have overlap and similarities. Both involve an outdoor or wilderness experience, but private campgrounds cater to couples and families who occupy tents, tent campers, trailers, and motorized recreational vehicles (RVs), and most private camps offer supervised programs in an outdoor setting primarily for youth. Private camps operate mainly during the summer months.

Passions—This is an area where it is easy to fall in love with the job. Those who glory in the out-of-doors and the natural environment will find much to attract them to this area. In both the campground environment and the summer camp program, there is an abundance of contact with people having fun and children being children. There is the opportunity to educate and create an environment full of fun, learning, and fulfillment.

Pay and Perks—Both camping areas are seasonal in nature, and that somewhat limits their ability to provide high compensation. For the few who are management level and full-time employees, compensation is similar to teaching and social work salaries. Those who own successful camps that attract a year-round affluent clientele do much better, but the real perks are in the lifestyle and low-key off-season, which allows a lot of freedom. Quite frequently, camp management personnel are offered lodging free or housing at a low rate.

Preparation—A degree in Parks and Recreation Management, Leisure Services, Education, or Outdoor Education is a good start. Courses in Child Development, Natural Sciences, and personal skills are helpful. The best preparation may come from the experience of actually camping or serving as a camp counselor while attending college. The American Camping Association holds conferences and workshops for camp staff and management.

Possibilities—Most camps and campgrounds are family owned, and operate with a small year-round staff. Most summer camps raise their own staff from counselors. There is little growth in the industry, so staff positions are rare. Also, there is a little or no growth trend in campgrounds, so opportunities are limited.

Campground Operations. While a large number of the country's more than 20,000 campgrounds are owned and operated by governmental agencies (National parks and forests, Bureau of Land Management, Corp of Engineers, state, county, and municipal government), over 3,900 campgrounds are operated as private enterprises, including quite a few that are located in public parks but are managed by private companies.

Privately owned campgrounds are located in every state of the nation and range in size from less than 10 campsites to over 1,000 campsites in a single business. Typically, they are open when weather and demand permit, which means some are year round, while others operate for only a few peak months.

For additional information about private, for-profit campgrounds and RV Parks, contact the National Association of RV Parks and Campgrounds www.arvc.org (703-242-8801). Possible jobs include campground manager, activity director, and facility manager.

Private Resident Camps. Many summer camps may be operated by non-profit organizations like YMCAs or Boy Scouts / Girl Scouts, but the overwhelming number of resident camps are privately owned and operated as private, for-profit enterprises.

While most camps operate in a limited 10- to 12-week period over the summer months, key staff and management have a full-time responsibility to recruit campers, maintain and improve facilities, and they recruit and train staff on a year-round basis. Many camps recruit summer staff from former campers, and full-time staff from the summer paid staff. Get a listing of camps near you from the American Camping Association (ACA), which certifies and evaluates resident camps. The ACA lists over 2,400 camps now accredited and in operation in the United States. ACA inspects these camps on over 300 standards involving health, safety, and program quality. There are 24 regional offices in the U.S. Web site: www.ACAcamps.org or phone: 765-342-8456. Camps hire counselors, waterfront directors, sports and activity directors, and specialty activity directors (Many camps specialize in certain activities).

Passions—Watersports-based activities have an almost automatic appeal to most people. Just look at the crowded beaches, fast boats, and multitudes of cars carrying canoes, fishing gear, and trailered boats. Everyone seeks the water. In spite of warnings to the contrary, check out the number (and severity) of suntans as you walk along almost any street in America. We are a culture of sun worshippers and water spirits. If this aquatic wanderlust haunts you daily, you are a prime candidate for a job in this sector.

Pay and Perks—This axiom applies: If your goal is to spend personal time surfing or fishing, you had best resign yourself to the title of beach bum or surfer dude. To find financial success in this area, you need to either be the very best at your trade, or you need to start with a goal to one day own your own company. Starting pay ranges from tips only to minimum wage. Many jobs are seasonal, but this is definitely a growth environment.

Preparation—As per most of these career areas, personal participation in water sports is the first introduction to the specific activities in this category. Your local YMCA, boating clubs, canoe clubs, scuba dealers, colleges, and private businesses can advance your skill levels in these activities. The Red Cross, American Canoe Association, and PADI offer advanced skills courses.

Courses will provide you with the basic skill set but will not provide you with the background you will need to operate the business successfully. A college degree in recreation management or business administration with courses in public relations, marketing, business, and finance will round out your preparation. Part-time and seasonal employment and participation in professional organizations are essential to your continued success.

Possibilities—Water-based activities seem to grow bigger and better from year to year. While economic conditions may temporarily hold down sales of costly equipment (boats, gear, canoes), the demand for learning and participating in water-based recreation moves steadily up.

This is an area where weather can make a significant difference in the season and consequently in the profitability of the business. A number of innovative companies have paired warm-weather activities with winter activities or indoor sports. For instance, I know of several ski and canoe shops that continue to produce business on a year-round basis.

Water-Related Businesses

Everybody loves the water. If you don't live on a lake, river, or sea, you probably want to go there for vacation. From this primal instinct to be on or near the water, many marine-based businesses have developed. Technology has added to the list of activities with the invention of sport kayaks, jet skis, kite boarding, and motorized scuba scooters.

This is a job area with a sustained growth pattern, but the boat and motor area is profoundly affected by economic downturns. However, the remainder of the market continues to enjoy good growth, and there are a number of opportunities for expansion.

Boating. This industry is booming and brings with it loads of opportunities for career employment. There are more than 17 million recreational boats registered in the U.S. (See chart below). Marinas, pleasure cruises, sailing schools, resort rentals, and charter boats are examples of the type of companies who need people to assist them in this fast-growing market. In virtually every city, town, or tourist spot with a water source nearby, there are from one to dozens of private companies offering the public sightseeing, naturalist, historical, or action boat tours.

For example, a Chicago tourism publication listed 17 different companies offering services for the public based from a boat. For a good list of marine, fishing, water sports, and boat organizations, contact: www.marinewaypoints.com.

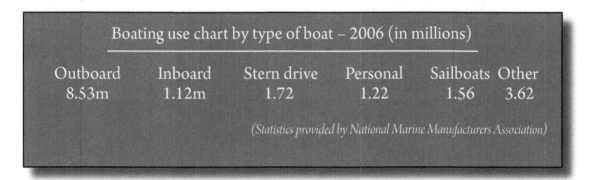

Boating use chart by type of boat – 2006 (in millions)					
Outboard	Inboard	Stern drive	Personal	Sailboats	Other
8.53m	1.12m	1.72	1.22	1.56	3.62

(Statistics provided by National Marine Manufacturers Association)

Dive and Snorkel Shops. One of the best opportunities in the commercial recreation field is the area of diving and snorkeling—recreation under the surface of the ocean. This fascinating activity introduces participants to the many wonders of marine life, fanciful coral formations, colorful tropical fish, and the company of sea predators such as sharks, barracuda, and rays.

Extensive in-service training is required to instruct in this potentially dangerous field. Most of this training is done through the Professional Association of Diving Instructors (PADI). According to PADI, more than 1,500 certified dive centers are now in operation around North America and the Caribbean. For more information see www.padi.com, 800-729-7234. Almost all of these business are privately owned and operated.

Most resorts and water-based hotels have dive and snorkel programs for their guests and the public. While some of the larger and more specialized lodging establishments operate their own programs, the vast majority of dive and snorkel programs at resorts and hotels are concessions, owned by individuals.

There is a segment of this industry we recommend you avoid. It is the cave diving segment. This has been one of the most dangerous activities of our times, and it is difficult, if not impossible to get liability insurance. The death rate is among the highest of all sports.

Canoe and Kayak Liveries and Guided Trips. The growth of sea kayaking as a recreational activity has expanded this area of recreation businesses greatly in recent years. Sales of recreational kayaks has increased fourfold over the last decade. There are many companies offering instruction in sea kayaking, day trips, and multiday expeditions. These enterprises supplement the traditional canoe rental and instructional business and make this area one of the fastest growing segments in America. There are canoe, kayak, and paddlesports liveries (rentals) and instructional programs in every state in the U.S. and in almost every country in the world. This sport has been particularly popular with the 40- to 60-year-old population of baby boomers and early seniors, and is in a strong growth position due to the age diversity of the population it draws upon.

An area of particular interest to entrepreneurs is the overseas kayak expedition business. Kayak owners are older, more affluent, and find the excursion to exotic locations very attractive. These excursions usually cost from $1,000 to $4,000 per person, and the high ticket price makes this area attractive to those who offer these trips. Many current kayak businesses offer trips worldwide to such exotic destinations as Costa Rica, Belize, Turkey, and Ireland.

In most areas, these businesses are seasonal in nature. (Try Florida, California, the Caribbean, or Arizona if you are looking for year-round employment.) Or many active persons combine a summer sport (canoe guide) with a winter sport (ski instructor) for year-round employment.

The Paddlesports Industry Association (PIA) is the trade organization for the growing business of canoeing, kayaking, and human-powered watersports. Their 1,000+ members are prime employers for those with a serious interest in the watersports business. For more information see www.paddlesportsindustry.org. or call 800-789-2202.

Whitewater Rafting and Kayaking. The whitewater industry is a dynamic portion of the adventure travel business, with whitewater rivers located in more than 30 states, and an estimated 12.4 million persons participating in this activity annually. Contact America Outdoors (www.americaoutdoors.com), 800-524-4814 for additional information about this job market. Many of the industry leaders in this field began as raft guides while in college and are now owners or managers for the more than 500 firms now offering whitewater adventures in the U.S.

Passions—This is the area where personal interests can meld into business success. If you have a particular sport, interest, or hobby that you love, you can fulfill your personal dreams and your financial dreams all at once if you have an entrepreneurial spirit. Doing a job you love and for which you have a personal passion increases your chances of ultimate success immeasurably. Thousands of small businesses exist today based upon serving the needs of leisure enthusiasts.

Pay and Perks—It all depends on you, and the fact that YOU can make the choices that ultimately will determine its success or failure. Working at an existing business to learn it may mean a minimum wage or slightly more. As you progress, you could become the manager of a local franchise and earn a comfortable living. Eventually, when you own and operate your own business, you could live quite comfortably on the profits. Owning your own business also has its perks. You often can legally charge many expenses to your business. You can also take perks that relate to the business instead of having to pay for them out of pocket. So, ownership has its privileges (along with some tax benefits).

Preparation—The same basic educational requirements of a bachelor's degree with an emphasis on recreation and business will set the stage for success. There are a number of college entrepreneurship programs that can hone your business senses. If you have another major, take advantage of some of their classes as a minor.

Ultimately, your best preparation for these areas is actual work experience, along with programs presented by industry related professional organizations.

Possibilities—Those with have a personal interest, talent and strong passion for a specialty commercial recreation business may find their life-long dream and the land of opportunity here. Remember, it takes an entrepreneurial spirit, good business sense and access to paying clients to make your career choice in this area become a reality. Your choices are as diverse and abundant in the specialty commercial recreation activities areas, and what follows are descriptions of four popular commercial recreation specialty business ideas.

Specialty Commercial Recreation Activities

Name an interest area where people spend their leisure time, and you will come up with a new and extensive list of opportunities for private recreation businesses. Whether it is running, exercise, model railroading, sewing, motorcycle riding, or cultural arts, there is a potential market for someone to make a living supporting that industry. Whether it be in retailing items the enthusiast needs to do the job, or offering instruction in how to do it properly, there is money to be made servicing people's leisure needs.

Horseback Riding and Dude Ranches. Riding stables and other recreational activities with horses are increasingly popular across America. Ellen Hargrove, Past President of the Colorado Dude Ranchers Association (www.duderanching.org), indicates that there are more than 2,400 permits currently in effect for commercial

Go Fly a Kite!

Kitty Hawk Kites started out in 1974 teaching a few people how to hang glide off the same sand dunes where the Wright brothers conducted the first successful airplane flight.

Now they have 13 stores all over the North Carolina outer banks offering kayaking, eco-tours, jet boat tours, hiking trips, kiteboarding, parasailing, and a never-ending variety of outdoor activities. Their 200-plus seasonal employees provide activities for over 15,000 people annually, but time has proven that their retail stores with outdoor apparel, kites to fly, and recreation gear are the main revenue producers for this unique recreational enterprise.

horseback riding on government lands, and that does not include all of the businesses who use only private land for their rides and trips. For further information on this industry, try www.horsecouncil.org or the American Quarter Horse Association.

Fishing, Hunting, and Backpacking Guides. Perhaps the ultimate job for a person who loves to fish, hunt, or hike is to be a wilderness guide. It is a profession one may more easily be born into than trained for. The fact is that a skilled fishing guide who knows where the fish are, or the backpacking guide who leads the youth group into unknown territory and away from danger, gain their expertise from doing and seeing rather than from some formal education.

But turning that "interest" into a successful "business" does require skills such as bookkeeping, marketing, social skills, computer skills, and more. In a world where supply is plenty, and demand is limited, the guide with a college education stands an excellent chance of making it in a difficult profession.

In many ways, the wilderness fishing or hunting guide has a fairly easy time starting his or her own business. The cost of a guiding business may be as little as several thousand dollars and a phone line and Web site. Some connections and insurance may be all an entrepreneur needs to get into business. Be aware, though, that a single-person business depends fully upon the full and total commitment of the founder, and the successes and failures in this area. In most areas, both permits and certification are required so do your homework.

Snow Skiing, Snowmobiling, and Winter Sports. If you live in (or want to live in) one of the snow belt areas of this country, or in Canada, you might want to look into winter sports. However, most companies who have businesses in this area of the for-profit recreation field use this as a supplement for other summer or year-round businesses. For instance, a Colorado couple rents skis and organizes ski trips for youth groups in their area as winter revenue. In the summers, they earn a living taking photos of families riding a commercial vintage steam train. The two businesses dovetail to provide a steady stream of income, which sustains them year round. Also, don't forget ice skating (and hockey), which can be operated on a year-round basis.

Bicycles and Motorcycles. Bicycling is the number-one leisure activity in the U.S. in which you are self-propelled. Over one billion bicycles were sold in 2009, half of them in China, and 30 million in the U.S. The industry produces $6 billion annually in sales. There are also 4,271 dealers selling motorcycles in America alone, producing $4.8 billion in revenues annually. and it is estimated that more than 120 million people participate in the U.S.A. alone today. Jobs are available selling, repairing, customizing, racing, and providing organized tours. Bicycle and motorcycle rental operations and multi-day tours offer opportunities for enthusiasts to start a career. Check out bicycle touring101.com for additional information.

Recreation Retail and Hobbies

Hobbies and their associated retail shops provide a fascinating and wide-open area where small business opportunities abound. Those with personal interests can turn those interests into a lifetime vocation. One of the most obvious successful examples of a hobby business is the Build-A-Bear Workshops.

The Bear that Built an Empire

In 1997, Maxine Clark had an idea. It certainly would be fun and maybe she could actually make a little profit if she opened a store that allowed children to stuff their own teddy bears and then dress them.

A short ten years later, Maxine has been crowned as "Entrepreneur of the Year," and she now has 274 Build-A-Bear Workshops in the U.S.A., and over 100 more overseas in Australia, Thailand, Russia, South Korea, Sweden, India, and a total of 18 countries, and they are opening scores of new stores every year!

Maxine is one of many Americans who took an idea based upon a personal hobby and turned it into a huge success.

Passions—There is nothing like doing exactly what you enjoy most, and making a living doing it!

Pay and Perks—Look through the list. It is as diverse as this country. There is something for everyone, and everything for someone. In this environment, it is most difficult to anticipate salaries or income. But the perks of owning your own business to support your participation in it and to share it with others is as great a perk as you can ever have!

Preparation—To be honest, the best preparation is learning by doing. You can increase your business sense by having basic math, economics, bookkeeping, and marketing courses, and learn from experts in your field by doing, but most of this education will be at the school of hard knocks!

Possibilities—Consult the individual activity descriptions for a list of pertinent professional associations and organizations in your specialty area. Active membership and attendance at professional conferences and training events will gain you good friends, better tips on how to succeed, and a wealth of information you may need to stay competitive.

Here are just a few of the areas where hobbies have led to gainful employment and/or business ownership:

- Ceramics shops
- Shooting galleries and target ranges
- Pet salons and pet training facilities
- Quilting and sewing classes and stores
- Miniature golf courses and driving ranges
- Sports instruction clinics

- Model train, car, and military diorama stores and clubs
- Video game parlors, competitions, and programming
- Musical instruction, performance, and sales
- Travel clubs and organized tours
- Fitness clubs, gyms, physical fitness trainers

The list goes on and on. Think of any hobby or leisure activity, and you can begin to see needs in that particular area where private enterprise could provide goods and services to satisfy demand.

This list of for profit (or commercial) recreation can be expanded to hundreds of interest areas, including hobby shops, ceramics and crafts, and such exotic activities as adventure racing, skate parks, go carts, game arcades, and virtually any other leisure activity you can imagine that can support commercial partnerships. Many astute operators began profitable businesses as a result of their own personal interests and hobbies.

SUMMARY OF COMMERCIAL RECREATION AND LEISURE BUSINESS CAREER POSSIBILITIES

Career	Passions	Pay and Perks	Preparation	Possibilities
Campgrounds and camps	Being in the outdoors and natural environment, of fun, learning, and fulfillment	Compensation similar to teaching and social work salaries.	Bachelor's degree in parks and recreation management, leisure services, education, or outdoor education	Seasonal, camp staff positions are limited, little or no growth trend in campgrounds, opportunities limited
Water-related business	Automatic appeal to most people who have a strong desire to be near the water	Seasonal, but a growth environment. Starting pay ranges from tips only to minimum wage. Many jobs are seasonal, but this is a growth environment. Start your own successful business and the sky's the limit!	Personal participation in water sports is the first introduction to the specific activities in this category. American Canoe Association and PADI offer advanced skills courses. A college degree in recreation management or business management, with courses in public relations, marketing, business, and finance round out your preparation.	Water-based activities seem to grow bigger and better from year to year. While economic conditions may temporarily hold down sales of costly equipment (boats, gear, canoes), the demand for learning and participating in water-based recreation moves steadily up.

Career	Passions	Pay and Perks	Preparation	Possibilities
Specialty commercial activities	Special interests can blend with business success when you are doing a job you love and for which you have a personal passion. This increases your chance of ultimate success.	Working at an existing business to learn it may mean earning around minimum wage. As you progress, you could become the manager and earn a comfortable living.	Bachelor's degree with an emphasis on recreation, college entrepreneurship programs to hone business sense. Best preparation is actual work experience, along with programs presented by industry-related professional organizations	Personal interest, strong passion, and entrepreneurial spirit make choices diverse and abundant in the specialty commercial recreation activities area.
Recreation and retail hobbies	There is nothing like doing exactly what you enjoy most and making a living doing it!	Difficult to anticipate salary or income. Perks of owning your own business to support your participation in it and to share it with others is as great a perk as you can ever have!	Best preparation is learning by doing. You can increase your business sense by having basic math, economics, bookkeeping, and marketing courses and learn from experts in your field by doing, but most of this education will be the school of hard knocks.	Consult the individual activity descriptions for a list of pertinent associations and organizations in your specialty area. Active membership and attendance at professional conferences and training events will gain you good friends, better tips on how to succeed, and a wealth of information you may need to stay competitive.

FUTURE OPPORTUNITIES, ISSUES, AND CHALLENGES

The Commercial Recreation field is very broad and diverse, so it is difficult to pinpoint opportunities, issues, and challenges. Suffice it to say that there are millions of people employed today in positions that allow them to work and earn money while pursuing a personal pastime. In times of economic downturn, people will vacation closer to home, so local commercial enterprises may do better. In times when the economy is better, people will travel farther and spend more. Thus, It's always important to do your research, stay on top of trends, and consider short-

and long-term patterns in order to capitalize on opportunities. Plan accordingly. In short: plan your business and work your plan.

As America's leisure appetite expands to new activities and pursuits, numerous job opportunities become available, and persons with the proper skills and experience are in a good position to take advantage of this and be promoted to higher positions quickly. A good example of this occurs in the amusement park field, where over 80% of supervisors holding top positions in parks such as Disney World, Great Adventures, and Busch Gardens have worked their way up the ladder quickly, and the average age of year-round supervisors is in the late 20s or 30s. Compare that to other fields where managers tend to be in their 50s and 60s.

If you have a passion for commercial recreation enterprise, look for opportunities to integrate your interests with your need for employment. Then after you learn the trade, you can attempt to make it your own through ownership or management opportunities.

RESOURCES AND GETTING INVOLVED

To drive home a key point: your own specific interests developed and confirmed as you learn more about your field of interest through part-time and seasonal work opportunities, Hands-on experience will be your greatest resource in this all-encompassing, generic segment of the leisure industry.

Professional Organizations

Every segment of the recreational business market has its national, regional, and local professional or interest organizations, as well as participant organizations. Google your activity area and, or use your yellow pages to start the search. Better yet, consult someone you know has interest and knowledge in your specific interest area. Here are some organizations to get you started:

Adventure Travel Trade Association (ATTA)
www.adventuretravel.biz/
ATTA is a thriving community of more than 560 responsible, profitable businesses, destinations, and media who transform customers and businesses alike into advocates for sustainability and justice worldwide. Members, spanning six continents and more than 60 countries, include tour operators, destination marketing organizations, tourism boards, specialty travel agents, guides, accommodations, media and service providers.

Resort and Commercial Recreation Association (RCRA)
www.rcra.org
The Resort and Commercial Recreation Association (RCRA) is an international non-profit, non-regulatory organization comprised of professionals, educators, and students in resort and commercial related industries. The mission of RCRA is to serve as a vehicle to communicate, educate and promote standards of professionalism within the industry and to provide opportunities for continuing education, networking and awareness of industry trends.

American Camp Association

www.ACAcamps.org

The American Camp Association is a community of camp professionals who, for nearly 100 years, have joined together to share knowledge and experience to ensure the quality of camp programs.

National Association of RV Parks and Campgrounds

www.arvc.org

ARVC is the only national association exclusively representing the interests of all commercial RV parks and campgrounds in the United States. Membership includes RV parks and campgrounds, cabin and lodge resorts, membership campgrounds and resorts, industry suppliers and park developers.

Professional Paddle Sports Association (PPSA)

www.paddlesportsindustry.org

PPSA is the premier trade association fostering paddlesports business. This organization"s mission is to provide information on safety, paddling locations, and paddling basics to enhance participants' paddling experiences. Another goal is to increase the number of people who participate in paddlesports and how often they go paddling.

Outdoor Industry Association (OIA)

www.outdoorindustry.org

OIA is the premier trade association for companies in the active outdoor recreation business. OIA provides trade services for over 4000 manufacturers, distributors, suppliers, sales representatives and retailers in the outdoor industry. The Outdoor Industry Association seeks to ensure a healthy and diverse specialty retail and supply chain based on quality, innovation and service.

National Association of RV Parks and Campgrounds (ARVC)

www.arvc.org

ARVC is the only national association exclusively representing the interests of all commercial RV parks and campgrounds in the United States. Membership includes RV parks and campgrounds, cabin and lodge resorts, membership campgrounds and resorts, industry suppliers and park developers.

Colorado Dude Ranchers Association

www.duderanching.org

The Colorado Dude and Guest Ranch Association offers benefits such as marketing, camaraderie, and education, along with the credibility of being a part of a reputable trade association.

National Ski Area Association – NSAA

www.nsaa.org

The National Ski Area Association is the trade association for ski area owners and operators. It represents 329 Alpine resorts that account for more than 90 percent of the skier/snowboarder visits nationwide. Additionally, it has over 400 supplier members who provide equipment, goods and services to the mountain resort industry.

Certifications and Licenses

Most recreation and leisure jobs offering skills instruction, or having an element of adventure, require some certification and training. Maine, Montana, New York, California, Idaho, and many other states license guides. In addition to college and university programs, the National Outdoor Leadership School (NOLS) provide training for outdoor leaders. Since many leisure activities are held on national and state parks and recreation area, permits for outside vendors are usually required, and you will be regulated by that state or federal agency. In most other activities, professional organizations such as the American Camp Association and the Professional Association of Dive Instructors (PADI) provide the appropriate certification.

Remember this: If you don't have all the credentials and permits you are required to hold, you are not a professional, so never put yourself in that position. If you do, you are begging for a civil suit and the loss of your business and your home. You should also have adequate liability insurance to cover yourself and your guests.

American Canoe Association (ACA)

www.americancanoe.org

The ACA offers skills courses and certification courses to paddlers of all skill levels in multiple different disciplines. These courses represent a body of knowledge, sets of skills, safety procedures and other materials deemed appropriate for the particular environments of the various disciplines.

Maine Guides Online

http://maineguides.com/become-a-guide

MaineGuides.com is a one-stop resource providing easy searches for Licensed Professional Maine Guides throughout the state or for any Maine recreational sport from Maine Bird Watching to Whitewater Rafting in Maine.

New York State Licensed Guide Certification

www.dec.ny.gov/permits/30969.html

The licensing of outdoor guides is regulated by the New York State Forest Rangers. In general terms, a guide is a person, at least eighteen years of age, who offers services for hire, part or all of which includes directing, instructing, or aiding another in fishing, hunting, camping, hiking, whitewater rafting/canoeing/kayaking, or rock and ice climbing.

National Outdoor Leadership School (NOLS)

www.nols.edu

NOLS is a 501(c)(3) not for profit educational institution that takes people of all ages on remote wilderness expeditions, teaches technical outdoor skills, leadership, and environmental ethics.

SCUBA Organizations and Certification

Professional Association of Dive Instructors (PADI)
www.padi.com
PADI is one of the world's leading scuba diving training organizations.

National Association of Underwater Instructors (NAUI)
www.naui.org
NAUI Worldwide is one of the world's most respected, largest non-profit diver training organizations. Established in 1959 as a membership association and organized solely to support and promote Dive Safety.

Scuba Diving International (SDI)
http://www.tdisdi.com/
SDI was created in 1999 and grew out of the success of its sister company, TD, which specializes in the more advanced disciplines of dive training. They have streamlined course materials to let students study the essential academics with an emphasis on practical diving skills learned in both the pool and open water environments.

Technical Diving International (TDI)
http://www.tdisdi.com/index.php?site=2
TDI is the largest technical certification agency in the world. As one of the first agencies to provide training in mixed gas diving and rebreathers, TDI is seen as an innovator of new diving techniques and programs, which previously were not available to the general public.

Handicap Scuba Association
http://www.hsascuba.com/
HSA was founded in 1981 and is now the world's leading authority on recreational diving for people with disabilities. Headquartered in California, HSA INTERNATIONAL extends its underwater educational programs worldwide.

Where to Get Experience

In an effort to make a living doing something they really enjoy, or for which they have a personal passion, graduates may enter these areas without a good business plan or adequate capital and quickly fall by the wayside as the business doesn't attract enough revenue to become viable.

To increase your chance of success in this field, plan to take a position in a currently successful leisure business for several years. Work your way up the ladder of responsibility until you know enough about the business aspects of the company to start your own company. At this point, you will have a much better chance of success in starting your own business. There is also a good chance of being chosen for a position with more responsibility in the company where you work or in another similar company. One of the best ways you can prepare yourself for advancement is to learn all aspects of the business, from the accounting to the reservations; from the ordering of equipment and supplies to the maintenance routines. In doing so, you make yourself more valuable to your current company, but also increase your capability to successfully start your own company.

Don't hesitate to let the business owner or manager know of your desire to learn the business and to make it a career. Personal communication of your goals to the management will provide you with opportunities to learn the business internally, as well as alerting management of your desire to be a career player.

Additional Online Resources

Explore job opportunities in the outdoor adventure industry at the sites below. Note that many of the professional associations listed previously also have career information and/or job bulletin Web links on their main sites.

Americas Job Bank
www.jobsearch.com.
Americas Job Bank is a search engine for jobs in the U.S.

Coolworks.com
www.Coolworks.com
Cool Works can help you finding a seasonal job or career in some of the greatest places on Earth. Get a summer job in Yellowstone, Yosemite, or another national park. Find a summer job as a camp counselor. Ski resorts, ranches, theme parks, tour companies and more are waiting for you. Let Cool Works.com show you the way to live out your own amazing adventure!

Outdoorindustryjobs.com
www.outdoorindustryjobs.com
OutdoorIndustryJobs.com enables the Outdoor, Bicycle, Winter and Snow Sports, ActionSports, Fishing, and Hunting Industries' job seekers and employers to network and connect. In these particular industries, a passion for the outdoors is the common denominator between the job seeker and the employer. Their mission is to provide the platform where "the passion can happen" for both job seekers and employers alike so they may form mutually beneficial life and business relationships.

MarineWaypoints.com
www.marinewaypoints.com
MarineWaypoints.com is a marine-related site dedicated to learning resources, a boating community, news and more. It is also a directory of marine-related websites, which include boating, diving, fishing, gear, sailing, weather and much, much more.

America Outdoors, Information Services for Outdoor Recreation Enthusiasts
www.americaoutdoors.com
America Outdoors is an outdoor information center and gathering area for outdoor recreationists for those who enjoy the great outdoors. America Outdoors offers numerous resources.

Fun Jobs
www.funjobs.com
Fun Jobs is dedicated to bringing together people who love their work and employers who love their people.

Mountain Resort Community Employment Connection
www.mountainjobs.com
Mountainjobs.com is a connection to ski jobs, summer jobs, seasonal and full-time professional careers.

CONCLUSION

Success is sweet and satisfying, especially for those who choose carefully and enter the commercial recreation field with adequate preparation. Even with knowledge of the limitations and obstacles, this calling has many benefits:

1. Doing something you personally enjoy and sharing that experience with others is very gratifying.
2. For many, having the off-season open so you can pursue personal goals or another job opportunity is a positive. A common application of this is beach lifeguards spending the winter on snow ski patrol or instructing skiing, or school teachers organizing hiking trips over the summer.
3. However, be cognizant that as your responsibility level increases in a company, the amount of off-season leisure time will probably decrease. And if you become the proprietor of a successful enterprise, the free time will likely disappear.
4. America loves its leisure. Even in times of recession, folks are likely to give up almost everything but their vacations and their leisure activities. This sector is growing by leaps and bounds. What better place to be than in the center of the fray, helping people have fun, and enjoying what you do while helping others have fun!

FOR FURTHER INVESTIGATION

Active Investigation

1. Do some research and a local site visit. Check Google, Bing, Ask, or any of the multitude of search engines on the Internet, and search for the activity or interest of your choice. Enter your local city or state along with the activity to find nearby service providers. After checking out the websites to determine if they really do the things in which you are interested, give the best of them a call, or stop by for a visit to see for yourself.

2. Conduct an informational interview. After you have satisfied yourself of the validity of the business, contact the owner or manager and ask if you can stop by for a visit. Explain that you are pursuing a degree in recreation management, and are interested in learning more about their specialty. Use the informational interview instructions in chapter 2 to prepare for your interview.

Whether this leads to future employment orro internship, or simply provides you with a future contact or additional information, you will find this direct and personal method to produce great results.

For More Research

1. Consult your curriculum advisor, someone working in the field, your school's career center, the library, or and the Internet to learn more about career opportunities in your area of interest. See what minors are available at your school to complement your major and interest in commercial recreation (e.g., business, marketing, public relations and so on).

2. Choose one area of interest in commercial recreation and determine what certifications and licenses would be an asset. Use the Internet to prepare a report detailing the type of training and experience needed to acquire the certification(s). Make sure your report includes a budget so you can determine how much it may cost you to pursue each certification.

3. Visit the website for the Resort and Commercial Recreation Association (RCRA), the professional organization of commercial recreation field, with a strong emphasis on the resort and tourism sector (www.rcra.org). See how much it costs to join as a student and make a list of the benefits you would receive from this membership. Also, check out the next conference and see if your school can support you and other students to attend.

4. Investigate potential jobs and salaries. Go to Coolworks.com (www.Coolworks.com) and Outdoorindustryjobs.com (www.outdoorindustryjobs.com) and locate at least five current job postings that interest you. Report on qualifications, salary range, and application requirements. Apply for one or more jobs for next summer.

Recommended Reading

Crossley, J., Jamieson, L., & Brayley, R. (2007). *Introduction to commercial recreation and tourism: An entrepreneurial approach* (5th ed.). Champaign, IL: Sagamore.
Introduction to Commercial Recreation and Tourism is a stepping-stone to understanding the scope, characteristics, entrepreneurial strategies, and management aspects of commercial recreation and tourism.

Goeldner, C. R., & Ritchie, J. R. B. (2009). *Tourism: Principles, practices, philosophies* (11th ed.). Hoboken, NJ: John Wiley & Sons, Inc.
Tourism examines how different components of the industry work together to create a unified, successful travel experience.

Bolton, W. K., & Thompson, J.L. (2000). *Entrepreneurs: Talent, temperament, technique.* Butterworth Heinemann, Oxford.
Entrepreneurs is the most comprehensive treatment of the entrepreneur on the market.

Bolton, W. K., & Thompson, J. L. (2003). *The entrepreneur in focus: Achieve your potential.* Thomson, London.
The Entrepreneur in Focus is about identifying and releasing entrepreneurial potential. Using the idea of character themes, it defines the entrepreneur in terms of six key themes, and provides readers with the opportunity to assess themselves in these areas.

"

Choose a job you love and you will never have to work a day in your life.

— CONFUCIUS

"

14

Preparing for a Career in Recreation

CRAIG M. ROSS
Indiana University

FOCUS QUESTIONS

Q. *How do I learn more about a career in recreation, park, and leisure services?*

A. Read, ask questions, and try it! Reading is the simplest way to learn more about career opportunities. Read the variety of resources that are available to you. Visit with your campus career services department for specific career resources, manuals, and guides or use the university/public library careers section. The Internet is also an excellent way to discover and research career opportunities. Once you have read the literature, ask professionals in the field for their perspective. The informational interview technique is a great way to speak with experts in the field. Also, job shadowing with current practitioners will give you a better understanding of what occurs behind the scenes. One of the best ways to assess if you would like a certain career in recreation, park, and leisure services is to try it. Seek practical, hands-on experience in typical jobs associated with your career choice while you are in college. Working part-time during the school year, being employed in a summer job, and volunteering or completing an internship for academic credit are excellent ways to see if you would enjoy the work and the environment.

Q. *How do I know what is the "perfect" career choice for me?*

A. In order to make good career choices and decisions, it is essential that you "know yourself." Self-assessment involves an honest, personal self-exploration in which you identify and prioritize your values, interests, skills, personality, and lifestyle. The more accurate you are during this phase, the better the chances of making good career decisions.

Q. *What if I don't know anyone working in this field; will I still be able to find a job?*

A. Absolutely! Since many jobs are never publicly advertised (known as the "hidden job market"), you as a future job seeker must actively seek out contacts in the field. Establishing and maintaining these contacts is called networking. Networking involves connecting with the right people at the right time. The old adage of "It's not what you know, but who you know" is certainly true in career preparation and the job search process. Developing a strong network of contacts early in your college education helps you become known to people in the field who may be hiring or may be in a position to refer you to someone who is hiring. Being an active member in a student or professional associations is an excellent way to start making contacts too.

KEY TERMS

Career planning
Career exploration
Values
Interests
Skills
Personality
Lifestyle
Informational interview
Campus career services
Technology
Student or professional organization
Networking

Job shadowing
Part-time work
Summer job
Volunteering
Internship
Certifications and licenses
Job search
Portfolio
Resume
Cover letters
Job interview

TESTIMONIAL LETTER

"Hello there! I hope you are doing well! Things are going great for me, which is why I'm writing you. I feel that my education and experiences paved the road to success. I have many suggestions and experiences that would be helpful to any upcoming graduate, or even someone who has graduated, but cannot seem to find their path.

Upon completion of an internship with a Tour company in Florida and graduation, I made my official move to Orlando, FL. My first position was a Sales Representative for a Tour company. I dealt with other tour operators who were bringing groups to Orlando yet needed a resource for hotels, attractions tickets, meal functions, etc. It was a great way to break into the travel/tourism industry.

A year later, I was brought on board by another, yet very different tour company. I became a Sales Manager, in charge of working with schools and groups directly. I provided tour packages for student groups to any destination throughout the country, our top markets being Orlando, NYC, Chicago, Washington D.C., New Orleans, Boston, etc. This gave me managerial experience, not to mention the freedom to manage my own accounts.

Next week, I am making another move to the Arizona area. I am the new Sales Manager for the Hard Rock Café! My responsibilities will include bringing large parties from various markets into the restaurant. I will also take part in promotions and community events. I am very excited about this position and the opportunities that exist in Arizona. The Hard Rock corporation is known throughout and has an outstanding reputation.

Throughout my short career, I have been employed by Disney. When I decided to make the move to Orlando, I knew that I was doing it all alone, so before I even moved here, I got a job as a server at Walt Disney World. This has been an invaluable experience, has taught me many lessons, and proved a network of friends. This weekend job also gave me the extra income, allowing me to live by myself. It has not always been easy. I work a 40+ work week, then go to work at 7:00 a.m. on Saturday and Sunday. However, it has all been worth it! I cannot stress enough how invaluable it is to hold a part-time job while also having a career. It forces you to be responsible and use your time wisely.

My point in sharing all this with you is that I am an example of how hard work and dedication truly pay off. Each position I have attained has been a promotion and a significant pay raise. However, I really put myself out there and did everything I could do to get the job/career that I desired. I witness other 24- to 30-year-olds and their quest to find a job. It seems to me that people truly do not know how to best look for a job. They simply send out a few resumes and claim they are unable to find a job. I found a job in Phoenix, while living in Orlando. Anything is possible! I encourage young people to send their resumes EVERYWHERE! Someone will pass it one to someone else, and so on. Post your info and resume on CareerBuilder and Monster. Go to Job Fairs. Do extensive research on CVB websites. Looking for a job is a job within itself.

Have a GREAT DAY!   (letter from a former student)

DISCOVER A PROFESSIONAL CAREER

Career planning is an individual journey of self-exploration in which one takes responsibility and control for his/her future as a professional. Career planning is not to be confused with job searching. Job searching, while extremely important, is just one aspect or component of career planning. Career planning is an ongoing life-long process that incorporates short-term and long-term career goals and objectives and a process that has many rewards and challenges. Career decisions you make today will largely determine life and work choices for the future.

While some students know exactly what professional career they want after graduation, most explore a variety of options while in college before deciding on the right career path. This **career exploration** process is a combination of learning about yourself as well as discovering all of the potential work environments that might be of interest to you. In many cases, career exploration is a systematic process of elimination…eliminating career options that are not well suited to you!

Thus, career planning is an individual process, or a way of thinking, about how to make informed decisions regarding the various career options throughout your college years and beyond. Remember the old adage, "If you don't know where you're going, any road will take you there." Every journey begins with the first step, but don't travel down just any road. Be focused and make informed decisions.

Your first step begins with an honest self-assessment of yourself. Socrates referred to this as "know thyself." Developing a better understanding of who you are—your values, interests, abilities, personal traits, and desired lifestyle—will put you in a better position to evaluate educational options and career alternatives best suited for you. It is also important to understand that the self-assessment and career exploration steps are ongoing processes and that are never really complete!

ASSESS YOUR VALUES, INTERESTS, SKILLS, PERSONALITY, AND LIFESTYLE

As discussed in greater detail in chapter 2, it is important to conduct and gather information about yourself in order to make an informed career decision. This is the first step in the career planning process and typically involves a personal self-exploration or self-assessment inventory of your values, interests, personality, skills, and lifestyles.

- **Values** are the principles and beliefs that you use when making important decisions in your life. You probably already have a core set of values that you have already developed as a youth and ones that you strongly believe are important.
- **Interests** are activities or experiences that you like to do and find rewarding and enjoyable. What are your interests in the classroom? Beyond the classroom? At work? To make a good decision about a future career, it helps to know what type of work you enjoy doing!
- **Skills** are those items that you might have learned from previous full- or part-time jobs, volunteer experiences, sport participation, or other school and social activities.
- **Personality** describes an individual's pattern of behavior, thoughts, feelings, and motivation. Since each of us has our own personality traits, it is very important to find a career that complements these personality characteristics, not conflicts with it.
- **Lifestyle** represents personal values of where and how you live, work, and play both now and how you see yourself in years to come. In most cases, your career choice will have a significant impact on your lifestyle!

Devote quality time and attention to the self-assessment phase of career planning. By being totally honest and sincere in your self-assessment, you become more aware of your existing skills and abilities and can learn and discover where your strengths (as well as weaknesses!) and interests lie. Once this inventory process is completed, you can then begin to identify the various recreation settings, organizations, and agencies that are a good fit with these qualities and make the best of your skills and abilities. Is it important to note in this career planning phase that it is not necessary to find the "ideal" job that perfectly matches all of your values, interests, skills, personality, and lifestyle. Rather, your goal is to begin to prioritize your values, needs, and wants and to make a more informed decision on a career path that is best for you. The more accurate your self-reflection is, the better the fit will be for a successful career choice.

Also, understand that no career choice is ever set in stone. You will soon find that the "real world" of work is constantly changing and evolving. What is a common practice in a career setting today may be obsolete by the time you graduate. On the other hand, so too will your personal life, lifestyles, and relationships change. The importance and priority that you place on some values today as an undergraduate may be totally different a few years from now as you continue to grow and mature. Subsequently, your career options will change because you will change. While it is very important for you to focus on one career direction for now, just know that studies show that the average working American will have three to five careers and between 10 to 12 jobs during his or her lifetime (Denham, 2009).

CAREER EXPLORATION: RESEARCH AND EXPLORE THE VARIOUS OCCUPATIONS IN RECREATION

Researching specific careers and their specific jobs and occupations allows you to make an informed decision about your career goals. During this phase of career exploration and development, you are interested in researching and gathering as much information and learning all that you can about what occupations will allow you to use your strongest skills and match your interests, values, and personality traits. Most career information will be found by observing and interacting with professionals in the field as well as reading various publications (books, newsletters, booklets, pamphlets, etc.) written by professionals and professional associations. The Internet is also an excellent resource, as are public and university libraries and college placement offices or career development centers. Other sources that have information about occupations include current newspapers, trade journals, professional magazines, and agency annual reports.

During this information-gathering phase, the systematic process of collecting and evaluating information ultimately results in making decisions on career choices. Depending on the individual and circumstances, this process could be condensed into a matter of a few weeks (not recommended!) or expanded to several years. There are a number of sources that you can use in gathering information. The easiest approach is to obtain information directly from the company or agency. Most will provide you with their most recent annual report, job descriptions, flowcharts, program policies, mission statements and various public relations documents. Another source is to talk with your friends, colleagues, career advisors, faculty mentors and alumni. Some Internet resources are listed below:

The Better Business Bureau
(http://search.bbb.org/)
The BBB gathers and reports information on fair and effective businesses and business practices across the country.

Annual Reports
(http://www.annualreports.com/)
This is a free Internet source that provides users with one of the most complete and up-to-date sites of annual reports from various companies.

Newspaper Articles, Press Releases and Periodicals
NewsLink (http://newslink.org/) provides easy state-by-state access to newspapers, magazines, and radio/tv resources.

NewsPaperLinks
(http://www.newspaperlinks.com/voyager.cfm) is a comprehensive gateway to newspaper websites around the world and provides local community information, news, and classified sections.

Nonprofit Organizations
GuideStar (http://www.guidestar.org) is a neutral source of nonprofit information for over 1.7 million nonprofit organizations.

Company Addresses and Phone Numbers
YellowBook (http://www.guidestar.org) is the largest, independent publisher of yellow pages which provides users with the most complete source of local buying information in print and online.

No matter what career path you finally choose, enjoy exploring and learning about the various career options during your undergraduate education. Gain practical experience and valuable networking opportunities along the way. Get involved in student and professional organizations and other extracurricular activities. Attend professional association conferences as a student. Solicit the help of a faculty mentor. By taking advantage of these diverse experiences and making networking connections with professionals in the field, you will become much more marketable when you begin the actual job search process.

INFORMATIONAL INTERVIEW

One of the most effective ways of obtaining more detailed information about a particular career in recreation, parks, and leisure services is to conduct an **informational interview** with people who work in a job or occupation in which you might be interested in pursuing. They are an invaluable resource for "insider" information regarding a job or occupation. The goal of the information interview is to gather information that will allow you to make an informed career decision. It is not designed as a job interview for a specific job! If conducted properly, information interviews will allow you to expand your professional network of colleagues, keep up-to-date on career information, and build confidence in your interviewing skills. Refer to chapter 2, a more specific referent for more details regarding the actual process and various questions that might be asked in an informational interview.

MAKE THE MOST OF YOUR FORMAL EDUCATION

Brainstorm as many college majors and career options as possible as you begin your educational pursuits. You will have an abundance of majors and careers from which to choose in recreation, parks, tourism, and leisure services. Formal education, in conjunction with practical experience, provides the knowledge, skills, and abilities necessary to work in this field. Making an informed decision on a major and/or career must align with your values, skills, interests, personality, and desired lifestyle that you identified in your self-assessment process.

Selecting a College and Major

Once you have identified potential college majors and career options, you need to learn more about them. Good career decisions require careful thought and consideration about all aspects of the choices before you. Gather as much specific information as you can, such as academic departments, typical academic courses, faculty, degree requirements, sample job descriptions, potential salary ranges for selected occupations, and employment outlook overviews, etc., for each career area you are considering. This will increase your chances of making good decisions.

It is very important to decide on an academic curriculum that is related to the job that you desire. Having subject matter expertise in a particular discipline is a requirement for most jobs in this field. For example, if you are planning a career in the tourism industry, you should orient your curriculum choices toward building fundamental skills in customer service, event planning, and managing business such as hotels, resorts, cruises, and casinos. However, there are many generalizable and transferable skills that cross content areas and mastery of these skills is key to having flexibility in one's career.

Utilize Campus Career Services

Depending on the size of the institution, most colleges and universities offer free career development services to their students by providing various programs, resources, and staff assistance to help you assess your career interests and assist in the job search process. **Campus career services** departments have a wide variety of resources for you to explore such as career advising, career-related job fairs and workshops, mock interview practice sessions, library and Internet resources, job listings, resume and cover letter preparation, and in some cases alumni mentorship and networking services.

TECHNOLOGY AND CAREER PREPARATION

Significant technological changes are occurring in society, in the recreation, parks, tourism, and leisure services fields, and in career preparation. **Technology** is changing not only the way we work, but also the way we get jobs. Advancing technology and the popularity and growth of the Internet have created a whole new dimension in the job search process and the use of technology is now an essential resource in career preparation and job searching. With the introduction of the second generation of the World Wide Web in the past several years, social networking and dynamic web pages are now replacing first-generation static web pages. Social networking technologies and tools available today are completely unique and have expanded to not only include the Internet but also mobile phone technology. "The tools of the networking trade are changing and moving online, where e-mail, IM, and social-networking websites such as LinkedIn, Facebook, and some specific to industry and careers are the means to make new contacts and interact with current ones" (Fogarty, 2009, p. 1).

GETTING INVOLVED: STUDENT AND PROFESSIONAL ORGANIZATIONS

Being a member of a **student or professional organization** can be an important factor in the success and enjoyment of your college experience and later years as a professional in the field. The American Society of Association Executives (ASAE) suggests that the specific purpose of an association is to "promote the interest, welfare, or common good of an industry, a profession, a field of interest or endeavor, or a group of members. To promote industry, provide education, foster professional conduct, gather and disseminate information, develop standards, etc." The large number of professional associations for recreation and leisure services providers exist to help members value and promote their profession as well as nurture their individual careers.

While academic learning of theories and concepts is the primary goal of a college education, extracurricular activities associated with student and professional organizations help you learn, develop, and grow beyond the walls of the classroom. They can provide you with hands-on training and encourage continuing educational and professional development opportunities to better prepare you for your future career. Student and professional organizations also provide many leadership opportunities. Involvement as an officer, committee member, presenter, or attendee at a local, state, or national conference, or just being an active member can earn acknowledgment from colleagues and professionals alike and offer the chance for you to gain leadership experience and to distinguish yourself from the "average" student who just attends classes.

There's much to gain from becoming a member of a student and professional organization. As a student, sure, it looks impressive on your resume, but there are far more valuable reasons for getting actively involved while in college such as:

Marketplace Resources

When it's actually time to start the job search process, you'll have valuable job-hunting resources available through the professional organization's career opportunities center website. Most organizations' websites provide marketplace resources such as: job announcements and job alerts, resume posting services, salary survey data, and other career and job resource tools.

Networking and Continuing Education

Student and professional organizations host meetings, seminars, regional and national conferences, and other events where you can interact with leaders and other professionals in the field. Most organizations provide a membership directory (either hardcopy or web version) that provides contact information for professionals in the association so that you can connect with peers in the association community and have them become a part of your professional network.

Updated Professional Information

Most associations provide journals, magazines, newsletters, or Listservs discussions that offer up-to-date information on important trends and issues facing the field. Professional organizations can give you firsthand access to great resources on the current state of your field.

There are a variety of associations and organizations to choose from. Figure 14.1 provides a sampling that are available in our profession as well as links to their respective websites.

NETWORKING: CONNECTING WITH THE RIGHT PEOPLE AT THE RIGHT TIME

Career planning is about making contacts and relationships. **Networking** is the formal term used to describe this process with people in the profession. It is a critical part of the career preparation and job search process and one of the most effective tools used in job hunting. "Approximately 80% of all job positions are filled without employer advertising" (JobStar, 2009). These positions are filled by word of mouth, personal contacts, and referrals. Networking, then, is the key to tapping into these "hidden job market" jobs. Trying to find a job without networking is difficult and frustrating. Start building relationships and a network as early as possible in your career planning process and academic program.

Getting involved with organizations and people who share your same career interests can advance networking. It is never too late to start! Proper networking will help you achieve your personal and professional career goals by opening up new avenues for you to pursue. Take the time to brainstorm possible networking sources and follow up on this list. Don't limit yourself geographically or be hesitant to talk to others about your skills and talents. Inform everyone you know that you are looking for employment (including parents' friends, former high school and college classmates, religious leaders, your dentist and physician, neighbors, part-time work colleagues, professional acquaintances, etc.). Have confidence in yourself and your abilities to be a great professional in the field of recreation, park, and leisure services. Remember, networking is a lifelong process of building relationships to help you succeed in reaching your goals. Here are some resources that can help you learn more about this important process:

Figure 14.1
A Sample of Professional Associations and Organizations in Recreation, Parks, Sport Management, Hospitality, and Tourism

Professional Association/Organization	Website
Adventure Travel Association (ATA)	http://www.adventuretravel.com
Aerobics and Fitness Association of America (AFAA)	http://www.afaa.com/
American Alliance for Health, Physical Education, Recreation and Dance (AAHPERD)	http://www.aahperd.org
American Association for Leisure and Recreation (AALR)	http://www.aahperd.org/aapar
American Association for Physical Activity and Recreation (AAPAR)	http://www.aahperd.org/aapar
American Association of Zoo Keepers (AAZK)	http://aazk.org
American Correctional Association (ACA)	http://www.aca.org
American Hotel and Lodging Association (AHLA)	http://www.ahla.com
American Therapeutic Recreation Association (ATRA)	http://www.atra-tr.ogr
Association for Experiential Education (AEE)	http://www.aee.org
Association of College Unions International (ACUI)	http://www.acui.org
Association of Destination Management Executives (ADME)	http://www.adme.org
Association of Outdoor Recreation & Education (AORE)	http://www.aore.org
Club Managers Association of America (CMAA)	http://www.cmaa.org
Council on Hotel, Restaurant & Institutional Education (CHRIE)	http://www.chrie.org
Cruise Lines International Association (CLIA)	http://www.cruising.org
Employee Services Management Association (ESM)	http://www.esmassn.org
International Association for Amusement Parks and Attractions (IAAPA)	http://www.iaapa.org
International Association of Assembly Managers (IAAM)	http://www.iaam.org
International Association of Exhibitions and Events (IAEE)	http://www.iaee.com
International Facility Management Association (IFMA)	http://www.ifma.org
International Festivals & Events Association (IFEA)	http://www.ifea.org
International Fitness Association (IFA)	http://ifafitness.com
International Health, Racquet, & Sports Club Association (IHRSA)	http://chs.ihrsa.org
International Special Events Society (ISES)	http://www.ises.com
Meeting Professionals International (MPI)	http://www.mpiweb.org
National Association for Girls and Women in Sport (NAGWS)	http://www.aahperd.org/nagws
National Association for Interpretation (NAI)	http://www.interpnet.com
National Association for Sports and Physical Education (NASPE)	http://aahperd.org/naspe
National Association of Recreation Resource Planners (NARRP)	http://narrp.org
National Association of State Park Directors (NASPD)	http://www.naspd.org
National Association of Youth Sports (NAYS)	http://www.nays.org
National Institute for Fitness and Sport (NIFS)	http://www.nifs.org
National Intramural–Recreational Sport Association (NIRSA)	http://www.nirsa.org
National Recreation and Park Association (NRPA)	http://www.nrpa.org
National Therapeutic Recreation Association (NTRA)	http://nrpa.org/ntrs.aspx
North American Society for Psychology of Sport and Physical Activity (NASPSPA)	http://www.naspspa.org
North American Society for Sport Management (NASSM)	http://www.nassm.org
Professional Convention Management Association (PCMA)	http://www.pcma.org
Resort and Commercial Recreation Association (RCRA)	http://www.rcra.org
Society of Corporate Meeting Professionals (SCMP)	http://www.scmp.com
Sportsplex Operators & Developers Association (SODA)	http://www.sportsplexoperators.com
Stadium Managers Association (SMA)	http://www.stadiummanagers.org
Travel and Tourism Research Association (TTRA)	http://www.ttra.com
World Leisure Association (WLA)	http://www.worldleisure.org
World Leisure Organization (WHO)	http://www.worldleisure.org/
World Waterpark Association (WWA)	http://www.waterparks.org

Networking Your Way to a New Job
(http://www.quintcareers.com/networking_guide.html)
This is a great article that describes the various steps to successful networking in the job search process.

Networking Techniques for Job Hunters
http://www.distinctiveweb.com/top.htm)
Basic networking strategies are outlined to gain access to the hidden job market.

Successful Job Search Networking
http://jobsearch.about.com/cs/networking/a/networking.htm
Sample job search networking letters and other networking tips and ideas on how to approach networking contacts are provided.

HANDS-ON EXPERIENCE

Career-related opportunities are so important in that they provide hands-on experience to acquaint and familiarize you with the various options in the recreation and leisure services field. In many cases, they simply offer a starting point for locating career and job opportunities. These hands-on type of opportunities allow one to contribute and excel outside of the formal classroom. Job shadowing, part-time work, summer jobs, volunteering, and internships all help build self-confidence and maturity and can equip you with specialized skills, as well as transferable skills, that are so important in today's workplace. These opportunities will have a tremendous impact on your career direction as well as the job search process upon completion of your academic degree program. Informational interviews and job shadowing generally only take anywhere from 30 minutes to a few days. Part-time jobs, career-related volunteering, and internships may last a summer, several semesters, or even longer. Prospective employers are focusing more and more on work experiences (both paid and volunteer) as a way to screen and assess candidates' skills and abilities before they consider them for a position.

Job Shadowing

Job shadowing is a career exploration strategy and is great for high school and college students alike. Many colleges have formal job shadowing programs where students are matched with alumni and professionals who work in related fields that may be of interest to them. Essentially, job shadowing involves spending a period of time with an expert in the field, observing firsthand what professionals actually do on a daily basis, what their working environments are like, and what kinds of people (customers, clients, participants, etc.) they interact with. By taking advantage of job-shadowing opportunities, you can observe the workplace atmosphere and get a behind-the-scenes view of the daily operation. The information and experience that you gather through job shadowing will help immensely when deciding upon a career.

Part-Time Work

Part-time work during college can be very valuable for a number of reasons. First, and most obvious, with the cost of college education increasing every year, any additional financial support is always welcomed! In addition to earning extra money, working part time allows you to learn responsibility, work ethic, and all kinds of lessons about the "real world." These experiences can be very beneficial in acquiring job skills, self-management skills, and transferable skills (i.e., budgeting, meeting deadlines, project planning, supervision, leadership, people skills, etc.) that can be transferred from one job or even one career to another. Being able to include these on your resume or discuss them during a job interview will certainly enhance your position later in the job search process.

Summer Jobs

Working at a **summer job** is an excellent opportunity to pursue a possible area of career interest and to learn and experience the daily operation of a particular organization or agency…not to mention a chance to earn extra money for school! A number of summer job opportunities in recreation and leisure services exist at the national, state, and local areas including parks, hotels/resorts, camps, YMCA/YWCA, theme parks, health and fitness centers, local pools, and regional theme water parks, and commercial recreation venues to mention just a few.

Volunteer Opportunities

Volunteering your time and service is a great way to gain experience and learn more specifics about a particular career field or interest that you may want to pursue. It also demonstrates your enthusiasm and potential leadership skills for the field. Serving as a volunteer provides exposure to a work setting and the various types of people and job tasks that are associated with this career setting. In addition, the knowledge, skills, and experience that you acquire as a volunteer will certainly enhance your resume and marketability later when you pursue full-time employment. Involvement with organizations outside of the classroom and paid work responsibilities provides a glimpse and insight to potential employers of the type of person you are and how you might contribute to their organization in the future. Volunteering at events is an excellent way to network with industry professionals and while gaining practical experience at the same time.

INTERNSHIPS

An **internship** as defined by the National Society for Experiential Education (2009) as: "A carefully monitored work or volunteer experience in which an individual has intentional learning goals and reflects actively on what he or she is learning throughout the experience." It is a capstone, hands-on experience, usually completed in the senior year of college, where a student is afforded the opportunity to apply theories and concepts learned in the classroom to a real-world work environment in order to gain and develop career-specific skills and experience.

Actual internships vary greatly from one agency or organization to the next. Traditionally, a sponsoring recreation, park, and leisure service agency works with the student to meet specific learning goals and outcomes developed by the student and his or her university faculty advisor and provide special mentoring or contact/networking opportunities. In exchange, the student intern agrees to assist the employer in meeting the specific department or programming needs in a variety of roles and responsibilities. Internships may be paid or unpaid, with or without academic credit, and can be completed in one semester, two semesters, a 14-week summer session, one year, etc. Having completed an internship experience prior to graduation gives you an edge over other candidates in a competitive job market. And, in many cases, organizations offer a full-time position to a successful intern.

Selecting Your Internship

The best way to approach the selection process is to treat the internship as if it were a full-time position. Research, preparation, and follow through, essential in the job search process, are also important elements that can make the difference in having a successful and enjoyable internship experience.

Once you have researched and identified the career setting that you are interested in pursuing, you should be ready to write specific internship objectives that will guide you through the search and selection process. You will notice that the possibilities are numerous and vary in degree of duties and responsibilities, so you want to examine these carefully in order to have a meaningful internship experience that meets your needs and wants.

In researching possible internship agencies, your faculty internship coordinator will play a significant role in the selection process and can provide valuable information about agencies that have hosted quality internships in the past. Collect as much information as possible about agencies that might host interns to see if that agency fits with your particular needs. Seek leads from faculty, friends, family, alumni, and students just completing their internship. Contact employers in your field of study to see if they have an existing internship program or inquire if they would be willing to discuss the possibility of an internship. Review your informational interviews to see if they have any suggestions or leads.

After you have collected your agency information and before making a decision to apply for an internship, it is time to ask yourself specific questions regarding the internship experience. Example questions include:

- When you do want to intern ... fall, spring or summer semester?
- Where do you want to work? What city, state, region of the country?
- Do you need to live at home or close proximity or can you live with family or friends in other parts of the country?
- How much money do you need to make during the internship summer? Would the agency or university allow you to combine an unpaid internship with a part-time job?
- What are the specific duties and responsibilities of the internship?
- What is the probability that the agency will offer you a position upon completion of the internship?

CERTIFICATIONS AND LICENSES

Professional associations grant credentials such as **certifications and licenses** to individuals who can demonstrate knowledge, problem-solving abilities, willingness to learn, and expertise in any given field. It is a way to ensure that professionals are qualified and can meet high standards of performance. The certification process consists of an individual voluntarily submitting his/her credentials to a board for review based upon competencies, criteria or standards that have been identified by that certifying agency. Some careers (i.e., therapeutic recreation) will require individuals to possess a particular certification before employment.

The National Recreation and Park Association (2009) suggests the following five reasons to become a certified professional:

1. Greater career opportunities and advancement.
2. Demonstration of your commitment to the parks and recreation profession.
3. Enhanced quality of parks and recreation services nationwide.
4. Recognition of your accomplishments and ability to meet national standards.
5. Expansion of your skills and knowledge through continuing professional development.

One of the leading and most recognized recreation certification programs in recreation, park, and leisure service is the Certified Park and Recreation Professional (CPRP) credential, administered by the National Recreation and Park Association (NRPA) and governed by the National Certification Board. Two other certifications are also offered by NRPA, and they include the Aquatic Facility Operator (AFO) certification for pool operators and aquatic facility managers and the Certified Playground Safety Inspector (CPSI) for individuals who inspect playgrounds for safety related issues. The National Council for Therapeutic Recreation Certification (NCTRC) provides an independent certification, the Certified Therapeutic Recreation Specialist (CTRS), for professionals who work with the mentally and physically disabled, as well as the elderly. There are a variety of other specialty certifications in recreation, park and leisure services.

As a student, earning certification credentials tells prospective employers that, in addition to earning your new degree, you have been tested by a national certification board on a wide range of practical knowledge and experiences and have shown dedication to your chosen profession through voluntary certification. Increasingly, employers are including certifications as a desirable (and in some cases a "must-have") part of a candidates' career portfolio. Regardless of what your particular area of career interest might be, speak with both your academic faculty and practitioners in the field to determine what credentials are necessary and advantageous for you to possess and get them.

JOB SEARCH STRATEGIES

The **job search** is the culmination of integrating and applying all that you learned during the career planning and exploration phases. It involves a systematic plan that consists of portfolios, resumes, cover letters, interviews, and job offers. Organizing your portfolio, creating your resume, developing a well-written cover letter, and practicing for job interviews are all things that should be done in order to be successful in the job search process.

Portfolios/Electronic Portfolios

A **portfolio** is an excellent job search tool that is used to capture your skills, abilities, and accomplishments. A portfolio is a "portable collection of materials that showcase your skills, achievements, experience, academic excellence, and anything else that is relevant for the interviewer to see. While the resume is a great toll for summarizing your background, the portfolio actual proves the existence and the depth of your skills, education, and other experiences" (Turner, 2009). Portfolios generally can include the following sections, with actual documentation, that highlight:

- education
- resume
- reference letters
- professional training including proof of all training certificates, licenses, certifications, workshops/seminars or specific courses such as first aid, CPR, WSI, etc.
- conferences you have attended
- thank-you letters from an association, customer and/or participant that appreciated your assistance
- letters of recommendation or testimonials
- articles/publications/presentations you have written an article for a professional publication
- in-house publications (i.e. health tips, etc.) news releases related to a program or special event that you coordinated or hosted past or current job descriptions that outline duties and levels of responsibility
- performance appraisals
- academic projects or other samples of work that you have completed while in college that might showcase your talents and/or competence

While the portfolio is a collection of your actual documents or artifacts, the "electronic portfolio (also known as an ePortfolio, e-portfolio, efolio, digital portfolio, webfolio, and so on) is essentially an electronic version of a paper-based portfolio, created in a computer environment, and incorporating not just text, but graphic, audio and video material as well" (Butler, 2006, p. 1).

Resumes

A **resume** is a summary of your professional and personal experiences that introduces you to a potential employer. The main purpose of the resume is to "get your foot in the door" of an agency so that they will be interested in personally interviewing you for the job. In most cases, the resume does not get you the job... it is at the interview that the job is won. However, the resume is usually the first impression that an employer has of you. It can be a deciding factor on whether you remain in the pool of qualified applicants, so it is extremely important that the resume be created, designed, and organized in a professional manner. Most importantly, resumes should be skills-based and clearly reflect your particular skills and accomplishments and how you have excelled and mastered these skills.

There are three common types of resume formats: chronological, functional, and combination. The chronological format is the most popular format and is a chronological listing of employment and employment-related experiences including specific employer names, locations, and dates of employment. The functional format highlights skills, experience, and accomplishments and is organized by functions or skills and qualifications rather than by employer and dates of employment. The last format is the combination format, which features a combination of functional attributes and includes a chronological listing of employment, education, and related experiences. Choose the format that best displays and showcases your strengths and accomplishments.

Regardless of the resume format that you choose, there are a number of basic principles that should be using in writing your resume. These include:

- Be brief but targeted...one to three pages is an acceptable length of a resume, especially for undergraduate students.
- Include basic content such as name, current and/or permanent address, telephone number (both landline and cell), and email address.
- More specific required content includes education, professional employment experiences—both paid and volunteer—honors, awards, licenses, and certifications, and professional memberships.
- Optional content can include job objective, presentations and publications, community activities, references, and special skills, hobbies, and interests.
- Use measurable outcomes and numerical values that can enhance your qualifications and accomplishments.
- Use action verbs when describing your work experience and job responsibilities.

Your resume should always be consistent with expectations of professionals in the field, free of spelling and grammatical errors, and above all, honest. Lastly, your resume should always be up to date and mirror your personal and professional development. As you grow professionally by gaining skills and experiences, so should your resume.

Cover Letters

Cover letters are a great way to introduce and personalize your resume and target your skills. They provide an opportunity for the employer to gain more insight into your interest in their position as well as for you to highlight and explain specific experiences and accomplishments that reinforces your strengths for the position that might not be evident in your resume. A cover letter, like the resume, should be free of spelling and grammatical errors and usually is only one page in length. Your cover letter should be addressed to a specific person that is responsible for conducting the review process that this position. If you do not know the specific name of the person to receive your application material, you may need to conduct a web search on the agency or place phone calls to the agency for further clarification.

The cover letter gives you an opportunity to direct the reader to your specific qualifications that meets their needs as well as to explain why you are interested in this particular job and agency. The content of the letter should include four general areas:

- A brief introductory paragraph of who you are, how you learned of the position opening, and why you are writing.
- A second paragraph highlighting your experience and education that makes you an ideal candidate for the position.
- The third paragraph explains in more detail your interests and motivation as to why you are interested in the position and agency and how your credentials meet their specific needs.
- The last paragraph is your chance to be pro-active and structure future follow-up steps on your part.

Interviewing

While a well-written resume and cover letter are essential in the job search process, it is the **job interview** that will make or break your chance of being selected for the position. There are a number of different types of job interviews that are used by employers, such as telephone screening, in-person screening, peer group interviews, luncheon interviews, stress interviews, and video conferencing. Regardless of the type of interview that you might experience, employers are looking for your communication skills, confidence, personality, accomplishments, and knowledge about the field and their particular organization. On the other hand, remember that the interview is a two-way street. It is also your opportunity to learn more about the organization and how you might fit in this work environment.

Some general pointers that may be helpful to you in order to be successful at the interview include:

- Be prepared. Research the organization prior to the interview.
- Be on time; arrive 10-15 minutes prior to your scheduled interview.
- Dress appropriately by selecting clothing appropriate to the job that you are applying for.

- Communicate your best image highlighting your experiences and accomplishments.
- Demonstrate your enthusiasm, excitement, and positive attitude for the position you are interviewing for as well as the field.
- Handle difficult questions by giving direct and honest answers.
- Follow-up in writing by sending a thank-you letter or note to each person with whom your interviewed.

CONCLUSION

The career planning process suggested in this chapter can be very exciting and interesting, and it will require a substantial amount of work on your part in order to be successful. The first step in the process is to complete an honest self-assessment of yourself (both personally and professionally) so that you can identify and match your skills and interests with occupations in the field. Once this is done, investigating a variety of student and professional organizations is a good place to begin developing a professional network. Acquiring practical, hands-on opportunities is essential in familiarizing and gaining experience with the various occupations in recreation, park, and leisure services. Job shadowing, part-time work, summer jobs, volunteering, and internships all help in building your self-confidence and establishing your credentials. Lastly, the actual job search is the culmination of the entire career planning process and consists of a developing and maintaining your portfolio, creating a resume, writing personalized cover letters, interviewing with potential employers, and then the ultimate prize: a job offer!

FURTHER INVESTIGATION

For More Research

1. Create a career overview for your ideal job position. Your career overview should include the following sections: websites, career paths, related job titles, required certifications, salary, possible networking contacts, and position questions.
2. Identify two professional associations and one student (on-campus) association related to your career interest. For each association, document the name of the association, address and contact information, the website address (if applicable), the purpose and goals of the association, membership costs for both a student membership as well as a professional membership, date and location of the next major association conference or meeting, and if the association has a career opportunities center.
3. Using your networking and job researching skills, locate three position announcements that describe your ideal job. Review the qualification requirements for each position. What qualifications do you possess? Where are the gaps that you need to narrow? Develop a plan of action to strengthen your qualifications for these positions.

Active Investigation

1. Spend at least one hour job shadowing a professional in the field of recreation, parks, and leisure services. As a part of this activity, research this career of interest (Internet, books, magazines, etc.) prior to your job shadow experience. After you have spent time with the professional, identify the specific skills that are required for that line of work. Compare and contrast your current skills, knowledge, and experience to the requirements of the job. If this is an area that you would like to pursue further, outline the steps you might take to prepare yourself for this career.
2. Begin planning and developing your career portfolio. As a part of this on-going process, you will need to complete an honest self-reflection on your current knowledge, skills, abilities, and experiences. Gather artifacts and other documents that would support your accomplishments such as letters of recommendation; list of service, leadership, or involvement activities; projects or papers from courses that you are really proud of; awards; pictures; or any other items that would give the reader important information about you.
3. Design a resume and write a cover letter for an actual position opening that you have found on the Internet or other job posting area.

Recommended Reading

Bolles, R. N. (2009). *What color is your parachute? 2010.* Berkeley, CA: Ten Speed Press.
A practical manual for job hunters and career changers has been annually updated for the past 40 years and is still considered one of the best-selling job-hunting and career planning books with its step-by-step plan and guide in mastering the career-planning process.

Bolles, M. E., & Bolles, R. N. (2008). *Job hunting online* (5th ed.). Berkeley, CA: Ten Speed Press.
A desktop guide that helps job seekers navigate the overwhelming amount of information available on the Internet to find the most useful sites and avoid common pitfalls. In addition, the book includes hundreds of annotated website recommendations geared to the job-search process.

Bureau of Labor Statistics. (2009). Occupational outlook handbook, 2008-2009 edition, http://www.bls.gov/OCO/.
This website provides excellent job-search tips, links to information about the job market in each state, as well as the training and education needed, earnings, expected job prospects, what workers do on the job, and working conditions for hundreds of jobs.

Enelow, W., & Kursmark, L. (2010). *Cover letter magic: Trade secrets of professional resume writers* (4th ed.). Indianapolis, IN: Jist Works.
This book provides the reader with excellent tips on resume preparation, e-mail and scannable cover letters, thank-you letters, and includes over 150 sample resumes as well as opening paragraphs for cover letters.

Reeves, E. G. (2009). *Can I wear my nose ring to the interview?* New York: Workman Publishing.
Written in an upbeat, positive, and non-intimidating style, this book serves as a good starting point that offers numerous practical suggestions and advice for new job hunters or college grads in the job-search process from start to finish.

Ross, C. M., Beggs, B. A., & Young, S. J. (2010). *Mastering the job-search process in recreation and leisure services* (2nd ed.). Sudbury, MA: Jones and Bartlett Publishers.
This book guides readers just starting out in the field of recreation and leisure services through each step of the job-search process, from both an employer's and applicant's point of view. Chapters cover researching an organization, portfolios, cover letters and resumes, interviews, internships, and navigating the transition from college to professional life.

Troutman, K. K. (2007). *Federal resume guidebook: Strategies for writing a winning federal electronic resume, KSAs, and essays* (4th ed.). Indianapolis, IN: JIST Works.
This guidebook provides a comprehensive federal government career resource for all job-seekers, including instructions, tips, and resume samples written to help readers write a comprehensive federal resume that can be used when completing online federal government applications

Recommended Career and Job Search Websites

CareerBuilder
(http://www.careerbuilder.com)
CareerBuilder offers both online and print networks to help job seekers connect with 9,000 employer career websites including 140 newspapers.

CollegeGrad
(http://www.collegegrad.com)
This is a career website that provides information on resume writing, networking, job searching, etc. for entry-level job searches conducted by college students and recent grads.

JobInterview.net
(http://www.jobinterview.net)
This is an excellent site that provides interview questions and answers, job interview tips, various interview techniques, and sample questions to ask the employer during a job interview.

JobStar Central

(http://jobstar.org)

Jobstar is a public library-sponsored guide for job seekers including resumes, cover letters, salary surveys, and career selection.

Monster

(http://www.monster.com)

Monster is one of the largest employment websites in the world and is the largest global job search engine with over a million job postings at any given time.

National Association of Colleges and Employers JobWeb

(http://www.jobweb.org)

This site offers career and job-search advice for new college graduates as well as updated salary surveys for new graduates.

Quintessential Careers

(http://www.quintcareers.com)

Various job search tools are provided, including expert advice, career articles, and some of the best job sites on the Web.

Riley Guide

(http://rileyguide.com)

This site is one of the oldest and most comprehensive directories of career and employment resources available online and provides a guide to the best the Internet has to offer for job search and career information.

USAJobs

(http://www.usajobs.com)

The official job site of the U.S. Federal Government and is the one-stop source for Federal jobs and employment information.

WetFeet

(http://wetfeet.com)

WetFeet provides insightful profiles of companies, careers, and industries to guide job seekers toward finding the right career and the right job.

REFERENCES

Denham, T. 2009). "The Truth About 15 Career Development and Job-Search Beliefs" Retrieved on November 14, 2009 from http://www.jobweb.org/studentarticles.aspx?id=758

Fogarty, K. (2009). "Can you Facebook your way to a new job?" Retrieved on November 6, 2009 from https://cdn.theladders.net/static/pdf/socialnetworkingThree.pdf

JobStar Central. (2009). "Hidden Job Market - What is it?" Retrieved November 1, 2009 from http://jobstar.org/hidden/hidden.php

National Recreation and Park Association. (2009). "Certification Programs" Retrieved October 29, 2009 from http://www.nrpa.org/Content.aspx?id=410

National Society for Experiential Education. (2009). "About Us" Retrieved November 10, 2009 from http://www.nsee.org/about_us.htm

Turner, V. K. (2009). "Portfolio: Add power to your job search with a portfolio" Retrieved November 1, 2009 from http://careercenter.missouristate.edu/assets/careercenter/Portfolio.pdf

" *Students are entering a vastly different world now from that even just 10 or 15 years ago. Today's new park and recreation professionals have been told they can do anything, and they want to make an immediate impact.*

—DOUGLAS VIARA, AUTHOR
Parks & Recreation Magazine

"

15

Recreation, Parks, Sport Management, Hospitality, and Tourism Careers:
Forces Shaping the Future

JAMES MURPHY
San Francisco State University

FOCUS QUESTIONS

Q: *How does the "Flat World Paradigm" relate to parks, recreation, and tourism?*

A: We live in a global environment created by the convergence of technological and political forces with a web-enabled playing field that allows for multiple forms of collaboration without regard to geography or distance or, eventually, even language. As the global playing field flattens, this new world order will require all service sectors to respond quickly to trends. Leaders will be required to become more technologically savvy and conscious of ever-changing desires fueled by multiple constituent groups that will be continually evolving with the ability to influence the direction of change.

Q: *In light of the rapidity of high-speed change in all aspects of our lives, what is the implication of electronic/wireless/virtual technology in the delivery of recreation, parks, sport management, hospitality, and tourism services?*

A: We live in a contrasting world of both **virtual leisure** and **in nature (direct) engagement** in real-time experiences. One might argue there will no longer be mass trends that encompass all of society because everyone has at their disposal, literally in the palm of their hand, a portal to the world. This empowers a person to both view virtual and real life events and to become interconnected with people next door, down the street, across the nation, and globally at an instant.

Q: *How does the increasing emergence of diversity in North America complicate or extend leisure expression? Career options?*

A: We live in an increasing multicultural society. The challenge for all societal institutions is to embrace subcultural, racial, ethnic, and lifestyle differences that will continue to represent a higher proportion of the population mix rendering Anglo-Saxon, heterosexual, Judeo-Christian majority perspectives less an overriding influential in setting community norms, mores, and institutional structures

Q: *How does the concept of **sustainability** influence recreation, parks, sport management, hospitality, and tourism?*

A: Those in recreation-related professions will be central to promoting the need to conserve the biodiversity of the planet through sustainable practices.

Q: *How does a future filled with ambiguity and uncertainty influence one's career choice?*

A: It will be incumbent for future professionals to be flexible, adaptive, inquisitive, at times "in the moment," and open to change in order to not only provide guidance to their participants/guests but to be able to manage their own personal lives.

KEY TERMS

Flat World Paradigm
Virtual leisure
In nature engagement
Sustainability
Macro themes
Micro themes
Pluralistic
Green profession
Carbon footprint
Augmented Reality Technology (ART)
Social media

For-benefit
Microtargeting
Long Attention Span (LAS)
Collaborative, boundary-free
Servant leaders
Temporal aspects
Environmental and social
  justice
Ecological model
Advocacy
Stewards
Deep recreation

FORCES SHAPING THE FUTURE

These are the best of times and these are among the most challenging of times. Recreation, parks, sport management, hospitality, and tourism have never been in such a strategic position, locally, regionally, nationally, and globally. Revenues generated from tourism continue to increase nationally and worldwide. There is increasing pressure at the federal level to preserve wilderness and parklands. Local governments and nonprofit agencies are becoming the focal point for promoting quality of life experiences for the community and simultaneously promoting the sustainable use of resources. While the threat of terrorism moderates all planning and delivery efforts, the second decade of the twenty-first century promises to be an exciting and profitable era for continued growth of careers in recreation, parks, sport management, hospitality, and tourism.

Any attempt to masterfully map the future will inevitably fall short of what will actually occur. The world is changing at such a rapid pace that we barely have time to embrace changing technology, societal structures, and emerging values while trying to adapt and adjust our personal and professional lives. However, we do know that change is inevitable, and the pace of change occurs at a faster rate than a generation ago.

This chapter will identify four key **macro themes** that are likely to influence institutions and therefore everyday life. The eventual outcome of each theme as forecasted will likely be moderated by unanticipated events. At the same time, there are perhaps even more influential **micro themes** caused by increasing freedom and the prevalence of individual choice that serve to buoy many kindred small, intense subgroups who aspire for more personally relevant forms of expression.

Macro themes appear to influence impacting society as a whole and are thus helping shape the future of parks, recreation, tourism and leisure service careers.

Macro Theme: Diversity

The challenge for recreation, parks, tourism, and leisure service organizations is to consider incorporating a **pluralistic** framework. That is, one that recognizes and accepts differences, while embracing and honoring various racial, ethnic, and lifestyles within an overarching national perspective.

Community life in North America will continue to be transformed in the years ahead by the influx of immigrants. Recreation, parks, sport management, hospitality, and tourism professionals will have a critical role in creating a welcoming environment for all community members, particularly immigrant groups. At the early part of the twenty -first century, "more than 60% of the net increase in minority population growth was due to immigration, with over 75% of the U.S. immigration originating from Asia and Latin America" (Floyd et al., cited in Murdock, White, Hoque, & Pecotte, 2003). Leisure professionals will need to know how leisure contributes to a sense of place and community and where communities are forming and restructuring due to immigration (Floyd et al., 2008, p. 14). In this regard, recreation, parks, sport management, hospitality, and tourism professionals may help provide insight into how world leaders can resolve global tensions. "Ethnic tensions and conflict occurring in the U.S., Europe, and other parts of the world show there are opportunities for race and ethnicity research to explore how leisure contributes to social conflict and community cohesion" (Floyd, et al., 2008, p. 14). It will be critical for future recreation, parks, sport management, hospitality, and tourism professionals to provide a place for all people in the community to have a safe haven to play and recreate and to also work to reduce racial and ethnic disparities in access to parks and various forms recreation expression. As recreation, parks, sport management, hospitality, and tourism professionals more reflect the overall population, there will be expanded opportunities both for individuals from varied cultural, racial, and ethnic backgrounds to become an important part of leisure services and for organizations to become increasingly relevant to their community constituents and guests.

Macro Theme: Sustainability

Leisure services will need to increasingly become a **green profession**. While sponsoring and initiating a myriad of activities and events and provision of facilities, buildings, and natural areas that use a considerable amount of energy and water, we must minimize the **carbon footprint** and increase efficiency and cost savings. Dustin and colleagues (2010) warn that "the increasing divide between humans and nature jeopardizes our health in significant ways" (p. 4). Dustin et al. (2010) comment that the "individual, through a healthier lifestyle, reduces his or her carbon footprint on the larger world, while the larger world reciprocates with cleaner air, cleaner water, and an abundance of health-restoring properties" (p. 7).

Recreation, parks, sport management, hospitality, and tourism professionals will be central to promoting the need to conserve the biodiversity of the planet. "Threats to biodiversity and the consequences of its losses, including the obvious ecological consequences, as well as the impact on aesthetic, ethical, sociological, and economical aspects of our world, reveal the reality of our dependence on a healthy planet." (Dustin et al., 2009, p. 9). Professionals will need to understand that these relationships extend from the global to the local level, affecting the health and well-being of the planet and all its inhabitants. Recreation, parks, sport management, hospitality, and tourism professionals will be at the forefront of conveying the need that each recreation experience, much like any other human activity, can have a negative effect on the ecosystem as a whole and is therefore intertwined and interdependent with other individual, family, community, national, and international systems.

Macro Theme: Health and Wellness

Concurrent with the evolution of recreation, parks, sport management, hospitality, and tourism becoming green professions is the recognition that recreation expression, physical engagement, and participation in community life improves ones' physical and emotional health. Linked to the other Macro trends, the availability and opportunities for all community members to engage in physical activity in programs and in natural settings.

Leisure service providers will play an important role in fostering healthy living, particularly for urban populations who often lead sedentary lifestyles. Dustin, Bricker, and Schwab (2010) argue that "our physical, mental, and emotional well-being can be improved by walking, hiking, biking, climbing, running rivers, skiing, snowboarding, snowshoeing" (p. 9). As such it will be cheaper to prevent health problems such as asthma and obesity than to pay for their medical treatment. Thus, recreation, parks, sport management, hospitality, and tourism providers must advocate for creation to be embraced as a part of a comprehensive health promotion strategy. It is important for service providers to recognize that low-income and racial/ethnic minority populations typically have less access than other population groups to parks and physical activity-friendly environments. Therefore, recreation, parks, sport management, and tourism professionals must work collaboratively with other community, regional, and federal partners to assure more equitable availability of, access to, and quality of resources for everyone (Taylor et al., 2007).

Macro Theme: Pace of Change and Technology

Change will continue to come rolling at us at a seemingly faster and faster pace. Many social institutions (church, schools, workplace, and family) do not often provide sufficient clarification and assistance for people to decipher and decode the signals that announce changes that are forthcoming and "land" before us. The messages that represent change, even when conveyed via the Internet, social network sites, or on cell phones, Blackberries/iPhones, etc., often leave people unable to make sense of them. People increasingly rely on their internal barometers to gauge the meaning of changes that appear daily. **Augmented reality technology (ART)** is emerging as a tool for interacting with the world. It layers virtual imagery and information over a real-world environment. ART provides information on objects, locations, and people automatically as it pops up in real time as you encounter them. The technology is conveyed through smart phones that leverage Global Positioning Systems data, a digital compass, a camera and wireless connectivity. "Everything you carry will have much more awareness about where it is and what's around it, whether you are interested or not" (Kim, p. 8). Recreation, parks, sport management, hospitality, and tourism professionals will need to be adept at dealing with instantaneous communication and a world without borders and provide insight, clarity, and even wisdom to their colleagues and constituents on how to live, even thrive. The twenty-first century recreation, parks, sport management, hospitality, and tourism professional will need a skill set that includes the ability to promote and advocate for removal of inequities in services via **social media** (Facebook, MySpace, Twitter, etc.), which will be as important as face-to-face expertise working with community members.

Will Technology Get Between People?

There is concern that technology will fracture connectivity between people. However, Naisbitt (1999) cites the community of Celebration, Florida, where technology is being used to more closely connect the community. Founded in 1994, with "a commitment to community, education, health, technology, and a sense of place," Celebration is fully wired and Internet ready for all residents. The town was created to provide residents the best of technology and humanity, with access to technology and community amenities. Each resident receives access to the Internet and a password to a local "Front Porch" Intranet to keep up to date on community events and happenings. *Based on book by John Naisbitt, High-Tech, High-Touch (1999).*

Macro Trend: The Fourth Sector

As mentioned in chapter two, the Leisure Service Delivery System is evolving into less discrete forms of service by type of participant or constituent to one that is more permeable (see Figure 2.1, page 37). In the past, the public agencies provided local, state, and federal government programs, facilities, and natural areas for people to enjoy; private, non-profit agencies have primarily provided youth and group membership forms of service; and commercial, for-profit organizations who have offered entertainment, festival, and theme park experiences. In essence, recreation, parks, sport management, hospitality, and tourism agencies are confronted by what the rest of society has been experiencing as the accelerated rate of change and the removal of "artificial" barriers between types of organizations, and there is a realization among all types of service providers that traditional structural boundaries no longer have relevance. Thus, the emergence of the "Fourth Sector."

What is the significance of the blurring of boundaries between commercial, for-profit, public, and non-profit sectors? How will this melting away of strictly defined organizational missions/service orientation impact recreation, parks, sport management, hospitality, and tourism services? As previously discussed in chapter 2, the mission and methods of an increasing number of organizations are becoming steadily more similar with an organizational landscape that integrates social purposes with business methods (refer back to Figure 2.1, the "Leisure Service Delivery System: Evolving Structure" and see Figure 15.1). The Fourth Sector is the result of the creation of hybrid organizations that "transcend the usual sectoral boundaries and resist easy classification within the traditional three sectors" (Sabeti, p. 2).

The Fourth Sector organization (or **"For-Benefit"** organization) may well best serve the leisure needs of communities in the future because at their core these are socially conscious entrepreneurs who may well help our society meet the requirement of sustainability—"the pursuit of lasting economic prosperity, social equity, and environmental well-being" (Sabeti, p.4). Further, these kinds of emerging organizations are equipped and dedicated to being a part of the broader community and can ideally affect systemic solutions.

Recreation, parks, sport management, hospitality, and tourism organizations are ideally suited for such a vision of service. Indeed, if they do not make such a conversion from their more rigid service structures, they will not be able to confront and ameliorate overcrowded recreation facilities, threatened riparian and wetland areas. A lack of conscious environmental planning that could lead to stifling, even ruining, recreation expression. As the increasing degradation of the planet occurs from global warming, increasing ill effects of urbanization, unhealthy obese and diabetic youth, and growing, out-of-control gang violence, the resolution of these and a multitude of other problems requires organizations to be more flexible and have the ability to influence policies that will cut across territorial boundaries of organizations to influence the direction of public/governmental, non-profit, and commercial, for-profit decisions done in narrow silos.

With the emergence of Fourth Sector organizations, leisure service professionals will need to have educational backgrounds and work experience that emphasize transparency, measureable impact, venture philanthropy, social investing, economic sustainability, program-related investments, and accountability. The Fourth Sector

FIGURE 15.1
PATTERNS OF ORGANIZATIONAL CHANGE:
EMERGENCE OF A FOURTH SECTOR

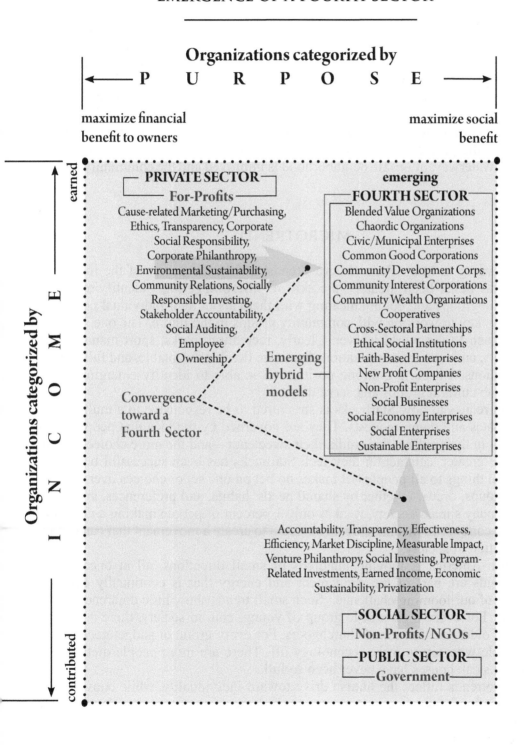

Organizations categorized by

← P   U   R   P   O   S   E →

maximize financial
benefit to owners

maximize social
benefit

Organizations categorized by   I N C O M E

earned

contributed

PRIVATE SECTOR
For-Profits
Cause-related Marketing/Purchasing,
Ethics, Transparency, Corporate
Social Responsibility,
Corporate Philanthropy,
Environmental Sustainability,
Community Relations, Socially
Responsible Investing,
Stakeholder Accountability,
Social Auditing,
Employee
Ownership

emerging
FOURTH SECTOR
Blended Value Organizations
Chaordic Organizations
Civic/Municipal Enterprises
Common Good Corporations
Community Development Corps.
Community Interest Corporations
Community Wealth Organizations
Cooperatives
Cross-Sectoral Partnerships
Ethical Social Institutions
Faith-Based Enterprises
New Profit Companies
Non-Profit Enterprises
Social Businesses
Social Economy Enterprises
Social Enterprises
Sustainable Enterprises

Emerging
hybrid
models

Convergence
toward a
Fourth Sector

Accountability, Transparency, Effectiveness,
Efficiency, Market Discipline, Measurable Impact,
Venture Philanthropy, Social Investing, Program-
Related Investments, Earned Income, Economic
Sustainability, Privatization

SOCIAL SECTOR
Non-Profits/NGOs

PUBLIC SECTOR
Government

is designed for sustainability, to benefit the owners, board members, and employees of For-Benefit organizations as well as the financial supporters and constituents of public and non-profit agencies. Therefore, this type of organization is dedicated to advancing the welfare of all its stakeholders. So, a For-Benefit organization does not interact with its stakeholders; it is its stakeholders.

Thus, in the future, recreation, parks, sport management, hospitality, and tourism professionals will not be in a quandary when a conflicting policy, discriminatory practice, or neglected segment of the population, is just outside the "boundary" of the agency's purview because an organization that deploys all of the evolving structure of the Leisure Service Delivery System is restructured as a For-Benefit organization. It will be an organic, strategic effort to lend leadership to the community to provide direct intervention and advocate positions that will remediate the problem so that the quality of life of the underserved population, polluted waterway, or unsafe neighborhood is improved and the community at large benefits.

MICROTRENDS

According to Mark Penn (Micro Trends, 2007), the power of the individual choice has never been greater—the skill of **microtargeting**—identifying small, intense subgroups and communicating with them about their individual needs and wants—is key to working with community groups in the future. The one size-fits-all approach to the world is over. Clearly, recreation, parks, sport management, hospitality, and tourism organizations that have flexible, adaptable, and full-service organizations will be in a strong position to be able to identify emerging trends among sub cultural groups and serve them.

Penn relates to how Starbucks is structured to be responsive to a multitude of coffee tastes and menu requests. They are governed by the idea that people make choices—in their coffee, their milk, their sweetener—and the more choices people have, the greater satisfaction they feel. Starbucks has been successful because it can be all things to all people—it makes no bet on one set of choices over another. Small groups, drawn together by shared needs, habits, and preferences, are on the rise. In today's mass society, it takes only 1 percent of people making a dedicated choice—contrary to the mainstream choice—to create a movement that can change the direction of society.

North America is moving hundreds of small directions, all at once. These microtrends are part of the excitement and energy that is continually evolving and part of our looming challenge. Such small trends show little deference to one another. For every high-profile group of young, chic in society, there is another group of older, old-fashioned churchgoers. For every group of gadget geeks, there are people who say turn the technology off. There are more people dieting than ever, but steak houses have never been so full.

Microtrends reflect the human drive toward individuality, while conventional wisdom often seeks to drive society toward the lowest common denominator. The original mass-produced industrial model of the economy is being replaced by the Starbucks economy—the multiplication of choice as the driver of personal expression and satisfaction. For every trend there is a countertrend. For every push to modernization, there is a drive to hold on to old values. For every dash to the Internet, there are those who want to escape to the outdoors for peace and quiet. For every push to have instant information, there are people who want it long, detailed, and thoughtful.

Examples of some of microtrends identified by Penn (2007) include:

- **Increase in individual and nature-based sports.** In the period between 1999-2005 skateboarders (167%), kayakers and rafters (117%), and snowboarders (114%) far outdistanced more traditional big sports such as baseball, which decreased 7%, and basketball, which fell .7% during the same timeframe (National Sporting Goods Association).
- **Thirty-something Video Game Players.** As of 2006, the average video game player was 33, up from 26 just four years earlier (National Software Association).
- **Homeschooling**. There has been a steady increase in the number of families who home school their children. In the period from 1999-2003, there was an increase of 30% of parents who homeschooled their children. This figure represented 2.2 % of the school-age population in the United States but 12% of finalists for the National Spelling Bee.
- **Slowing down.** While there is a surge in Internet use, Twittering, YouTube and Facebook social networking site participants and texters, allowing users to obtain immediate information and be connected to their family and friends instantly, there are also people who have **long attention spans (LAS)**. They are represented by marathoners who take hours to finish a race, golfers who take four and one-half hours to play a round, readers who enjoy books of 400 and 500 pages, and moviegoers who enjoy sitting through films of one and one-half to two and one-half hours.
- **Linguistically isolated households**. One in 25 households (25 million people) in the United States has individuals and families where no one speaks English very well or at all. While most mainstream work settings require workers to speak in English, there are a number of communities where lower wage earners in particular, can work, play, shop, and socialize entirely in Spanish, Mandarin, or Hindi.

Microtrends and Leisure

Microtrends are accelerating the fragmentation of community life. We are watching groups of dedicated, intensely interested people express their individuality in new ways, putting stress on politics, religion, popular culture, family structure, and leisure service organizations. We are witnessing a disaggregation of society and the breaking down of boredom and expansion of freedom of choice that is becoming more of the cornerstone of people's overall life choices. Leisure expression has never been more central to people's way of living. The potential for personal satisfaction due to individual choice is at its highest level ever. Even with a change from more materialistic forms of leisure (represented by consumerism) people are recognizing that leisure as experience, one in which they are more conscious of and care more about, has value (White Hutchinson Leisure and Learning Group, 2009).

People's growing desire for leisure experience has resulted in a desire to strengthen their bonds and pursue enjoyment with family and friends and for knowledge and self-improvement. White Hutchinson (p. 7) conveys that the increasing desire for transformation (or self-actualization) is premised on the ideas that people recognize that experiences contribute to making you a better person beyond just the purchase of things or engaging in non-enriching experiences. The desire for transformational experiences is underscored due to the higher education levels of people 30-34 compared to the generation of those 70-74. This microtrend shows us that leisure expression is becoming more and more like classical leisure, as discussed in chapter 1.

Some people have argued that the rise in choice and synchronization (i.e., transformational leisure) threatens social cohesion. Can there be no unity, no community, no single America or Canada? The numbers of people in contemporary society in contrast of 50-60 years ago are so much more numerous, but rather they are dividing along lines of personal choice rather than circumstance, like race, gender, homeownership, etc.

More and more actions will be based on 51% coalitions rather than a broadly unified public, because personal choices tend to pull in opposite directions and make it harder to bring people together on anything. It can be argued that we are moving away from a mass society. This mass society was a faceless society, with people forced into conformity—everyone looking alike, dressing alike, and being required to think alike. Penn argues that are we are now heading in the opposite direction—a future of choices, driven by individual tastes—in which those choices are reinforced by the ability to connect and communicate with communities of even smaller niches with individuals looking more and more different by the minute.

Re-Inventing America: Can Art Save a Mall?

In suburban St. Louis, a huge shopping mall was scheduled for demolition as half its stores stood empty and it faced the same crisis that has bankrupted more than one in 10 of the nation's 1,100 enclosed malls. However, Crestwood's owners had an idea—instead of tearing it down, why not open its more than 200,000 square feet to artists? "Members of arts groups were ecstatic—opportunities like this simply don't happen. We held an open house, and over 200 artists showed up," recalled Leisa Son, the mall's leasing director (p. 18). Today, the mall displays the work of artists, contains a dance studio, and a children's art museum. Of course, ArtSpace still has its share of problems. Since space was rented on a first-come, first-served basis, it lacks a clear theme. There are unfilled spaces and crowds at times. It's unknown yet whether this will be a permanent solution, because at present the owners are subsidizing the artists. Fine points out, "Crestwood's daring choice could enliven malls around the country, ending the sameness from which they suffer. Integrating artists into the mall gives shoppers another reason to visit. A trip to Callahan or Jeanne Johnston weaves the entire mall deeper in the community." This idea is growing, and art instead of commerce isn't a new idea. But the idea of a mall built just to sell things becoming an art center is. *Based on Parade Magazine story by Susan Fine, November 22, 2009.*

MELDING OF MACRO AND MICRO THEMES:
TRENDS EMERGING FROM A SYNERGY OF CLASHING THEMES

There is no clear direction of the future for recreation, parks, sport management, hospitality, and tourism agencies, given the magnitude of at times clashing macro and micro trends. It is likely that for leisure service organizations to function effectively, let alone flourish, they will be required to recognize that mainstream culture and national expectations of mass conformity will not resonate with the hundreds of subcultural groups and may even alienate most everyone.

Recreation, parks, sport management, hospitality, and tourism organizations will need to acknowledge the multiplicity of small niche interest (many are viewed as leisure) groups within their community boundaries and adopt the **collaborative, boundary-free** leisure service delivery system approach that promotes and encourages its front-line professional staff to seek out various interest groups for their input on program ideas and ways to engage them directly or remotely and to facilitate people's desires they view as beneficial in the community.

Servant Leadership

Leisure service delivery must utilize the full range of leadership roles that embrace tolerance, outreach, developmental tasks, removal of barriers to participation and advocacy for people's rights to enable them to engage fully in all aspects of community life. **Servant leaders** are best suited for this challenge as they have a desire to serve first (not promote organizational mechanisms)—the conscious choice that brings one to aspire to lead. Some characteristics of servant leaders include:

- Commitment to the growth of people
- Building community
- Stewardship
- Empathy and healing capacity
- Awareness
- Foresight—understanding the lessons of the past
- Entrepreneurial
- Flexibility and adaptability

The concept of servant leader was originally articulated by Robert Greenleaf. According to Greenleaf, "the first priority of a leader should be one of service and putting others first" (Greenleaf cited in Peete, 2005, p. 8). The leadership emphasis of servant leaders is on empowering and helping others. Servant leaders recognize the full continuum of leisure service delivery—direct service, information-referral, enabling/facilitation, entrepreneurship, and advocacy—are all necessary for any organization to be most responsive to the great diversity of interests, lifestyles, and subcultural values that exist in most communities. Servant leaders seek, above all, to provide services that result in public benefit. Thus, servant leaders are more likely to be able to comprehend the complexities of a world that increasingly is evolving in ways that require flexible, visionary, compassionate, and socially conscious leaders.

Servant leaders will play an enormous role in blending the competing forces that both enhance and decimate recreation opportunities. Where do we as professional recreators go from here? According to Dustin (2006) "…we human beings are biologically ill-equipped to deal effectively with the environmental problems confronting the world of today… there is a fundamental mismatch between the nature of these problems and our ability to perceive them and do something about them; and that if we are to have any hope of turning things around, we must better understand the causes of the mismatch so that we might begin to act in the light of our limitations as a species as well as our potentials" (p. 205).

The City of San Leandro, California Recreation and Human Services Department embraces the full continuum of leisure service delivery. It provides a full array of recreation services and events; social service resource information; and supports community-based nonprofit organizations whose services and programs meet San Leandro's social service needs. The City supports organizations that offer preventative education, crisis intervention and basic needs services (housing, mental health, legal assistance, disability, alcohol and drug services, etc.). In this way, the City of San Leandro recognizes that it must provide a full spectrum of services that includes everyone and holds itself accountable to do so. Their commitment to building community by enhancing belonging and inspiring pride for all residents is more likely ensured through the utilization of a comprehensive recreation and human service delivery system. *Based on City of San Leandro, California, Recreation and Human services website (http://ci-San–Leandro.ca.us/)*

Slowing Down in Order to Keep it Together

To Dustin (2006), we, as humans, are increasingly out of step with our own nature. Our success as a species has not been in adapting to our understanding the natural world, but in transforming that world to make it a more hospitable place. He argues that politicians are ill-suited to offer leadership to solve our environmental problems. In this regard, one can't be a leader for constructive, sustainable change unless he or she views the end result on behalf of the community, not as a way to receive a vote. Recreation, parks, sport management, hospitality, and tourism professionals of the future, embracing the fullness of the leisure service delivery system (particularly collaboration and advocacy), can emerge into the forefront as recognizable catalysts and champions for habitable, quality of life that serves the total good. Dustin offers the following recommendations for all community members and as such, for recreation, parks, sport management, hospitality, and tourism professionals, to enhance and support:

1. **Slowing down.** Live less frantic lives and become more aware of one's total surroundings and the impact we each have on the planet.
2. **Scaling down.** Downsize our list of necessities, live more consciously below our means. "We need to measure the fullness of our lives not by the number of

our possessions, but by the quality of our relationships with others and by the degree to which we continue to learn and grow intellectually, spiritually, and emotionally" (Dustin, p. 212).

3. **Disengaging from our anthropocentric pedestals.** We should assume a more humble position among the creations of the Earth. He suggests cultivating a lifestyle characterized by reverence and restraint.

Godbey (2006) cautions that there will be competing trends that will on the one hand promote more personalized (customized) uses of time and on the other restrict time use (See Table 15.1 below).

Table 15.1	
Factors CreatingFactors Creating More Urbanization of Time	**Contingent Time Use**
More Choice	Less Choice
Changing nature of work	Health problems of older population
Working patterns (part-time, flextime, work at home)	Increased care giving
Increased urbanization and population density	Increased global warming and extreme weather
Technology which operates in real time	Terrorism and responses
Massive increases in immigration	Transportation gridlock
Concentration of immigrants within small regions of a country	Tourist sites reach capacity
Decline of standardized life styles	Massive government debt, restructuring of retirement, health benefits
Transfer of demand for customized products to demand for customized time schedules	
Differences in perceived time scarcity	

*Godbey, Geoffrey (2006), "The Future of Work and Leisure: More Customized and Contingent Across Time, p. 17.

Godbey anticipates that the **temporal aspects** of leisure and tourism behavior will become more diverse, complex, and uncertain. Godbey (2006) states: "For leisure and tourism providers, the provision of services will become more complex, agile, and information rich. The extent to which the information about the customer or visitor is collected and used will increase greatly. Demands for temporally customized leisure services will increase dramatically, which will, in turn, customize work schedules for employees in leisure and tourism services much further" (p. 26). He anticipates that temporal planning and schedules will move toward customization at an individual level. Life will become more complex and, in some ways, more free. He believes, though, that there is no guarantee with such freedom that it will be accompanied by the notion of the "common good."

Environmental and Social Justice

Recreation, parks, sport management, hospitality, and tourism professionals will be in the forefront in the future to the degree they embrace **environmental and social justice**, ensuring that there will be a sustainable planet and all people, regardless of race, ethnicity, income, national origin, or educational level, will receive equitable treatment and opportunities to meaningful involvement in community life. Recreation, parks, sport management, hospitality, and tourism professionals will continue to play a vital role in assuring the reduction of racial and ethnic disparities by promoting physical activities in public parks, playgrounds, and other recreation facilities. By incorporating an **ecological model**, that is, one that includes consideration of environmental and policy variable as determinants of recreation expression, is important to assuring full access. (Taylor et al., 2007)

Similar to Dustin (2006), Taylor et al. (2007) recognize that it is fundamental to acknowledge that recreation and park systems are public goods and are provided as a matter of public policy: "[First] they are an important function of government and are found at all levels government (municipal, county, state, and federal). Eighty-percent of the U.S. citizens report using public parks, and nearly one in four use them frequently. Second, the use of parks and recreation opportunities is associated with numerous benefits, including psychological (e.g., stress reduction), social (e.g., family bonding), economic (e.g., increased property values), environmental (e.g., open space), and health (e.g., benefits of exercise) " (p. S53).

The Need for Advocacy

Recreation, parks, sport management, hospitality, and tourism professionals have not viewed **advocacy** as a legitimate leadership role. But as there is increased recognition of the impact that recreation, parks, sport management, hospitality, and tourism have on communities, the necessity increases for professionals to become more influential and viable partners with other community services. The role of advocate means ensuring that all constituents are served and promoting sustainable living patterns. Advocacy, and becoming a core member of the community, has emerged as an essential role and will likely continue to be in the years ahead.

The California Parks and Recreation Society (CPRS) have made strides in enabling the profession to demonstrate why parks and recreation is an essential service. CPRS (1999) developed an action plan for the profession highlighted by nine missions that park and recreation programming and facilities should demonstrate:

- Strengthen community image and sense of place
- Support economic development
- Strengthen safety and security
- Promote health and wellness
- Foster human development
- Increase cultural unity
- Protect environmental resources
- Facilitate community problem solving
- Provide recreational experiences

Any of these items can be used to advocate convincingly for recreation, parks, sport management, hospitality, and tourism. To achieve these recognized missions, CPRS identified nine core competencies that professional leaders must be: resourceful, knowledgeable of community, creator of experiences, partnership and coalition builder, mediator, facilitator, skilled in working with people, flexible, and multi-tasker (See Figure 15.2, Strategic Planning Framework for Parks and Recreation). Servant leaders understand that they have an important responsibility to develop collaborations and partnerships with internal public service departments, public safety and other leading organizations, build community through volunteerism, public meetings, and focus groups, and gain legislative support by being an advocate (Clark, 2006).

CONCLUSION: WHAT DOES THIS MEAN AND WHAT SHOULD WE DO ABOUT IT?

So, where are recreation, parks, sport management, hospitality, and tourism headed as a profession? Daniel Dustin (2009) offers both an exciting and a daunting challenge to current professionals and those individuals aspiring to enter this critically important career area:

1. Parks, recreation, sport management, hospitality, and tourism can make a substantial contribution to the quality of life.
2. The best way to articulate those contributions is in the context of health promotion.
3. Our society is fundamentally "out of synch" with what is really healthy for human beings and the environment. Our society must serve the American Dream in a way that is socially and environmentally sustainable over the long haul.
4. Parks, recreation, and tourism ought to be treated as a public good, as something that everyone in our culture should have access to, like public education.
5. When that access is compromised, it is an ethical or moral problem (i.e., this must be remedied and must be viewed in the shaping of social and environmental justice).
6. Ultimately, the biggest professional challenges for parks, recreation, sport management, hospitality, and tourism professionals is to speak to the general public in a way that is so compelling that they will recognize the need to redefine number 3 above so that discussing number 5 is unnecessary.

The profession faces ethical and moral dilemmas. There is a need to maintain a delicate balance between fostering recreation expression, ensuring access to parklands and facilities, while being **stewards** of the environment that will guarantee future generations will be able to realize their human potential and quality of well-being on a fragile Earth landscape. Dustin, McAvoy, and Schultz (2002) believe park, recreation, and tourism professionals are in a unique position to champion human fulfillment in the future. As such they state, "in the name of human fulfillment, park and recreation professionals can contribute to the creation

FIGURE 15.2
STRATEGIC PLANNING FRAMEWORK FOR PARKS AND RECREATION

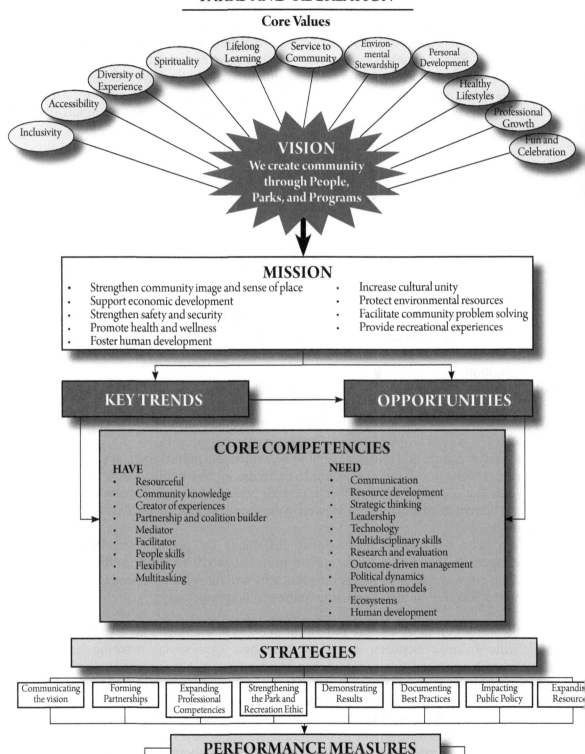

Core Values

Inclusivity · Accessibility · Diversity of Experience · Spirituality · Lifelong Learning · Service to Community · Environmental Stewardship · Personal Development · Healthy Lifestyles · Professional Growth · Fun and Celebration

VISION
We create community through People, Parks, and Programs

MISSION
- Strengthen community image and sense of place
- Support economic development
- Strengthen safety and security
- Promote health and wellness
- Foster human development
- Increase cultural unity
- Protect environmental resources
- Facilitate community problem solving
- Provide recreational experiences

KEY TRENDS → **OPPORTUNITIES**

CORE COMPETENCIES

HAVE
- Resourceful
- Community knowledge
- Creator of experiences
- Partnership and coalition builder
- Mediator
- Facilitator
- People skills
- Flexibility
- Multitasking

NEED
- Communication
- Resource development
- Strategic thinking
- Leadership
- Technology
- Multidisciplinary skills
- Research and evaluation
- Outcome-driven management
- Political dynamics
- Prevention models
- Ecosystems
- Human development

STRATEGIES

Communicating the vision | Forming Partnerships | Expanding Professional Competencies | Strengthening the Park and Recreation Ethic | Demonstrating Results | Documenting Best Practices | Impacting Public Policy | Expanding Resources

PERFORMANCE MEASURES

Community | Professional

of an environment which nourishes human potential. We, as much as any farmer, physician, carpenter, or scientist, can play a vital role in orchestrating an atmosphere of hope for humankind. We serve as principle architects of a new beginning of this planet." (p. 116)

Dustin et al. (2002) suggest four guidelines for action in what recreation, parks, sport management, hospitality, and tourism professionals can do when confronted with the myriad challenges that will require them to balance the materialistic, tangible behaviors desired to achieve self-fulfillment with sustainable, minimal impact expressions that not only benefit individuals but the broader society as well.

1. **Ideal of individual freedom.** "We should act on the environment, both the internal one of the organism and external one of society, and make it compatible with the expression of that freedom…[society]…must give [individuals]…room to grow and develop, to succeed and fail, to express their initiative, creativity, and fulfillment as individual human beings. [And individuals]…must accept responsibility for [their] behavior." (p. 117)
2. **Commitment to expanding opportunities**. "The park and recreation professional should be committed to the ideal of expanding opportunities for choice." (p.117). Although some opportunities may be in conflict with service providers ideas/values, "the opportunities should be made available as long as they are socially acceptable" (p. 117)
3. **Supporting the overall good of the community.** "On occasion matters of personal preference clash with matters of social principle." (p. 117). At times, recreation, parks, sport management, hospitality, and tourism professionals will experience conflicts of individual preferences among different lifestyle and interest groups but they should "support the social principle governing the situation." (p. 118)
4. **Ethical principle: reconciliation of competing individual and societal interests.** "There is an interplay between one's freedom to act and one's responsibility to society for one's actions… one's behavior must be in accordance not only with the welfare of humankind, but also with the welfare of the larger community of life." (p. 118)

Recreation, parks, sport management, hospitality, and tourism professionals contribute to the survival of the Earth. Dustin et al. (2002) "believe this profession is indispensable to the quality of life. In this sense, park and recreation professionals do indeed contribute to the very survival of humanity" (p. 118). The stakes are high for leisure service professionals, and in this regard, the world community will look to and rely upon the capable decisions being made by socially conscious servant leaders on behalf of a profession whose primary goal is to promote human dignity and fulfillment while sustaining the fragile natural world and parklands for future generations to enjoy. There are immense possibilities for the recreation, parks, sport management, hospitality, and tourism profession in the years ahead that can result in an enormous emergence of the leisure service fields as a fulcrum for supporting and helping to facilitate recreation experiences that foster culturally relevant, personally satisfying, and environmentally sustainable **"deep recreation"** (Murphy, 2007). This idea, sometimes called flow, is representative of personal desires that embrace freely chosen, intense, challenging, transformational, and intrinsically motivational experiences.

The prognosis for employment opportunities for recreation, parks, sport management, hospitality, and tourism workers in the future by 13 to 35 percent well into the teens in the twenty-first century is projected to increase, which is as fast as the average for all occupations. To the degree that leisure service organizations recognize the full array of ways in which people desire various forms of leisure expression, ranging from deep forms of intense, challenging, and transformational experiences to quick, momentary forms of engagement, in both direct and remote contexts, they will have an important role to play in community life and job opportunities both organizationally driven and self-run, entrepreneurial businesses should be viable.

FOR FURTHER INVESTIGATION

For More Research

1. Identify, research, and write a paper about macrotrends affecting recreation, parks, sport management, hospitality, and tourism in your community. How does the influence of a macrotrend intersect with other, possible competing or contrary microtrends in your community? Are they reconcilable?
Recommended websites:
http://childandnature.org/blog/
http://www.google.com/Top/Society/Future/Predictions
http://www.markpenn.com/microtrends/
http://www.microtrending.com/
http://naisbitt.com/
http://newblaze.com
http://slowisbeautifulcecile.blogspot.com/
http://www.theyear2012.blogspot.com/

2. Select something from the recommended reading list. Read it and write a paper about what you learned and how you believe these lessons will impact recreation, parks, sport management, hospitality, and tourism.

Active Investigation

1. Choose a cause, write and send an advocacy letter supporting an issue (that might be controversial) that will contribute to individual/community well-being.
2. Interview one or more professionals about the trends they see and how they believe they will affect the future of recreation, parks, sport management, hospitality, and tourism. Choose a professional who has been in the field for 10 or more years to get a long-range view. Example interview questions:
   • How have you seen your job change over the years?
   • How have your customers changed? Do you believe that your agency or business has done well keeping up with customers' changing needs?

- What is the biggest challenge you see facing recreation, parks, sport management, hospitality, and tourism today? What do you think it will be five and 10 years from now?
- Review the sections on Macrotrends and Microtrends—ask the professional how some of these are affecting his or her agency or business.

3. Go online and navigate to one of the websites listed above and join in and participate in a blog related to an issue of interest to you and see how others react to your views.

Recommended Reading

Andrews, C. (2006). *Slow is beautiful: New visions of community, leisure and joie de vivre.* Gabriola Island, B.C., Canada: New Society Publishers.
Happiness is on the decline even though we are the most affluent country in the world, yet no one seems to know how to exit the fast lane. Andrews helps us understand the forces taking the joy out of our existence and provides a vision for a more fulfilling life.

Chivian, E., & Bernstein, A. (Eds.). (2008). *Sustaining life: How human health depends on biodiversity.* New York, NY.: Oxford University Press.
This book was motivated by its UN sponsors' sense of the world's indifference to the consequences of environmental degradation. It covers a collaborative survey of biodiversity issues written and/or reviewed for accuracy by more than 100 scientists, and the authors collectively warn that present extinction rates are abnormally high.

Chouinard, Y. (2005). *Let my people go surfing: The education of a reluctant businessman.* NY.: Penguin Group.
As the founder of Patagonia, Chouinard provides a fascinating look inside its history. His book provides a guide for anyone interested in creating a "new style of responsible business."

Hartig, T., Mang, M., & Evans, G. (1991). Restorative effects of natural environment experiences. *Environment and behavior, 23* (1), 3-26.
These research studies offer evidence of the restorative effects that arise from experiences in nature.

Louv, R. (2005). *Last child in the woods: Saving our children from nature-deficit disorder.* Chapel Hill, NC.: Algonquin Books.
Last child is an inspiring must-read book that proves children need nature as much as nature need children.

Poscente, V. (2008). *The age of speed.* Austin, TX: Bard Press.
Posente explains that work is no longer a place but rather a state of mind. He explains how speed is both the cause of the problem and the solution to the ambiguity we face when trying to resolve the competing demands of career and personal life.

Roberts, N., Chavez, D., Lara, B., & Sheffield, E. (2009). *Serving culturally diverse visitors to forests in California: A resource guide.* General Tech. Rep. PSW-GTR-222. Albany, Ca.: U.S. Department of Agriculture, Forest Service, Pacific Southwest Research, 76 pp. Available at http://www.fs.fed.us/psw/publications/documents/psw_gtr222/psw_gtr222.pdf
Changing demographics make is essential that recreation managers understand how to both attract and serve ethnically diverse visitors to our forest resources. The guide provides numerous materials, best practices and practical application tips.

Robert Wood Johnson Foundation. (2000). *Healthy places, healthy people: Promoting public health and physical activity through community design.* Princeton, NJ: Robert Wood Johnson. Available at http://www.rwjf.org/files/publications/other/HealthyPlaces.pdf
This expert's report is a white paper from a meeting that summarizes the best thinking about how the problem of physical inactivity can be addressed. Successful interventions must target both the individual and the environments in which people work and live.

Schwartz, B. (2004). *The paradox of change: Why less is more.* NY: Harper Collins Publishers, Inc.
This psychology professor provides convincing evidence that we face too many choices on a daily basis. The bewildering array of choices is stressful because it exhausts our brains and erodes our sense of well-being. The author offers practical suggestions for reducing stress during decision-making.

Van den Berg, A., Hartig, T., & Staats, H. (2007). Preference for nature in urbanized societies: Stress, restoration, and the pursuit of sustainability. *Journal of Social Issues, 63* (1), 79-96. Available at http://www.agnesvandenberg.nl/jsi.pdf
These environmental psychology researchers demonstrate that people's desire for contact with nature serves and important function—that of psychological restoration. Suggestions are offered for designing communities to balance settlement density with satisfactory access to nature experiences. The authors conclude that urban nature is a viable design option that promotes urban sustainability.

REFERENCES

California Parks and Recreation Society. (1999). *Creating community in the 21st century: An action plan for parks and recreation.* Sacramento, California.
Clark, J. (2006). *Human resources: Servant leadership and the parks and recreation professional.* Unpublished paper.
Dustin, D., Bricker, K., & Schwab, K.(2010). People and nature: Toward an ecological model of health promotion. *Journal of Leisure Sciences,* 32:1, 3-14.
Dustin, D., McAvoy, L., & Schultz, J. (2002). *Stewards of access/custodians of choice.* Champaign, IL: Sagamore.
Dustin, D. (2009). Personal correspondence. October 22, 2009.
Dustin, D. (2006). *The wilderness within.* Champaign, IL: Sagamore.

Fine, S. (2009, November 22). Can art save a mall? *Parade Magazine*, New York: Parade Publications, p. 18.

Floyd, M., Bocarro, J., & Thompson, T. (2008). Research on race and ethnicity in leisure studies: A review of five major journals. *Journal of Leisure Research. 40*:1-22.

Friedman, T. (2007). *The world is flat: A brief history of the twenty-first century.* New York: Picador/Farrar, Straus and Giroux.

Godbey, G. (2006). The future of work and leisure: More customized and contingent across time. In Weiermair, K., T. Bieger, & H. Pechlander (Eds.), *Time shift, leisure and tourism.* Berlin, Germany: ESV Publishing.

Kim, R. (2009). Augmenting how we see the world. *San Francisco Chronicle.* October 26, 2009.

Kritt, D.W. (Fall, 2001). Technology's covert socialization of children: High-tech toys. *Journal of Thought, 36* (3) 53-61.

Murdock, S., White, S., Hoque, N., & Pecotte, B. (2003). *The new Texas challenge: Population change and the future of Texas.* College Station, TX: Texas A & M University Press.

Murphy, J. (2007). *Whither organized parks and recreation?* Bay Area Institute, District IV, California Parks and Recreation Society, Redwood City, California.

Peete, D. (July, 2005). Needed: Servant leaders. *Nursing homes/long-term care management*, pp.8-9.

Penn, M. (2007). *Microtrends: The small forces behind tomorrow's big changes.* New York: Hachette Books Group.

Sabeti, H. (2009). *The emerging fourth sector.* Washington, D.C.: The Aspen Institute.

Support for the great outdoors America. (September, 2009). Marienville, PA.: National Association of Recreation Resource Planners.

Taylor, W., Floyd, M., Whitt-Glover, M., & Brooks, J. (2007). Environmental justice: A framework for collaboration between the public health and parks and recreation fields to study disparity in physical activity. *Journal of Physical Activity and Health, 4*:S50-S63.

The future of leisure time: A new value equation. (2009). White Hutchinson Leisure and Learning Group. Retrieved from http://www.whitehutchinson.com/news/knews/2009_august/article 103.shtml on September 10, 2009.

Viara, D. (May, 2010). Talking About My Generation. *Parks & Recreation, 45*(5), pp. 40-42.

Index